D1241792

Casino Gaming in the United States

A Research Guide

Thomas R. Mirkovich
and
Allison A. Cowgill

The Scarecrow Press, Inc.
Lanham, Md., & London
1997

SCARECROW PRESS, INC.

Published in the United States of America
by Scarecrow Press, Inc.
4720 Boston Way
Lanham, Maryland 20706

4 Pleydell Gardens, Folkestone
Kent CT20 2DN, England

British Cataloguing-in-Publication Information Available

Library of Congress Cataloging-in-Publication Data

Mirkovich, Thomas R., 1954–
    Casino gaming in the United States : a research guide / Thomas
R. Mirkovich, Allison A. Cowgill
        p.   cm.
    Includes index.
    ISBN 0-8108-3230-5 (hardcover : alk. paper)
        1. Casinos—United States—Bibliography. 2. Casinos—United
States—Research—Handbooks, manuals, etc. 3. Gambling—United
States—Bibliography. 4. Gambling—United States—Research—
Handbooks, manuals, etc. I. Cowgill, Allison A., 1950- . II. Title.
    Z7164.G35M57   1997
    [HV6711]
    016.795—dc20   96-31864

ISBN 0-8108-3230-5 (cloth : alk.paper)

♾™ The paper used in this publication meets the minimum
requirements of American National Standard for Information
Sciences—Permanence of Paper for Printed Library Materials, ANSI
Z39.48–1984. Manufactured in the United States of America.

For Kate, Sam, and Lara

Thomas R. Mirkovich

For Virginia Boucher,
longtime friend and mentor

Allison A. Cowgill

CONTENTS

ACKNOWLEDGMENTS

The authors want to thank Aaron Abbey, Bob Ball, John H.C. Barron, Susan Biery, Nan Bowers, Ida Bowser, Ann Brinkmeyer, Anne Cowgill, Pat Deadder, Paul Depp, Roberta Depp, Sandy DeVaney, Steve Fitt, Tom Fry, Beth Gable, Adolph Gannoe, Jennifer Garcia, Russell Guindon, Shelley Heaton, Bob Hyland, Susan Jarvis, Peggy Jobe, Margaret Johnson, Annie Kelley, Jeff Kintop, Michael Kucher, Myoung-ja Lee Kwon, Linda Leong, Mary McCoy, Edmond Mignon, Lara Mirkovich, Janet Perry, Kathy Rothermel, Margaret Scott, Matt Simon, Carol Ann Swatling, Bill Thompson, Terry Violette, Sidney Watson, Laura Witsche, and the staffs of the Council of State Governments, National Conference of State Legislatures, and University of Nevada, Las Vegas, Special Collections.

PREFACE

The dramatic proliferation of casino gaming throughout the United States has been a controversial issue for several years. While heated debate about gambling's place in this society is ongoing, Americans wagered $324 billion in casinos in 1994, making casino gaming one of the largest and fastest-growing industries in the United States. Nearly twenty-five states now offer some form of casino gaming, and many more are considering legalization. It is estimated that by the year 2000 all Americans in the continental United States will be able to drive to a casino in less than four hours.

Casino gaming is certainly a high-interest topic, and information on all aspects of this subject can be found in a wide variety of sources. A single work bringing much of this information together, however, was not available. To produce this reference guide and selective survey, the authors examined many of these varied sources. Foremost were the holdings of the libraries of the University of Nevada, Las Vegas, which contain the country's premier collection on gaming and gambling. Special efforts were also made to collect citations for state and local documents which can be particularly useful but difficult to identify. Collegial relationships between the Nevada State Library and Archives and other governmental agencies and organizations made access to these materials possible. Additionally, a thorough search of the social sciences literature, both print and on-line, and a survey of gaming industry trade publications provided many of the references included here.

This book is for government officials at all levels, industry personnel, scholars and researchers, business consultants, planners and developers, community groups, religious leaders, students, and any others interested in the social, economic, political, and legal aspects of the American casino gaming industry.

The contents include bibliographic citations or references for periodical articles, government publications, monographs, manuscripts, newspaper articles, and electronic resources from CD-ROMs, on-line services, and the Internet. In addition to this data, directory listings for governmental agencies, associations, experts and consultants, Indian gaming locations, and industry sources related to casino gaming are included. The authors' intent was to bring together a variety of useful information in one source. Though a short bibliography on how to play casino games is provided, this work is not intended as a reference tool for the recreational or professional gambler.

The bibliographic portion of this book is divided into separate sections on the casino industry, Indian gaming, riverboat gaming, casinos and the law, casinos and economic development, casinos and American society, and casinos and crime. Sources from 1985 through 1994 were surveyed. Materials were selected based on their representative subject content, uniqueness, and scholarship. Earlier materials, materials about other countries, and materials about other forms of gambling, such as lotteries, are included if they are particularly significant or informative. Every effort was made to represent a broad variety of views on casinos and gambling, and if a bias is perceived, it reflects the sources surveyed. The authors intended to present neither a pro-gaming nor anti-gaming stance.

Casinos, once very disreputable and suspect, are now part of mainstream America. As their presence in the United States continually increases, the need for accurate information about their impact is more important than ever. The authors hope this work will be useful to numerous readers by providing valuable information on industry operations and the complex controversies and important issues surrounding casino gaming.

INTRODUCTION

GAMING OR GAMBLING?

The recent and rapid growth of legalized gambling has resulted in a great deal of literature on casinos and their meaning for the United States. Although information on this industry and its myriad effects on American society can be found in many places, this book came about when the authors realized that no single reference work existed to bring these data together.

The first decision to be made concerned semantics. What should the title be? Does the book deal with "gaming" or "gambling?" What is the difference? Reference librarians at the Nevada State Library and Archives occasionally get questions about this distinction, primarily from out-of-state tourists who want to argue that the word "gaming" is an artificial way to improve the somewhat disreputable image of "gambling," Nevada's primary industry.

In her 1994 *New York Times Magazine* article on gambling, Gerri Hirshey says:

> "Gambling," the term that once conjured up green visors, cigar smoke and gumball-size pinky rings, has been buffed with warm fuzzies. We call it *gaming* these days.[1]

Catholic leader Edward B. Geyer views the "gambling" versus "gaming" issue differently. Gaming is "defined as the wagering of one's discretionary or recreational income" and does not jeopardize a person's economic status or well-being. Gambling, however, is "considered sinful" because it can put a person's livelihood at risk.[2]

A third opinion is found in William N. Thompson's *Legalized Gambling: A Reference Handbook:*

> Gambling may be defined as an activity in which a person subjects something of value—usually money—to a risk involving a large element of chance in the hopes of winning something of greater value, which is usually more money. . . . The term "gaming" is usually associated with the activities found in casinos. Herein, the terms "gambling," "gaming," and "wagering" will be used somewhat interchangeably.[3]

Major businesses, such as Smith Barney, and major business publishers, such as Standard and Poor's, use the phrase "gaming industry." Additional proof of this phrase's acceptance: the Nevada "Gaming" Control Board, the New Jersey Division of "Gaming" Enforcement, and the title of *International "Gaming" and Wagering Business*, a standard industry publication.

After debating the issue, the authors decided the book's working title would be *Casino Gaming in the United States: A Research Guide.* This wording was selected because the book would not focus only on the casino industry; it would also review materials on the many social and economic effects this industry has on the United States. While public acceptance of gambling increases every year, casino gaming raises complex issues which can involve extremely divergent viewpoints and deeply held beliefs.

Now that the title was chosen, the real research could begin. Incidentally, the exhaustive literature review done to complete this work was not particularly enlightening about very specific uses for "gambling" and "gaming." This distinction can still be confusing, and as William N. Thompson noted in his work, these words are used "somewhat interchangeably" here as well.

RESEARCH METHODOLOGY

For this book, the authors reviewed a wide variety of literature and indexing from 1985 through 1994. A very large number of books, periodical articles, databases, and government publications offer a great deal of information on all aspects of the casino gaming industry and its social and economic effects on American society. In fact, initial efforts provided an overwhelming amount of material, and it quickly became apparent that many difficult selection decisions would be necessary due to space limitations. Any section in chapter 3 could have been a book-length bibliography in itself. Since only a certain number of citations could be included, the authors identified the following selection criteria:

Scholarship and importance: the work is a major contribution to the literature on the casino industry and its social and economic effects on the United States. The author is a widely respected expert on the subject; the work may be repeatedly cited in other sources.

Accuracy: the work presents valid, substantiated information on the casino industry and its social and economic impacts. Accurate information is critical to sound research.

Timeliness and relevance: the work contains the latest information or statistics on the gaming industry for current evaluation or analysis. Older materials can be relevant and applicable in spite of their publication dates.

Usefulness: the work contains information which is particularly clear and applicable and includes bibliographical references that provide worthwhile direction for additional research.

Uniqueness: the work presents or compiles information or viewpoints on the gaming industry and its social and economic effects not readily found elsewhere. Many of the

bibliography's state and local government publications fall
into this category because they are frequently very useful
while very difficult to identify.

Variety: the work represents the diverse sources which
contain information on casinos and their social and economic
impacts; these are materials which many might overlook in a
comprehensive research effort.

Availability: the work may not be truly unique but may
be available locally; while some of the annotations, for
example, contain similar information or viewpoints, researchers may have ready access to one and not the others.
Local availability becomes critical when information is needed immediately. Also, many of these materials will be
available by interlibrary loan through local libraries. Contact
them for information on interlibrary loan.

Although this list may seem obvious, a research project
of this magnitude requires many evaluations and decisions.
While the authors made every effort to identify key sources,
it must be stressed that the bibliography found here is very
selective, not exhaustive. Its intent is to bring together in
one source a wide variety of accurate and useful information
on the varying viewpoints and major issues raised by this
country's rapidly growing gaming industry.

NOTES

1. Gerri Hirshey, "Gambling Nation," *New York Times
Magazine* (17 July 1994): 36.
2. Canon Edward B. Geyer, *The Atlantic City Experience: Gaming and the Church* (Atlantic City, N.J.: Diocese
of New Jersey, Atlantic City Mission, 1993): 2.
3. William N. Thompson, *Legalized Gambling: A
Reference Handbook* (Santa Barbara, Calif.: ABC-CLIO,
1994): 2.

CHAPTER 1

The Casino Industry:
An Overview

The American casino industry has grown tremendously since 1988, experiencing the "most widespread liberalization of gaming entertainment in its history."[1] For most of this century, casinos were found only in Nevada, whose state legislature legalized gambling in 1931. Forty-five years later, New Jersey approved casino gambling in Atlantic City to improve its severely depressed economy. The city's first operation opened in 1978, two years after the vote. South Dakota then opened low-stakes casinos in Deadwood in 1988 to increase tourism revenues, and Colorado soon followed by legalizing similar operations in three mountain towns in 1991.[2] Only a few years later, casinos are found throughout the country. Some form of casino gambling is now available in twenty-three states, reservation-based Indian gaming is now found in nineteen states, and riverboat casinos now operate in six states.[3]

Public attitudes about gambling have certainly changed. Once perceived as a disreputable pursuit, associated with immorality and organized crime, gambling is now a mainstream activity and the fastest growing component of this country's multi-billion-dollar entertainment industry. Grouped with theme parks, sporting events, movies, and boating, gambling has become a recreational pursuit for many Americans. Over the last ten years,

> entertainment and recreation have claimed a steadily increasing share of consumer spending. . . . Since 1991, consumers have boosted their outlays on

entertainment and recreation by some 13%, adjusted for inflation—more than twice the growth rate of overall consumer spending.[4]

The growth of the casino industry obviously reflects an increase in gambling activity by Americans. The following statistics show how America's attitudes toward gambling have changed:

U.S. casino revenue increased from $8.3 billion in 1990 to $12.9 billion in 1993.[5]

Americans spent $28 billion on all forms of legal gambling in 1993.[6]

The amount of total casino wagers has grown at an annual rate of 10.27 percent since 1982.[7]

92 million people visited casinos in 1993, twice the 1990 figure of 46 million.

In 1993, more than half of the adults (51 percent) in the United States found casino entertainment "acceptable for anyone," and another 35 percent found it "acceptable for others, but not for me."[8]

"Casino gaming can be a fun night out," according to three out of four U.S. adults in 1993.[9]

Casino entertainment now ranks ahead of attendance at many other popular forms of entertainment, including major league baseball games, arena concerts, and Broadway shows.[10]

Why has this industry been so successful? Besides growing public acceptance, many elected officials and citizens alike think casinos are a "solution to their declining economies, lack of tax base, and shortage of jobs for central city residents."[11] One well-managed operation can add millions of dollars to a state's budget in a single year. Gaming on reservations, first begun in the late 1980s, has brought sudden prosperity and independence to several Native American tribes formerly entrenched in extreme long-term poverty. Many credit the advent of riverboat casinos with revitalizing areas around the southern shores of the Mississippi and its tributaries.

America's interest in gambling is not a recent phenomenon. People have gambled throughout history. Evidence of gambling can be found in Egyptian pyramids, Greek and Roman histories, and in both testaments of the Bible. Western American folklore conjures up legendary images of cowboys sitting in saloons playing poker, frequently with fatal results. A long history of betting on horse racing, dice, playing cards, and lotteries demonstrates how people are attracted to chance and risk-taking, particularly when financial gain is in the offing.

In his work *Legalized Gambling: A Reference Handbook*, William N. Thompson traces the evolution of gambling from ancient times to the 1990s. He discusses noted authority I. Nelson Rose's cyclic theory on the three waves of gambling activity in European-American history:

> Gambling activity has ebbed and flowed with varying intensities throughout history. In what has appeared to be a love-hate relationship between the public and gambling promoters, several "waves" of permissiveness have rippled through North America, only to subside with prohibitionary regulation.[12]

Each wave precipitated or represented public acceptance of gambling. These three waves are:

1. The colonial period: characterized by lotteries, horse racing, and card games;

2. The post Civil War era: characterized by lotteries, horse racing, and card games;

3. The 1960s: characterized by the first modern state lottery in New Hampshire in 1964.[13]

Lotteries, in what is obviously a popular pattern, have a long history of being "used to supplement government treasuries."[14] New Hampshire's legalization was the first major indication that public support for gambling was resurfacing in the United States.

Nevada's legalization of gambling, while radical at the time, was a little ripple rather than a wave. Passage of the required legislation really reflected the state's small population, relative isolation, unique circumstances, and economic needs. It did not precede any spreading acceptance of gambling. Indeed, the state's actions were condemned by the rest of the country, and the Nevada casino industry's initial links to organized crime and corruption only worsened gambling's already negative image.

Nevada's experiences, however, play an important role in the recent growth of the casino industry and its operation today. The state's casinos and its government's long-term involvement in gaming showed New Jersey it was both profitable and manageable, adding momentum to legalization efforts nationwide. Nevada, like gambling, has "gone mainstream." Briefly tracing the industry's evolution in this state highlights some noteworthy developments.

From the 1930s to the 1960s, Nevada's casinos were run by families or small partnerships. Gambling debts were legally uncollectible, and banks were reluctant to get involved in casino finance. Significant state legislation, passed in 1969, changed the casino business. "Prompted by the industry's need to maintain and upgrade facilities, and continuing need to improve the state's image," it allowed publicly held corporations to own casinos.[15] This legitimization opened the industry's access to new capital, allowing it to develop at a much greater speed.

New Jersey officials astutely studied Nevada's casino laws and regulations before implementing legalized gambling in Atlantic City. The enabling legislation, the New Jersey Casino Control Act of 1977, benefited from Nevada's long-

standing experiences with the industry. Subsequent New
Jersey legislation improved on Nevada law by allowing
casinos to collect gambling debts, a major step for industry
operators who previously had no legal recourse. Nevada
soon enacted a similar law.

In the 1970s, the casino industry matured in both places.
Important Las Vegas industry figures like Jay Sarno,
William Bennett, and Stephen A. Wynn focused on
changing their industry's image:

> The attitudinal sea change toward "casino entertain-
> ment" owes much to Wynn's well-executed excesses
> here. Nobody does it better—and with cannier
> timing. While Jay Sarno's Circus Circus can be
> credited with offering the first free "themed"
> entertainment in the mid-70's . . . it was Wynn's far
> grander vision that jump-started the Vegas transfor-
> mation.[16]

Wynn's view of gambling as entertainment is certainly
evident in his very elaborate and successful Mirage and
Treasure Island hotel-casinos with their Disney-like
attractions. Las Vegas's ongoing success as a major
worldwide tourist destination for all kinds of people can be
largely attributed to Wynn's "respectable" entertainment and
recreation emphases. Gambling destinations are fun places,
certainly still glamorous, but now that glamour and
excitement are available to almost everyone.

Wynn's marketing and financial acumen had a major
influence on the casino industry's growth. In the mid-
1970s, he convinced Drexel Burnham and Lambert bond
trader Michael Milken to support his Golden Nugget Casino
in Atlantic City. This relationship "set the stage for quarter-
billion-dollar forays into the junk market by other emerging
gambling outfits like Elsinore (Hyatt's gaming branch),
Trump, Hilton, Circus Circus and Merv Griffin's Resorts
International."[17]

While the casino industry was experiencing rapid trans-
formation and growth, many state governments continued to

turn to lotteries to improve state finances. By the end of 1994

> The number of states without lotteries is now about a dozen, basically some states in the deep South and a few Western states. Repeal of existing lotteries isn't under consideration anywhere, but there are serious moves to adopt a lottery in nearly every state without one.[18]

This governmental involvement and citizen support of one form of gambling legitimized it for many people with little previous exposure. These lotteries and an increasingly respectable and visible gaming industry are two important factors which helped change this country's perceptions about gambling, greatly increasing the force of that third wave of gambling acceptance.

For many Americans, gambling is now a recreational pastime with public approval seeming to increase every year. There are exceptions, however; not everyone applauds the rapid spread of legalized gambling in this country. Some people question the industry's integrity and future prospects or express serious concerns about its short and long-term effects on America's economy and society. Many of the issues it raises are very complex and involve extremely divergent viewpoints and deeply held beliefs and attitudes. The issues the casino industry and legalized gambling raise underscore gambling's increasing importance in this country.

CASINO INDUSTRY ISSUES

Since land-based and riverboat gaming continues to grow at a rapid rate, the industry's overwhelming concern is ever-increasing competition:

> After years of aggressive expansion, gambling companies face the prospect that the capacity of

casinos will eventually outpace the number of players to fill them.[19]

Industry officials are identifying ways their operations can remain competitive here and around the world. Issues include ways to attract and retain customers; affect enabling legislation so it does not limit casino profits or patronage; minimize scandals so the industry's image is not tarnished; modernize management practices to improve performance at all levels; apply state-of-the-art computer technologies to casino operations and games; participate in federal and state regulatory processes to minimize complicated and costly changes; identify locations worldwide for expansion into new markets; and continue to improve public opinion in the United States so gambling initiatives win voter approval.

According to the April 1995 *Standard and Poor's Industry Surveys* "Leisure Time: Basic Analysis," continued growth in the casino industry depends on

> further loosening of state laws and investment in new facilities . . . if one state approves casinos, adjacent areas are increasingly likely to do the same in an effort to protect their share of consumer spending, jobs, and taxes. . . . However, casinos are not always met with open arms. Gaming proposals in New York and Texas, for example, have failed to win legislative approval thus far.[20]

It is also important to note that "evidence is mounting that success of new forms of gambling are coming in part at the expense of older forms."[21] State lottery and parimutuel racing have shown profit declines in some states where casinos have recently opened. While Indian gaming is a major part of the industry as a whole, its increase poses unique concerns because complicated sovereignty and rights issues now protect reservation activities from any private sector interference.

According to a variety of sources, the overall outlook for the U.S. casino industry continues to remain positive. *The Harrah's Survey of U.S. Casino Entertainment 1994* states:

> casino entertainment will continue to experience robust growth over the next decade, propelled primarily by riverboats and Indian reservation casinos . . . U.S. casino revenues will double in the next decade.[22]

The effects of increasing competition, however, are already appearing. In December 1994, reporter Rick Alm wrote a story on riverboat casino competition in Mississippi, where operation began in 1992. In Biloxi, for example,

> casino owners battle for survival in a market that is overbuilt and, experts say, ripe for a fall. The state's economic fortunes depend on how far and how fast that fall occurs. Gaming regulators in other states are learning from Mississippi's saturated gambling market. A handful of the weakest casinos already have been squeezed out. Several others are teetering with shrinking profits.[23]

Gambling legalization has also experienced difficulties. The November 1994 elections indicated strong public opposition. Voters' sound rejection of casino gaming in Florida was a major defeat for the industry, which spent over $18 million on its support. *Financial World* writer Dan Cordtz explains why this referendum was critical: "Not a single state's citizens have voted to pursue the riches—and notoriety—that big-time casinos brought to Las Vegas and Atlantic City."[24] Industry officials hoped legalization in Florida would encourage larger states like New York and Texas to follow. In other locales:

> Rhode Island voters turned back casinos for Providence and four other communities. And Navajos rejected casinos for their reservation, which

stretches over parts of Arizona, New Mexico, and Utah.[25]

The Center for State Policy Research, a private organization focusing on state legislative and regulatory issues, released a report in December 1994 which predicts that thirty-six states will probably consider some type of gambling legalization in 1996. Eleven of these states are now looking at casino operations, and six are interested in riverboat gaming.[26] A frequently repeated rationale for government support is the fear that legalization in nearby states prompts residents to spend their money in those jurisdictions, not at home. "Newly-elected governors in Connecticut, New York, and Pennsylvania have expressed interest in legalized gambling" to head off increasing competition from adjacent areas.[27]

While government-sanctioned expansion seems to be the rule, the report argues that the gaming industry will probably face increasing government regulation and more organized opposition. Noted gaming consultant Nancy Todd said she anticipates the industry's maturing "to cap out by the end of the century. . . . Setbacks aren't unexpected in an industry where voter approval is often required for success."[28] According to Ray Paulick, however, industry leaders envision a "future with slot machines and card tables in virtually every section of the country."[29]

In a different scenario, "to get around U.S. gambling laws, the first on-line casinos are setting up their card tables offshore."[30] *Time* author Joshua Quittner describes recent gambling opportunities on the Internet, which "reaches tens of millions of people around the world, and it's growing faster than a Las Vegas bar tab."[31] Other entrepreneurs are developing interactive television programing for wagering:

NTN is testing an interactive service in Carlsbad, Calif. For $9.95 a month, subscribers can buy a package that includes betting on horse races at a Los Angeles-area track and table-game gambling. But all the wagering is done with points, not money.[32]

The industry could be redefined, since participants in these gambling activities do not have to leave home to engage in some traditional casino games.

Since public opinion and state governments can be unpredictable, individuals following gaming issues can only wait to see what unfolds. Even as statistics show increased public support for gambling, many people are uncomfortable legalizing casinos in their states because "they do not want one in their backyards."[33]

INDIAN GAMING ISSUES

Indian gaming became a significant casino industry force after the 1987 *State of California v Cabazon Band of Mission Indians* case. This U.S. Supreme Court decision allows Indian tribes to conduct gaming operations for profit on reservation lands. The following year, the Indian Gaming Regulatory Act of 1988 (IGRA), Public Law 100-497, was enacted to provide a framework for regulating these activities. The law was widely promoted as a much needed economic development tool for this country's frequently impoverished Native American tribes.

While too involved to describe in detail here, chapter 3's Indian Gaming section provides a sense of the confusion and controversy which followed; most of the legal materials referred to in this book deal with some aspect of this legislation and its ramifications. Central issues include Indian sovereignty and states' rights. Indian tribes can only offer on their lands the same types of gambling which are allowed by the state in which they are located. While this provision has been frequently debated, the law also demands that tribes wanting to conduct gaming operations reach agreements or compacts with state governments, mandating unprecedented cooperation between these groups.

The United States Congress has held frequent and often impassioned hearings on implementing and amending the Indian Gaming Regulatory Act since its passage. At the end of 1994, newspapers reported that Congress had

adjourned without reforming the National Indian
Gaming Regulatory Act of 1988, leaving the
Supreme Court as the next likely forum for states and
tribes to try to settle their differences on reservation
gambling.[34]

One major issue is the Act's attempt to settle negotiation
problems between tribes and states. When a tribe requests
the negotiation necessary to operate casinos, the state must
participate in good faith. When a state declines, the law
declares district courts will preside over any actions brought
against that state by Native Americans . The United States
Constitution's Eleventh Amendment, however, does not
allow Indian tribes to take action against or sue state governments, and, in reality, tribes have no real legal recourse.[35]
    In October 1994, the Supreme Court asked the admin-
istration's Justice Department for their opinion on

> whether federal courts have the authority to oversee
> gaming negotiations between tribes and states. . . .
> The issue before the Supreme Court is whether states
> are protected by the 11th Amendment from being
> sued by tribes for refusing to negotiate gaming
> compacts. . . . The losing side in the Supreme Court
> cases may turn to Congress for help, but right now
> state and tribal officials seem to prefer letting the
> courts resolve the Indian gambling dispute instead of
> Congress.[36]

Reservation casinos continue to operate, and Indian leaders
continue to resist any government intervention in casino
management.
    Many Indian casino operations are enjoying great
success. According to Judy Zelio, National Conference of
State Legislatures, casino gaming "has transformed some
tribes into heavyweight economic players in their states and
localities."[37]   Zelio reports that as of June 1994, "19 states
and 84 tribes have nearly 100 agreements about the conduct

of Indian gaming."[38]   Most noteworthy, perhaps, is the immense success of Connecticut's Mashantucket Pequots' Foxwood Casino, now the most profitable in the United States.

In addition to the legal disputes noted above, Indian gaming has generated other kinds of controversy. Tribal leaders who support this industry cite impressive statistics about the economic benefits it affords their members. Unemployment on many reservations has dramatically decreased, and profits are being spent on such reservation improvements as new roads, schools, and health centers. Many Native Americans agree with Ojibwa leader Marge Anderson when she says that Indian gaming

> is the only economic development that's ever worked in Indian country. Period. And without gaming, we were losing our culture, we were losing our language. We wouldn't survive.[39]

Other Native Americans disagree so strongly that lives have been lost. One such conflict occurred in 1990 on the Mohawk Indians' St. Regis Reservation, located in New York, Quebec, and Ontario. While some tribal members endorsed gaming to fund tribal programs, others argued that casinos cause a variety of social problems and generate little profit. This clash, resulting in one gun battle and two deaths, was complicated by a "bitter power struggle between competing tribal councils" and the reluctance of U.S. and Canadian officials to involve Mohawks in their efforts to resolve the conflict.[40]

Some Native Americans have expressed deeply felt beliefs against Indian casinos. They are seriously concerned that tribal traditions and heritage will be lost and sacred areas will be destroyed by outsiders. Along with profits come increased underage gambling, compulsive gambling, alcoholism, and drug abuse. Although Native Americans have a cultural basis for many games of chance, Indian opponents also question tribal involvement in "mainstream" American casino action.

Some industry leaders have criticized Indian gaming. They think it is susceptible to corruption and mismanagement, since operations may be run by individuals with no gaming experience. Donald Trump, one vociferous opponent, has been accused of fearing the competition Indian gaming threatens. Also, while government agencies outside of the gaming industry normally monitor and regulate state-sanctioned casino activities, the Indian Gaming Regulatory Act basically turns this responsibility, and power, over to the Indian operators themselves.

While all signs point to continued expansion of Indian gaming, any resolution of the legal and tribal controversies just discussed may impose limitations. Currently, however,

the notable success of some tribal casinos has spurred the expansion of nontribal gaming as competition increases for gambling dollars. . . . The siting of tribal casinos also may create a "domino effect" as nearby jurisdictions begin to vie for the co-economic benefits offered by gaming.[41]

Many communities were initially resistant to the spread of reservation-based casinos, perhaps due to a variation of the "not in my backyard" theme differently worded as the "not in back of my community" argument.

The most successful tribal casinos have had significant effects on their non-Indian neighbors. Job creation, increased tax revenues, and entertainment potential have been real advantages. . . . Increased casino employment at a Wisconsin Winnebago operation has been estimated to save the state over $2.2 million in welfare costs per year.[42]

Zelio concludes, "The 'state vs. tribes' theme now sounds a little tired in the face of the economic realities that are realigning communities."[43]

The outlook for Indian gaming is strongly positive, even as moral and economic controversies continue and legal issues have yet to be resolved. Observers may have to again adopt that wait and see attitude. As with most gambling enterprises, accurately predicting its future can be difficult.

LEGAL AND REGULATORY ISSUES

Casino gaming is one of the most heavily regulated industries in the United States. The Casino Law and Regulation section in chapter 3 covers most of the legal and regulatory issues casinos raise. Many of the annotations there examine or compare how states have regulated gambling or are considering regulation if gambling is legalized. Some authors analyze specific aspects of legislative or regulatory language, while others describe the administrative roles governments and their regulatory agencies have adopted. These references should particularly interest public administrators and lawmakers in states or locales where legalized gambling is being considered or current law is being amended. The impacts of such federal legislation as the Money Laundering Control Act of 1986 are also examined.

Regulating and controlling computerized gaming devices is a central issue in recent literature. Ever-changing computer applications have revolutionized gambling for both operators and players. Ensuring fair play is particularly difficult when highly complicated, computerized machines determine wagering outcomes. State law must address such complex issues as fair, defect-free machines, restricted access to machines and servicing, and accurate collection and accounting mechanisms.[44]

According to Joseph Maglitta, many gambling opponents use these developments in their fight against legalization:

Critics worry that the wildfire growth of new and emerging technologies—including computerized Keno and video poker games, 800- and 900-call services, multimedia racetrack systems, and interactive gaming channels on the "information highway"—will turn the $329 billion gambling industry into a huge digital monster.[45]

He describes some recent computer glitches that have adversely affected both operators and bettors and stresses that these technologies raise new, ethical "questions for systems professionals involved in building and supporting gaming systems."[46] Furthermore, the increasing availability of more attractive, easier-to-play games may result in increases in gambling by the poor, by adolescents, and by compulsive gamblers. While some state governments are now looking at these issues, officials may have trouble keeping up with the rapid technological developments which promise to quickly increase gambling behavior and industry profits.[47]

ECONOMIC DEVELOPMENT AND SOCIAL ISSUES

As noted earlier, gambling legalization raises serious concerns for many people regardless of the form it takes. Lotteries, casino gambling, parimutuel betting, and local poker parlors have all prompted strong opposition from a variety of people. This discussion combines economic development and social issues, since many works in the bibliographies emphasize this interrelationship.

Foremost, perhaps, opponents question legalizing gambling as an economic development tool, the major reason increasing numbers of states approve or consider it. Are its promises fulfilled? Who benefits most from gambling profits, citizens or casino owners in distant states? Some annotations in chapter 3 demonstrate how viewpoints on a single location differ dramatically. The debate surrounding legalization of riverboat gaming in Tunica County, Mississippi is an excellent example of this divergence. Some say it has dramatically improved one of this country's poorest areas, a place Jesse Jackson called "America's Ethiopia." Janet Plume, for example, describes how the area's riverboat casinos attract thousands of players and bring millions of dollars into the local economy.[48]

U.S. News & World Report writer James Popkin agrees with Plume to an extent. He notes that "ninety-five percent of all adults now work, and the median family household income has nearly tripled."[49]   Conversely, housing costs have soared, more people are unable to pay their bills, drunk-driving arrests have increased 500 percent, and compulsive gambling problems are beginning to surface.[50]

A third author, *Southern Exposure's* Jenny Labalme, totally disagrees with both Plume and Popkin. She says that contrary to popular belief, Tunica's casinos have done little to raise the local standard of living. Also, the county has spent much on road, water, and sewer improvements without financial assistance from the casinos which necessitated these changes.[51] As noted earlier, increasing competition has already adversely affected Mississippi's gaming industry; some operations have closed and others are barely surviving.

Atlantic City casinos have prompted similar disagreements. A 1987 Touche Ross & Company report cites numerous statistics on how gaming has benefited New Jersey.[52]   Others, like Randy Diamond, see a different outcome. He calls Atlantic City a "picture of urban America at its worst," where "slums by the sea sit next to shiny glass-and-steel towers."[53] Gambling opponents frequently cite Atlantic City's problems as reason to keep casino gaming illegal. John D. Wolf, for example, describes that city's experience with "increased crime, prostitution, corruption, and drug trafficking" as grounds not to support casinos in Gary, Indiana.[54]

Readers should critically review articles like the ones listed above. Further research is necessary to substantiate the merits and validity of such differing viewpoints.

Two other concerns about casinos as economic development tools need to be mentioned. Like many others, Steven D. Gold argues that the gaming industry's success will greatly diminish due to increasing competition:

As casinos open in ever more states, their potential
for producing state revenue and stimulating economic

development diminishes. Casinos are most
beneficial when they attract many residents from
outside states. As more states have casinos, more
competition will exist among them, and fewer out-of-
state residents will be attracted to any particular
state.[55]

Phillip Longman raises this concern as well. He also
explains why legalization, to retain gamblers' dollars inside
their own states, does not improve government revenues.
Any local revenue gains are offset by social costs and the
diversion of money from area businesses to casinos. People
who gamble have less money to spend on those goods and
services which raise sale and excise taxes. He concludes,
"states cannot build economic strengths on the mental
weaknesses and anti-capitalist urges of their citizens."[56]
    In addition to the various views represented above, other
social and economic considerations about casino gaming
abound. A simple list highlights major issues:

Concerns about the ethics and morality of gambling
activities and particularly their support and endorsement
by governments;

Concerns about increased crime rates and prostitution in
areas which approve casinos;

Concerns about increased rates of alcoholism and drug
abuse in areas which approve casinos;

Concerns about dramatically growing rates of
compulsive gambling due to increases in opportunities
and the negative effects this addiction has on individuals,
their families, their employers, and communities;

Concerns about increasing rates of underage gambling,
which sets teenagers up for compulsive gambling
problems in later life;

Concerns about the equity or regressive nature of casino gambling taxes; some studies have shown lower income households gamble larger percentages of their incomes than those with higher incomes;

Concerns about the increased crowding, traffic congestion, and noise and air pollution casino development causes and the possible long-term environmental effects on specific locations;

Concerns about increases in public assistance because casino locations may attract people who either cannot find work or do not remain consistently employed due to the vagaries and seasonal nature of much casino tourism;

Concerns about radical changes in community identities which may force local residents to leave;

Concerns about the large number of low wage, unskilled jobs casinos provide which offer employees little chance for advancement or training applicable to other kinds of work;

Concerns about the destruction of small, local businesses either displaced by casinos or unable to compete with services, such as restaurants, which they provide;

Concerns about historic preservation when casinos are placed in or near significantly historic areas;

Concerns about emphasizing seemingly effortless financial gains in a society founded on the work ethic.

Although this list is not complete, it does reflect many of the social and economic problems people have associated with legal casino gaming. In many cases, researchers and writers weigh the economic benefits casinos offer against the social costs which result. Studies that cover ways to identify and quantify these social costs repeatedly appear in literature opposing gaming, and some of the studies in chapter 3 explain what they mean for American society.

While space limitations do not allow greater analysis of all significant issues associated with casino gaming, this discussion highlights most major concerns. Ongoing discussion about the impacts of casinos, from both supporting and opposing views, are well covered in the bibliographies found later in this work, and readers are urged to look there for more information. Even as casinos proliferate throughout the country and public opinion seems increasingly to approve their presence, there is no evidence that the controversies about their place in United States society are decreasing. As with the industry itself, it is difficult to predict how, or even if, these issues will change during the next few years, years that will certainly interest everyone with any stake in either the industry's successes or failures.

NOTES

1. *Global Gaming Almanac 1995* (N.p.: Smith Barney, December 1994): 9.

2. William N. Thompson, *Legalized Gambling: A Reference Handbook* (Santa Barbara, Calif.: ABC-CLIO, 1994): 2.

3. *The Harrah's Survey of U.S. Casino Entertainment* (Memphis, Tenn.: Harrah's, 1994): 4.

4. Michael J. Mandel, Mark Landler, and Ronald Grover, "The Entertainment Economy—America's Growth Engines: Theme Parks, Casinos, Sports, Interactive TV," *Business Week* 3362 (14 March 1994): 59.

5. *The Harrah's Survey of U.S. Casino Entertainment* (Memphis, Tenn.: Harrah's, 1994): 4.

6. Michael J. Mandel, Mark Landler, and Ronald Grover, "The Entertainment Economy—America's Growth Engines: Theme Parks, Casinos, Sports, Interactive TV," *Business Week* 3362 (14 March 1994): 60.

7. *Global Gaming Almanac 1995* (N.p.: Smith Barney, December 1994): 7.

8. *The Harrah's Survey of U.S. Casino Entertainment* (Memphis, Tenn.: 1994): 12.

9. *Harrah's Survey* (1994): 12.

10. *Harrah's Survey* (1994): 11.

11. "Gambling Sweeping the Country," *State Policy Reports* 12 (September 1994): 3.

12. William N.Thompson, *Legalized Gambling: A Reference Handbook* (Santa Barbara, Calif.: ABC-CLIO, 1994): 6.

13. Thompson, *Legalized Gambling* (1994): 8.

14. Thompson, *Legalized Gambling* (1994): 6.

15. Thompson, *Legalized Gambling* (1994): 69.

16. Gerri Hirshey, "Gambling Nation," *New York Times Magazine* (17 July 1994): 43.

17. Hirshey, "Gambling Nation," 44.

18. "Gambling Sweeping the Country," *State Policy Reports* 12 (September 1994): 2.

19. Barry Meier, "Casinos in Pursuit of New Players," *New York Times* (29 December 1994): D1 (L).

20. "Leisure-Time: Basic Analysis," *Standard & Poor's Industry Surveys* (April 1995): L37.

21. "Gambling Sweeping the Country," *State Policy Reports* 12 (September 1994): 18.

22. *The Harrah's Survey of U.S. Casino Entertainment* (Memphis, Tenn.: Harrah's 1994): 12.

23. Rick Alm, "Miss. Riverboat Casinos Barely Staying Afloat," *Las Vegas Sun* (7 December 1994): 1.

24. Dan Cordtz, "High Noon for High Rollers," *Financial World* 13 (8 November 1994): 60.

25. "Voters Give Gaming Measures Mixed Reception," *Las Vegas Review-Journal* (13 November 1994): 7F.

26. Dennis Camire, "Report: Expansion May See More Hurdles," *Reno Gazette-Journal* (19 December 1994): 3.

27. Camire, "Report," 3.

28. Camire, "Report," 3.

29. Ray Paulick, "Games People Play," *The Blood-Horse* 120 (8 October 1994): 4762.

30. Joshua Quittner, "Betting on Virtual Vegas," *Time* 145 (12 June 1995): 63.

31. Quittner, "Betting on Virtual Vegas," 63.

32. Don Cox, "Firms Bet on Bringing Gambling to the Home," *Reno Gazette-Journal* (9 December 1994): 5.

33. Dave Palermo, "Selling Gaming Not Easy," *Las Vegas Review-Journal/Sun* (6 November 1994): 17E.

34. Tony Batt, "Indian Gaming Unsettled," *Las Vegas Review-Journal* (6 November 1994): 17E.

35. Peter T. Glimco, "The IGRA and the Eleventh Amendment: Indian Tribes Are Gambling When They Try to Sue a State," *John Marshall Law Review* 27 (1993): 197.

36. Tony Batt, "Indian Gaming Unsettled," *Las Vegas Review-Journal* (6 November 1994): 17E.

37. Judy Zelio, "The Fat New Buffalo," *State Legislatures* 20 (June 1994): 38.

38. Zelio, "The Fat New Buffalo," 38.

39. Mark Marvel, "Gambling on Reservations: What's Really at Stake?" *Interview* 24 (May 1994): 114.

40. Joelle Attinger, "Mohawks, Money and Death," *Time* 135 (15 May 1990): 32.

41. Judy Zelio, "The Fat New Buffalo," *State Legislatures* 20 (June 1994): 39.

42. Zelio, "The Fat New Buffalo," 39.

43. Zelio, "The Fat New Buffalo," 43.

44. Cory Aronovitz, "Comments—To Start, Press the Flashing Button: The Legalization of Video Gaming Devices," *Software Law Journal* 5 (December 1992): 795.

45. Joseph Maglitta, "High-Tech Wagering: Jackpot or Jeopardy?" *Computerworld* 28 (7 February 1994): 28.

46. Maglitta, "High-Tech Wagering," 28.

47. Maglitta, "High-Tech Wagering," 28

48. Janet Plume, "Little Las Vegas Sprouting in Tunica," *Casino Journal* 7 (September 1994): 79.

49. James Popkin, "A Mixed Blessing for 'America's Ethiopia,'" *U.S. News & World Report* 116 (14 March 1994): 52.

50. Popkin, "A Mixed Blessing for 'America's Ethiopia,'" 52.

51. Jenny Labalme, "The Great Riverboat Gamble," *Southern Exposure* 22 (Summer 1994): 10-11.

52. *Casino Industry's Economic Impact on New Jersey* (Newark, N.J.: Touche Ross & Co., 20 October 1987): 2-3.

53. Randy Diamond, "Atlantic City Seeks Life Beyond Gambling," *Christian Science Monitor* 86 (19 January 1994): 8.

54. John D. Wolf, "Taking a Gamble on the Casino Industry," *Christian Science Monitor* 107 (17 January 1990): 38.

55. Steven D. Gold, "It's Not a Miracle, It's a Mirage," *State Legislatures* 20 (February 1994): 28.

56. Phillip Longman, "The Tax Mirage," *Florida Trend* 37 (June 1994): 67.

CHAPTER 2

Research Methods

Finding information quickly on casino gaming and its social and economic effects on the United States is really quite easy. Thorough research, of course, is much more time consuming. For this book, the authors did an exhaustive search in a wide variety of print and nonprint sources, and quickly discovered that there was an overwhelming amount of material on this high interest topic published since 1985. A quick check of recent sources indicates that the quantity of information increases each year, naturally reflecting the proliferation of casinos and their growing presence in this country. Gaming-related issues are regularly covered in newspapers, periodicals, government publications, monographs, and print, CD-ROM, and on-line indexes for the social sciences. This chapter will briefly highlight several sources which are particularly useful for research on this topic.

First, almost everything on casinos and their impact on the United States will be found in social sciences literature. The main subject headings, keywords, or descriptors are "gambling" and "casinos." Books on how to gamble, such as how to play blackjack, are not covered here.

The following discussion is arranged by categories of reference materials with brief lists of some key sources in each area. There are a great number of library reference sources, much too numerous to fully list or describe here, that will help researchers find information on this topic. New reference books and indexes are constantly being published, and over the last several years, many sources have been issued in more than one format, including paper, CD-ROM, and on-line. Some reference titles may duplicate, in part or completely, the scope and information found in other standard materials.

Because of the myriad sources available, the list below is not at all comprehensive. In fact, it is very selective and is simply intended to give readers some direction for beginning their own research on this topic. Many of these sources will be found in larger public and academic libraries, and librarians are there to direct researchers to relevant sources. If the items below are unavailable, librarians may be able to suggest valid alternatives which are in their collections or refer researchers to other libraries that own them. Due to space limitations, entire bibliographic citations and lengthy descriptions have not been included. In every case, the sources listed are found in many libraries nationwide, and the exact titles should provide enough information either to locate them or identify other items with similar coverage.

First, there are a wide variety of general handbooks on how to find information in libraries. Many libraries also publish guides on how to find information in their specific institutions. Librarians will recommend particular sources and search strategies. It is helpful, though, if researchers have a clear sense of what they want and are able to articulate this need clearly. In her book *Popular Entertainment Research: How to Do It and How to Use It*, Barbara J. Pruett includes a lengthy first chapter on the research process. She states that research is really a two-part process: (1) Finding and collecting the information you need; and (2) Studying and analyzing of that information.[1] She provides useful pointers on defining the research project, identifying the type of research necessary, and organizing the results while the research is being done. Although Pruett focuses on entertainment, her clear suggestions are applicable to any research pursuit. As noted, there are many other equally useful works which offer brief or in-depth information on resources and search strategies; library staffs and catalogs will direct researchers to sources in their collections.

GENERAL SOURCES

Books in Print: lists of books currently available for sale in the United States. The subject volumes arrange titles by topic. Available on-line, CD-ROM, print.

Encyclopedia of Associations: lists a wide variety of associations and organizations in this country; good key-word access to organization names and concise descriptions of their purposes. Most of these groups provide information on their activities or refer inquiries to other relevant sources. Separate volumes for U.S. regional associations and international associations. Many entries have publication lists which can be particularly useful. On-line, print. Note: though the *Encyclopedia of Associations* is an excellent general resource, a more comprehensive list of gaming-related associations and organizations is included in chapter 5 of this research guide.

Library Catalogs: contain bibliographical information for books found in particular collections; most larger public and academic libraries now have on-line catalogs, although older holdings may still appear in traditional card catalogs.

Ulrich's International Periodicals Directory: lists peri-odicals published worldwide, arranged in broad subject categories. Note: because of their highly specialized and often fleeting nature, many gaming periodicals are not listed in *Ulrich's.*   Appendix A of this research guide provides information on many of these hard-to-find titles.

SELECT SOURCES ON THE CASINO INDUSTRY

These print titles provide information and statistics on gambling and the casino industry; citations and annotations for all but one are found in chapter 3. The bibliographies in that chapter include many books that are available in libraries.

Gambling. San Diego, Calif.: Grehaven Press, 1995. Provides overview information on casinos, gambling, and their social and economic effects. Not included in the bibliography because it was published after 1994.

Global Gaming Almanac 1995. N.p.: Smith Barney, 1994. Provides a wide variety of statistics and information on gambling activities worldwide.

The Harrah's Survey of U.S. Casino Entertainment, 1994. Memphis, Tenn.: Harrah's, 1994. Provides statistics on gaming and gambling behavior which are frequently quoted in a variety of sources. Annual.

"Leisure Time: Basic Analysis." In *Standard & Poor's Industry Surveys.* New York: Standard and Poor's Corp., 1973-. Quarterly. Provides concise overview information on the casino industry and the major issues it faces; contains a variety of statistics.

GENERAL PERIODICAL INDEXES

Magazine Index: provides indexing for 400 popular and general interest magazines and some newspapers; includes the *Wall Street Journal* and the *New York Times* . On-line, CD-ROM.

New York Times Index: the *New York Times* regularly covers important casino-related events. On-line, CD-ROM, print. (Many of the general indexes here also index this prominent newspaper.)

Newsbank: indexes articles from newspapers of over 450 U.S. cities. Print, CD-ROM.

ProQuest: indexes a variety of periodicals and some newspapers, including the *New York Times* and the *Wall Street Journal.* On-line, CD-ROM.

National Newspaper Index: indexes the *New York Times, Christian Science Monitor, Los Angeles Times, Wall Street Journal,* and the *Washington Post.* On-line, CD-ROM.

NEWSSEARCH: provides access to current articles and wire stories from over 1,800 different sources; includes information for only the previous fourteen to forty-five days. On-line.

Readers' Guide to Periodical Literature: a very general periodical index and standard source found in libraries of all sizes. On-line, CD-ROM, print.

SPECIAL GUIDES: SOCIAL SCIENCES LITERATURE

This is a very select listing of some standard research guides on the social sciences in general and business in particular. They cite and summarize most of the sources listed here as well as many others. There are other similar titles not included here.

Daniells, Lorna M. *Business Information Sources.* 3rd ed. Berkeley, Calif.: University of California Press, 1993.

Freed, Melvyn, and Virgil P. Diodato. *Business Information Desk Reference: Where To Find Answers to Business Questions.* New York: Macmillan, 1991.

Ganly, John, ed. *Data Sources for Business and Market Analysis.* 4th ed. Metuchen, N.J.: Scarecrow Press, 1994.

Sproull, Natalie L. *Handbook of Research Methods: A Guide for Practitioners and Students in the Social Sciences.* Metuchen, N.J.: Scarecrow Press, 1995.

SPECIALIZED INDEXES

This is a very select list of specific social sciences and business indexes that routinely provide access to information on gambling and gaming. The formats included at the end of each summary could change at any time.

ABI/Inform: indexes over 800 business and trade journals, providing information about companies, products, trends, business conditions, corporate strategies, and management techniques in a variety of business fields. On-line, CD-ROM.

American Statistics Index (ASI): indexes statistical information found in publications of the U.S. Government; very thorough, useful, and easy to use. On-line, print.

Business Periodicals Index: indexes a very select number of business periodicals; a standard library source. On-line, CD-ROM, print.

Dissertation Abstracts International: lists doctoral dissertations completed in this country. Also titled *Dissertation Abstracts On-line* and *Dissertation Abstracts OnDisc.* On-line, CD-ROM, print.

International Hospitality and Tourism Database: indexes and abstracts several key gaming trade publications not indexed elsewhere along with a variety of hotel, restaurant, and travel publications. CD-ROM.

LEXIS/NEXIS: contains indexing and full-text access to hundreds of business journals, newspapers, and popular magazines. Also contains full text of federal, state, and local laws and regulations pertaining to all subjects. On-line.

Psychological Abstracts: indexes information on psychology and behavioral sciences; particularly useful for information on compulsive or addictive gambling behavior. Also titled *PsychINFO* on-line, and *PSYCHLIT* on CD-ROM (*PSYCHLIT* covers most of the information found in the print source). On-line, CD-ROM, print.

Public Affairs Information Service (PAIS): indexes a wide variety of social sciences materials on such subjects as business, government, international relations, political science, public administration, and finance. Includes some federal, state, and local government publications. On-line, CD-ROM, print.

Social Science Citation Index: indexes the literature of the behavioral and social sciences; very thorough. Also titled *SOCIAL SCISEARCH* on-line. On-line, CD-ROM, print.

SOCIOFILE: Indexes over 1,600 sociology journals worldwide and includes dissertations in the field; this CD-ROM product is the equivalent of *Sociological Abstracts* and *Planning/Policy and Development Abstracts*. On-line, CD-ROM.

Sociological Abstracts: indexes sociology journals, reports, and presentations. On-line, CD-ROM (see above), print.

Statistical Reference Index (SRI): indexes statistical information not found in U.S. Government publications; does include state government, association, and trade publications. Provides some access to state government statistical reports on casinos and gambling. Print.

Wall Street Journal Index: indexes the *Wall Street Journal*, which regularly covers gaming industry news; as noted above, this newspaper is also indexed in a variety of other sources. Print, CD-ROM, on-line.

Westlaw: provides access to legal information, including journals, case law, etc.; for practicing attorneys; found in law libraries and larger law firms. On-line.

INFORMATION ON U.S. COMPANIES

As with the previous sections, this is a highly selective, and by no means complete, listing of information sources on specific companies. Lorna Daniells's *Business Information Sources*, cited before, will have additional information. Librarians can recommend many sources for various kinds of information on this topic. Widely available series are published by Moody's, Dun & Bradstreet, and Standard & Poor's; the series and services these three companies issue are too numerous to mention here. The appendices in this book include a list of publicly held companies which deal with gaming or gaming equipment.

Compact D/SEC: provides financial and management information compiled from annual reports and other financial disclosure statements for approximately 12,000 U.S. public companies. To be included, companies must have filed an SEC document within the last eighteen months and must have at least 500 stockholders and assets of at least 500 million dollars. On-line (*Disclosure*), CD-ROM.

Investext: includes over 30,000 company and industry research reports on over 11,000 U.S. and international companies; the industry reports cover fifty-three industries. On-line, CD-ROM.

GUIDES TO GOVERNMENT SOURCES

The titles listed below are just two of the available guides or handbooks that explain how to find specific kinds of information in the wide variety of sources the United States government publishes each year. U.S. government publications are found in libraries throughout the country; almost every state has at least one library which receives all depository items distributed each year. Again, many librarians can direct researchers to these titles.

Morehead, Joe, and Mary Fetzer. *Introduction To United States Government Information Sources*. 4th ed. Englewood, Colo.: Libraries Unlimited, 1992.

Sears, Jean L., and Marilyn K. Moody. *Using Government Information Sources: Print and Electronic*. 2nd ed. Phoenix, Ariz.: Oryx Press, 1994.

FEDERAL GOVERNMENT SOURCES

Code of Federal Regulations: contains all regulations governing federal government activities; these regulations, by definition, also affect state and local governments as well. Accompanied by an index. A privately-published index, with much broader coverage, is also available; it contains numerous references under such headings as "Gambling Operations," "Gambling Winnings," and "Gambling Devices."

Federal Register: contains proposed or adopted regulatory changes for the U.S. Government; includes information on the Indian Gaming Regulatory Act, when related regulatory changes occur, and lists names of Native American tribes which have obtained tribal/state compacts. Accompanied by an index; a privately-published index, with broader coverage, is also issued. Full text of the *Federal Register* is available on-line in a variety of sources, including *GPO Access* and *LEXIS/NEXIS*.

GPO Access: provides on-line access to proposed and final federal legislation and includes full text access to such publications as the *Federal Register*. Also includes the Monthly Catalog, described below, from January 1994 to date. Available at depository libraries and on the Internet (World Wide Web: http://www.access.gpo.gov/su_docs).

Monthly Catalog of United States Government Publications: lists a wide variety of materials issued by the federal government and distributed to select libraries throughout the country. Excellent subject access; particularly useful for materials on laws, hearings, and reports on gambling and casinos. Many federal publications are included in this book's bibliography. Various companies, such as Marcive and Silver Platter, issue this from 1976 to date on CD-ROM, and CARL and Dialog are just two of the vendors which provide on-line access. Print, CD-ROM, and Internet (See *GPO Access* above).

United States Code: contains all laws for the United States, including such important legislation as the Indian Gaming Regulatory Act and the Money Laundering Control Act. Includes index.

United States Statutes at Large: contains exact text of the laws, as passed, and is arranged numerically by congressional session and the sequentially-assigned public law number. Later editions include brief legislative histories which are particularly useful for thorough research; these references refer readers to the *Congressional Record* and specific House and Senate reports.

FEDERAL GOVERNMENT INFORMATION

CIS Index: provides detailed subject access to all congressional activities, hearings, reports, etc. Later annual cumulations contain a separate volume listing all public laws passed during the year with legislative histories that provide references for related government publications. An indispensable source of information on the U.S. Congress. Monthly, with annual cumulations.

LEGI-SLATE: provides on-line access to a wide variety of U.S. legislative information, including full texts of the *Congressional Record*, the *Federal Register*, and proposed and passed legislation.

STATE GOVERNMENT INFORMATION

Much of the legal activity surrounding gambling legalization occurs at the state level. A very select list of print sources follows. It is critical for researchers to remember that state and local governments publish a great deal of useful information about legalizing casino gaming; unfortunately, these publications can be difficult to identify. A serious effort was made to include a variety of them in chapter 3.   Chapter 4 contains a thorough listing of regulatory agencies found throughout the country; almost all of them will respond to direct inquiries about their publications and activities. The Nevada Gaming Control Board, for example, distributes on demand a list of several publications they sell at moderate cost.

The collected laws for each state that has legalized casino gambling contain a great deal of information. Sets of these laws, for states or for regional parts of the country, are found in larger law libraries. Nearly all library collections contain the set for their state.

Since so much activity concerning gambling legislation occurs in state legislatures, chapter 4 also includes lists of legislative libraries and legislative hotlines that can provide information on all aspects of the legislative process or refer callers to appropriate sources.

Book of the States: provides a great deal of information on state legislatures, including stop and start dates for legislative sessions, members' names, etc. A very useful and easy-to-use source.

State Elective Officials and the Legislatures: contains names and information about state legislators and identifies their political responsibilities.

State Legislative Sourcebook: contains a wide variety of information on state legislatures. Biennial.

The associations below provide assistance to their primary clientele—state government agencies or state legislatures—as indicated by their names. They may provide some brief information or referrals for individuals outside of these groups, as time permits.

> National Conference of State Legislatures
> 1560 Broadway, Suite 700
> Denver, Colorado 80202
> Telephone: (303) 830-2200

> Council of State Governments
> Headquarters Office
> 3560 Iron Works Pike
> P.O. Box 11910
> Lexington, Kentucky 40578-1910
> Telephone: (606) 244-8000

INTERNET SOURCES

Including sources on casinos and gambling found on the Internet is a somewhat risky business. This international computerized network changes daily, and finding much of the information it offers requires training, skill, and a high degree of interest and motivation. Increasing numbers of larger libraries provide Internet access and assistance for their users, and many Americans are accessing it in their homes through a variety of subscription services.

Internet guides and handbooks are being issued constantly. Below is a very selective list of some books which will help novices with this complex resource.

Gross, Michael. *A Pocket Tour of Law on the Internet.* The Sybex Instant Reference Series. San Francisco: Sybex, 1996.

Hoffman, Paul E. *The Internet Instant Reference.* 3rd ed. San Francisco: Sybex, 1996.

Rosenfeld, Louis, et. al. *The Internet Compendium: Subject Guides to Social Sciences, Business and Law Resources.* New York: Neal-Schuman, 1995.

Tittle, Ed, and Margaret Robbins. *Internet Access Essentials*. Boston, Mass.: AP Professionals, 1995.

Zakalik, Joanna, ed. *Guide to Internet Databases*. Detroit, Mich.: Gale, 1995.

Computer and library publications frequently offer articles on finding Internet information on particular topics. The following articles are examples of what may be found in a variety of periodical indexes.

Makulowich, John S. "Internet Company Information: A Business Buffet." *Database* 18 (April 1995): 79-80.

Mallory, Mary. "Network Access to State Legislative Information," *DTTP: Documents to the People* 23 (June 1995): 72-77. This is a particularly useful article for anyone who searches the Internet for state-level legislative information. These Internet addresses provide on-line access to states' legislative information systems, which should provide current information on any pending or recently-passed gambling and casino legislation.

Morgan, Keith, and Deborah Kelly-Milburn. "Internet Resources for Economics." *C&RL News* 55 (September 1994): 475-478.

For the last two years, it seemed that much of the information on casino gaming on the Internet dealt with casino locations or discourses on how to gamble. A search done in August 1995, however, turned up some Internet sources which are applicable to this book's scope. A search of *WebCrawler*, using the query "gaming," turned up 617 hits, a wide variety of files; while the authors did not read each one of these, it appears that there is some useful information on the business and regulatory aspects of casino gaming. A *Lycos* search, using the query "casinos," turned up 502 hits, another wide variety of files. Again, the authors did not read each one of these; it does appear that there is some information on the business and regulatory aspects of casino gaming. Another *Lycos* search, http://lycos.cs.cmu.edu, found a large number of hits on Indian gaming and investing in gaming. Other worthwhile Internet addresses include:

gopher://earth/usa.net—provides information on the Indian Gaming Regulatory Act.

http://www.halycon.com/FWDP/fwdp.html—provides information on Native Americans and Indian gaming.

Chapter 1 of this book includes a reference to a 1995 *Time* article on gambling on the Internet, in which the author predicts that this phenomenon will increase over the next several years.

SPECIAL LIBRARY COLLECTIONS

The University of Nevada, Las Vegas, Gaming Resource Center holds one of the world's premier collections of gaming-related literature. The collection is open to the public. Internet access to the library's on-line catalog is available through neon@nevada.edu. Full address information for the Center is provided in chapter 5.

As stressed at the beginning of this chapter, readers can find a great deal of information about casino gaming, and its social and economic effects on the United States, in a wide variety of standard library resources. Again, the sources listed above are by no means exhaustive; they are included here only to offer some suggestions which can be particularly useful to readers who want additional information on this controversial and high interest topic.

NOTES

1. Barbara J. Pruett, *Popular Entertainment Research: How To Do It and How To Use It*. (Metuchen, N.J.: Scarecrow Press, 1992): 1.

CHAPTER 3

Casino Gaming
Bibliography

For this book, the authors reviewed a wide variety of literature, indexing, and on-line sources dating from 1985 through 1994. The primary intent was to identify and selectively list significant materials focused on casino gaming and its social and economic effects in the United States. The following bibliography contains references for periodical articles, government publications, monographs, manuscripts, and newspaper articles.

Criteria utilized in selecting materials are listed and explained in the introduction: scholarship and importance; accuracy; timeliness and relevance; usefulness; uniqueness; variety; and availability. Materials written before 1985, about other countries, or about other forms of gambling are included if they are particularly significant or informative.

A few notes about the bibliography:

Citations are arranged alphabetically by author, or title if no author is present, under seven subject headings: the casino industry, Indian gaming, riverboat gaming, casino law and regulation, casinos and economic development, casinos and American society, and casinos and crime. As with any subject divisions, overlap occurs. Materials are placed in the category that seemed most appropriate based on their predominant subject emphases.

Serious effort was made to compile a thorough and useful index. While a review of all citations in a broad category provides a great deal of information on one of these areas, readers are strongly encouraged to review the index for additional materials of interest that may be found in other parts of the bibliography. Index headings are arranged alphabetically; the corresponding numbers refer to entry numbers, not page numbers. The separate author index also refers to entry numbers.

This is a selective, not exhaustive, bibliography. While most citations are fully annotated and indexed, the authors chose to include additional citations for other materials which are valuable but could not be summarized due to space restrictions. These references are found under a separate heading, Supplemental Materials, at the end of each subject section. While the authors of these unannotated citations are indexed, subject indexing is not included.

While materials at University of Nevada, Las Vegas Special Collections are noncirculating, many other items cited here will be available on interlibrary loan; researchers should contact their local library for information on how to obtain items of interest.

Materials containing transitory information, or information without long-term value, are not included in the bibliography. While the rise and fall of various gaming stocks' values, for example, may command immediate attention, their ongoing variations were considered of short-term interest only.

Chapter 2, Research Methods, lists some key sources useful for researching the gaming industry and its economic and social effects in the United States.

SECTION A

The Casino Industry

Casino gaming is one of the fastest growing and most dynamic industries in the United States. Widely considered recession proof, it has become an attractive economic development tool in twenty-three states, and many others are considering it. Ninety-two million Americans visited casinos in 1993, more than the number of people who attended major league baseball games and arena concerts. This section provides access to literature about casino gaming written by industry operators, investment analysts, consultants, scholars, reporters, and others. Myriad aspects of casino operations, from accounting to strategic planning, are addressed; industry overviews and statistical sources are provided; and major developments are covered.

1.   Abelson, Alan. "Up & Down Wall Street." *Barron's* (10 May 1993): 1, 37.
       Discusses Donald Trump's legal efforts to ban Indian gaming in New Jersey. Calling Trump "Big Chief All Bull" in this negative tongue-in-cheek analysis, Abelson chides him for resisting any competition to his Atlantic City casinos.

2.   Alexandar, Blair, et al. *The Gaming Hotel Industry*. Business Policy MBA Capstone Paper. Santa Clara, Calif.: Santa Clara University, Leavey School of Business, 1991. 141 pp.
       Analyzes the casino-resort industry from the perspective of market opportunities and structural analysis. This report spotlights Circus Circus and Caesars World Incorporated along with their contrasting market focuses and operating philosophies and explores each firm's strategic

planning process and product portfolio. Bibliographical references.

3.   Ambiel, Terry. *Casino Math? A Professional's Guide to Reading Cheques and Stacks: Craps, Roulette, Twenty-One.* Revised ed. Sparks, Nev.: T. Ambiel, 1994. 94 pp.
     Helps casino dealers quickly calculate payoffs for such table games as craps, roulette, and twenty-one. The technique involves instantly knowing the value of a stack of chips and memorizing ways to calculate quickly the amount to be paid out for a particular type of bet. This is a technical training manual for casino dealers. Charts, illustrations.

4.   Avansino, Raymond C., Jr. *Hilton and the Worldwide Proliferation of Gaming.* University of Nevada, Las Vegas, Special Collections. 1993. 8 pp.
     Contends the proliferation of gaming is directly caused by America's need for new jobs, tax revenues, and increased tourism, and that a similar need exists in Europe, Asia, and Latin America. "Globalization" is at the heart of Hilton's corporate strategy, and it plans to manage gaming operations worldwide. In addition to its domestic operations, the company is involved in casinos in Australia, Uruguay, Puerto Rico, Canada, and Turkey. Avansino is President and Chief Operating Officer of Hilton Hotels Corporation.

5.   Brewer, Pearl, and Leslie Cummings. "Information Systems for Gaming—Slot Tracking Technology." *The Bottomline* 9 (December 1994/January 1995): 6-7, 29.
     Explains how slot tracking systems embody the "ever-increasing use of technology in casinos." The authors call the slot machine a "composite device" because it is "both the product and the data entry device for the product's sales." They discuss how it provides very accurate information for the "four managerial functions of slot systems: accounting, security, maintenance, and marketing." Each function is then discussed individually. Slot tracking systems provide accounting information, for example, on

wagers or "coin-in," payouts or "coin-out," and the number of games played on a specific machine for any specific time period.

6.   Britton, David Ross. *A Casino Supervisor's Guide to Effective Performance Evaluation.* Las Vegas, Nev.: Britton, 1988. 87 pp.
        Provides lower and middle-level casino supervisors with a practical guide for the evaluation of their subordinates. Job analysis and description, appraisal instruments, and evaluator training are covered. Bibliographical references.

7.   Brock, Floyd, George L. Fussell, and William J. Corney. "How To Optimize Casino-Hotel Revenue." *Journal of Business Forecasting* 9 (Summer 1990): 2-5, 10.
        Describes how managers can analyze "customer migration in a casino-hotel," determine how such movement affects revenues, and then manipulate it to improve profits. Their simulation procedure includes the following steps: "identify stops for customer migration" where people "spend time or money" such as gift shops or restaurants; "build a mathematical model that specifies the nature of the stops" and "links their pathways"; create a computer program for the model with "simulation languages like Simscript II.5," QuickBASIC or Turbo Pascal; run the program to decide if it is "doing what it is supposed to be doing"; and "run the simulation with different assumptions (scenarios) and test their results." Tables give a sample list of destinations in a hotel/casino and information on "guest migration paths." Tables, bibliographical references.

8.   Brown, Terrence E., and Michael M. Lefever. "A 50-Year Renaissance: The Hotel Industry From 1939 To 1989." *Cornell Hotel and Restaurant Administration Quarterly* 31 (May 1990): 18-25.
        Covers growth in the hotel industry and puts developments in historical context. Placing casinos in resort hotels is one of several landmarks listed. Hilton Hotels led the way with two Las Vegas locations in the early 1970s,

and Holiday Inn became the largest concern by 1980 with Harrah's in Las Vegas, Lake Tahoe, and Atlantic City. Industry insiders "speculated that casino properties pointed the way to the hotel industry's future."

9.   Brownell, Judi. "Opening the 'Taj': The Culture of Fantasy." *Cornell Hotel and Restaurant Administration Quarterly* 31 (August 1990): 19-23.
       Shows how leaders "can influence organizational culture" to achieve desired outcomes. Brownell describes Donald Trump's development of Atlantic City's Taj Mahal Casino Resort. "Trump symbolizes his concern for grandeur by paying obsessive attention to it." He stresses the importance of "providing maximum space, maximum equipment, and maximum service." The author lists ten "essential principles of culture leadership" which build "a strong, healthy organizational culture" by communicating vision and principles to employees.

10.   Brubaker, John M. *Eye in the Sky: A Casino Surveillance Guide for Management, Directors and Other Casino Executives and Personnel.* University of Nevada, Las Vegas, Special Collections. 1993. 132 pp.
       Addresses the seemingly countless ways dishonest customers and employees cheat casinos and recommends how to stop them. Chapters cover such topics as employee files, complimentaries, cheats and scams, table games, gaming equipment, slot machines, customer credit, marketing, purchasing, currency transaction reports, forgery and counterfeiting, money counts, chips, surveillance equipment, evidence control, door security, pit procedures, bank deposits, and found money. Brubaker stresses that strict adherence to procedures will limit losses. This is an outstanding handbook for casino security professionals. Bibliographical references.

11.   Bruzzese, Anita. "Hedging Their Bets." *Incentive* 166 (September 1992): 36-38, 43.
       Describes incentive marketing techniques casinos use to attract people. "Taking good care of customers" involves

"offering the bettors the extras they want." Hotel-casinos employ computer databases, for example, to record customers' preferences for rooms, food, casino games, and size of wagers, information which will be used to encourage their repeat business. Incentive "comp packages can include everything from discount rooms to special gambling packages." Several successful casino promotions, done during slow business periods, are also covered. Includes a sidebar on "how to make a promotion a safe bet."

12.	Charleton, James H. *Recreation in the United States: National Historical Landmark Theme Study*. Washington, D.C.: U.S. Department of the Interior, National Park Service 1986. 831 pp.
	Covers the history of U.S. recreational locations selected for possible National Historic Landmark designation. These sites include baseball parks, amusement parks, circuses, resort hotels, racetracks, world's fair sites, zoos, and public parks. Reno's Mapes Hotel and Casino, built in 1947 and 1948 and operational until 1982, is the only casino chosen for inclusion. This section, pages 721-736, provides an architectural summary of the art deco building, interior and exterior descriptions and illustrations, a brief history of gambling in Nevada, and information on the state's prominent Mapes family. This hotel has a three-part vertical composition. The lower level contains casino space, restaurants, banquet facilities, shops, and a hotel lobby. The body of the building contains guest rooms, and the uppermost floor provides space for entertainment, dancing, dining, drinking, more gambling, and a wedding chapel. Until recently, nearly all Nevada casino design followed the Mapes three-part plan. Map, bibliographical references.

13.	Christiansen, Eugene Martin, Patricia A. McQueen, and Sebastian Sinclair. "93 Gross Annual Wager." *International Gaming and Wagering Business* 15 (5 August 1994): 14-44.
	Examines the financial side of the gaming industry with detailed information on gross wagering, market shares,

and revenues. Every form of legal gaming and every
gaming jurisdiction in the United States are thoroughly
covered. This report also discusses costs or "negative
externalities" associated with the expansion of gaming.
Charts, tables.

14.   Christiansen/Cummings Associates, Inc. *Legal
Gambling in Connecticut: Assessment of Current Status and
Options for the Future.* 2 vols. New York: Christiansen/
Cummings, 1992.
       Provides exhaustive coverage of current legal
gambling, impending developments, and potential new
gaming options in Connecticut. A lengthy evaluation and
recommendations are also provided. Christiansen/
Cummings recommends that the state enhance its current
lottery product portfolio, privatize off-track betting
operations, and introduce state authorized casino gaming.
Bibliographical references.

15.   Davis, Bertha. *Gambling in America: A Growth
Industry.* New York: Franklin Watts, 1992. 112 pp.
       Presents an overview of the world of gambling, with
discussion of the gaming industry, types of gambling,
betting, people who gamble, compulsive gambling, and the
issues surrounding legalization. Though cataloged as
juvenile literature, the text is well researched and
informative. Bibliographical references.

16.   Davis, Mike. "Armageddon at the Emerald City:
Local 226 vs. MGM Grand." *Nation* 259 (11 July 1994):
46-50.
       Examines the heated labor dispute between Kirk
Kerkorian's MGM Grand and Culinary Workers Local 226,
"the 40,000-member affiliate of the Hotel and Restaurant
Employees International." Robert Maxey, "MGM's fa-
mously unionbusting C.E.O.," announced the Las Vegas
resort "would open without a contract." Asking if Las
Vegas is the "last union town in America," Davis reviews
union activity and strikes there and explains how the
phenomenal growth of casino gaming in the city has affected

labor. "Local 226, reflecting the revolution in the size and composition of the gaming work force, is in the midst of a profound transition"; now minorities outnumber whites, and lower-wage workers exceed higher-wage ones. Even as union leaders fear the MGM Grand signals the death of Local 226, they are actively recruiting members and training them to be a "a disciplined street army." The "union's research department has also been transformed into an offensive weapon."

17.   Dell'Orto, Benedict. *The Structure, Conduct and Performance of Nevada's Slot Route Industry.* Master's thesis, University of Nevada, Las Vegas, 1993. University of Nevada, Las Vegas, Special Collections. 51 pp.
        Examines Nevada's highly specialized slot route industry which is composed of firms that provide gaming machines to non-traditional gaming establishments such as bars, gas stations, and convenience stores. While seventy percent of the industry is controlled by four publicly traded companies, United Gaming, Jackpot Enterprises, International Game Technology (IGT), and Electronic Data Technology (EDT), profits are not extraordinary. The author explores possible explanations for this anomaly. Bibliographical references.

18.   Demos, Peter G., Jr. *Casino Supervision: A Basic Guide.* Hayfork, Calif.: Panzer Press, 1991. 204 pp.
        Provides information on casino supervision. With twenty years in the casino industry, Demos shares his knowledge of supervision, accounting duties, public relations, game protection, and how to get ahead in the organization. This book also includes a collection of columns on related subjects written for *Casino Journal.*

19.   Denkberg, Nate. *Hotel/Casino Job Title Classifications.* Las Vegas, Nev.: Camelot Consultants, 1988. 185 pp.
        Contains concise job descriptions of the hundreds of positions required to operate a hotel-casino. Casino departments include management, promotions, junkets, 'eye

in the sky' or security surveillance, the cage, and various casino games. Nearly half of the book consists of organizational charts that illustrate the relationships between the positions that are defined. Restaurant positions are also included.

20.   Doocey, Paul. "Truck Stops Enter the Gaming Fast Lane." *International Gaming and Wagering Business* 15 (5 October 1994): 51-52, 54.

Discusses the explosion of truckstop video poker in Louisiana following legalization in 1991. By 1994, legislation designed to inhibit this truckstop gaming was enacted after the industry was rocked by a scandal linking it with organized crime. A court case found most of the regulations designed to control the industry unconstitutional.

21.   Eadington, William R., and Judy A. Cornelius, comps. *Gambling and Commercial Gaming: Essays in Business, Economics, Philosophy, and Science*. Reno, Nev.: Institute for the Study of Gambling and Commercial Gaming, College of Business Administration, University of Nevada, Reno, 1992. 656 pp.

Contains forty articles on gaming by economists, psychologists, mathematicians, business faculty, industry officials, consultants, and theologians. This anthology is divided into five sections titled: Studies in Casino and Gaming Management; Marketing and Regulation; Analysis of Sports Betting, Lotteries, and Parimutuel Racing; Understanding the Rationale of Gambling and the Gambler; and Scientific Studies and the Analysis of Games and Other Wagering Opportunities. A vibrant anthology of current research on commercial gaming and scientific analysis of gambling situations and behavior. Bibliographical references.

22.   Eder, Robert W. "Opening the Mirage: The Human-Resources Challenge." *Cornell Hotel and Restaurant Administration Quarterly* 31 (August 1990): 25-31.

Describes how Las Vegas's Mirage successfully recruited and trained 5,000 new employees so it "would be

fully operational and staffed within ten days of its opening."
Eder identifies the challenges facing pre-opening staff and
examines how the hotel's human resources plan was
developed, how the opening went, and how management
handled "employee relations, staffing, turnover, training,
and stress management." Key elements included careful
advertising, recruiting, and hiring practices, flexible staffing
plans, and special training and orientation programs. "Part
of the Mirage's solution was to focus on clear structure,
personal communication, team bonding, and a trusting
management style that respects employee needs." The
author credits this successful "lesson in the importance of
analysis, planning, and execution of an integrated human-
resources strategy" to owner Steve Wynn's emphasis on the
importance of managing employees "to obtain competitive
advantage in the marketplace."

23.   Empson, Elizabeth A. "Casino Credit: Claridge
Casino." *Credit World* 74 (May/June 1986): 22, 24, 25-28.
       Discusses application and record-keeping procedures
for individual credit privileges at Atlantic City's Claridge
Casino. The author, director of casino credit operations,
also looks at the influence of the Casino Control
Commission's regulations which "prohibit the cashing of
any checks for the purpose of gambling"; credit privileges
allow patrons to gamble without cash. She argues that
recently imposed regulations adversely affect casino
employees who make credit decisions and the casino
industry itself.

24.   Fine, Adam. "Colorado: Gaming in Flux." *Casino
Journal* 7 (March 1994): 40-42, 44-45, 48.
       Provides a detailed account of casino operations in
Central City, Cripple Creek, and Black Hawk, Colorado
since their introduction in 1991. Revenues and patronage
continue to increase in spite of such restrictions and
limitations as parking problems, poor roads, table limits, and
historic preservation requirements.

25.   Francoeur, Louise. *Applying the Theme of "Luck" to a Destination Resort With Casino.* University of Nevada, Las Vegas, Special Collections. 1992. Master's thesis, Cornell University. 103 pp.

Explores the sociological meaning of "luck" and identifies it as an important element of a casino's image. Casinos which convince people they are lucky places to gamble have a considerable advantage over their competition. Understanding luck, symbols, and super- stition, and incorporating them in the decor and atmosphere of a property, are sound casino marketing strategies. Bibliographical references.

26.   Friedman, William. *Casino Management.* Rev. ed. Secaucus, N.J.: Lyle Stuart, Inc., 1982. 542 pp.

Considered a trusted handbook for casino executives and employees since it was originally published in 1974. Friedman's book includes sections and detailed chapters on casino organization, personnel and financial structure, credit and collection, hotel marketing, hosting and comps, junkets, room sales, advertising, entertainment, accounting procedures for casino games, regulation, licensing, and taxation. Although dated, this is still an important reference work.

27.   *Gambling in the Single Market: A Study of the Current Legal and Market Situation.* 3 vols. University of Nevada, Las Vegas, Special Collections. 1991.

Provides a country-by-country report on the European Community's "betting, gaming, and lottery market." As an industry, gaming ranks twelfth in Europe, ahead of the computer and office equipment industries. Casinos, lotteries, horse racing, gaming machines, and bingo are highlighted. Taxation, revenues, licensing, and regulation are also discussed.

28.   Gardner, Jack. *Gambling: A Guide to Information Sources.* Detroit, Mich.: Gale Research, 1980. 286 pp.

Lists and describes hundreds of works on gambling. Compiled by a respected Las Vegas librarian, this is one of the most comprehensive annotated bibliographies on gambling ever published. While emphasis is on modern how-to-play materials, Gardner also provides a wealth of information on legalized gaming operations in Nevada and New Jersey. This work is also useful for historical research; many references are for nineteenth-century works and some are even from the fifteenth century. Bibliographical references, index.

29.   Gelbtuch, Howard C. "The Casino Industry." *Appraisal Journal* 59 (April 1991): 179-190.
        Explains how the recent proliferation of gaming affects the appraisal industry. The author first describes how "the gaming industry has gained both credibility and visibility over the past twelve years" and why it should "continue to enjoy success." The real estate industry, however, is "ignoring the potential for spectacular growth in some markets as well as the stagnation and decline in other" ones. This concise and thorough review of gaming provides figures on industry performance and growth and specific statistical summaries for Las Vegas and Atlantic City. Outlooks are included for those two areas as well as for Laughlin, Reno, Lake Tahoe, Deadwood, and Mississippi riverboat casinos. Tables.

30.   *Global Gaming Almanac, 1995.* N.p.: Smith Barney, December 1994. 560 pp.
        Contains detailed statistics on gaming markets worldwide. The introduction covers industry highlights, domestic and international overviews, a list of 1994 setbacks, and investment strategies. Most of the text is arranged geographically under headings for the United States, Canada, Asia and Australia, the Caribbean, Europe, South and Central America, the Middle East, and Africa. Each part has a market overview, followed by discussion of individual states or countries in these areas. The U.S. overview provides a great deal of information, including industry highlights, summary gaming statistics, and figures on emerging markets. Also reviews major gaming companies such as Bally Gaming, Mirage Resorts, and

MGM Grand. A very informative and useful compendium. Maps, tables, graphs.

31.   Goodall, Leonard E. "Market Behavior of Gaming Stocks: An Analysis of the First Twenty Years." *Journal of Gambling Studies* 10 (Winter 1994): 323-337.

Studies the "price movement patterns of gaming stocks compared with the broader market for six stock market cycles between 1973 and 1992." Goodall concludes, "gaming stocks tend to be more volatile than the market as a whole and this has been true throughout the twenty-year period." Gaming stocks have outperformed the general market, have benefitted from the opening of new jurisdictions, and are particularly sensitive to the effect oil availability and pricing have on the market.

32.   Gordon, Gil E. "Beating the Odds Against High Turnover." *The Human Resources Professional* 3 (Summer 1991): 29-33, 41.

Describes how an unnamed Atlantic City hotel-casino increased staff retention by "emphasizing management accountability." As a hired consultant, Gordon first distinguished "controllable and uncontrollable turnover" using payroll separation codes and found "only three percent turnover could be attributed" to such uncontrollable reasons as death, retirement, and relocation. He then estimated turnover costs "came to more than $2.8 million, using relatively conservative cost estimates." Working with human resources staff, he identified a set of assumptions; one, for example, noted turnover "is usually the combined effect of many small problems, each of which must be addressed." He explains how a select number of retention strategies were used, including "recruiting and selection improvements" and "improved company orientation." In service industries, "it is absolutely essential to keep jobs filled with employees who are trained, confident, and competent." Since business objectives could not be met without these "people objectives," this hotel-casino "began a process to treat retention like any other business objective."

Contains useful information that could be readily applied by other business management. Chart.

33. Greenlees, E. Malcolm. *Casino Accounting and Financial Management.* Reno, Nev.: University of Nevada Press, 1988. 378 pp.

Presents a fiscal overview of casino operations, including taxation, licensing and regulation, revenue flows, auditing, financial reporting, and managerial accounting. Accounting for specific casino operations, including table games, slot machines, keno, bingo, cardrooms, sports and race books, credit accounting, and central cashiering is thoroughly covered. Bibliographical references, index.

34. Gros, Roger. "The Great Experiment." *Casino Journal* 7 (June 1994): 26-28, 30.

Highlights the opening and operational success of the Casino Windsor in Windsor, Ontario. Gros provides information on how the operation is run and how management seeks to maximize benefit to the Canadian economy by relying on local suppliers and the local work force. Casino Windsor is government owned and operated by Hilton Hotels, Caesars World, and Circus Circus.

35. *The Harrah's Survey of U.S. Casino Entertainment 1994.* Memphis, Tenn.: Harrah's Casinos, February, 1994. 20 pp.

Covers the results of an annual industry sponsored survey on American casinos first conducted under this title in 1993. The report includes an overview of "U.S. casino destinations," a description of survey methodology, a brief executive summary, a list of survey results, and the "Harrah's casino entertainment outlook." This contains a wide variety of statistics on casino revenues, employment, tax contributions, and development by city and state. Statistics on gambling behavior note that the "percent of U.S. households that gambled in a casino within the last year (penetration) was 27 percent or 28 million households in 1993, up from 22 percent or 23 million households in 1992" and in 1993, "U.S. households made 92 million visits

to casinos, nearly twice the 1990 number—46 million."
Two frequently quoted statements from this publication are:
"casino entertainment ranks ahead of attendance at many
other popular forms of entertainment, including major league
baseball games, arena concerts, and Broadway shows" and
"casino gaming can be a fun night out according to three out
of four U.S. adults in 1993." Industry officials predict that
"U.S. casino revenues will double in the next decade."
Includes additional statistics on gambling behavior by
median age, median household income, region and
educational level and reservation and riverboat gaming.
Maps, tables.

36.   Hart, Steve. *The Professional in Casino Credit.*
University of Nevada, Las Vegas, Special Collections.
1983. 119 pp.
       Acts as a primer on casino credit and customer
relations. This book was designed as a textbook for the
author's Casino Credit and Host program which is part of
the Resort Technology Curriculum at the Community
College of Southern Nevada. Credit policies, procedures,
and controls are outlined. Tips on how to provide customer
service to high rollers are discussed. Also includes basic
information on how casino table games are played.

37.   Hevener, Phil. "Has Deadwood Overdeveloped?
The Town is Full of Cookie-Cutter Casinos, But Not Much
Else." *International Gaming and Wagering Business* 13 (15
March 1992): 1, 69.
       Describes Deadwood, South Dakota as a gaming
venue that is overpopulated with little, unprofitable casinos
that lack identity. Though gaming has rescued the small
town from economic decay, intense speculation on the value
of casinos and too many licenses have led to severe financial
problems and market saturation. Estimates indicate that sixty
of the eighty casino operations there are unprofitable.

38.   Hirshey, Gerri. "Gambling Nation." *New York
Times Magazine* (17 July 1994): 34-44, 50-51, 53-54, 61.

Describes the growing popularity and rapid proliferation of legalized gambling throughout the country. On a
"journey through the noisy, neon nation, total handle $330
billion," Hirshey covers such venues as Mississippi
riverboats, Connecticut's Mashantucket Pequots' casino,
Oklahoma "bingo palaces," and Las Vegas resorts, with a
great deal of background information and many quotes from
a wide variety of customers, operators, and government
officials. She discusses, for example, Steve Wynn's hand
in successfully redefining Las Vegas as a family-oriented
tourist destination and how "the industry can now count
government among its most forceful allies" as growing
numbers of states legalize gambling. "Casinos are one of the
few ways left for America to experience Saturday night
live," she states, "with fewer and fewer 'sure things,' the
timing is right for a large-scale flirtation with Lady Luck."
An anecdotal and informative overview of the casino
industry. Illustrations.

39.   Holden, Anthony. "Where Kitsch Is King." *World
Magazine* 54 (November 1991): 62-66.
       Discusses tourist attractions of Las Vegas's Caesars
Palace. The resort offers an elaborate Greco-Roman setting,
nine gourmet restaurants, exciting entertainment, and
luxurious rooms. Responding to competition from the
nearby Mirage, Caesars has planned to create a shopping
mall with ninety stores as upscale as Beverly Hills shops.
Includes six illustrations.

40.   International Game Technology. *Getting Started in
Gaming*. 3rd ed. Las Vegas, Nev.: International Game
Technology, 1994. 47 pp.
       Provides a general overview of the gaming industry,
including who gambles and why, the evolution of video and
reel slot machines, and the market share held by various slot
machine manufacturers. Casino design and marketing,
casino security, and the mechanics and components of slot
machines are also discussed. This company is the world's
largest manufacturer of slot machines and video poker
machines.

41.   Johnston, David. *Temples of Chance: How America Inc. Bought Out Murder Inc. to Win Control of the Casino Business*. New York: Doubleday, 1992. 312 pp.

Criticizes the casino industry and the agencies that regulate it. Johnston, an investigative reporter, finds that corruption, dirty dealings, and greed abound, as he cites junk bond swindles, casinos' use of "subtle psychological techniques that invite addictive behavior," cutthroat corporate maneuvering, and intentional encouragement of minors to drink and gamble. Though he concedes that gaming is no longer controlled by the mob, Johnston portrays casino gaming as a disreputable business. Index.

42.   Karlen, Neal. "Dice, Drinks and a Degree." *Rolling Stone* 588 (4 October 1990): 144-145, 147-148.

Discusses the University of Nevada, Las Vegas, William F. Harrah College of Hotel Administration. Students gain a variety of experiences working at Las Vegas hotel-casinos while going to school. According to student Steve Guinn, "they make you read the latest textbooks on hotel and casino management. But they also make you live in the real world. A mile away from campus, we've got 70,000 hotel rooms to use as a laboratory." According to Karlen, "UNLV's hotel college graduates 1,500 students a year from virtually every state and forty foreign countries"; it has become "the academic jewel of the university" whose "reputation is overshadowed only by its Ivy League archrival: Cornell's School of Hotel Administration" in Ithaca, New York.

43.   Klebanow, Andrew M. *Employee Substance Abuse in the Hotel/Casino Industry: An Analysis of Rehabilitation Effectiveness*. Master's thesis, Cornell University, 1991. University of Nevada, Las Vegas, Special Collections. 64 pp.

Examines the problem of substance abuse and treatment efforts in the hotel-casino industry. This study also includes a cost-benefit analysis of substance abuse programs at Mirage Resorts and Resorts International. Klebanow concludes that employee assistance programs

(EAPs) produce substantial savings. Mirage Resorts realized a savings of at least $700,000, and worker productivity and employee morale increased. Bibliographical references.

44.   Klebanow, Andrew M., and Robert W. Eder. "Cost Effectiveness of Substance Abuse Treatment in Casino Hotels." *Cornell Hotel & Restaurant Administration Quarterly* 33 (February 1992): 56-67.

Demonstrates how employee substance abuse programs save money by "retaining successfully treated workers and increasing their productivity." After noting drug abuse is a "particularly acute problem for the hospitality industry," the authors present a cost-benefit analysis of employee assistance programs (EAPs) at Las Vegas's Mirage and Atlantic City's Resorts International Hotel-Casino. The discussion covers factors used to measure EAPs success; ways to determine substance abuse costs of absenteeism and turnover; comparisons of these two programs; and guidelines for establishing and monitoring an EAP. In this study, Resorts International, for example, saved $71,500 by reducing absenteeism and $219,000 by reducing turnover. Tables, bibliographical references.

45.   Koentopp, Juli. "The Mirage Concerning Hotel Security." *Security Management* 36 (December 1992): 54-60.

Describes the advanced security system at Las Vegas's Mirage casino. This fully integrated system, a "new dimension in security management," covers a 100-acre location with three 30-story towers, more than 3,000 rooms, two ballrooms, many meeting rooms, and an erupting volcano, waterfalls, and natural animal habitats. Security is particularly critical because millions in cash are handled daily, and "strict compliance with gaming laws and established casino procedures is controlled by close supervision, surveillance, and carefully monitored audits." The Polaroid ID-2000 system, the operation's central component, "combines advanced database, computer, and electronic imaging technologies." Koentopp explains how employee identification cards are quickly produced and how they provide work hours and payroll information. She also discusses the system's use in accounting and auditing procedures.

46.   Kuriscak, Steve. *Casino Talk: A Rap Sheet for Dealers and Players*. N.p.: Steve Kuriscak/Screenwriters Guild, 1985. 57 pp.
        Provides definitions for the hundreds of slang terms and phrases that have evolved around casino gaming tables. As the author states, "to really understand the game requires an understanding of the gamers. Knowing their language isn't a bad start."

47.   LaCoste, Mary. "Casino Credit: John Ascuaga's Nugget." *Credit World* 74 (May/June 1986): 20-22.
        Discusses commercial credit operations at John Ascuaga's Nugget, Sparks, Nevada. LaCoste, assistant credit manager, manages credit approval and collection for the company's meat plant, hotel, convention center, internal credit cards, and casino. While the Nugget has access to five major databases, TRW, Trans Union, Chilton, Pinger, and CBI, the author focuses on the company's use of Central Credit, a "credit reporting company of international scope geared toward the gaming industry." She also addresses application of the Fair Credit Reporting Act and Nevada Gaming Control Board regulations to credit activities.

48.   Lambert, Pam, Doris Bacon, and Maria Eftimiades. "High Roller." *People Weekly* 40 (6 December 1993): 75-77.
        Profiles Stephen Wynn, successful Las Vegas casino owner and developer of the Mirage and Treasure Island. Some acknowledge Wynn for the city's shifting focus from gambling to family-oriented 'Disney-like' theme attractions. This change is credited for maintaining Las Vegas's status as a major tourist destination worldwide, even as casinos spread throughout this country.

49.   Lampert-Greaux, Ellen. "MGM Grand Hotel: Architecture 94." *TCI* 28 (May 1994): 44-47.

Describes the architecture and interior design of Las Vegas's MGM Grand Hotel created by architect Veldon Simpson. Opened in December 1993, it "calls itself the world's largest hotel, casino and theme park, with 5,005 guest rooms in four 30-story emerald-green glass towers." The author discusses the colors, lighting, special effects, and decoration of the "four different themed areas: the Emerald City, Hollywood, Monte Carlo, and Sports."

50.   Lee, Daniel R. *Betting on Betting.* New York: First Boston, 1991. 95 pp.

Spotlights casino gaming as a hot growth industry worthy of an investor's dollar. Lee gives an overview of how casinos operate and background and performance information on ten industry leaders: Aztar Corporation, Bally Manufacturing (now Bally Entertainment), Caesars World, Inc., Circus Circus Enterprises, Golden Nugget (now Mirage Resorts), Hilton Hotels Corp., MGM Grand, Promus Companies, Inc., Resorts International, and Showboat.

51.   Legato, Frank. "All That Glitters: Interior Designers Strut Their Stuff." *Casino Journal* 7 (April 1994): 62, 64-65.

Explains how interior design firms profit from the proliferation of casino gaming. As one designer states, "casinos provide some of the most fantastic fantasy facilities an architect or designer could ever run across." Designing a large property is similar to designing a whole city under one roof. Projects by Morris & Brown and Marnell Corrao Associates are discussed.

52.   Legato, Frank. "Consulting: Helping the New to Help Themselves." *Casino Journal* 7 (March 1994): 52-54.

Recommends that operators of new gaming facilities hire consultants to assist them with planning and operating casinos. Gaming is not like other businesses and requires specialized knowledge. Also, understanding Nevada's

gaming business will not necessarily prepare operators for
doing business in other jurisdictions which have different
regulations and different markets. The role of the consultant
is thoroughly discussed.

53.   Loro, Laura. "Casinos Chance Targeted Ads."
Advertising Age 60 (20 February 1989): 50MW.
        Reports on increases in casino advertising budgets
because of growing competition. Targeted direct marketing
campaigns are gaining popularity over the more costly use of
mass media. Since the Federal Trade Commission prohibits
communication of "information about gambling across state
lines," out-of-state mailings sell resorts, hotels, entertainment, and restaurants. A sidebar notes that advertising
employment is growing in Las Vegas, due in part to
gaming's growth.

54.   Lubove, Seth. "Token Appreciation." *Forbes* 154
(21 November 1994): 20.
        Describes briefly how Las Vegas casino employees
try to explain tipping to first-time visitors. "The Nevada
Casino Dealers Association has paid for a series of new
billboards . . . that remind visitors it's good sport to leave a
few chips on the table." Many tourists do not realize that
"most dealers, like restaurant workers, earn a minimum
wage and depend upon tips, or 'tokes,' to supplement their
income." Tips made by the city's dealers have decreased 33
percent since the 1970s.

55.   Luna, S.M. "Growth: A Watchword for Northern
Nevada Casinos." *Nevada Business Journal* 8
(November/December 1993): 12-13.
        Discusses casino development in Northern Nevada.
Although recent reports have focused on Las Vegas's
growth, several casinos in northern Nevada are planning to
expand their current facilities, including Reno's Hilton,
Flamingo Hilton, Eldorado Hotel and Casino, Harrah's, and
Peppermill. Harvey's, Lake Tahoe plans to open a casino in
Las Vegas as well as one in Colorado. As in Las Vegas,
"theme areas" are becoming more popular.

56.   Macomber, Dean M. "Development Quicksand: The Mistakes That Become Apparent After It is Too Late." *International Gaming and Wagering Business* 14 (15 September 1993): 38, 40, 43; and 14 (14 November 1993): 48-51, 72.

Discusses errors in the casino development process which can cause customer dissatisfaction and even financial failure. In this two-part article, Macomber suggests ways to avoid the most common errors which include building to overcapacity; support elements not meeting casino capacity; inadequate support of "front of the house" operations; inaccurate cash flow projections; cutting costs in ways that negatively affect customers; and building without considering future expansion.

57.   Maglitta, Joseph. "High-Tech Wagering: Jackpot or Jeopardy?" *ComputerWorld* 28 (7 February 1994): 128-29.

Analyzes how computerized technology has affected the gaming industry and gambling behavior. "Critics fear the wildfire growth of new and emerging technologies . . . will turn the $329 billion gambling industry into a huge digital monster." The author looks at such advances as electronic Keno games, video lotteries, and interactive television gambling. Opponents worry that computerization, by making gambling easier and more accessible, will increase problem gambling, particularly among lower income groups and the young who can afford it least. It also raises serious concerns about the fairness and control of the computer systems themselves and, in many cases, the governments which monitor them. Includes sidebars on adult gambling statistics, new gaming technologies under development, and specific "computer glitches" affecting wagering outcomes.

58.   Mandell, Michael J., Mark Landler, and Ronald Grover. "The Entertainment Economy—America's Growth Engines: Theme Parks, Casinos, Sports, Interactive TV." *Business Week* 3362 (14 March 1994): 58-64.

Explains how entertainment and recreation industries have grown steadily over the last ten years. Data from the

Bureau of Labor Statistics shows that these groups "added 200,000 workers in 1993—a stunning 12 percent of all net new workers"; also, "since 1991, consumers have boosted their outlays on entertainment and recreation by some 13 percent, adjusted for inflation—more than twice the growth rate of overall consumer spending." Gambling is the fastest growing component; the U.S. Department of Commerce states people spent $28 billion on it in 1993. "Gambling, once a vice, is now part of a family outing." Also discussed are concerns that these trends raise for the economy and American society. A sidebar describes how these industries may help distressed urban areas; some casino revenues are used for special improvement projects. An excellent overview. Tables.

59.   McQueen, Patricia A. "North American Gaming at a Glance." *International Gaming and Wagering Business* 15 (5 September 1994): 20-22, 24, 28.
        Examines legalized gaming in jurisdictions within the United States and Canada. Recent developments in card rooms, casinos, Indian gaming, sports betting, video lottery terminals, parimutuels, and other forms of gaming are discussed. This report is published annually.

60.   Meier, Barry. "Casinos in Pursuit of New Players." *New York Times* (29 December 1994): D1, D17 (L).
        Explains why casinos are trying to attract new customers. "After years of aggressive expansion, gambling companies face the prospect that the capacity of casinos will eventually outpace the number of players to fill them." The new Las Vegas Hard Rock Cafe is one example of the industry's efforts to attract younger people. Established leaders are planning "bigger attractions . . . to pull in the casual tourist" in the United States while considering new markets worldwide. Although money spent on gambling has increased "about ten percent annually," there are potential problems ahead. Last fall, Florida voters soundly defeated an amendment legalizing gambling, casino investments continue to be risky, and the effects of increasing competition are difficult to predict.

61.   Mills, John. "The Money Laundering Control Act and Proposed Amendments: Its Impact on the Casino Industry." *Journal of Gambling Studies* 7 (Winter 1991): 301-312.

   Analyzes how the Money Laundering Control Act of 1986 "resulted in significant compliance costs for casinos" which many states do not consider when legalizing gambling. This act "requires financial institutions to report cash transactions over $10,000 to the federal government"; after passage, it was estimated that larger Nevada casinos were "spending an additional sixty staff hours a month to comply," and the state's Gaming Control Board hired an additional fifty agents for the resulting paperwork. Mills clearly lists currency reporting requirements and gives examples of how complicated compliance can be for casino employees. Bibliographical references.

62.   Minnesota. Gambling Control Board. *Gambling Manager's Handbook.* St. Paul, Minn.: State of Minnesota Gambling Control Board, 1994. 163 pp.

   Explains Minnesota's licensing processes and operational procedures for all forms of legal charitable gaming operations. Under present regulations, Minnesota allows qualified nonprofit organizations to offer bingo, raffles, paddle wheels, tipboards, and pulltabs.

63.   Morrison, Robert S. *High Stakes to High Risk: The Strange Story of Resorts International and the Taj Mahal.* Ashtabula, Ohio: Lake Erie Press, 1994. 378 pp.

   Documents the rise of James Morris Crosby from an obscure paint company owner to gambling developer in the Bahamas. After making his fortune, Crosby began construction on Atlantic City's Taj Mahal casino only to die suddenly before its completion. The story chronicles Donald Trump's acquisition of the project through junk bonds and easy credit and his organization's serious financial miscalculations. The author owns the fiberglass company that created the ornate towers and elephants which adorn the Taj Mahal, and he has still not received three million dollars owed him for this work. Index.

64.   Nordheimer, Jon.   "Behind the Lights, Casino Burnout: Atlantic City Dealers Feel Trapped in Tense, Dead-End Jobs." *New York Times* (5 August 1994): B1-B2 (L).
     Describes problems Atlantic City dealers routinely face.   Nordheimer says it is "high-pressure work, as stressful on a daily basis as being a big-city cop or an emergency room nurse, and signs of wear and tear on casino workers are becoming more pronounced." Major causes of stress include varying work shifts; boring jobs requiring alertness and accuracy; the "constant audio and visual overload" of casino interiors; difficult customers; few promotion opportunities; and seemingly uncaring management.   Compulsive gambling problems can also be a dangerous threat to dealers because constantly handling money seems to lessen its value for many people.

65.   Nordling, Christopher W., and Sharon K. Wheeler. "Building a Market-Segment Accounting Model to Improve Profits." *Cornell Hotel & Restaurant Administration Quarterly* 33 (June 1992): 29-36.
     Describes how one hotel-casino correlated "different market segments" to profits. The authors, two Las Vegas Hilton executives, explain how an employee team designed and implemented a "market-segment accounting model" to "account for revenues, costs, and profits by market segment as well as by hotel department." They cover how the concept was developed, market segments were defined, the methodology was formatted, and revenues were categorized. They conclude the most important outcome is the "contribution percentage" that "represents each market segment's contributions to total operating income." Excellent tables highlight how this process works. Tables, bibliographical references.

66.   "North American Gaming Report 1994." *International Gaming and Wagering Business* 15 (5 July 1994): 1-80.
     Provides a state-by-state and province-by-province account of gaming in North America.   A brief news summary for each jurisdiction is accompanied by total

handle, prize payout, and gross revenue figures for casinos, lotteries, parimutuels, and other legal forms of gambling. This supplement appears annually and is frequently referred to in other sources. Tables, graphs.

67.   O'Donnell, John R., and James Rutherford. *Trumped: The Inside Story of the Real Donald Trump, His Cunning Rise & Spectacular Fall.* New York: Simon & Schuster, 1991. 348 pp.

Provides a window into the world of high stakes casino management and finance. The author was president of the Trump Plaza Hotel & Casino in Atlantic City from 1987 to 1990 and describes a progression of poor business decisions that lead to the collapse of the Trump empire. By overbuilding the Atlantic City gaming market, Trump not only lost huge amounts of money with the Taj Mahal but drew customers and revenue away from his boardwalk casinos. Index.

68.   Ortiz, Darwin. *Gambling Scams: How They Work, How to Detect Them, How to Protect Yourself.* New York: Dodd, Mead, 1984. 262 pp.

Examines casino cheating from both sides of the table, including craps, backgammon, three-card monte, and a host of other scams. Techniques for cheating at various casino games are thoroughly discussed and illustrated; the precautions taken by casinos to deter cheating are also covered. Includes a glossary of the colorful terminology of the card mechanic, dice hustler, grifter, and con artist.

69.   Painton, Priscilla. "The Great Casino Salesman." *Time* 141 (3 May 1993): 52-55.

Profiles prominent Las Vegas casino owner/developer Stephen Wynn. Painton states that Wynn is on a "mission to gentrify gambling in America, cleansing it of its associations with high life and low life." Due in part to his efforts, legalized gambling is losing its negative reputation, making possible its growth throughout the country. With casino gambling becoming an "innocuous middle-class" activity, Wynn says he is in the "recreation business." A review of Wynn's professional life is preceded by a brief look at legalized gambling's growth and profits.

70.   Paulick, Ray. "Games People Play." *The Blood-Horse* 120 (8 October 1994): 4762-4763.
        Presents a racing industry report on Las Vegas's 1994 World Gaming Congress and Expo. While the focus was on the gaming industry's increasing growth and power, "pro-casino speakers warned that the entire parimutuel racing industry would very likely wither and die" if it did not share the gambling industry's view of a future "with slot machines and card tables in virtually every section of the country." Discussion of parimutuels focused on "the mix of casinos and gaming machines with racetracks, and the future of racing as it relates to off-track betting" was frequently stressed as the major thrust for the years ahead. Louisiana Downs, an example of casinos' effect on racetracks, experienced "substantial on-track business declines" after three riverboat casinos opened nearby. Purses are down 15 percent, while on-track attendance and handle are even lower. One speaker discussed how this track has promoted racing and incorporated traditional casino games by adding video poker machines. Other participants "saw growth potential for parimutuel racing without expansion into casino gaming," such as live racing on cable television. Unfortunately, some of the necessary changes, such as campaigns to attract younger customers, can be expensive. Includes information on casino initiatives and technological advances.

71.   Popkin, James. "Tricks of the Trade." *U.S. News & World Report* 116 (14 March 1994): 48-52.
        Describes how casinos "part bettors from their cash." Since "the longer a player gambles, the greater the house's chance of winning," many efforts are designed to retain customers by keeping them comfortable. Gamblers like the new slot machines with "built-in bill acceptors," for example, because they eliminate waiting in line for change; casinos like them because "they keep slot hounds glued to their stools." Other strategies include piping special scents

into casino areas to make them more pleasant; using deep,
dark interior colors to "trigger a strong response in slot
players"; distributing chips in lower denominations to
encourage betting, since players are more reluctant to part
with more valuable ones; and offering "frequent-gambler
cards" that "record all play—handy for marketers." New
games have been developed with "stunning house odds" that
are even greater than usual, such as double exposure and
multiple action blackjack. Sidebars outline the architectural
"anatomy of a casino," define casino employee jargon, and
list some insider comments on casino operation. A good
introduction to how casinos "manipulate" customers.

72. Reimann, Bernard C. "The Newest Game in Vegas
Is Strategic Management." *Planning Review* 21 (January
1993): 38-40, 49.
    Reports on the gaming industry's current emphasis
on strategic management, which was the focus of a 1992
Academy of Management conference. The recent
proliferation of gambling opportunities has forced Nevada
operators "to become more strategically focused" to remain
competitively ahead of Indian, riverboat, and video gaming.
Speaker Alan Stutts, University of Nevada, Las Vegas,
states "advantages can be sustained to the extent that they are
based on intangible, hard-to-duplicate resources . . . human
resources, brand name," and "research and development."
In his description of these factors, Stutts said Australian
casinos use the "latest video imaging and graphics" much
more than their American counterparts. Executives from
Harrah's and MGM describe how these companies are
implementing human resource management plans to improve
their performance. While acknowledging the industry
efforts highlighted at this meeting, Reimann had "doubts
about how effectively" the industry "could leverage their
resources (tangible or intangible) into other endeavors."

73. Romero, John. *Casino Marketing*. New York:
International Gaming & Wagering Business, 1994. 268 pp.
    Gives the reader a wild ride through casino advertising
and marketing. Romero's light and humorous approach

belies the wealth of information he provides. This is a rich
source of information on direct marketing, advertising, and
the fine art of courting customers in a highly competitive
industry.

74.   Scarne, John. *Scarne's Guide to Casino Gambling*.
New York: Simon and Schuster, 1978. 352 pp.
    Provides considerably more information than how to
play casino games. John Scarne is one of the best-known
authorities on games of chance, and this work established
him as a leading expert on casinos in general. Here he
discusses the history of legal and illegal casinos, the
National Gambling Commission, and the media's coverage
of gambling. He also covers the mathematics and science of
casino gambling and how to play blackjack, craps, roulette,
baccarat, and a host of other casino games. Index.

75.   "Sexual Harassment in the Casino Workplace."
Gaming Law 1 (15 July 1992): 1-2.
    Describes casino management's obligation to resolve
employee sexual harassment issues.   Noting that "the
Clarence Thomas hearings raised the question of what is
sexual harassment," the article explains how courts identify
it, and how, in Nevada, it can jeopardize casino licenses and
casino careers. "To owners and management, affirmative
guidelines and programs to report and remedy sexual
harassment charges are essential."

76.   Sifakis, Carl. *Encyclopedia of Gambling*. New
York: Facts on File, 1990. 340 pp.
    Lists and defines gambling terms and slang from
"Ace-Deuce Standoff," the excessive house edge for craps,
to "Zombie," a draw poker variation. This detailed work
also includes biographical sketches of notorious gamblers,
descriptions of famous casinos and gambling halls, the rules
for hundreds of card, dice, casino, and other games, and
descriptions of myriad cheating techniques and scams. A
glossary is included. Index.

77.   Sodak Gaming Supplies. *Getting Started in Indian Gaming*. 2nd ed. Rapid City, S. Dak.: Sodak Gaming Supplies, 1991. 72 pp.

Provides a general overview of the gaming industry, including who gambles and why, the evolution of video and reel slot machines, and the market share held by various slot machine manufacturers. How to design and market a casino, casino security, and the mechanics and components of slot machines are also discussed. Sodak Gaming Supplies is the distributor for International Gaming Technology, Reno, Nevada.

78.   Sprecher, C. Ronald, and Mars A. Pertl. "Intra-Industry Effects of the MGM Grand Fire." *Quarterly Journal of Business and Economics* 27 (Spring 1988): 96-116.

Investigates the effect of Las Vegas's 1980 MGM Grand fire on the stock returns of other hotels and casinos. This disaster "was a highly publicized event with damage amounts estimated in the hundreds of millions of dollars and more than 80 lives lost." While noting that the fire resulted in substantial building code and fire regulation changes nationwide, Sprecher and Pertl decided to determine if it adversely affected major hotels and casinos in other ways. After explaining their hypotheses and methodology, the authors conclude there was "no intra-industry effect . . . the marketplace viewed the MGM fire as a nonsystematic event that only affected MGM" because the costs of additional insurance and loss control efforts did not have a "measurable impact on the returns of firms in the hotel-casino industry." Bibliographical references.

79.   Taucer, Vic. *Blackjack Dealing and Supervision: A Complete Manual to Instruct Dealing and Supervising Casino-Style Blackjack*. Las Vegas, Nev.: Casino Creations, Inc., 1993. 121 pp.

Provides a complete overview of blackjack dealing and supervision, including chapters on rules, card handling, take and pay procedures, and cheating. Taucer is an instructor in casino management at the Community College of Southern Nevada and a twenty-year veteran of the casino industry. This well-organized work is an excellent training manual for students and employees. Index.

80.   Tegtmeier, Ralph. *Casinos.* New York: Vendome Press: Distributed by Rizzoli International Publications, 1989. 190 pp.
        Presents a richly illustrated history of casinos. Photographs and paintings emphasize the glamour and beautiful architecture of nineteenth century European gaming palaces. Attention is also given to casinos now in the United States and around the world. Bibliographic references, index.

81.   Thompson, William Norman. *Crapping Out in the Executive Suite: The Potentialities for Disaster in the Casino Industry.* University of Nevada, Las Vegas, Special Collections. 1993. 15 pp.
        Explains how the casino industry can experience a variety of disasters. Things that can go wrong in casinos include natural disasters; accidents; theft; organized crime; bad business decisions, such as poor location choices; bad economic conditions; top personnel turnover; bad loan practices; failure to keep undesirable players out; and governmental regulation. According to Thompson, government regulation poses the largest threat to casinos. He also argues that casinos in many jurisdictions fail to improve the local economy as anticipated, which results in a potential anti-casino backlash. This paper was presented to the New Avenues in Risk and Crisis Management Conference, University of Nevada, Las Vegas, August 12, 1993.

82.   Turner, W. Bruce. *It's a Whole New Ballgame: An Examination of Nevada Casino Activity.* New York: Salomon Brothers, 1994. 14 pp.
        Spotlights the explosive growth in Las Vegas with the openings of the Luxor, Treasure Island, and the MGM Grand. These three properties added 16,000 gaming positions to a base of 165,000 positions in one year, creating a "marketwide supply shock." Surprisingly, Las Vegas has easily absorbed the shock just as it has absorbed earlier

building booms. Turner is confident that the city will be able to absorb four more mega-resorts that are planned for 1996 and 1997 openings. This report supplies retrospective quarterly data on revenue, number of gaming positions, and win-per-position-per-day figures for the Las Vegas Strip, Downtown Las Vegas, Laughlin, Lake Tahoe, and Reno. Tables.

83.   Turner, W. Bruce. *The Wall Street Transcript Roundtable Discussion: Gaming Stocks.* New York: Salomon Brothers, 1994. 10 pp.
        Analyzes the current state of the gaming industry. This report focuses on Mississippi casino operations, future prospects for the industry, industry leaders, and the potential for mergers and acquisitions.

84.   Uphoff, John P., and W. Bruce Turner. *The Dramatic Growth of Legalized Gaming in North America.* St. Petersburg, Fla.: Raymond James & Associates, 1991. 22 pp.
        Surveys the rapid expansion of casino gaming in the United States, including video lottery machines, Indian operations, and riverboat gaming. Uphoff and Turner also provide an overview of operations and regulatory environments in various jurisdictions including Colorado, South Dakota, Iowa, Illinois, Louisiana, Mississippi, Montana, and Oregon.

85.   Vignola, Margo L. *Atlantic City: Challenge Prompts Change.* New York: Salomon Brothers, 1992. 29 pp.
        Examines Atlantic City's viability in an increasingly competitive marketplace. Twelve Atlantic City casinos generate $3 billion in revenues annually and are generally profitable; however, the introduction of gaming in Connecticut and other jurisdictions is threatening their profits. Vignola maintains that Atlantic City is vulnerable because of the city's dilapidated infrastructure, over-regulation, and lack of hotel rooms. She thinks the recent regulatory change allowing twenty-four hour gaming and

plans for a new airport and convention facilities will be good for business.

86.   Vignola, Margo L. *Gaming Industry: Entering the Mainstream*. New York: Salomon Brothers, 1992. 29 pp.
        Traces the growth of legalized gaming from a cottage industry in the 1940s to a $26 billion behemoth in 1991. Gambling's move from the shadows of organized crime to mainstream American entertainment is analyzed. Key investment points, long-term industry issues, and new markets are also discussed.

87.   Vignola, Margo L. *Gaming Industry: The Battle for Glitz...with Spoils for All*. New York: Salomon Brothers, 1990. 35 pp.
        Covers casino finance, regulation, gaming markets, and key public companies. The explosive growth of Nevada markets in Las Vegas, Laughlin, and Reno is emphasized.

88.   Vignola, Margo L. *Las Vegas: The Mother Lode of Gambling*. New York: Solomon Brothers, 1992. 27 pp.
        Examines Las Vegas's role in an increasingly competitive marketplace. Vignola concludes that Las Vegas is a "middle-market vacation mecca" which shows remarkable economic resilience, even during economic downturns. Credit is given to the city's excellent infrastructure that includes modern highways and an outstanding airport, the industry's shift to entertainment, the city's domination of the convention market, and affordable lodging, meals, and entertainment. Long-term issues, threats, and future prospects are discussed.

89.   Vinson, Barney. *Las Vegas: Behind the Tables*. 2 vols. Grand Rapids, Mich.: Gollehon, 1986, 1988.
        Tracks the phenomenal evolution of Las Vegas from the early Bugsy Siegel and Howard Hughes periods through the arrival of corporate America during the late 1960s and early 1970s. This discussion also looks at Las Vegas as the "Entertainment Capital of the World" and covers the many entertainers who perform there, the many movies that are

filmed there, and the amazing collection of roadside attractions that casinos create to lure customers. Vinson, who spent twenty years in the city's casino industry, also addresses the occupations and working conditions of various casino employees; casino games; players; surveillance; comps and credit; and the ways casinos handle large amounts of cash. Bibliographical references.

90.   Vogel, Harold L. *Entertainment Industry Economics: A Guide for Financial Analysis.* New York: Cambridge University Press, 1986. 457 pp.

Discusses the business economics of major entertainment industries. Gaming and Wagering, pages 239-297, begins with a short history of gambling in the United States followed by sections on financial and operating characteristics of lotteries, tracks, and casinos, profit principles, performance standards, casino management and accounting policies, and utility-function models. An appendix briefly covers major casino games of chance, such as blackjack, craps, slots, and roulette. Charts, glossary, bibliographical references, index.

91.   Walton, Roger Alan. *Colorado Gambling: A Guide.* Lakewood, Colo.: Colorado Times, 1991. 130 pp.

Traces gambling throughout Colorado history and emphasizes the recent legalization of casinos in three of the state's mountain towns. The evolution of public policy toward parimutuel betting, bingo and raffles, the lottery, private gambling, and casinos are also discussed.

92.   Waters, Gary A. *Job Satisfaction of Slot Department Shift Managers in Las Vegas Casinos.* Master's thesis, University of Nevada, Las Vegas, 1988. University of Nevada, Las Vegas, Special Collections. 109 pp.

Identifies reasons for dissatisfaction among slot department shift managers and recommends how morale and customer service could be improved. This study concludes that job satisfaction could be increased by using organizational norms to accomplish goals and emphasizing teamwork among employees. Waters embraces industry

implementation of W. Edwards Deming's Total Quality
Management principles and Management by Values to
improve casino operations and profitability. Bibliographical
references.

93.   Watson, Jerome R. "Employer Liability for the
Sexually Harassing Actions of Its Customers." *Employee
Relations Law Journal* 19 (Winter 1993-1994): 227-237.
        Explains how employers can be "held liable for acts
of sexual harassment committed by their customers or other
nonemployees against their employees." Watson describes
the court case *Powell v Las Vegas Hilton.* The plaintiff, a
casino dealer, sued the casino for not stopping sexual
harassment by customers; this case illustrates the intricacies
and complexities of such situations. After covering the
evolution of sexual harassment law and other "cases holding
employers liable for the harassing actions of nonemployees,"
Watson lists considerations in "determining employer
liability" and "practical actions" employers can take to protect
themselves. Bibliographical references.

94.   Yoshihashi, Pauline. "Standing Pat: Crusty
Revolutionary in the Casino Industry Battles Against Time."
Wall Street Journal (1 April 1994): A1, A4.
        Profiles Circus Circus Enterprises chairman William
G. Bennett and his role in the company's success. Circus
Circus, based on high volume, low prices, and strict cost
controls, was influential in changing the "image of casino
gambling from vice to mass-market entertainment." While
Bennett has discussed retirement, he has no intention of
leaving until a successor is chosen. Yoshihashi shows the
influence one individual can have on a company and an
industry.

SUPPLEMENTAL MATERIALS

95.   "All Systems Go for the Bally Slot Data System."
Nevada Business Journal 8 (November/December 1993):
14-15.

96.   American Institute of Certified Public Accountants. *Audits of Casinos with Conforming Changes as of May 1, 1994*. Chicago: Commerce Clearinghouse, 1994. 6 pp.

97.   Bayus, Barry L., Robert L. Banker, Shiv K. Gupta, and Bradley H. Stone. "Evaluating Slot Machine Placement on the Casino Floor." *Interfaces* 15 (March-April 1985): 22-32.

98.   Border, Gary A. "High Stakes Direct Marketing." *Direct Marketing* 50 (April 1988): 36-38.

99.   Byrne, Harlan S. "Jackpot Enterprises: Serving Nevada's Gaming Locals." *Barron's* (18 May 1992): 40-41.

100.   C&S Consulting. *Infrastructure Impact Study on the Rivergate Casino Site*. New Orleans: C&S Consulting, 1992. 21 pp.

101.   Caesars World Resorts of Louisiana, Inc. *New Orleans Casino Proposal: Submitted to the City of New Orleans*. Los Angeles, Calif.: Caesars World Resorts of Louisiana, Inc., Caesars World Resorts, Inc., Caesars World, Inc., 1992. Unpaged.

102.   Carnival Management Services. *New Orleans Proposal*. Miami, Fla.: Carnival Management Services, 1992. Various pagings.

103.   Casino Orleans Consortium. *Financial Incentive and Business Plan*. Baton Rouge, La.: Casino Orleans, Inc., 1992. 94 pp.

104.   Casino Orleans Consortium. *Request for Qualifications and Proposal*. University of Nevada, Las Vegas, Special Collections. 1992. Unpaged.

105.   Collier, Lynn. "The 'New' Vegas: For Many, the Old Shows Still Work Best." *Las Vegas Business Press* 11 (7 March 1994): 1, 8.

106.   Comte, Elizabeth. "Casinos Resort to Sports Events for Extra Revenue." *The Sporting News* 209 (25 June 1990): 48.

107.   Connor, Matt. "Can Harness Racing Survive in the 1990s? Proliferation of Casinos Forces Industry to Adapt or Else." *International Gaming and Wagering Business* 15 (5 March 1994): 1, 38, 40.

108.   Connor, Matt, and Paul Doocey. "Gaming Explosion to Continue in 1994." *International Gaming and Wagering Business* 15 (5 January 1994): 19-20, 25.

109.   Dandurand, Lawrence. "Market Niche Analysis in the Casino Gaming Industry." *Journal of Gambling Studies* 6 (Spring 1990): 73-85.

110.   de Lisser, Eleena. "Mississippi's Casino Industry is Seeking a Better Hand Amid Changing Market." *Wall Street Journal* (3 October 1994): A5.

111.   Di Ilio, John. "Parimutuels and Gaming, a Primer: How To Plan an Integrated Facility." *International Gaming and Wagering Business* 14 (15 May 1993): 42-44.

112.   Duboff, Rob, and Curt Smith. *Marketing of Gaming Properties*. University of Nevada, Las Vegas, Special Collections. 1986. 26 pp.

113.   Eadington, William R. "Possible Effects of the California Lottery on Nevada's Casino Industry." *Nevada Public Affairs Review* 2 (1986): 7-11.

114.   Eadington, William R. "The Casino Gambing Industry: A Study of Political Economy." *Annals of the American Academy of Political and Social Science* 474 (July 1984): 23-35.

115.   Ebner, Mark. "From Dino to Dinosaurs: Las Vegas's Shifting Sands." *Spy* 8 (September/October 1994): 50-55.

116.   Edwards, Jerome. "Nevada Gambling: Just Another Business Enterprise." *Nevada Historical Society Quarterly* 37 (Summer 1994): 101-114.

117.   Evans, Lance W. "Rollin' With the River: Banking on Their Colorado River Location, Laughlin Boosters Have Rolled the Dice and Come Up Winners." *Nevada Magazine* 51 (January/February 1991): 58-61, 63-66.

118.   Fine, Adam. "1993: The Year in Review." *Casino Journal* 7 (January 1994): 40-41, 43-45, 47-49, 51, 62.

119.   Frey, James H. "Labor Issues in the Gaming Industry." *Nevada Public Affairs Review* 2 (1986): 32-38.

120.   "Gambling Sweeping the Country." *State Policy Reports* 12 (September 1994): 2-9.

121.   "Gaming Industry: The Good News Keeps on Coming: A Special Sponsored Section." *Institutional Investor* 28 (February 1994): 2-45.

122.   "The Grand Portfolio: From Minnesota to Mississippi, Aggressive Grand Casinos Emerges as a Leading Operator in New Gaming Jurisdictions." *Casino Journal* 7 (February 1994): 24-27, 59.

123.   Gros, Roger. "A Tunica Tale: Northern Mississippi's Casinos Transform Rural South." *Casino Journal* 7 (April 1994): 69.

124.   Gros, Roger, and Mike Epifanio. "Getting a Piece of the Pie: An Analysis of American Gaming in 1994." *Casino Journal* 7 (February 1994): 35-37, 39, 41, 58.

125.   Grover, Ronald. "Can Hilton Draw a Full House? It's Gambling on Casinos—Hoping They'll Prop Up Weak Hotels." *Business Week* 3269 (8 June 1992): 88-89.

126.   Grover, Ronald. "No Honeymoon in Vegas: The Bitter Frontier Strike Is Pitting Hotel Owners Against Each Other." *Business Week* 3284 (21 September 1992): 38.

127.   Grover, Ronald, and Chris Roush. "Will Too Many Players Spoil the Game? As Gambling Spreads, Some Operators May Have to Fold Their Hands." *Business Week* 3341 (October 18 1993): 80, 82.

128.   Haines, Kimberly A. "Trump Taj Mahal: High Stakes Security." *Security Management* 34 (September 1990): 116-122.

129.   Harrah's. *Harrah's New Orleans World Casino.* Memphis, Tenn.: Promus Companies, Inc., 1992. Unpaged.

130.   Hilton Hotels Corporation. *Response to Request for Qualifications and Proposal: (RFQ/P) To Develop the 6.47 Acre Rivergate Casino Site in Downtown New Orleans.* University of Nevada, Las Vegas, Special Collections. 1992. Unpaged.

131.   ITT Sheraton Corporation. *Response, Request for Proposal, City of New Orleans.* Boston: ITT Sheraton, 1992. Various pagings.

132.   Jesitus, John. "Caesars World Hits It Big in New Orleans." *Hotel & Motel Management* 207 (14 December 1994): 3, 40.

133.   Johnson, Kirk. "Casino Owner Offers Lure: $140 Million in New Taxes." *New York Times* (12 February 1993): B5 (L).

134.   Kent, Bill. "The Bold Man and the Sea: Donald Trump's Billion-Dollar Bet Could Be a New Beginning—or the Beginning of the End in Atlantic City." *Philadelphia* 81 (May 1990): 130-139.

135.   Klein, Howard J. "Tired Brains . . . Tired Games: Casinos Could Learn a Lot From Video Arcades." *International Gaming & Wagering Business* 13 (15 July 1992): 14-15.

136.   Koselka, Rita. "The Last Pharaoh: Once the Envy of the Gambling Business, Circus Circus Is Trying to Make a Comeback but Its Strategy Is Unclear." *Forbes* 153 (11 April 1994): 118-119.

137.   Kuriscak, Steve. *Casino Cafeteria.* N.p.: Cognac Press, 1992.   96 pp.

138.   La Fleur, Teresa, and Bruce La Fleur. *La Fleur's 1995 World Gambling Abstract.*   Boyds, Md.: TLF Publications, Inc., 1994.   145 pp.

139.   Legato, Frank. "Slot Futures: The World's Largest Slot Manufacturers Reveal Their Latest Innovations to Attract Gamblers and Increase Casino Revenues." *Casino Journal* 7 (September 1994): 48-52, 54, 102, 103.

140.   Legato, Frank. "Tracking For Tomorrow: Systems Manufacturers Bring Today's Business Technology to the Slot Department." *Casino Journal* 7 (June 1994): 44-45, 51.

141.   Macomber, Dean M. "Management Policy and Practices in Modern Casino Operations." *Annals of the Academy of Political and Social Science* 474 (July 1984): 80-90.

142.   Marcial, Gene G. "Slot Machines That Take Bills: IGT's Jackpot?" *Business Week* 3382 (25 July 1994): 80.

143.   McAvoy, Kim. "Casino Advertising Permitted by Infohighway Bill: Provision Would Create Revenue Stream for Broadcasters To Use Toward New Consumer Services." *Broadcasting & Cable* 124 (22 August 1994): 32.

144.   McKee, Jamie. "Gaming: The Shakeout May Have Begun." *Las Vegas Business Press* (26 December 1994): 1, 7-8.

145.   Mills, R.G.J., and D.M. Panton. "Scheduling of Casino Security Officers." *Omega: International Journal of Management Science* 20 (1992): 183-191.

146.   Mirage Resorts, Inc. *Casino Royal, New Orleans: Qualifications and Proposal Submitted to the City of New Orleans for the Rivergate Site: A Presentation.* 2 vols. University of Nevada, Las Vegas, Special Collections. 1992.

147.   *Nationwide Directory of Licensed Gambling Establishments.* Gainesville, Fla.: Outcalt & Associates, Inc., 1994. 240 pp.

148.   Nevada. Legislature. Subcommittee to Study the Future of Gaming in Nevada. *Subcommittee to Study the Future of Gaming in Nevada: Work Session Document.* University of Nevada, Las Vegas, Special Collections. 1991. 8 pp.

149.   "N.J. Paper Gets Casino Info." *Editor & Publisher* 127 (13 August 1994): 35.

150.   Nossiter, Adam. "The Video Poker Truck Stop: Ante Up and Fill 'er, Too." *New York Times* (11 October 1994): A17 (L).

151.   *Ownership of the Casino Industry.* Memphis, Tenn.: Promus Companies, November 11, 1993. 7 pp.

152.   "Perini Builds a New Las Vegas." *F.W. Dodge Construction Profile: Supplement to ENR* (24 January 1994): 41-50.

153.   Peters, Shannon. "HR Helps Mirage Resorts Manage Change." *Personnel Journal* 73 (June 1994): 22, 26, 29-30.

154.   Plume, Janet. "Gambling Ads vs. FCC." *Adweek: Southwest Edition* 16 (22 August 1994): 5.

155.   Plume, Janet. "House Rules: Broadcasters Fight Casino Ad Limits." *Adweek: Southwest Edition* 16 (22 August 1994): 1, 33.

156.   Plume, Janet. "Little Las Vegas Sprouting in Tunica." *Casino Journal* 7 (September 1994): 79-81.

157.   Pollesche, Eric. "Internal Controls in a Casino Environment." *Casino Journal* 7 (December 1994): 22.

158.   "Rhode Island Aide in Casino Talks Held GTech Shares." *Wall Street Journal* (2 September 1994): A2.

159.   Riggle, David. "Hotels Join the Parade: Resorting to Recycling." *BioCycle* 33 (October 1992): 37-39.

160.   Rowe, Megan. "Las Vegas' Big Gamble: Facing Steeper Competion for Tourists' Dollars, Las Vegas Continues to Reinvent Itself. How Will the Latest Wave of New Hotels Fare?" *Lodging Hospitality* 50 (February 1994): 26-28, 30.

161.   Russell, Deborah. "Hard Rock Betting on Vegas Casino & Hotel." *Billboard* 106 (10 September 1994): 13, 119.

162.   Salomon, Alan. "Gambling Is Winner for Mississippi." *Advertising Age* 65 (18 July 1994): 10.

163.   Sims, Calvin. "Family Values as a Las Vegas Smash." *New York Times* (3 February 1994): D1, D8 (L).

164.   Spain, William. "Despite Family Tug, Vegas Reasserts Roots: Attraction Building Spree Sets Tone, but Casino-Revenue-Per-Room Drives Engine." *Advertising Age* 65 (27 June 1994): 31, 37.

165.   Stein, M.L. "Publisher Joins Board of Casino Operator." *Editor & Publisher* 127 (10 September 1994): 8, 10.

166.   Stuart, Lyle. *Winning at Casino Gambling*. New York: Barricade Books, 1994. 320 pp.

167.   "Survey Shows Gambling's Popularity." *Hotel & Motel Management* 209 (21 March 1994): 3, 28.

168.   Tait, Thomas G. "Positioning for Leadership: Nevada in the Next Century." *Nevada Business Journal* 8 (November/December 1993): 25-26.

169.   Taylor, John. "Fantasy Island: My Weekend at the Taj." *New York* 23 (21 May 1990): 48-55.

170.   "Theme Parks: Feeling the Future." *Economist* 330 (19 February 1994): 74, 79.

171.   Troy, Timothy N. "Flexibility a Key for Vendors Betting on Casinos." *Hotel & Motel Management* 209 (19 September 1994): 27, 33.

172.   Troy, Timothy N. "Getting in While the Gaming's Good." *Hotel & Motel Management* 209 (1 February 1994): 24-25.

173.   Troy, Timothy N. "High Stakes Technology." *Hotel & Motel Management* 209 (19 September 1994): 27, 30.

174.   Turner, W. Bruce. *Casino Gaming Outlook for the Mississippi Gulf Coast: Storm Clouds Rising*. St.

Petersburg, Fla.: Raymond James & Associates, 1993. 30 pp.

175.   Tyler, Ralph. "The High Life of the High Roller: A Report From the Inside." *Variety* 336 (9 August 1989): 66.

176.   U.S. Congress. House. Committee on Education and Labor. Subcommittee on Labor-Management Relations. *Oversight Hearing on Labor Relations in the Entertainment and Gaming Industry: The Frontier Hotel Strike: Hearing Before the Subcommittee on Labor-Management Relations of the Committee on Education and Labor.* 103rd Cong., 1st sess., 1 October 1993. 50 pp.

177.   "Using Cards for Credit in Casinos Is Approved." *New York Times* (14 December 1993): B4 (L).

178.   Weatherford, Mike. "Where Themes Come True." *Nevada Magazine* 53 (January/February 1993): 10-14.

179.   Whalen, Jeanne. "Out-of-Home Follows the Gambling Flow: As Casinos Sprout Through the Midwest, Highway Boards Entice High, Low Rollers." *Advertisting Age* 64 (22 November 1993): S2.

180.   Wolfe, Frank. "Capital Gaming International Lost a Big One in Last Month's Rhode Island Elections. So . . . Why is Jack Davis Smiling?" *Forbes* 154 (19 December 1994): 84.

181.   "Year in Review." *International Gaming and Wagering Business* 15 (5 December 1994): 3, 38, 40, 41-42, 44-45, 56, 62.

182.   Yoshihashi, Pauline. "The Gambling Industry Rakes It in as Casinos Spread Across the U.S." *Wall Street Journal* (22 October 1993): A1, A9.

183.	Yoshihashi, Pauline. "ITT Delays Indefinitely Plans to Build a $750 Million Casino in Las Vegas." *Wall Street Journal* (17 October 1994): C18.

184.	Zimmerman, Kevin. "Fountain of Youth Fills Vegas Venues." *Variety* 343 (27 May 1991): 1, 101.

SECTION B

Indian Gaming

Indian gaming is a controversial, explosive growth sector within the casino industry. Since the passage of the Indian Gaming Regulatory Act of 1988 (Public Law 100-497), nearly 100 casinos have opened on reservations in twenty-two states, raising issues of tribal sovereignty, states' rights, social welfare, management, and regulation. The citations that follow were selected from a wide variety of sources. Effort was made to provide thorough coverage of the complex issues raised by Indian gaming.

185. "Agency Says Tribal Status Is in Doubt." *New York Times* (4 December 1993): A26 (L).
    Discusses the U.S. Department of the Interior's proposed denial of federal tribal recognition to New Jersey's Ramapough Mountain Indians, preventing their involvement in casino gaming. Chief Ronald Van Dunk believes they were treated unfairly, especially since New Jersey Representative Robert G. Torricelli knew about this decision before he did. Torricelli opposes Indian gaming because it competes with Atlantic City casinos.

186. Attinger, Joelle. "Mohawks, Money and Death." *Time* 135 (14 May 1990): 32.
    Discusses conflicts about casinos on the Mohawk Indians' St. Regis Reservation located in New York, Quebec, and Ontario. While some view such revenues as an "easy way to fund tribal welfare programs," others argue that casinos cause a variety of social problems and generate little profit. The clash, resulting in one gun battle and two deaths, is complicated by a "bitter power struggle between competing tribal councils" and the reluctance of U.S. and

Canadian officials to involve Mohawks in efforts to resolve
the conflict.

187.   Baker, James N., and Debra Rosenberg. "Gambling
on the Reservation." *Newsweek* 119 (17 February 1992):
29.
        Announces the opening of the $58 million dollar
Foxwoods High Stakes Bingo and Casino on Connecticut's
Mashantucket Pequot Reservation which will greatly benefit
both the tribe's 200-plus members and the community. After
a brief look at Indian gaming's history and growth, the
authors state that many tribes continue to resist government
intervention in their management of gambling operations
although regulatory problems have decreased since the 1988
Indian Gaming Regulatory Act and its creation of the
National Indian Gaming Commission.

188.   Baumgold, Julie. "Frank and the Fox Pack." *Esquire*
121 (March 1994): 88-96.
        Examines the success of the Foxwoods High Stakes
Bingo and Casino on Connecticut's Mashantucket Pequot
Reservation. About a "tenth of the population of the United
States" lives within driving distance, and with a profit
margin of almost 45 percent, it is one of the country's richest
casinos. Frank Sinatra's appearance in the showroom is one
sign of success. A history of the tribe and the casino's
development highlights the ingenuity of tribal leaders, the
casino's impact on tribal members, and the tribe's
relationships with state and local government.

189.   Belliveau, James J. "Notes—Casino Gambling
Under the Indian Gaming Regulatory Act: Narragansett
Tribal Sovereignty Versus Rhode Island Gambling Laws."
Suffolk University Law Review 27 (1993): 389-424.
        Explains how Indian gaming regulation "raises
important issues regarding state law enforcement authority,
the need for proper regulation of gaming activities, and the
strong interests of Indian tribes in self-government and
economic development." The author focuses on settlement
agreements with Rhode Island's Narragansett Indian Tribe to

show how complex and difficult these issues are. His
discussion covers the development of reservations, the
concept and limitations of tribal sovereignty, the history of
the Indian Gaming Regulatory Act and "recent judicial
interpretations of its provisions," and case law's effects on
"the inevitable legal confrontation" between this tribe and the
state. Belliveau concludes, by "applying the analysis of
recent court decision, it appears that the Narragansetts will
be able to circumvent the state's civil regulatory laws and
proceed with their casino plans." A clearly written
explanation of complicated legal matters. Bibliographical
references.

190. Bezpaletz, Reuben D. *The Impact of the Indian
Gaming Regulatory Act on State-Tribal Relations: Issues for
the Nineties.* Issue Memorandum 94-42. Pierre, S. Dak.:
South Dakota Legislative Research Council, September 27,
1994. 6 pp.
    Identifies current issues affecting the future of Indian
gaming in South Dakota. After reviewing gaming there, the
author briefly summarizes the following concerns: tribal
sovereignty; off-reservation casino sites; public opposition;
casino management; utilization of casino profits; tribal land
acquisition; casino expansion; state-tribal litigation; tribal
politics; and perceived racism. He concludes that while
Congress is best equipped to address and resolve most of
these issues, there are many areas which are the legitimate
domain of state-tribal relations, and neither the tribes nor the
state "should allow congressional inactivity to distract them
from their mutual responsibilities."

191. Briancon, Pierre. "Betting With the Indians." *World
Press Review* 40 (December 1993): 36-37.
    Outlines the growth of legalized gambling throughout
the United States, focusing on Indian reservation casino
operations and riverboat gaming as two examples.
Gambling promises an easy way to improve government
coffers, and in today's climate, moral issues surrounding the
issue no longer seem to be a shared public concern.

192.   "Bugsy and the Indians." *Economist* 322 (21 March 1992): 27-28.

Discusses the Agua Caliente Cahuilla Indian Tribe's plan to open a casino in Palm Springs, California. While Indian gaming has a "mixed reputation" due to mismanagement and corruption, the article notes it is spreading across the United States and is very successful in some locations. Competition, not corruption, may be the major threat to that success; as legalized gambling increases, more operations compete for gamblers' interest and money. A sidebar looks at casinos' adverse effects on rural Colorado.

193.   "Californian Indians: Buffalo Stakes." *Economist* 328 (24 July 1993): 25-26.

Examines the spread of legalized gaming on Indian reservations. Since California's constitution bans slot machines and the Indian Gaming Regulatory Act restricts reservation games to those allowed elsewhere in the state, Indians are unable to operate lucrative machines. Tribes were recently encouraged, however, when a federal judge ruled that the state's lottery and slot machines "offered an essentially similar form of gambling," opening the way for lucrative "Las Vegas-style casinos."

194.   Carlson, Arne H., Hubert H. Humphrey III, and Tribal-State Compact Negotiating Committee. *Report to the Legislature on the Status of Indian Gambling in Minnesota.* St. Paul, Minn.: The Governor, 1991. 111 pp.

Provides an overview of Indian gaming activities in Minnesota and a summary of the federal law that forms the basis for Indian gaming. This report also identifies concerns, including an overtaxed regulatory system, and the link between the growth of non-Indian gaming and the legal basis for the further expansion of Indian gaming operations. Includes full text of two tribal-state compacts for video poker and blackjack.

195.   Carter, Irl. "Gambling With Their Lives: American Indians and the Casinos." *CURA Reporter* 22 (August 1992): 2-6.

Focuses on the phenomenal growth of reservation-based casinos in Minnesota and the profits and problems that followed. While many Indian leaders point to the economic advantages of increased income and employment, others are concerned about a variety of potentially negative outcomes affecting tribal structures and members. Included are compulsive gambling, adolescent gambling, and adverse effects on tribal traditions. This succinctly covered debate among Minnesota's tribal leaders is followed by a brief analysis of the future of Indian casinos. Bibliographical references.

196.   Cashen, Henry C., and John C. Dill. "The Real Truth About Indian Gaming and the States." *State Legislatures* 18 (March 1992): 23-25.

Analyzes the Indian Gaming Regulatory Act of 1988 and argues that state governments can affect gambling on Indian lands. This law establishes three categories of games; casino gambling and slot machines are in the category which requires a tribal-state compact. A discussion of Connecticut's experience with the Pequot Indians notes that the state did not understand its rights and responsibilities under this law, resulting in critical mistakes during the negotiation process.

197.   "Casino Profits Help Indians Get Degree in Gaming." *New York Times* (2 March 1994): B8 (L).

Notes that Wisconsin's Minominee Indians are using gaming profits to support a local community college's gambling program. The College of the Minominee Nation's associate of arts degree covers "gaming law, casino management, casino security, and personnel management." Other U.S. tribes are now sending members to this school to take these courses.

198.   Clark, Steven D. "Before You Sign on the Dotted Line." *Indian Gaming* 4 (September 1995): 10, 11, 23, 24.

Gives advice on selecting an Indian gaming management company or lender. The author has worked with dozens of tribes throughout the western United States and Canada.

199.   Clines, Francis X. "Indian Tribes Close Ranks to Protect Casinos From Cheats and Rivals." *New York Times* (25 December 1993): A6 (L).

Looks at increase of unparalleled cooperation among various Indian tribes to prevent corruption and cheating at reservation casinos. One example is Wisconsin's Indian Gaming Intelligence Association which includes seventeen casinos that share information on corrupt employees and players, casino management practices, accounting procedures, and security systems.

200.   Clinton, Robert N. "Sovereignty and Jurisdiction." In *Native America in the Twentieth Century: An Encyclopedia*, edited by Mary B. Davis. Reference Library of Social Science: Vol. 452.   New York: Garland, 1994.

Covers the history and development of tribal sovereignty and jurisdiction in the United States. In this section, pages 605-611, the author shows how colonialism "gradually changed the legal and political status of Indian tribes from sovereign independent nations to domestic dependent" ones. While the "modern remnant of those colonialist legal doctrines continues to treat Indian tribes as sovereign nations" and tribes view themselves as sovereign nations, there has been "significant erosion in tribal jurisdiction, often in favor" of greater roles for state and local government. Clinton anticipates that this "political dynamic" will continue to cause "tensions and disputes among tribal, federal, and state governments." Although this article does not directly deal with gambling activities, it provides a clear, useful overview of the sovereignty issues so central to Indian gaming controversies. Bibliographical references.

201.   Connor, Matt. "Corruption on the Reservation: Cause for Concern?" *International Gaming and Wagering Business* 14 (15 October 1993): 55-56, 58-59.

Exposes possibly disreputable deals being made between corrupt tribal leaders and dishonest casino management companies. The federal government appears to be reluctant to investigate allegations of wrongdoing because of tribal sovereignty.

202.   Connor, Matt. "Indian Gaming: Prosperity, Controversy." *International Gaming & Wagering Business* 14 (15 March -14 April 1993): 1, 8-10, 12, 45.

Explains how the proliferation of tribal casinos has enhanced life on Indian reservations. Profits have provided "improved road and water systems and health-care centers," and "job training, scholarships and both home and business loans to tribal members." The National Indian Gaming Association predicts that "within a few years, nearly every Indian reservation in the U.S. will operate some kind of gaming facility." Controversial effects include "opposition from state governments, other non-Indian gaming venues, and pressure groups outside the Indian community" and arguments among various tribes. Indian gaming operates in a "maze of conflicting interests, legal questions, and political maneuvers." Includes sidebars with brief definitions of relevant terms found in the U.S. Constitution and the Indian Gaming Regulatory Act, a list of tribes with compacts by state, and a chronology of Indian gaming's evolution. Tables.

203.   Cruise, Cathy. "Federal Officials Refute Trump Allegations; Committee Members Offended by Remarks." *Indian Gaming* 3 (November 1993): 3, 18.

Presents Donald Trump's tirade against Indian gaming before the House's Native American Affairs Subcommittee. Trump charged that organized crime was "rampant" on reservations and some tribes should not be allowed to operate a reservation because "they don't look like Indians to me and they don't look like Indians to

Indians." This article also provides responses from various congressmen to Trump's allegations.

204.   Eadington, William R., ed. *Indian Gaming and the Law*. Reno, Nev.: Institute for the Study of Gambling and Commercial Gaming, College of Business Administration, University of Nevada, Reno, 1990. 298 pp.
        Presents a collection of writings on the politics and enforcement of the Indian Gaming Regulatory Act which captures many of the conflicting perspectives on the issue. Contributors include Stewart L. Udall, former Secretary of the Interior; Harry Reid, Senior Senator from Nevada; Harold Monteau, Tribal Attorney for the Chippewa-Cree Tribe; and Nora Garcia, Chairperson of the Fort Mojave Tribe. Bibliographical references.

205.   Enos, Gary. "Betting on Casinos." *City & State* (15-28 February 1993): 1, 22.
        Describes how many "casino-averse government officials" are now "trying to exert some control over" Indian casinos because of the economic benefits they provide. Connecticut's Mashantucket Pequot Tribe, for example, agreed to "pay the state at least $100 million a year in slot-machine revenue, or 25 percent of what it expects to raise from the popular games," funds earmarked for "distressed municipalities." He concludes that governments "have ample opportunities to reap some winnings."

206.   Filzer, Paul N. "Can Indian Tribes Remain Competitive? The Future of Off-Reservation Gaming Under The Indian Gaming Regulatory Act of 1988: Michigan Governor Purports to Reject Detroit Tribal Gaming Project." *Indian Gaming* 4 (November 1994): 8-9, 18-19.
        Focuses on efforts by the Sault Ste. Marie Tribe of Chippewa Indians to obtain land in Detroit, Michigan for a tribal gaming project. Though approved by Secretary of the Interior Bruce Babbit, the request was killed by Governor John Engler. Filzer challenges Engler's justification for stopping the Detroit project.

207.   George Washington University. National Indian
Policy Center. *Reservation-Based Gaming*. Washington,
D.C.: National Indian Policy Center, George Washington
University, 1993. 45 pp.
    Surveys public opinion regarding Indian gaming
obtained in a 1992 Harris Poll. The survey suggests that
sixty-eight percent of Americans believe that Indians should
be allowed to have casino gaming on tribal lands, while only
forty-four percent favor legalized gambling off reservations.
This report also provides a description of tribal-state gaming
compacts for class III gaming, an analysis of the economic
impacts of Indian gaming, and a summary of case law
interpreting the Indian Gaming Regulatory Act. Bibliographical references.

208.   Glimco, Peter T. "The IGRA and the Eleventh
Amendment: Indian Tribes Are Gambling When They Try to
Sue a State." *John Marshall Law Review* 27 (1993): 193-
237.
    Argues that "recent federal district court decisions
prevent Indian tribes" from establishing the tribal-state
compacts the Indian Gaming Regulatory Act (IGRA)
requires. Glimco first stresses that the purpose of this law is
to help tribes achieve "economic independence through
gambling." When a tribe requests the negotiation necessary
to operate casinos, "the state must negotiate this agreement in
good faith." When a state declines to participate in the
process, U.S. "district courts have jurisdiction over any
action brought by an Indian tribe." Since the Eleventh
Amendment, however, "bars any action by an Indian tribe
against a state or state official," tribes have no legal recourse.
Glimco shows how the current law perpetuates this
conundrum and "how Congress can and should rectify this
deficiency." Moving the law's authority from the Indian
Commerce Clause to the Interstate Commerce Clause would
give tribes "a forum in which to raise their contentions" and
thus fulfill IGRA's intent. Bibliographical references.

209.   Greenberg, Pam, and Judy Zelio. "States and the Indian Gaming Regulatory Act." *State Legislative Report* 17 (July 1992): 1-18.

Analyzes the impact the Indian Gaming Regulatory Act has had on tribal-state relations. Background on the act is provided along with a discussion of the classes of gaming defined in the act. Tribal requirements under the act and the role of state legislatures are also discussed. A state-by-state summary of Indian gaming activity is provided along with a list of state statutes concerning tribal-state compacts.

210.   Gros, Roger. "Indian Impact: How Will Indian Gaming Affect Gaming Industry?" *Casino Journal* 7 (August 1991): 16-17.

Argues that Nevada and New Jersey fear competition from tribal casinos. Las Vegas's Steve Wynn "believes that the success of Indian gaming will be its downfall, for when public officials see the revenue they are losing to the tribes, they will legalize taxable gaming in their states." Mashantucket Pequot casino president Al Luciana thinks their success will affect Atlantic City because they appeal to "people in the middle," not the high rollers New Jersey attracts; how each area markets itself will be the decisive factor. Members of the Nevada Resort Association are concerned that business will be adversely affected by Indian gaming in nearby states whose citizens now come to Nevada to gamble. Gros concludes that "ready or not, however, Indian gaming is about to hit, and the casino industry had better be prepared."

211.   Hill, Rick. "Indian Gaming Allows Tribes to Rediscover and Protect Their Traditions." *Indian Gaming* 3 (October 1993): 3, 17.

Contends that gaming is helping Indians reestablish their cultural identities. "Historically, poverty has forced many Indian people to leave their reservations and lose their connections to their people. Now gaming is bringing them, and the traditional ways, back to our Indian communities."

212. Hill, Rick. "Sixty Minutes' Full Color Yellow Journalism." *Casino Journal* 7 (December 1994): 21.
Rebuts the negative image of Indian gaming portrayed on *60 Minutes*. Aired by CBS-TV on September 18, 1994, the show is purported to be "littered with inaccuracies, half truths, and innuendo." This official response from the National Indian Gaming Association provides a good overview of the economic benefits which Indian gaming has brought to Connecticut and New England. In Connecticut, for example, $500 million of goods and services are purchased and over $120 million paid to the state each year because of Indian Gaming.

213. "Indian Gaming Resolution From the National Governor's Conference." *Indian Gaming* 3 (April 1993): 19.
Provides the full text of a resolution passed at the 1993 National Governor's Conference. This resolution calls for increased flexibility for states in negotiating tribal-state compacts, greater control over the types of games offered on reservations, and more authority for states to impose stipulations on agreements involving land taken into trust for gaming purposes.

214. *Indians, Indian Tribes and State Government.* Corrected ed. St. Paul, Minn.: Minnesota House of Representatives, Research Department, February, 1993. 79 pp.
Compiled to introduce Minnesota legislators to the major issues in the relationship between Indian tribes, Indians, and state government. After providing some basic data on Indians and tribal gaming in Minnesota, this report contains a series of papers on specific legal issues. They cover the following areas for "Indian country": criminal jurisdiction; civil jurisdiction; gaming regulation; liquor regulation; control of natural resources; environmental regulation; taxation; health and human services for Indians; and education law affecting Indian students. These sections may include background information, legal references and definitions, brief discussions of pertinent federal law, and

summaries. This report brings together a great deal of information that affects all states, not just Minnesota. Maps, tables, bibliographical references.

215.   Israel, Daniel. "Analysis of Proposed Amendments to the Indian Gaming Regulatory Act." *Indian Gaming* 4 (July 1994): 3,6,11,16, 23.

Attacks proposed 1994 amendments to the Indian Gaming Regulatory Act as serious threats to tribal sovereignty and the profitability of Indian gaming operations. Israel's biggest concern is a measure that would significantly increase the budget and authority of the National Indian Gaming Commission.

216.   Johansen, Bruce E. *Life and Death in Mohawk Country*. Golden, Colo.: North American Press, 1993. 189 pp.

Chronicles the virtual civil war that erupted on the Awkesasne Indian Reservation in the summer of 1990 and sheds light on the roots and aftermath of this deadly conflict. At the core of this dispute are Mohawk tribal members' efforts to bring gaming operations to the reservation and the extreme opposition they faced from tribal elders seeking to preserve traditional values and culture. Bibliographical references.

217.   Keechi, Charles. "Keechi Responds to Safire." *Indian Gaming* 3 (March 1993): 5.

Reacts to several essays written by syndicated newspaper columnist William Safire. Keechi, Chair of the National Indian Gaming Association, takes strong exception to these pieces, titled, "The Wigwam Casino (30 May 1991); "Redskins' Revenge" (6 January 1992); and "Now: Bet While You Booze" (11 January 1993). Keechi argues that Safire demonstrates a vulgar ignorance of Indian gaming.

218.   Kinsey, Jean, and Todd Gabe. "Casinos and Income in Non-Metropolitan Minnesota." *Minnesota Agricultural Economist* 677 (Summer 1994): 1, 4-7.

Analyzes legalized gambling's economic effects on Minnesota. For this study, the authors "estimated the impacts of various economic indicators, including the presence of a casino, on four measures of per capita income in all rural Minnesota counties . . . (1) overall per capita income, (2) income per person earned by workers in the bar and restaurant industry, (3) income per person in the hotel/motel industry, and (4) income per person in the amusement industry." Results show there "was no relationship between the presence of a casino and overall per capita personal income." They conclude that while it is too soon to understand the "full economic implications of Indian gaming," counties with reservation casinos show little increase in per capita income. An interesting, concise, and useful article. Sidebars include tables on the history of gaming in Minnesota, information on casino activity in state counties, and charts showing contributions to county wide per capita income and increases in income after casinos. Tables, bibliographical references.

219.   Liberman, Si. "Helping Casinos to Acquire Licenses." *New York Times* (28 November 1993): NJ3 (L).
Profiles G. Michael Brown, former director of the New Jersey Division of Gaming Enforcement, who now advises corporations and Indian tribes on licensing and operating casinos. He recently received a three-year contract as chief executive of Connecticut's Foxwoods High Stakes Bingo and Casino.

220.   "List of Indian Gaming Operations." *Indian Gaming* 4 (December 1994): 14-15.
Provides a state-by-state directory of Indian gaming operations throughout the United States by tribes and their locations. This column appears regularly in *Indian Gaming*.

221.   Lombardi, Michael. "Office of Inspector General's Report on Indian Gaming." *Indian Gaming* 3 (February 1993): 8.
Criticizes the media for focusing on the negative aspects of a report by the Assistant Inspector General for

Audit of the U.S. Department of the Interior. The report, titled *Implementation of the Indian Gaming Regulatory Act,* is highly critical of the National Indian Gaming Commission's failure to regulate casino gaming on reservations and charges that revenues are being improperly taken by corrupt operators and suppliers. However, the report also acknowledges that gaming has had a positive economic and social impact on certain tribes.

222.   Lueders, Bill. "Buffaloed: Casino Cowboys Take Indians for a Ride." *Progressive* 58 (August 1994): 31-33.
        Examines the "unlucky alliance between" Wisconsin's St. Croix Indians and casino partners Roy Palmer and Ronald Brown of Buffalo Brothers Management, Inc. "In 1992, the pair raked in $13.8 million in profits, more than twice the $6.5 million that went to the tribe." Lueders describes this unfortunate relationship to illustrate how Indian gaming "has been a mixed blessing." The rapid growth of reservation casinos has resulted in outside exploitation of tribal members, mistakes by tribal governments unfamiliar with gaming, increased access to alcohol and dangerous drugs, unwanted and unexpected tribal debts, poor casino management practices, and vulnerability to corruption. Unscrupulous individuals, for example, have leased gaming machines to tribes at ridiculously high rates that deplete their profits. "In 1993, the Office of the Inspector General for the U.S. Department of the Interior found excessive fees totaling $62 million in eighteen of the twenty-seven tribal management contracts it viewed." He concludes that "the determination of white outsiders to cash in on Indian gaming appears as strong as ever."

223.   Magnuson, Jon. "Casino Wars: Ethics and Economics in Indian Country." *Christian Century* 111 (16 February 1994): 169-171.
        Presents a Christian perspective on Indian gaming. The author, a Lutheran pastor, identifies three concerns voiced by religious leaders. First, in response to the moral issues gambling raises, Magnuson responds that it "is

unsettling that there has been so little opposition by church leaders to the proliferation of state lotteries." Noting how many tribes benefit economically from their casinos, he states it "might be good to clean one's own house before suggesting Native Americans clean theirs." A second response is "often moral indignation and masked anger" that the "noble American Indian" engages in gambling, a view he considers to be "rooted in an unconscious sentimentalizing and romanticizing of that which a dominant culture has destroyed." Finally, some suggest gambling offers unfair advantages to Indian tribes; Donald Trump, for example, has vociferously opposed their casinos, in truth, because of the competition they present. An historical understanding of Indian sovereignty, economic history, and relationships to the federal government refutes this fairness issue. These "responses to Indian gaming reflect deeper issues about ethics, spirituality, and the complex face of racism."

224.   Marvel, Mark. "Gambling on the Reservations: What's Really at Stake?" *Interview* 24 (May 1994): 114.
        Contains an interview with Marge Anderson, Ojibwa tribal leader and head of one of the country's most successful American Indian casinos. She responds to questions about controversies surrounding Indian gaming, Trump's testimony against Indian gaming at a House subcommittee hearing, and the economic benefits Indian gaming provides. She stresses that gaming "is the only economic development that's ever worked in Indian country. Period. And without gaming, we were losing our culture, we were losing our language. We wouldn't survive." It has brought back self-esteem, self-sufficiency, and self-determination.

225.   McKay, Nancy. "Comment: The Meaning of Good Faith in the Indian Gaming Regulatory Act." *Gonzaga Law Review* 27 (1991/1992): 471-486.
        Analyzes the use of the phrase "good faith" in the Indian Gaming Regulatory Act (IGRA). While Congress did not define this, the law says states "must negotiate in good faith" with tribes that want to operate gambling activities.

McKay summarizes relevant IGRA legislative history
pertaining to good faith, reviews related case law interpreting
this provision, explores "possible meanings of good faith as
derived from other areas of the law," and looks at
Washington state court interpretations of the concept.
Includes an analysis of a complaint the Spokane Tribe filed
against that state in 1991. She concludes that "the objective
test," rather than the subjective test, will help the courts
implement congressional intent because it "utilizes the
standard of reasonableness in fair, honest, and objective
dealings." Bibliographical references.

226.   Michigan Indian Gaming Enterprises. *Economic
Impact of the Hannahville Indian Community's $2 Bill
Payroll*. Prepared by University Associates, Carol
Bergquist. Wilson, Mich.: Hannahville Indian Community,
1993. 36 pp.
        Describes an interesting experiment and publicity
campaign. Michigan Indian Gaming Enterprises, a tribal
casino operator, paid employees with two-dollar bills to
track the distribution of the company's payroll in the
community in order to evaluate and demonstrate the economic importance of this area's chief employer. Provides a
model that others may find useful.

227.   Midwest Hospitality Advisors. *Impact: Gaming in
the State of Minnesota: A Study of the Economic Benefits
and Tax Revenue Generated*. Minneapolis, Minn.: Midwest
Hospitality Advisors, 1992. 58 pp.
        Analyzes Indian gaming's effect on tribal and local
economies in Minnesota and the tax revenues it generates for
the state and federal government. Welfare roles and
unemployment diminished significantly in jurisdictions
where casino gaming was introduced. Information was
taken from interviews with all Indian gaming operators and
from figures provided by various state agencies.

228.   Minnesota Indian Gaming Association. "MIGA
Responds to Inspector General's Report." *Indian Gaming* 3
(February 1993): 9.

Attacks the Assistant Inspector General for Audit of the U.S. Department of the Interior's report, *Implementation of the Indian Gaming Regulatory Act*, as a flawed document designed for political sabotage. This editorial identifies a sequence of events that suggest a deliberate campaign to "weaken tribal gaming and undermine the sovereignty of tribal governments."

229.   Minnesota Indian Gaming Association, and KPMG Peat Marwick. *Economic Benefits of Tribal Gaming in Minnesota*. Minn.: Minnesota Indian Gaming Association, 1992. 24 pp.
Presents data gathered from six of the eleven Indian tribes operating casinos in Minnesota. This study concludes that gaming, on its way to becoming one of the state's largest employers, now ranks twentieth among the top twenty-five corporate employers. The study also shows that while Minnesota's Aid to Families with Dependent Children has increased since 1987 in urban counties, it has decreased significantly in the four counties containing major tribal gaming operations.

230.   MN Planning. *High Stakes: Gambling in Minnesota*. St. Paul, Minn.: MN Planning, 1992. 86 pp.
Provides an overview of gambling in Minnesota. This report discusses the social and economic aspects of gambling, policy issues, Indian gaming, charitable gaming, the state lottery, parimutuel wagering, and gambling in neighboring states.

231.   MN Planning. *Minnesota Gambling, 1993*. St. Paul, Minn.: MN Planning, 1993. 42 pp.
Reviews gambling in Minnesota with emphasis on Indian gaming. MN Planning recommends that the expansion of video gaming devices be stopped, regulation and monitoring be improved, efforts to prevent and treat problem gambling be intensified, and cooperation between tribal governments, the state, and business groups be strengthened.

232.   Moore, W. John. "A Winning Hand?" *National Journal* 25 (17 July 1993): 1796-1800.

Discusses casino gaming's advantages for Indian tribes. Minnesota's Grand Casino owned by the Ojibwa Indians, for example, has added "millions of dollars to tribal coffers," and with 800 tribal members working at the casino, unemployment has dropped from sixty percent to practically nothing. Revenues are used for building homes, roads, schools, and a health clinic. Moore looks at the spread of Indian gaming nationwide, the Indian Gaming Regulatory Act, and proposed federal legislation that would limit it, citing concerns of those who favor it and those who oppose it. Tribal sovereignty and government intervention are central issues. Included is an analysis of Indian gaming's effect on states and their other businesses. A sidebar contains a brief historical overview of the legal relationships between Indian tribes and the federal government.

233.   Morales, Leslie Anderson, comp. *American Indian Gaming and Gambling: A Bibliography*. Public Administration Series: Bibliography P 3081. Monticello, Ill.: Vance Bibliographies, 1991. 8 pp.

Collects over 110 bibliographic citations on Indian gaming and gambling from magazines, newspapers, Congressional hearings, and federal publications. These "citations address issues of economic development, unemployment, crime, and traffic." They are arranged alphabetically by main entry and do not include abstracts.

234.   Moran, Kimberly A. *1994 State Legislation on Native American Issues*. Denver, Colo.: National Conference of State Legislatures, September, 1994. 35 pp.

Reviews 1994 state legislative activities related to Native Americans. The introduction briefly explains tribal sovereignty, how it confuses "most citizens of the United States," and how much proposed state legislation attempts "to clarify and improve the relationship and preserve the rights of the states, the tribes, and the people of both." Out of 344 relevant bills introduced in state legislatures prior to September 1994, twenty-six dealt specifically with Indian gaming, thirty-four with sovereignty, fourteen with state-tribal relations, and six with tribal status recognition. Legislative summaries arranged by state are followed by specific bill numbers and bill summaries, a list of state legislators of "Native American Indian heritage," and Native American population figures by state from the 1990 census.

235.   Newton, Nell Jessup, and Shawn Frank. "Gaming." In *Native America in the Twentieth Century: An Encyclopedia*, edited by Mary B. Davis. Reference Library of Social Science: Vol. 452. New York: Garland, 1994.

Reviews current status, issues, and controversies surrounding Indian gaming. In this section, pages 205-207, the authors concisely cover the evolution and growth of Indian gaming, the legal issue of Indian sovereignty, the mandates of the Indian Gaming Regulatory Act, and the benefits tribes receive from their operations. They also look at how gaming has caused problems among tribes and "sparked intense controversy between tribal and state governments." They conclude that "Indian gaming continues to be a powerful means towards stimulating economic growth in many tribal communities, enabling some tribes to become increasingly self-sufficient financially." Bibliographical references.

236.   Nyberg, Debra. "Gambling Casinos Benefit American Indian Tribes and Cities." *Minnesota Cities* 76 (November 1991): 12-14.

Explains how Indian gaming provides "economic growth for those cities near reservations and throughout" Minnesota. Nyberg discusses how the state's municipalities can work with tribal governments "to make gambling a part of a city's development strategy," describes how the economic rewards of Indian gaming benefit the state's cities, and outlines what "tribes are doing to insulate themselves from a possible recession in gambling." She urges officials to treat Native Americans politely, respectfully, and without suspicion. It is essential that "people remember that a tribal government is a sovereign nation, not a corporation." Includes sidebars with a map showing Minnesota's Indian

casino locations and a chart showing how legalized gambling
has grown there.

237.   Opel, Fritz. "Key Issues in Media Relations for
Native American Gaming." *Indian Gaming* 2 (February
1992): 8-9.
        Identifies four important public relations points for
reservation casino operators. Opel first stresses that Indian
gaming "represents one of the toughest marketing challenges
. . . the media's image of your tribe and the media's
perceptions of your gaming operation will always be
inextricably woven together." He urges tribal leaders to
"promote Indian gaming as a legitimate and attractive leisure
activity"; publicize how Indian gaming economically benefits
tribal members; "create public support" through involvement
in civic, business, charitable, and community associations;
and "look at your operation the way a camera crew might
view it." He then includes positive statements about Indian
gaming used by other tribes.

238.   Pevar, Stephen L. *The Rights of Indians and Tribes:
The Basic ACLU Guide to Indian and Tribal Rights.* 2nd ed.
An American Civil Liberties Union Handbook. Carbondale,
Ill.: Southern Illinois University Press, 1992.
        Examines federal Indian law and the history of
federal Indian policy. Chapters cover such topics as relevant
legal definitions, treaties, state power over Indian affairs,
taxation, the Indian Civil Rights Act, criminal and civil
jurisdiction on Indian lands, and tribal self-government.
Although this work does not discuss tribal casinos, it does
provide easily understandable background information on
tribal sovereignty and the legal and civil rights of Native
Americans essential to the study or understanding of Indian
gaming.

239.   Reeser, Ralph, ed. *Manual of Indian Gaming Law,
Annotated.* 3 vols. Fairfax, Va.: Falmouth Institute, 1992.
Looseleaf.
        Provides up-to-date information on the legal status of
Indian gaming operations. Sections include: Indian Gaming

Regulatory Act (IGRA) as amended; National Indian Gaming Commission; related federal laws, federal regulations, and issuances; court decisions; IGRA legislative history; tribal-state compacts; and updates. The section titled Other Federal Laws includes excerpts from the *United States Code* on gambling in general, transportation of gambling devices, Internal Revenue Service code revisions, gambling jurisdiction provisions, contracting restrictions, Freedom of Information Act revisions, judicial review, immigration and nationality, and criminal code provisions. The Other Regulations and Issuances section has various memoranda and letters from the Department of the Interior and sections from the *Code of Federal Regulations* regarding the Department of Justice and the Federal Communications Commission. A section on Lottery Matter (18 U.S.C. 1302) from the Postal Service Domestic Mail Service Manual is also provided.

240. Rose, I. Nelson. "Indian Gaming in California." *International Gaming and Wagering Business* 15 (5 July 1994): 22-25.
    Lists specific forms of gaming that are allowed on California Indian reservations and provides a directory of tribes offering gaming. A summary of California case law on Indian gaming is included.

241. Rose, I. Nelson. "The Future of Indian Gaming." *Journal of Gambling Studies* 8 (Winter 1992): 383-399.
    Examines "competitive conflicts" Indian gaming causes and offers "some speculation" about its future. Rose reviews the development of reservation casinos, the legal status of Native Americans, the limits on allowable games imposed by the Indian Gaming Regulatory Act, and the issue of sovereignty and "state versus federal control." Select court cases and Congressional testimony are also covered. He concludes that Indian casinos have revitalized reservations economically and "have the potential to be major competitors to all other forms of legal gambling." Congress, however, "will realize the door it opened and will move to limit new high stakes games." Bibliographical references.

242.   Santoni, Roland J. "The Indian Gaming Regulatory Act: How Did We Get Here? Where are We Going?" *Creighton Law Review* 26 (February 1993): 387-447.

Focuses on the right of Indian tribes to govern themselves and regulate the affairs and conduct of their members on tribal lands. Santoni gives a legal overview of the Indian Gaming Regulatory Act (IGRA) and provides a review of major Indian gaming cases. He concludes with recommended amendments to the IGRA. Bibliographical references.

243.   Sokolow, Gary. "The Future of Gambling in Indian Country." *American Indian Law Review* 15 (1990): 151-181.

Discusses the legislative and legal issues surrounding Indian gaming. Sokolow first provides an overview of Indian gaming, followed by an examination of federal government involvement and legislation and an analysis of existing case law. He illustrates his argument that the "expansion of gaming into Indian country and the recent proliferation of court decisions on the subject have aroused the interest of both the states and the Congress" with a review of significant public laws and legal decisions. He concludes that "one sure fact of Indian law is that it is a fluid concept, subject to few permanent and enduring concepts." Indian tribal sovereignty "is subject to gradual erosion as Indians and non-Indians live closer together, in ever-increasing numbers." Bibliographical references.

244.   Strate, Larry D., and Ann M. Mayo. "Federal Control of Indian Lands v State Control of Gaming: Cabazon Bingo and the Indian Gaming Regulatory Act." *Journal of Gambling Studies* 6 (Spring 1990): 63-72.

Addresses Indian gaming following the Supreme Court case, *State of California v Cabazon Band of Mission Indians,* which barred states from regulating Indian gaming. The analysis also examines the Indian Gaming Regulatory Act that established a three-tiered regulatory system. This article focuses on sovereignty, state interests, federal interests, and states that have regulated, non-tribal gaming industries.

245.   Thompson, William Norman. *A Suggested State Response to the Onslaught of Indian Reservation Casinos: Chill-out and Savor.* University of Nevada, Las Vegas, Special Collections. 1991. 36 pp.

Argues that since trying to stop Indian gaming is futile, states should start exploiting the opportunities Indian gaming provides. These benefits include the opportunity to develop a sound regulatory system that could be used for non-Indian gaming, the chance to study the feasibility of developing non-Indian gaming, the development of tourism, increased employment, and a reduction of government aid to certain Indian populations. This paper was presented at the Western Regional Conference, American Society of Public Administration, the Golden Nugget Resort, September 10, 1991.

246.   Thompson, William Norman. *Custer's Next Stand: The Indian Gaming Regulatory Act of 1988 and the Constitution.* University of Nevada, Las Vegas, Special Collections. 1989. 27 pp.

Discusses the Indian Gaming Regulatory Act (IGRA) and the constitutional issues the Act raises, including Indian sovereignty, judicial power, and licensing. Harshly critical of IGRA, Thompson suggests that the state-tribe compact method of regulating class II and class III gaming operations should be replaced by federal oversight by the National Commission on Indian Gaming, and he offers numerous ways to "clean up the Act."

247.   Thompson, William Norman, and Diana R. Dever. "A Sovereignty Check on Indian Gaming." *Indian Gaming* 4 (April 1994): 5-7, and 4 (May 1994): 8-9.

Examines how Indian gaming has affected tribal sovereignty and self-determination. The authors show how gaming has generated money and economic opportunities that have significantly enhanced tribes' abilities to provide housing, social services, and employment for their members. It has also resulted in educational opportunities, the return of homelands and culture, and greater political autonomy. They warn, however, of a potential downside due to exploitation by casino management firms; increases in crime; conflict among tribal members over the gaming issue; and culture stripping caused by hordes of visitors to reservations.

248.   Topa, John A. *Indian Gaming in Florida and Other States*. Tallahassee, Fla.: Florida House of Representatives, Committee on Regulated Industries, October 1992. 73 pp.
        Reviews recent proliferation of Indian casinos and provides an overview of the Indian Gaming Regulatory Act. Topa reports that when the Seminoles began negotiations for a gaming compact, the Governor assumed responsibility for representing the state, a role not designated in statute. The Legislature is urged to formally correct this ambiguity. Following provisions on such negotiations found in other states' statutes, Topa argues where this statutory authority should appear in three chapters of Florida state law.

249.   Turner, W. Bruce, and Scott M. Renner. *Native American Casino Gaming: A National Perspective*. St. Petersburg, Fla: Raymond James & Associates, 1992. 74 pp.
        Discusses the legal evolution and economic benefits of Indian gaming on tribal lands. The Indian Gaming Regulatory Act is explained, and a state-by-state summary of Indian gaming activities is provided.

250.   Turner, W. Bruce, and Scott M. Renner. *Native American Casino Gaming Update*. St. Petersburg, Fla.: Raymond James & Associates, 1993. 57 pp.
        Provides an overview of Indian gaming from August 1992 through August 1993, including the "land in trust" issue, Indian gaming at the national level, competitors in the Indian gaming market, a market forecast, and a state-by-state summary of Indian gaming activities. This work updates an earlier report, *Native American Casino Gaming: A National*

Perspective (see entry 249). Combined, they offer an excellent overall view of Indian gaming.

251.   U.S. Congress. *Indian Gaming Regulatory Act, Annotated.* Washington, D.C.: Hobbs, Straus, Dean & Wilder, 1989. 236 pp.
      Provides the full text of the Indian Gaming Regulatory Act, related Senate and House proceedings, a Federal Communications Commission rule implementing a portion of the Act [FCC NO. 89-124, 47 CFR Parts 73 and 76], Revenue Rule 85-194, and Secretary of Indian Affairs guidelines which cover tribal bingo management contracts.

252.   U.S. Congress. House. Committee on Natural Resources, Subcommittee on Native American Affairs. *Oversight Hearing Before the Subcommittee on Native American Affairs on Implementation of Public Law 100-97, the Indian Gaming Regulatory Act of 1988.* 103rd Cong., 1st session, 2 April 1993-22 April 1994. 7 pts., various pagings.
      Provides testimony on the Indian Gaming Regulatory Act and concerns about its implementation. This is a very controversial issue for tribes, state governments, and gaming industry officials.

253.   U.S. Congress. Senate. Committee on Indian Affairs. *Hearing Before the Committee on Indian Affairs on Amendments to the Indian Gaming Regulatory Act,* 103rd Cong., 2nd sess., 19 July 1994. 649 pp.
      Contains testimony on one day of hearings on proposed amendments to the Indian Gaming Regulatory Act, a controversial and disputed issued for tribes, state governments, and gaming officials.

254.   U.S. Congress. Senate. Committee on Indian Affairs. *Hearing Before the Senate Committee on Indian Affairs on the Need for Amendments to the Indian Gaming Regulatory Act,* 103rd Cong., 2nd sess., 20 April , 26 April , and 17 May 1994. 3 pts., various pagings.

Includes three days of testimony on the need for amendments to the Indian Gaming Regulatory Act. This legislation and any proposed changes especially interest Indian tribes, state governments, and gaming industry officials.

255.   Vizenor, Gerald. "Gambling With Sovereignty." *American Indian Quarterly* 16 (Summer 1992): 411-413.
Argues that Indian gaming could ruin tribal sovereignty. Vizenor describes how lethal violence erupted over gambling at one Mohawk reservation. Even as "tribal leaders maintain that casinos are located on sovereign tribal land," in 1992 for example, "federal agents raided casinos and seized machines to enforce the gaming laws on five reservations in Arizona." He concludes that the "tension between the idea of limited sovereignty and assimilation could be resolved by congressional resolutions in favor of state governments. Casinos could be the last representation of tribal sovereignty; the winners could become the losers."

256.   Ward-Smith and Company, Ken Adams, and the Gilmore Research Group. *The Feasibility of Starting and Operating a Profitable Gaming Casino on the Tulalip Reservation.* Seattle, Wash.: Ward-Smith and Company, 1990. 62 pp.
Explores the feasibility of a casino gambling facility in the Seattle-Everett, Washington metropolitan area. This study assesses market demand and income and profit potential. It also recommends how a casino should be developed. The authors emphasize the importance of slot machines, now illegal in Washington, and the need to provide amenities to attract and retain customers, including restaurant and cocktail facilities, hotel rooms, and entertainment. Risk factors such as competition and managerial competence are also discussed.

257.   Wilkins, Beth M., and Beth R. Ritter. "Will the House Win: Does Sovereignty Rule in Indian Casinos?" *Great Plains Research* 4 (August 1994): 305-324.

Identifies current debate surrounding Indian gaming as the most recent manifestation of long-term conflict between states, the federal government, and tribal sovereignty. The authors review the complex concept of sovereignty, the variances of federal Indian policy, the difficulties of tribal-state relationships, the recent emphasis on tribal self-determination, and the impact of the Indian Gaming Regulatory Act on tribal economies, all with a special focus on Midwestern Indian nations. They conclude that "carefully managed casinos and gaming revenues have the potential to empower the tribes to endure the pitfalls on the road to tribal sovereignty" by providing them with an economic base which can "free them from the purse strings of federal control." Bibliographical references.

258. Williams, John. *Questions and Answers on Indian Gaming*. House Research Information Brief. St. Paul, Minn.: Minnesota House of Representatives, House Research Department, November, 1992. 5 pp.

Briefly outlines Indian gaming's basic issues in question and answer format. Topics include the federal basis for Indian gambling, its locations, types of gambling allowed, states' rights, Minnesota's tribal-state compacts, and that state's Indian casinos.

259. Worsnop, Richard L. "Native Americans." *CQ Researcher* 2 (8 May 1992): 387-407.

Reviews major issues currently facing Native Americans. He discusses how the "Columbus quincentenary has spawned acrimony" in Indian communities and how Native American population, visibility, activism, and pride have increased. One section of this article briefly covers the proliferation of Indian reservation casinos, the gaming limitations imposed by the Indian Gaming Regulatory Act, resulting conflicts over tribal sovereignty and federal and state involvement, gaming's economic benefits, and the controversies it creates among the tribal members. Includes sidebars on Indian censuses, the ten largest American Indian tribes, and geographical breakdowns on where Native Americans reside. A concise and useful overview of

important Native American concerns.   Charts, maps,
bibliographical references.

SUPPLEMENTAL MATERIALS

260.   Aamot, Gregg. "Redwood Falls Hits the Jackpot:
Casino Spurs Development in Southwest Minnesota Cities."
Minnesota Cities 79 (March 1994): 8-12.

261.   Alley, Tom. *Report of the Special Ad Hoc
Committee to Study Legal Gambling on Indian Reservations
in Michigan.* Lansing, Mich.: Michigan State Legislature,
May 1986. 7 pp.

262.   Bolinski, Dorissa. "Mediation Brings Peace to
Community." *Dispute Resolution Journal* 49 (March 1994):
46, 78.

263.   California. Legislature. Senate. Committee on
Governmental Organization, and Assembly Committee on
Governmental Organization. *Informational Hearing on: Part
I. Indian Gaming in California. Part II. Review of the
Attorney General's Proposal to Create a State Gaming
Commission.*   Sacramento, Calif.: Senate Publications,
1993. Various pagings.

264.   "Charging in from the Outside: Sodak Gaming
Carves a Niche for Itself in Supplying the Indian Gaming
Industry." *Casino Journal* 7 (January 1994): 54.

265.   Christiansen, Eugene Martin, and North American
Conference on the Status of Indian Gaming, 1989. *The
Regulation of Reservation Gambling.* University of Nevada,
Las Vegas, Special Collections. 1989. 5 pp.

266.   Clines, Francis X. "The Pequots: It's One Thing for
Tribal Casinos to Strike it Rich, but When a Tiny Band of
Nearly Extinct Indians Beats the Industry at Its Own Game,

They Strike a Nerve." *New York Times Magazine* (27 February 1994): 49-52.

267.   Clines, Francis X. "Where Profit and Tradition Mingle: Oneida Nation's C.E.O. Runs New York's First Indian Casino." *New York Times* (2 August 1994): B1, B5 (L).

268.   Clines, Francis X. "With Casino Profits, Indian Tribes Thrive." *New York Times* (31 January 1993): 1, 42 (L).

269.   Clinton, Robert N., Nell Jessup Newton, and Monroe E. Price. *American Indian Law: Cases and Materials.* Charlottesville, Va.: Mitchie/Bobbs-Merrill, 1991. 1,378 pp.

270.   Connor, Matt. "State's Role, Politics, Sovereignty Are Hot Issues in the Regulation of Indian Gaming." *International Gaming and Wagering Business* 15 (5 June 1994): 50-51.

271.   "A Conversation With Timothy Wapato, Executive Director of NIGA: Tribes 'Will Not Stand' for Further Gaming Restrictions." *International Gaming and Wagering Business* 15 (5 January 1994): 17.

272.   Corl, Alex, and Norm Kur.   "Focus on Indian Gaming in Connecticut." *Casino Journal* 7 (June 1994): 22,70.

273.   "Court Backs States in Indian Gambling Dispute." *From the State Capitals: Federal Action Affecting the States* 48 (4 July 1994): 3.

274.   Doyle, Michael. "Bingo! Indian Tribes Strike It Rich." *California Journal* 20 (May 1989): 211-216.

275.   Eisler, Kim I. "Revenge of the Indians: Gambling Has Made the Once-Poor Pequots Rich, and Other Tribes

Are Getting in on the High-Stakes Casino Action."
Washingtonian 28 (August 1993): 65-67, 141-142.

276.   Enos, Gary. "Tribes Hit on Gaming: Congress' Help
Sought to Curb Proliferation of Indian Casinos." *City &
State* 10 (12 April-25 April 1993): 1, 22.

277.   Erickson, Connie F. *Gaming in Indian Country.*
Helena, Mont: Montana Legislative Council, December
1991. 7 pp.

278.   Fettig, David. "Gambling's Booty Extends Beyond
Reservation to Neighboring Community: Redwood Falls
Gains From Casino's Jackpot." *Fedgazette* 4 (July 1992): 8-
9.

279.   Forman, George. "Dispelling Myths About Indian
Gaming." *Indian Gaming* 3 (July 1993): 22-23.

280.   Gartner, Michael. "Viewpoint: Indian Tribes
Shouldn't Bet Their Future on Casinos." *Wall Street Journal*
(28 June 1990): A15.

281.   Hill, Rick. "Using Economic Studies to Dispel
Indian Gaming Myths." *Indian Gaming* 3 (January 1993):
3.

282.   Holstrom, David. "Native Americans Closely Watch
Moves to Regulate Casino Gambling." *Christian Science
Monitor* 86 (26 August 1994): 1, 4.

283.   Hornung, Rick. *One Nation Under the Gun.* New
York: Pantheon Books, 1991. 294 pp.

284.   "Indian Gaming." *From the State Capitals: Lottery,
Pari-Mutuel & Casino Regulation* 5 (11 July 1994): 2-3.

285.   Johnson, Kirk. "New Game for Pequots: Party
Politics." *New York Times* (30 August 1994): B1-B2 (L).

286.   Jones, Richard S. "Gambling on Indian Reservations." *Congressional Research Service Review* 7 (October 1986): 13-15.

287.   Kading, Linda King. "State Authority to Regulate Gaming Within Indian Lands: The Effect of the Indian Gaming Regulatory Act." *Drake Law Review* 41 (1992): 317-338.

288.   Kaufman, Michael T. "A James Bond With $100 Tries Out a Tribal Casino." *New York Times* (18 March 1994): C1, C16 (L).

289.   Keechi, Charles. "A Message from Charles Keechi, Chairman, National Indian Gaming Association." *Indian Gaming* 3 (April 1993): 3.

290.   Leonard, Saul. "Canadian Indians Play Fast Catch-up on Casinos." *International Gaming and Wagering Business* 14 (15 September 1993): 110.

291.   Leonard, Saul. "Comment: Let's Make Peace With the Indians Again." *Gaming and Wagering Business* 12 (15 December 1991-14 January 1992): 27, 36.

292.   Lorber, Leah L. "State Rights, Tribal Sovereignty, and the 'White Man's Firewater:' State Prohibition of Gambling on New Indian Lands." *Indian Law Journal* 69 (Winter 1993): 255-274.

293.   Maloney, Paul L. *Statement of Paul L. Maloney, Senior Counsel for Policy Criminal Division before the Select Committee on Indian Affairs, United States Senate, Concerning the Indian Gaming Regulatory Act.* University of Nevada, Las Vegas, Special Collections. 1992. 6 pp.

294.   Mashantucket Pequot Tribe. *Proposal of the State of Connecticut for a Tribal-State Compact Between the Mashantucket Pequot Tribe, Plaintiff, v State of Connecticut, et al., Defendants.* Hartford, Conn.: U.S.

District Court for the District of Connecticut, 1991. Various pagings.

295.   McCulloch, Anne Merline. "The Politics of Indian Gaming: Tribe/State Relations and American Federalism." *Publius: The Journal of Federalism* 24 (Summer 1994): 99-112.

296.   Murray, Marjorie. "California County Battles Indian Casino Plan." *City & State* 10 (13 September-26 September 1993): 4.

297.   North Dakota Legislative Council Staff for the Judiciary Committee. *Tribal-State Gaming Compacts.* Bismark, N.D.: North Dakota Legislative Council, September 1994. 7 pp.

298.   Oaks, Dan, and Eric Pollesche. "Coopers & Lybrand's U.S. Gaming Trends: Focus on Indian Gaming in Arizona." *Casino Journal* 7 (February 1994): 42-43.

299.   Oleck, Joan. "Tribal Warfare." *Restaurant Business* 92 (10 June 1993): 56, 58, 62, 66.

300.   O'Neil, Jack. "'Cashless' Casino, Thanks to Computers: Mashantucket Pequot Tribe's Casino Is Networked to the Hilt." *LAN Times* 9 (28 September 1992): 57-58, 63.

301.   Opel, Fritz. "Lighting the Fire: Why the Message of Economic Impacts Is Crucial to Protect Indian Gaming." *Indian Gaming* 3 (May 1993): 13-14.

302.   Pasquaretta, Paul. "On the 'Indianness' of Bingo: Gambling and the Native American Community." *Critical Inquiry* 20 (Summer 1994): 694-714.

303.   Passell, Peter. "Foxwoods a Casino Success Story: Indian Owners Clear $400 Million a Year." *New York Times* (8 August 1994): D1, D4 (L).

304.   Pico, Anthony R. "The New Indian Land Wars."
Indian Gaming 4 (December 1994): 3, 22.

305.   Popkin, James. "Gambling With the Mob? Wise
Guys Have Set Their Sights on the Booming Indian Casino
Business." *U.S. News & World Report* 115 (23 August
1993): 30-32.

306.   Prescott, Leonard. "Stop Picking on Indian
Gambling, Ignore Wild Claims Like Donald Trump's: Tribal
Operations Provide Benefits On and Off Reservations."
Indian Gaming 3 (January 1993): 8-9, 18.

307.   "Republican Seeks Inquiry on Donation by a
Casino." *New York Times* (18 August 1994): B7 (L).

308.   Rose, I. Nelson. "Gambling and the Law." *Indian
Gaming* 2 (January 1992): 12-14.

309.   Ross, Elizabeth. "Rhode Island Tribe Wants Casino
To Help Reduce High Jobless Rate." *Christian Science
Monitor* 85 (8 June 1993): 7.

310.   Sandler, Gregory. "Jackpot: The Pequot Indians
Plan To Open Their $50 Million Foxwoods Casino This
Month." *New England Business* 14 (February 1992): 20-23,
47.

311.   Schnaiberg, Lynn. "Indian Tribes Put Their Money
On Gaming to Boost Education." *Education Week* 14 (7
December 1994): 1, 10-11.

312.   Segal, David. "Dances With Sharks: Why the Indian
Gaming Experiment's Gone Bust." *Washington Monthly* 24
(March 1992): 26-30.

313.   Serwer, Andrew E. "American Indians Discover
Money is Power." *Fortune* 127 (19 April 1993): 136-140,
142.

314.   Strate, Larry D. *The Regulation of Gaming on Indian Land*. University of Nevada, Las Vegas, Special Collections. 1987. 21 pp.

315.   Swanson, Eric J. "The Reservation Gaming Craze: Casino Gambling Under the Indian Gaming Regulatory Act of 1988." *Hamline Law Review* 15 (Spring 1992): 471-496.

316.   "Sycuan Indian Leaders Create 'Loaned Executive Program' to Assist Morongo Tribe." *Indian Gaming* 2 (January 1992): 6-7.

317.   Thompson, Sherry M. "The Return of the Buffalo: An Historical Survey of Reservation Gaming in the United States and Canada." *Arizona Journal of International and Comparative Law* 11 (1994): 521-555.

318.   Torricelli, Robert G., and Daniel K. Inouye. "At Issue: Is the Indian Gaming Regulatory Act (IGRA) Unfair to the States?" *CQ Researcher* 4 (18 March 1994): 257.

319.   *Tribal Gaming*. Memphis, Tenn.: Promus Companies, Feburary 6, 1993. 9 pp.

320.   *Tribal Information for Those With Approved Tribal-State Compacts*. Washington, D.C.: Indian Gaming Management Staff, Office of the Commissioner, Bureau of Indian Affairs, Irregular. Request from the Indian Gaming Management Staff, Office of the Commissioner, Bureau of Indian Affairs, 1849 "C" Street NW, Mail Stop 2070 MIB, Washington, DC 20240. Phone: (202) 219-4068.

321.   "Tribes Can Sue States in Federal Court Over Gambling." *From the State Capitals: Federal Action Affecting the States* 48 (18 July 1994): 4.

322.   "Tribes 'Will Not Stand' for Further Gaming Restrictions: A Conversation with Timothy Wapato, Executive Director of NIGA." *International Gaming & Wagering Business* 15 (5 January 1994): 17.

323. U.S. Congress. House. Committee on Interior and Insular Affairs. *Implementation and Enforcement of the Indian Gaming Regulatory Act, Public Law 100-497: Oversight Hearings Before the Committee on Interior and Insular Affairs.* 102nd Cong., 2nd sess., 4 February 1992. 235 pp.

324. U.S. Congress. House. Committee on Interior and Insular Affairs. *Indian Gambling Control Act: Hearing Before the Committee on Interior and Insular Affairs.* 98th Cong., 2nd sess., 19 June 1984. 328 pp.

325. U.S. Congress. House. Committee on Interior and Insular Affairs. *Indian Gambling Control Act: Hearings Before the Committee on Interior and Insular Affairs.* 99th Cong., 1st sess., 25 June 1985. 151 pp.

326. U.S. Congress. House. Committee on Natural Resources. Subcommittee on Native American Affairs. *Implementation of Indian Gaming Regulatory Act: Oversight Hearing Before the Subcommittee on Native American Affairs.* 103rd Cong., 1st sess., 25 June 1993, 27 June, 1993. Various pagings.

327. U.S. Congress. Senate. Committee on Indian Affairs. *Indian Gaming Regulatory Act: Hearing Before the Committee on Indian Affairs.* 103rd Cong., 2nd sess., 20 April 1994. Various pagings.

328. U.S. Congress. Senate. Committee on Indian Affairs. *Indian Gaming Regulatory Act: Report Together With Additional Views (to Accompany S. 555).* 100th Cong., 2nd session, 3 August 1988. S. Rept. 100-446. 36pp.

329. U.S. Congress. Senate. Committee on Interior and Insular Affairs. *Indian Gaming Regulatory Act: Hearing Before the Committee on Interior and Insular Affairs, House of Representatives.* 100th Cong., 1st sess., 25 June 1987. 492 pp.

330.   U.S. Congress. Senate. Select Committee on Indian
Affairs. *Establish Federal Standards and Regulations for the
Conduct of Gaming Activities Within Indian Country:
Hearing Before the Select Committee on Indian Affairs.* 99th
Cong., 2nd sess., 17 June 1986. 673 pp.

331.   U.S. Congress. Senate. Select Committee on Indian
Affairs. *Gambling on Indian Reservations and Lands:
Hearing Before the Select Committee on Indian Affairs.* 99th
Cong., 1st sess., 26 June 1985. 708 pp.

332.   U.S. Congress. Senate. Select Committee on Indian
Affairs. *Gaming Activities on Indian Reservations and
Lands: Hearing Before the Select Committee on Indian
Affairs.* 100th Cong., 1st sess., 18 June 1987. 512 pp.

333.   U.S. Congress. Senate. Select Committee on Indian
Affairs. *Implementation of the Indian Gaming Regulatory
Act: Hearing Before the Select Committee on Indian Affairs :
Oversight Hearing on the Status of Activities Undertaken to
Implement the Gaming Regulatory Act.* 102nd Cong., 2nd
sess., 5 February 1992, 6 May 1992. Various pagings.

334.   U.S. Congress. Senate. Select Committee on Indian
Affairs. *To Establish Federal Standards and Regulations for
the Conduct of Gaming Activities on Indian Reservations
and Lands, and for Other Purposes: Report (to Accompany
H.R. 1920).* 99th Cong., 2nd sess., 1986. S. Rept. 99-493.
32 pp.

335.   Walke, Roger. *Gambling on Indian Reservations.*
Washington, D.C.: Congressional Research Service, Library
of Congress, 1989. 10 pp.

336.   Walker, Reid, and Allen Carrier. "NIGA Public
Relations Update." *Indian Gaming* 3 (April 1993): 9.
337.   Warrior, Robert Allen. "Indian Country Crap-
Shoot." *Christianity and Crisis* 52 (11 May 1992): 142-143.

338.   Wiegand, Steve. "The Canvas Casino: California, Indian Tribes Battle Over Gambling." *California Journal* 24 (August 1993): 25-27.

339.   Wilson, Jerome L. "Perspective: State Should Challenge Indian Casino Law." *New York Law Journal* 212 (15 July 1994): 2.

340.   Zelio, Judy. "The Fat New Buffalo." *State Legislatures* 20 (June 1994): 38-39, 41, 43.

SECTION C

Riverboat Gaming

Riverboat casinos now operate in six Midwestern and Southern states. Some thirty dockside casinos in Mississippi form the third largest casino market in the country, after Nevada and New Jersey. This section provides a variety of books, articles, and reports on many of the issues unique to the riverboat gaming industry. Social, economic, and regulatory aspects of riverboat gaming are also covered.

341. "1994 Riverboat Almanac." *International Gaming and Wagering Business* 15 (5 November 1994): 39-40, 42, 44, 46-48, 50, 52, 54, 58, 60, 62-64, 66-68.
    Provides an "annual state-by-state, boat-by-boat analysis of the floating casino industry." Includes "name, location, phone number, launch date, revenue, admission and other statistics of all riverboats in operation as of Sept. 1, 1994."

342. Better Government Association. *Statement on Riverboat Gambling to the Metro Ethics Coalition.* Chicago, Ill.: Better Government Association, 1994. 21 pp.
    Identifies economic development, promised by politicians and casino owners alike, as the driving force behind legislation to legalize riverboat gaming in Illinois. However, riverboat gaming in Illinois has proven to be nothing more than a taxation opportunity that generates revenue for the state. This survey suggests that it has done little to boost tourism or local businesses, and it has not brought new life to Illinois rivers or beautified their banks. Those expectations were unrealistic. The Association argues that any future expansion of gambling in Illinois should be based on solid economic evidence. Charts.

343.   Boothe, C.D.R. Chip. "Casino Riverboats Need More Than Dice and Dealers." *Proceedings of the Marine Safety Council* 49 (September-October 1992): 38-40.
    Summarizes the U.S. Coast Guard's concerns about passenger safety on riverboat casinos. The large vessels required for gaming raised significant concerns about inspection requirements, vessel weights, pilot licensing, crew sizes, maneuverability, and fire protection. The *Dubuque*, one of the largest riverboat casinos in operation, is as large as a medium-sized ocean liner.

344.   Buelt, Jamie Gottula.   "Roulette on the River." *Iowan* 40 (Spring 1992): 13-18.
    Looks at the success of Iowa's first five riverboat casinos where people bet almost $65 million in 1991, thirty percent more than projected. Economic advantages for local communities are briefly described. Iowa law put strict wager limits in place; the "maximum bet is $5 and the most anyone can lose on one excursion is $200." A one-page sidebar provides a short history of Mississippi River gambling.

345.   Cabot, Anthony. "Location, Location, Location." *Casino Journal* 7 (November 1994): 14.
    Explains why casino locations are regulated. Cabot looks at the following areas: Nevada, which restricts casinos from neighborhoods in order to suppress gambling by local residents; France, which places casinos in resort towns where it is assumed that mostly those with discretionary funds will gamble; and Mussolini's Italy, which placed casinos on the national borders to help stop the flight of *lire*. In the United States, Cabot argues, campaigns for riverboat casinos have been far more successful than land-based casino campaigns because of their politically advantageous locations.

346.   *Dockside Versus Excursion Riverboat Gaming.* Memphis, Tenn.: Promus Companies, 1 January 1993.   4 pp.

Compares excursion and dockside riverboat gaming from the industry's viewpoint. While both models are successful, the advantages of dockside riverboats are emphasized. They do not restrict customers to specific cruise schedules that limit attendance, and increased attendance means more revenues, jobs, and shore side business development. This paper also argues that moored boats are safer for passengers and cause less traffic congestion. Includes a brief history of the legalization of riverboat gaming.

347. Doocey, Paul. "Better Legislation Leads to Fewer Problems Down the River." *International Gaming and Wagering Business* 15 (5 December 1994): 46, 48.

Offers advice on how to avoid riverboat gaming problems caused by faulty legislation. Five pieces of advice are: give absolute control to a regulatory body; dictate capacity through the tax rate; keep burden of proof on the applicant; seek input from local government but give them no decision-making power; and keep the legislation simple.

348. Doocey, Paul. "Did Iowa Miss the Boat? Combination of Bad Laws, Low Population and Too Much Competition May Torpedo an Industry." *International Gaming and Wagering Business* 15 (5 April 1994): 1, 39, 40, 42, 44.

Relates the steep decline in revenues experienced by Iowa's riverboat gaming operations since their tremendous opening in 1991. Gaming supporters blame restrictive $5 bet/$200 maximum loss limits and competition from other jurisdictions for the migration of several Iowa riverboats to more lucrative venues in nearby states.

349. Eckert, Toby. "Riverboat Gambling: Panacean or Picayune?" *Illinois Issues* 17 (August/September 1991): 37-39.

Discusses projected outcomes of legalized riverboat gaming in Illinois from supporters' and opponents' viewpoints, shortly before the first boats "hit the water." Processing licenses delayed riverboat casino openings for

many months allowing neighboring states to start their own
operations. Competition for gambling dollars is already
heated, and the industry's future is difficult to predict. The
article includes information on Illinois's licensing and
regulatory problems.

350.   *Final Report: Riverboat Gambling Study Committee.*
Des Moines, Iowa: Iowa Legislative Council, Riverboat
Gambling Study Committee, January 1987. 19 pp.
      Covers the establishment and recommendations of
Iowa's legislative Riverboat Gambling Study Committee,
created to consider legalizing riverboat gaming. A brief
discussion of committee activities is followed by the text of a
bill draft, which committee members amended and supported, legalizing riverboat gaming.

351.   Fishkind & Associates, Inc. *Riverboat Gaming:
Economic Impacts in Florida.* Orlando, Fla.: Fishkind &
Associates, Inc., 1993. 12 pp.
      Provides an overview of the riverboat gaming
industry and concludes that Florida would benefit from
hosting similar operations. The state could support eighteen
riverboats with 28.5 million annual passenger admissions.
Total economic impact could be $3.0 billion, and approx-
imately 62,900 jobs could be created.

352.   Gaming Consultants Group. *Report to Urban
Redevelopment Authority of Pittsburgh (Pennsylvania)
Regarding Riverboat Gaming Zoning and Land Use Issues.*
Minneapolis, Minn.: Gaming Consultants Group, 1994. 12
pp.
      Surveys gaming operation zoning and land use
issues in several cities around the country as a guide for the
possible introduction of riverboat gaming in Pittsburgh. The
Group explored conditional use permits, protection of
riverfront assets, parking concerns, transportation concerns,
pedestrian movement, commercial impacts, and business
impacts. Gaming Consultants found that few cities have
introduced riverboat gaming with a comprehensive plan, and

thus these processes were largely reactive rather than proactive.

353. Grinols, Earl L. "Bluff or Winning Hand? Riverboat Gambling and Regional Employment and Unemployment." *Illinois Business Review* 51 (Spring 1994): 8-11.

Investigates the gaming industry premise that gambling creates significant numbers of new jobs. Early studies of a proposed riverboat-casino complex in Chicago, for example, stated there would be 12,400 new jobs in the area. The author compares employment and unemployment figures taken before and after eight midwest areas implemented riverboat gaming to determine if such claims are valid. Stating that job gains or losses depend on "whether gambling attracts more dollars to the region than it takes out," Grinols finds that gambling frequently moves jobs from one place to another within areas and takes jobs from other employers in the same region. He concludes that such economic benefits are unsubstantiated. Tables.

354. Guskind, Robert. "Casino Round the Bend." *National Journal* 23 (14 September 1991): 2205-2209.

Analyzes riverboat gaming in Davenport and Bettendorf, Iowa and nearby Moline and Rock Island, Illinois. Residents, while happy about sudden prosperity, are discovering the "perils of big-time development politics." Small communities that back these casinos with public funds may be left with severe economic problems because the industry's future is uncertain due to rapidly increasing competition and the possibility it is a short-lived fad. Many deals have already been broken, and unlike their land-based counterparts, these casinos can be easily moved to more profitable locations. A one-page sidebar discusses the rapid growth of state-sponsored gambling.

355. Harp, Lonnie. "States Bet on Riverboat Casinos for New Revenue." *Education Week* 13 (16 March 1994): 13, 16.

Looks at rapid and widespread growth of riverboat casinos on the Mississippi River and how some states are using incoming revenues to fund school improvements. Mississippi's education budget, for example, will increase almost $300 million due to legalized gaming. In Illinois, however, state educational funding has fallen while riverboat casinos have prospered; lawmakers are putting these funds elsewhere. When possible, educators rush to take advantage of whatever increases occur before these revenues "eventually flatten out."

356.   Hinds, Michael deCourcy. "Riverboat Casinos Seek a Home in Pennsylvania." *New York Times* (7 April 1994): A18 (L).
        Lists projected advantages and disadvantages of legalized gambling on Pennsylvania rivers and the intense political rivalry this issue caused. The benefits of increased revenue, employment, and waterfront development are weighed against the possibilities of more crime, compulsive gambling, traffic congestion, and local business failures, all of which Atlantic City has experienced. One often repeated argument is that states without legalized gambling lose revenues when their citizens go elsewhere to bet. New Jersey, for example, will go to great lengths to protect its casinos from competition in Pennsylvania.

357.   Johnson, Craig R. "Riverboat Gaming: The First 1,000 Days." *International Gaming and Wagering Business* 15 (5 October 1994): 1, 67-68, 70, 72.
        Evaluates the status of riverboat gaming since its inception in 1991. In 1994, riverboats enjoyed a 20 percent share of the $16.2 billion casino market. Johnson finds that the industry healthy, though ripe for "industry rationalization, including both horizontal consolidation and perhaps vertical restructuring." Despite the negative spin on riverboat gaming found in some academic research, the author believes that these boats are responsible for dramatically improving employment and local tax bases in several jurisdictions.

358.   Johnson, Craig R. "State Lotteries and Riverboat Gaming: Will the Boats Torpedo the Golden Goose?"

International Gaming and Wagering Business 15 (5 March 1994): 12-14, 42.

Analyzes how riverboat gaming may affect state lotteries. Though evidence is largely anecdotal, statistics from Illinois and other states suggest that riverboats have a negative impact on lottery revenues. However, states that offer both lotteries and riverboat gaming have realized a dramatic increase in overall gaming revenues.

359.   Labalme, Jenny. "The Great Riverboat Gamble." *Southern Exposure* 22 (Summer 1994): 10-14.

Evaluates riverboat gaming's adverse effects on Tunica, Mississippi, a largely black community ranked among America's poorest. Contrary to popular argument, the casinos have "done little to raise the local standard of living." While the usual wagering tax rate is twenty percent, this state offered a very low eight percent to attract casinos, and most profits go to the Nevada companies that own them. Tunica has spent much on road, water, and sewer improvements without assistance from the casinos which necessitated these changes. The town has also experienced rapid increases in living costs, property values, alcoholism, compulsive gambling, traffic congestion, and highway fatalities.

360.   Lee, Anita. "Mississippi Stakes All on Riverboat Gambling." *Planning* 59 (December 1993): 8-13.

Examines the history, growth, and regulation of Mississippi's riverboat casino industry. In order to benefit economically, local communities must immediately begin planning for such factors as rapid growth in population, construction, and traffic volume. While some cities locally regulate riverboats to their advantage and have wisely anticipated their effects, others have not, with serious consequences. Zoning laws, for example, help cities balance the needs of their residents with those of the gaming industry. Includes a sidebar titled "Rules for Cities to Follow When Dealing With the Gaming Industry" by Sylvia Lewis.

361.   Legato, Frank. "Interior Designers Define New Venues." *Casino Journal* 7 (May 1994): 44-45, 51.

Covers interior design on riverboats and the challenges presented by marine design. Several firms specializing in marine design, including Directions in Design and Interior Design International, are highlighted. This article continues Legato's "All That Glitters: Interior Designers Strut Their Stuff." *Casino Journal* 7 (April 1994): 62, 64-65. (See entry 51)

362.   Legato, Frank. "The Making of a Floating Casino: Building a Riverboat from Concept to Delivery." *Casino Journal* 6 (June 1993): 40-42.

Explains how casino operators do not have as much control over the design of floating casinos as they do with land-based properties. Design parameters are heavily influenced by the type of vessel chosen and by the requirements of city and state regulations, historic commissions, urban design boards, and the United States Coast Guard. This article highlights several ship building firms, including Trinity Marine Group and Bender Shipbuilding which provide turnkey construction capabilities.

363.   Long, Ray, and Peggy Boyer. "Gambling on Illinois Riverboats: Morally Wrong or Profitably Right?" *Illinois Issues* 15 (October 1989): 16-17, 20.

Looks at the intense debate on legalizing riverboat gambling in Illinois. Proponents in the legislature argue that gambling will provide added revenues and prevent potential losses of gamblers to nearby Iowa. Opponents stress "long term social costs are created" when governments support it; compulsive gambling, for example, is a serious problem. Local government officials, such as the mayors of Chicago, Peoria, and Beardstown, also disagree on the industry's merits.

364.   Louisiana. Riverboat Gaming Commission and Staff. *Compiled Materials of Louisiana Riverboat Gaming Commission: Emergency Rules for Factfinding Meeting.*

University of Nevada, Las Vegas, Special Collections. 1992. 47 pp.

Promulgates emergency rules for the immediate implementation of Louisiana's riverboat casinos because the state was losing millions of dollars due to the rapid proliferation of gaming elsewhere on the Mississippi Gulf Coast. It was thought that Mississippi was drawing tourists away from Louisiana and collecting gaming revenues and fees that should have stayed there. If the state did not soon implement a riverboat gaming plan, riverboat operators would choose locations in other states.

365.   McCormack, Patrick J. *Riverboat Gambling*. St. Paul, Minn.: Senate Counsel and Research, 11 September 1991. 6 pp.

Reviews Iowa's legislation on riverboat casinos as a possible model for legalization in Minnesota. The author first summarizes Iowa's restrictions on games, wagering limits, excursions and locations, and regulations concerning employment, salaries, county approval, and taxes. In Minnesota, development issues focus on potential profits, revenues, and employment and increasing competition from Indian casinos and gaming in nearby states. Opponents are concerned about potential increases in compulsive gambling. The author concludes that while riverboat casinos have so far been lucrative for Iowa, Minnesota must "make its own decisions about legalization." Existing legislation and related regulation from other states can be adapted for use there if riverboat gaming becomes legal.

366.   McLaughlin, John. "Placing Their Bets." *Restaurant Business* 92 (20 November 1993): 34, 36.

Describes anticipated revenues from riverboat gaming in Chicago and what the city's restaurant operators expect from their arrival. In other places, local restaurants have lost profits because casinos offer inexpensive meals. In Chicago, however, several important owners are already negotiating food service contracts with gaming companies, and even those not directly involved think business will improve.

367.   Michaelis, Laura. "Fighting for River Gold." *Governing* 7 (May 1994): 27-28.

Looks at bitter state rivalries over water boundaries due to the advent of riverboat casinos. In 1943, Nebraska and Iowa "finalized an agreement designating the center of the Missouri River channel as the boundary of the two states"; if an Iowa-based riverboat goes down the river's center, it is then operating illegally in Nebraska. Kentucky and Indiana are also involved in such conflicts. "Jurisdictional water fighting" worsens as riverboat profits increase and states compete for customers.

368.   Mississippi Institutions of Higher Learning, Center for Policy Research and Planning. *Economic Impacts of Mississippi Casino Gaming*. Jackson, Miss.: Mississippi Institutions of Higher Learning, March, 1994. 18 pp.

Analyzes the effects of Mississippi's riverboat gaming industry on the state's economy and tax revenues. For fiscal year 1994, industry income is estimated at $1 billion, and general fund revenues are estimated at $170 million. While the industry's future in Mississippi is hard to foresee due to increasing competition from nearby areas, the report predicts that the state's tax revenue may increase at a "moderate rate, reach a plateau and then level off in a few years." Also includes a listing of all riverboat casinos in Mississippi and their total square footage, gross revenue, employee counts, payroll expenditures, and operational costs. Tables, charts.

369.   Moreau, Dan. "Rollin' on the River." *Kiplinger's Personal Finance Magazine* 45 (August 1991): 69-71.

Explains how riverboat casinos attract tourists to Iowa. These boats offer low wagers, supervised children's activities, "Las Vegas-style shows," restaurants, and such games as slot machines, blackjack, craps, and roulette. Since skill often has little to do with a game's outcome, the author stresses that players need only know the rules and remember that the "odds favor the house." Also includes brief descriptions of various riverboats and telephone numbers for more information and reservations.

370.   Murren, James. "Mississippi: R.I.P.? Managing the Growth of Gaming in Mississippi." *International Gaming and Wagering Business* 15 (5 November 1994): 34-35, 37.
    Paints a much more positive picture of gaming in Mississippi than many other sources. Murren approves of the state's open licensing policy and open Nevada-style regulations. Though casinos will come and go, the industry itself is healthy and is likely to stay that way. The biggest problems facing these casinos are a lack of hotel rooms, parking, and entertainment.

371.   Murren, James. *The Rise of the Riverboat.* New York: C.J. Lawrence, 1992. 9 pp.
    Explains how riverboat casinos' advantages over land-based operations make them good investments. At a cost of $10-$30 million, riverboats are relatively inexpensive. They are also capable of moving to lucrative markets, and they attract customers with inexpensive scenery, not high-priced white tigers, erupting volcanos, and other forms of Vegas-style kitsch. With operating costs lower than most land-based casinos, riverboats bring more revenue to the bottom line.   Includes a state-by-state summary of riverboat operations.

372.   Nevada. Gaming Control Board. Gaming Research. *Legalized Gaming in the State of Illinois.* Carson City, Nev.: Gaming Control Board, Gaming Research, 1990. 12 pp.
    Provides a detailed overview of gaming in Illinois, including charitable gaming, parimutuel wagering, the state lottery, and riverboat gaming. Regulations and licensing requirements are discussed in enough detail to interest corporations considering operating in Illinois. An economic and demographic profile of the state is also provided, and Indian gaming activities are mentioned.

373.   Nevada. Gaming Control Board. Gaming Research. *Legalized Gaming in the State of Iowa.* Carson City, Nev.: Gaming Control Board, Gaming Research, 1990. 12 pp.
    Provides a detailed overview of gaming in Iowa, including charitable gaming, parimutuel wagering, the state

lottery, and riverboat gaming. Regulations and licensing requirements are discussed in enough detail to interest corporations considering operating there. An economic and demographic profile of the state is also provided, and Indian gaming activities are mentioned.

374.   Nevada. Gaming Control Board. Gaming Research. *Legalized Gaming in the State of Mississippi.* Carson City, Nev.: Gaming Control Board, Gaming Research, 1990. 14 pp.
        Provides a detailed overview of gaming in Mississippi, including charitable gaming and casino gaming on cruise ships. Regulations and licensing requirements are discussed in enough detail to interest corporations considering operating there. An economic and demographic profile of the state is also provided, and Indian gaming activities are mentioned.

375.   Norris, Floyd. "In Mississippi, Bondholders Cry Fraud." *New York Times* (20 November 1994): 3p, 1 (L).
        Reports on the first riverboat casino bankruptcy in Mississippi. Thirteen months earlier, Belle Casinos borrowed $75 million by issuing bonds through Bear, Stearns & Company. Initially called mortgage bonds, Belle Casinos "now says there was no mortgage," since their casinos' barges were not ships, making ship mortgages invalid. Bondholders, thus, "have no claim to the casino built with their money." Norris argues this is not the last such bankruptcy, and the situation resulted from "Wall Street faddishness and foolishness, inept marketing and ruinous competition."

376.   *An Overview of Riverboat Gaming in the United States.* Memphis, Tenn.: Promus Companies, 15 February 1994. 6 pp.
        Describes the gaming industry's view on the development, structure, and success of riverboat casinos. Several states have legalized gambling to boost revenues, and surveys show that the public increasingly thinks gambling is a "legitimate form of social recreation." After

citing other reasons supporting riverboat gaming, the report
notes that Iowa's riverboat casinos decreased in number
because the state's regulations made these operations less
competitive than ones in nearby locations. Includes a brief
list of regulations and riverboat operations in Iowa, Illinois,
Mississippi, Louisiana, Missouri, and Indiana.

377.   Pillsbury, Dennis H. "Insuring Gambling Boats: A
Growing Market That Needs to Be Approached With Care."
Rough Notes 137 (October 1994): 26, 28.
       Looks at difficulties surrounding the insurance needs
of riverboat casinos. A single boat and its contents can be
worth up to $15 million or more, resulting in substantial
property coverage costs; underwriters are also anxious about
catastrophes, such as severe hurricane potential in southern
states, which could cause major property damage and
personal injuries. Other issues include insurance to "cover
the cost of an interruption in business"; market saturation,
suggesting that some enterprises are risky because they
could go out of business; the boats' very high passenger
capacities; and limited "facilities for ship repairs" if major
damages occur.

378.   Plume, Janet.   "Little Las Vegas Sprouting in
Tunica." *Casino Journal* 7 (September 1994): 79-81.
       Describes the "frenzied pitch" of casino competition
in Tunica, Mississippi, where casino operators are either
coming and going or expanding and downsizing. Once
called "America's Ethiopia" by Jesse Jackson, Tunica now
hosts ten casinos which attract thousands of players and
bring millions of dollars into the local economy.

379.   Popkin, James. "A Mixed Blessing for 'America's
Ethiopia.'" *U.S. News & World Report* 116 (14 March
1994): 52, 56.
       Describes how Tunica, Mississippi, one of the
country's poorest areas, has changed since riverboat casinos
arrived. "Ninety-five percent of all adults now work, and
the median family income has nearly tripled." While most
residents earn minimum wage, they are at least employed.

Conversely, however, housing costs have soared, more people are unable to pay their bills, drunk driving arrests have increased 500 percent, and problems with compulsive gambling are beginning to surface. Some economists fear that money is moving from the area to "faraway bank accounts." Others disagree, however, and more casinos are being planned.

380.   "Rolling the Dice on the Delta: Mississippi Betting on Gambling as its Economic Saviour." *From the State Capitals: The Outlook* 48 (17 January 1994): 1-4.
    Reviews the debate on legalizing riverboat casinos in Mississippi. Proponents argue that the economic benefits gambling brings can be used to improve public services. Riverboat casinos created almost 8,000 jobs in Natchez, Vicksburg, Tunica, and Greenville, for example, and in the last six months of 1993, the state received $24.4 million in gaming taxes. City officials believe that they make areas more competitive for "tourism and convention dollars." Others disagree, arguing that the social costs are too high. This article also looks at Mississippi legislative activity, Mississippi Gaming Commission actions, and a Louisiana regulation that forces customers to wait forty-five minutes before boarding, an irritating delay which sends them to nearby Mississippi sites.

381.   Romano, Carmine P. "Riverboats' Big Wheels Keep on Turning." *National Underwriter* 98 (17 January 1994): 11-12.
    Argues that insuring the rapidly growing riverboat gaming industry is "an underwriter's dream come true." According to the author, innovative and experienced inland marine underwriters deal best with a "property-type cover on an inland waterway," bringing together elements from both marine and inland/property underwriting. The unique insurance concerns of riverboat casinos are briefly outlined.

382.   Rose, I. Nelson. "Sinking Riverboats." *New Jersey Casino Journal* 7 (August 1991): 44.

Argues that Iowa's riverboat casino industry is an example of "what happens when a state legislature" operates "without having the slightest idea what it is doing." Rose states that Iowa's extreme regulatory restrictions on riverboat gambling ruin prospects for success. Low wagering limits, for example, take "the casino's mathematical edge and turns it into a massacre," putting players at extreme disadvantage. He looks at the odds of winning casino games with repeatedly low wagers to illustrate this point. While these limits were created to protect the players, the "reality is that virtually every player will lose his entire stake," and steady losers are not steady customers. Many people have already complained because they think the games are rigged.

383. Smolowe, Jill. "River Towns Take a Risky Gamble." *Time* 137 (10 June 1991): 76-77.
    Tracks the legalization of riverboat gaming and discusses the economic appeal of floating casinos to Midwestern jurisdictions experiencing revenue shortages. The romantic, historic allure of riverboats also makes them attractive, and they are much less threatening to communities than land-based Las Vegas-style casinos. Large profits, however, may be offset by the negative impacts of increasingly fierce competition among states and such social problems as crime, prostitution, and compulsive gambling.

384. Souter, Gavin. "Few Insurers Gambling on Riverboat Casinos." *Business Insurance* 28 (17 January 1994): 3, 27.
    Lists major reasons insurance risk managers and underwriters are cautious about riverboat casinos. While this industry is expected to grow a great deal, there are major concerns about deductible levels, premium costs, and "the lack of established loss figures." After a brief comparison of water-based and land-based casino rates, some insurance company executives identify the unique difficulties riverboats pose.

385.   Taylor, Gary F. "Murky Liability Status Sets Waterfront Gambling Adrift." *National Law Journal* 17 (21 November 1994): B1-B2.

Reports on the confusion surrounding dockside riverboat casinos and legal efforts to determine if they are boats or buildings. If they are vessels, the federal Jones Act that governs maritime law applies; their employees are then crew members and have the right to file negligence suits. If buildings, state workers' compensation laws apply with much different results. Attorneys are finding that state gaming legislation did not cover maritime law application to riverboat operations, raising serious questions about the status of casino employees and operator liability. While waiting for this issue to be resolved in the courts, many riverboat operators are purchasing "the more expensive Jones Act" insurance coverage.

386.   Thalden, Barry. "Design Issues for Riverboat Gaming." *International Gaming and Wagering Business* 14 (15 September 1993): 68, 70.

Examines the unique problems of riverboat casino design. Floors, for example, are not flat, which makes slot machine mounting difficult. Other factors include the importance of weight and stability; bulkheads, which cannot be moved as easily as ordinary walls; electrical equipment which is difficult to ground; lower ceilings which require more surveillance cameras; and fire safety codes which are very strict. Design parameters are often dictated by a host of state and municipal requirements.

387.   Thalden, Barry. "Successfully Competing for Riverboat Gaming Sites." *International Gaming and Wagering Business* 15 (5 January 1994): 35-39.

Provides advice to companies submitting "Requests for Proposals" (RFPs) for riverboat gaming sites. Cities and states are becoming increasingly restrictive because officials are very concerned about over expansion and market saturation. A quality RFP is critical to securing a gaming license.

388. "A Threat to Nevada? America's Heartland Sets Sail for Gaming." *Casino Journal* 6 (March 1993): 14-17.

Looks at riverboat gaming, its recent history, and its economic and political environment. This discussion covers regulations, winnings, and taxation in various jurisdictions along the Mississippi and its tributaries.

389. Turner, W. Bruce. "Gaming Industry: New Life on the Mississippi: Sponsored Section." *Institutional Investor* 28 (February 1994): 29-32.

Tracks the growth of legalized riverboat gaming from the investor's viewpoint in this "Sponsored Section." These casinos have achieved wide acceptance because people think they are easier to manage and control than land-based casinos, and riverboats, which once played important roles historically, are now increasing the revenues of state and local governments. While the success of this gaming industry is expected to continue, investors are cautioned that "public policy issues relating to gambling . . . can be highly emotional," and it will never be legal in many locations.

390. Turner, W. Bruce. "Mississippi at the Breaking Point: Is Mississippi the Correct Model for the Gaming Industry in the 1990s?" *International Gaming and Wagering Business* 15 (5 November 1994): 32-33.

Questions whether Mississippi's free market approach to gaming is an appropriate model for the industry's future. Market saturation and over development there have created considerable instability for both investors and operators. The author discusses whether tighter licensing control or a "pure monopoly structure" would be better alternatives.

391. Turner, W. Bruce, and Scott M. Renner. *New Life on the Mississippi—and Elsewhere: The Promising Potential of Modern Riverboat Gaming.* St. Petersburg, Fla.: Raymond James & Associates, 1993. 40 pp.

Discusses the appeal and economic effects of riverboat gaming, and provides a state-by-state overview of the industry. Turner and Renner view riverboats as a source of needed state and local tax revenues that also generate employment and ancillary services. Regulation and control play an important role in the success of operations; the authors state, for example, that Iowa's strict limits on betting have forced riverboat operators to relocate to Illinois to improve profits. Key players in riverboat gaming are: Mirage Resorts; Hilton Hotels; The President Riverboat Casinos, Inc.; Grand Casinos; Showboat; Players International; Casino Magic, Inc.; Casino America, Inc.; Sands Regent; and Argosy Gaming, Inc.

392.   Walters, Laurel Shaper. "A Mississippi County Grows Casinos Instead of Cotton." *Christian Science Monitor* 86 (13 September 1994): 10.

Reports how installing riverboat casinos altered Mississippi's wetlands. In 1990, the Legislature passed a law restricting casinos to riverboats floating on the Mississippi River in order to control waterfront development. Environmentalists argue that it would "have been better to have them anywhere other than in the state's sensitive wetlands." Operators dig ditches for increased riverboat stability, and "casinos often end up far from the river sitting on barges barely floating in several feet of water." Conservation groups and federal agencies involved in environmental issues are trying to compromise on how to balance industry and environmental needs to counteract the industry's negative impact.

393.   Williamson, Lonnie. "A Dicey Development." *Outdoor Life* 193 (April 1994): 44, 46.

Examines how riverboat casinos adversely affect Mississippi's dwindling wetlands. The Army Corps of Engineers announced that the Sheraton Tunica Corporation "would destroy only 2.5 acres of wetlands"; in fact, the corresponding development of hotels, highways, and parking lots will impact much more. The accumulative effects on wildlife, plant life, and water resources are not being considered in the rush to legalize such casinos, and undoing the ecological damage will be difficult, if not impossible.

SUPPLEMENTAL MATERIALS

394.   Collis, Cheri. "Casinos Roll the River." *State Government News* 34 (March 1991): 8-11.

395.   Coughlin, Kenneth M. "Riverboat Gambling on the Hudson." *New York Times* (29 May 1994): CY13.

396.   "Crown Casino Corp.: Company Challenges Zoning Blocking Riverboat Casino." *Wall Street Journal* (19 September 1994): A9.

397.   Doocey, Paul. "Good Year for Riverboats in Illinois." *International Gaming and Wagering Business* 15 (5 October 1994): 74, 76.

398.   Doocey, Paul. "Is Vicksburg Destined to Become the Next Casino Hub in the State?" *International Gaming & Wagering Business* 14 (15 November-14 December 1993): 14-15, 62.

399.   Doocey, Paul. "An Overview of Riverboat Gaming: Full Steam Ahead." *International Gaming and Wagering Business* 14 (15 November-14 December 1993): 1, 38, 39.

400.   Eichenwald, Kurt. "In Mississippi, Riverboat Gambling Rides Rougher Waters." *New York Times* (15 July 1993): F9 (L).

401.   "Gambling as Salvation: Glad to Get It." *Economist* 329 (20 November 1993): 28.

402.   "Gambling: A Punt on the River." *Economist* 326 (13 March 1993): 37.

403.   Greenberg, Pam. "Midwest States Wager on Historic Riverboat Gambling." *State Legislatures* 17 (March 1991): 17.

404. Illinois. Gaming Board. *Adopted Rules.* Springfield, Ill.: Illinois Gaming Board, July 1993. Unpaged.

405. Jacobs, Charles. "Gambling Boats: A Proposal That Is Clinging to Life." *New York Times* (8 May 1994): NJ1, NJ13 (L).

406. Jereski, Laura. "Problems With Tiny Belle Casinos Illustrate How Junk-Bond Funds' Tactics Could Backfire." *Wall Street Journal* (2 August 1994): C2.

407. "Louisiana: Will the Good Times Go on Rolling?" *Economist* 331 (18 June 1994): 30-31.

408. Peat Marwick Main & Co. *Economic Impact Analysis of Riverboat Gambling to the Quad City Area.* Prepared for the Quad Cities Riverboat Gambling Task Force. Minneapolis, Minn.: Peat Marwick Main & Co., 1990. Various pagings.

409. Plume, Janet. "What's Coming Down the River?" *New Orleans Magazine* 28 (June 1994): 62-63, 105, 107-108.

410. "St. Louis to Host the First Riverboat Gaming Congress." *International Gaming and Wagering Business* 12 (15 July-14 August 1991): 1, 7.

411. Swanson, Leslie Charles. *Riverboat Gamblers of History.* Moline, Ill.: L.C. Swanson, 1989. 60 pp.

412. Thalden, Barry. "Successfully Competing for Riverboat Gaming Sites." *International Gaming and Wagering Business* 15 (5 January 1994): 38-39.

413. Walters, Laurel Shaper. "Dicey Days for River Gambling." *Christian Science Monitor* 86 (31 March 1994): 20.

414.   Wilhite, Ed. *The Winner's Guide to Riverboat Gambling: Travel and Gambling Guide.* 1st ed. New York: Cardozo, 1992.   128 pp.

SECTION D

Casino Law and Regulation

Few industries are as heavily regulated, restricted, and taxed as the casino industry. With few exceptions, casinos are welcome only with the most stringent safeguards and the promise of substantial reward for the host. The conditions, or regulatory environment under which casinos operate, are critical to both the industry and society. This section includes materials on law, regulation, and public policy that are of particular interest to government officials, casino executives, attorneys, planners, and regulators.

415.   Abrams, Robert. *Report of Attorney General Robert Abrams in Opposition to Legalized Casino Gambling in New York State*. Albany, N.Y.: N.p., 1981. 24 pp.
    Analyzes the suitability of casino gaming in New York state. Proponent Abrams was forced to change his mind following intense debate on the issue. After studying Nevada and New Jersey, he concluded that the crime and social degeneration associated with casino-based economic enterprises outweigh the economic benefits.

416.   Aronovitz, Cory. "Comments—To Start, Press the Flashing Button: The Legalization of Video Gaming Devices." *Software Law Journal* 5 (December 1992): 771-796.
    Addresses legal concerns raised by the recent proliferation of video gambling devices. Aronovitz discusses the "origins of computerized gambling" and notes that states "want to be sure that video gambling devices play fairly, account accurately, and that the software operating the devices is secure from alteration." Ensuring fair play is particularly difficult when computerized machines determine

outcomes. State law must address such complex issues as fair, defect-free machines, restricted access to machines and servicing, and accurate "accounting mechanisms and collection" systems. Especially useful for public officials drafting legislation legalizing video gambling. Bibliographical references.

417. Baltzer, Harry W., Thomas G. Brownell, and Mary B. Magnuson. *A Report to the Legislature on Whether the State Should Implement a Sole Source System for the Distribution of Gambling Equipment.* St. Paul, Minn.: Minnesota Gambling Control Board, 31 January 1992. Various pagings.

Questions if all gambling equipment in Minnesota should be purchased from the state or from suppliers who contract with the state. The authors identify possible legal and fiscal outcomes from four options: sole distributor, sole supplier, contracts with distributors, and contracts with manufacturers. They conclude that these choices would all be implemented at considerable expense to the state and organizations currently conducting legalized gambling and recommend the continuation of their state-of-the-art system that thoroughly tracks equipment from the manufacturers to the organizations which use it. This report is a follow-up to, and includes, the KMPG Peat Marwick report, *Four Methods for the Distribution of Gambling Equipment in Minnesota: An Analysis* (see entry 442).Tables.

418. Barton, Babette B. "Legal and Tax Incidents of Compulsive Behavior: Lessons From Zarin." *Tax Lawyer* 45 (Spring 1992): 749-782.

Analyzes the legal ramifications of one person's extreme financial losses at an Atlantic City casino. *Zarin v Commissioner* involved an individual who lost $2.5 million of his own money and more than $3 million in casino credit over a two-year period due to his compulsive gambling problem. After Zarin settled the casino debt with $0.5 million, he faced "an income tax assessment of ten-fold that amount attributable to the canceled portion of the debt." This article will especially interest industry officials concerned with the effects of large losses by compulsive gamblers. Bibliographical references.

419.   Biscoe, Andre. *Legalized Poker Games.* LORL Inquiry No. 0711-90.   Harrisburg, Penn.: House of Representatives. Legislative Office for Research Liaison, 2 November 1990. Various pagings.
    Summarizes law and legislation permitting legalized poker games in California, Oregon, and South Dakota. This overview includes brief descriptions of legislative activity and includes pertinent state laws and texts of specific legislative bills.

420.   Bowers, Michael W., and A. Costandina Titus. "Nevada's Black Book: The Constitutionality of Exclusion Lists in Casino Gaming Regulation." *Whittier Law Review* 9 (Spring 1987): 313-330.
    Examines the constitutionality of Nevada's right to bar persons of "notorious or unsavory reputation" from the state's casinos.   The authors argue that individuals are unfairly assigned a "status" without proof that they have engaged in any misconduct.   They also explore the concept of freedom of association guaranteed in the First Amendment, overbreadth, and the due process and equal protection clauses of the Fourteenth Amendment.   Bowers and Titus conclude that Nevada's Black Book and a similar New Jersey list unfairly punish persons based on reputation, denying them equal protection under the law and the right to free association, speech, and movement.

421.   Brenner, Reuven, and Gabrielle A. Brenner. *Gambling and Speculation: A Theory, a History, and a Future of Some Human Decisions.* New York, N.Y.: Cambridge University Press, 1990.   286 pp.
    Advocates legalized gambling based on an historical analysis of the changing and frequently distorted perceptions of gambling, how those perceptions affected its regulation, and how gambling reflects human nature and society.   The authors cover such topics as why people gamble, how confusion about gambling resulted in its prohibition, how

crime and gambling are related, and how gambling differs from other forms of speculation. Also included are their recommendations for public policy, lotteries and states, and problem gambling. Bibliographical references, tables, index.

422.   Cabot, Anthony. "Avoiding the Impact of Scandal." *Casino Journal* 7 (May 1994): 12.
Predicts how a giant scandal will occur in a state that has recently legalized gaming, how it will involve corrupt government officials, and how it will put the future of gaming in that state and elsewhere at risk. Cabot explains that such a scenario is highly unlikely in Nevada because the design of Nevada's regulatory system separates regulators from the political process. States that fail to adopt a similar model are at risk.

423.   Cabot, Anthony N. *Federal Trial and Appellate Court Cases on Gambling.* Las Vegas, Nev.: Lionel, Sawyer & Collins, 1990. Various pagings.
Presents a collection of twenty-eight court cases pertaining to gambling culled from the pages of the *Federal Supplement* and the *Federal Reporter, 2nd Series.* These cases involve a wide variety of issues, including Nevada's Black Book, breach of contract, and Indian sovereignty.

424.   Cabot, Anthony N. *Gaming Contracts: Customer Disputes and Gaming Debt Collection in Nevada.* Las Vegas, Nev.: Lionel, Sawyer & Collins, 1986. 13 pp.
Discusses gambling debts and how they are administered in Nevada. Cabot's clearly presented historical approach helps readers understand these complex issues. Until 1983, gambling debts were considered legally uncollectible. After 1983 legislation, casinos were granted essentially the same rights awarded to any company seeking just recompense. For patron complaints against casinos, such as failure to pay jackpots, this 1983 statute allows limited judicial review in addition to the traditional Gaming Control Board review.

425.   Cabot, Anthony N. *The Law of Casino Gaming: A Selective Bibliography From 1970-1989.* Las Vegas, Nev.: Lionel, Sawyer & Collins, n.d. 16 pp.

Contains over 175 bibliographic citations for materials on casino gaming law. While Cabot does not include summaries, he groups this information under such headings as advertising, communications, and commercial speech; bankruptcy and federal law; marketing, junkets, and complimentary services; crime; economics; gambling debt enforcement; federal tax; service industries; social policy; and U.S. gaming laws.

426.   Cabot, Anthony N., ed.   *Casino Credit and Collection Law.* Las Vegas, Nev.: International Association of Gaming Attorneys, 1989. 170 pp.

Explores the role of casinos as credit agencies and the unique nature of casino credit. Information covers gambling debt collection in Nevada, New Jersey, and Great Britain. Chapter titles include Defense to the Enforcement of Gaming Debts; Special Defense—Compulsive Gambling; Interstate Collection; and Transnational Enforcement of Gaming Debts. Bibliographical references, index.

427.   Cabot, Anthony N., William N. Thompson, and Andrew Tottenham, eds. *International Casino Law.* 2nd ed. Reno, Nev.: Institute for the Study of Gambling and Commercial Gaming, College of Business Administration, University of Nevada, Reno, 1993. 565 pp.

Presents a monumental overview of gaming in the United States and around the world. Forty-two contributors provide information on authorized games, regulations, licensing, operational requirements, taxes and fees, economic conditions, history, and crime, for every country and jurisdiction with legal casino operations. Bibliographical references, index.

428.   Christiansen/Charterhouse. *Financial Stability: Contract #A-50289.* New York: Christiansen/Charterhouse, 1991. Various pagings.

Recommends a definition of "financial stability" for use in New Jersey's casino regulations. Four core tests of financial stability are identified: casino minimum bankroll, operating expenses, capital expenditures, and gaming privilege tax obligations. Applicants or licensees unable to satisfy these requirements should not hold casino licenses. Christiansen/Charterhouse's definition is derived from specific provisions of the Casino Control Act and the Casino Reinvestment Act; both laws are discussed in detail. This report was prepared for the New Jersey Casino Control Commission.

429.   Colorado. Division of Gaming. *What Are the Facts?: Limited Gaming Information Booklet.* Denver, Colo.: Colorado Division of Gaming, October 1991. 24 pp.

Provides basic information on the Colorado Division of Gaming. This overview includes information on Division staff, background investigations, applications, licenses, the limited gaming fund, and pertinent sections from Colorado's constitution. Tables.

430.   Continuing Legal Education in Colorado, Inc., and the Gaming, Entertainment and Sports Law Forum of the Colorado Bar Association. *Roll of the Dice: Past, Present and Future of Colorado Gaming.* Denver, Colo.: CLECI, 1993. Various pagings.

Acts as a manual for attorneys who want to keep abreast of Colorado's casino industry. High interest topics include shutdowns; foreclosures and bankruptcies; disclosure requirements; and disciplinary actions by the Division of Gaming.

431.   Cordtz, Dan. "High Noon for High Rollers." *Financial World* 163 (8 November 1994): 58, 60-61.

Describes the gaming industry's participation in legalization efforts in Florida. In a brief overview of recent gaming legislation nationwide, Cordtz notes that "not a single state's citizens have voted to pursue the riches—and notoriety—that big-time casinos brought to Las Vegas and Atlantic City." Industry officials think that legalization in

Florida will "provide that big breakthrough"; states like New York and Texas would soon follow. Although the industry spent $9 million to get this amendment on the ballot and millions more on intense advertising, it is not expected to pass due to opponents' efforts and gambling's unsavory reputation.

432.   *The Development of the Law of Gambling: 1776-1976.* Washington, D.C.: U.S. Department of Justice, Law ⚔ Enforcement Assistance Administration, National Institute of Law Enforcement and Criminal Justice, 1977. 934 pp.
     Examines gambling statutes and cases from 1776 to 1976 for all states and the federal government. It places these developments in economic, social, and political contexts to provide policy makers with the historical and legal frameworks necessary to evaluate proposals for suppressing or legalizing gambling. One major conclusion stresses the need to view different forms of gambling as separate activities and to understand that effective methods of control vary accordingly.

433.   Dombrink, John, and William N. Thompson. *The Last Resort: Success and Failure in Campaigns for Casinos.* Nevada Studies in History and Political Science No. 27. Reno, Nev.: University of Nevada Press, 1990. 220 pp.
     Examines casino gambling campaigns, both successful and unsuccessful, waged between 1976 and 1986. Despite opinion polls showing strong public support for casinos, the authors conclude that these movements fail when faced with strong opposition from attorneys general and other political leaders. Rival commercial interests, notably horse track betting, also contribute to the defeat of gaming measures, as do economic upswings which tend to deflate the demand for casinos as tools for economic revitalization. This work discusses campaigns in Florida, New York, New Jersey, New Hampshire, Connecticut, Illinois, Rhode Island, Arizona, Colorado, Washington, Hawaii, California, and Louisiana. Bibliographical references, index.

434.   *The Do's and Don'ts of Casino Legislation: Lessons From the Field.* Memphis, Tenn.: Promus Companies, January 1, 1993. 9 pp.

Lists industry guidelines on how states should enact legislation legalizing casinos. This report first explains how "economic development and public acceptance" are the "two most important drivers of casino legislation." The law must establish a strong regulatory framework and an environment conducive to commercial success. Suggestions include setting casino size requirements, identifying casino location restrictions, establishing strict application and licensing requirements, and instituting few restrictions on wagers or bets.

435.   Downey, William J. *Problems in Determining the Suitability of a Casino License Applicant: Legal and Ethical Issues.* Reno, Nev.: University of Nevada, Reno. Bureau of Business and Economic Research, 1981. 13 pp.

Discusses philosophical problems inherent in issuing gaming licenses under New Jersey's Casino Control Act. Debate centers on the clause that states an applicant must prove his or her "good character," and the complexities of deciding upon a workable definition of "good character."

436.   Eadington, William R. *Emerging Public Policy Challenges From the Proliferation of Gaming in America.* University of Nevada, Las Vegas, Special Collections. 1992. 11 pp.

Criticizes the lack of a rational approach to gambling legalization in the United States which, according to the author, allows its dangerous proliferation. Eadington argues that jurisdictions which do not have the ability to "hold a monopoly on gambling for some period of time" cannot sustain it for economic development. Uncontrolled competition for the gambler's dollar will ultimately lead to failures with severe long-term economic and social costs.

437.   Eadington, William R., and Judy A. Cornelius, comps. *Gambling and Public Policy: International Perspectives.* Reno, Nev.: Institute for the Study of

Gambling and Commercial Gaming, College of Business Administration, University of Nevada, Reno, 1991. 688 pp.

Examines various ways gambling is regulated and controlled worldwide. Trends in the legalization of commercial gaming, objectives and effects of regulation, historical and social perspectives on gaming, law enforcement issues, compulsive gambling and public policy, and risk taking are discussed in thirty-seven articles written by a variety of gambling scholars and experts. Bibliographical references, index.

438.   Fazzalaro, John J. *Traffic Improvements for Casinos.* Hartford, Conn.: Connecticut General Assembly, Office of Legislative Research, 6 January 1994. 9 pp.

Describes road improvements Connecticut made due to heavy traffic caused by the Mashantucket Pequot tribe's Foxwoods High Stakes Bingo and Casino. In this memorandum, Fazzalaro explains that state law requires developers of major traffic generators to obtain permits from the State Traffic Commission (STC) before opening their facilities. The tribe's sovereign nation status, however, makes it unclear whether these requirements are applicable. While the tribe has not contested the state's authority in this area, it has also not agreed to the state's jurisdiction. The existing relationship is a fairly cooperative one which has avoided legal confrontation over the state's authority. Includes a list of STC improvements, permits, and traffic count increases.

439.   Franckiewicz, Victor J. "The States Ante Up: An Analysis of Casino Gaming Statutes." *Loyola Law Review* 38 (1993): 1123-1157.

Reviews casino gaming law in ten states. The author first describes casino control mechanisms, state-by-state, for Colorado, Illinois, Iowa, Louisiana, Mississippi, Missouri, Montana, Nevada, New Jersey, and South Dakota. He then compares state policies on legalized gambling; licensing processes; location facility and operational requirements; and operation controls. Includes a brief discussion of the "multitiered, state/federal/tribal system" governing "reservation gaming under the Indian Gaming Regulatory Act" and constitutional issues raised by a select list of key court cases. An excellent overview of state law and regulation. Bibliographical references, tables.

440.   "Gambling and the State." *Economist* 323 (11 April 1992): 21-24.
Argues that state governments should not "run gambling" because "they make it a state monopoly." After reporting on how gambling has grown in this country, the article focuses on lotteries and notes states are now "America's biggest promoters of gambling" due to the revenue it generates. The author concludes if states exerted only regulatory control, gambling would "find its own level, without the distortions imposed by governments' confused intervention." The resulting competition and "efficiencies of the private sector" could even increase tax revenues.

441.   Goodwin, John R. *Gaming Control Law: The Nevada Model—Principles, Statutes and Cases.* Columbus, Ohio: Publishing Horizons, 1985. 198 pp.
Traces the history and evolution of gambling and gambling law in Nevada from territorial days through the modern era. By examining important court cases, statutes, and administrative codes, Goodwin provides a wealth of information on Nevada gaming regulatory agencies, law, licensing, taxation, judicial review, corporations and partnerships, and the state's infamous Black Book. Bibliographical references, index.

442.   KMPG Peat Marwick. *Four Methods for the Distribution of Gambling Equipment in Minnesota: An Analysis.* University of Nevada, Las Vegas, Special Collections. 1990. 35 pp.
Identifies four ways Minnesota can distribute pulltabs and other gaming devices. The principal concern is that pulltab machines will enter Minnesota's gaming market without proper registration, thereby evading taxation and regulation. The four alternatives discussed include the state

or private firm as the supplier to distributors; the state as the central purchasing agent; the state as sole distributor; or increased compliance and enforcement activities. This report is followed by *A Report to the Legislature on Whether the State Should Implement a Sole Source System for the Distribution of Gambling Equipment,* by Harry W. Baltzer, et al. (See entry 417).

443. "The Law of the Slot Machine." *Gaming Law* 1 (15 July 1992): 5-6.

Describes three actual gaming disputes in Nevada to illustrate how that state's law operates. The first two involve slot machine payoffs, and the third involves a blackjack dealer's error. Nevada's law and regulations which establish "procedures for deciding player disputes" resemble contract law. Casinos and customers "form a contract if one party makes an offer and the other party accepts the offer." The article succinctly explains how and why casinos won two of these three cases.

444. *Lawful Gambling.* St. Paul, Minn.: Minnesota Office of the Legislative Auditor, Program Evaluation Division, January 1990. 98 pp.

Notes that "charitable gambling" is the fastest growing gambling activity in Minnesota. The Legislative Audit Commission directed its Auditor to study how proceeds from lawful gambling are being used and determine if controls to prevent fraud and abuse are adequate. Although not directly concerned with casino gaming, the work's methodology, evaluation, and conclusions provide a framework useful to those studying and evaluating the control of legalized gambling.

445. Lee, Barbara A., and James Chelius. "Government Regulation of Labor-Management Corruption: The Casino Industry Experience in New Jersey." *Industrial and Labor Relations Review* 42 (July 1989): 536-548.

Analyzes how New Jersey's Casino Control Act of 1977 affected the casino industry and its unions. The authors interviewed "casino managers, union represen-

tatives, state regulatory agency officials, and attorneys."
They conclude that strict state regulation and the
"comparative simplicity of the industry's structure" (which
involves only a few key organizations) have kept casinos
"free of direct influence of organized crime." However,
efforts to keep unions free from organized crime are
hampered by "links between some unions and organized
crime that predate the casino industry, protection afforded
unions under federal law, the membership of non-casino
employees in locals representing casino employees, and the
continued activity in union business of ousted officials."
This mixed success does not "inspire emulation."
Bibliographical references.

446.   Lehne, Richard. *Casino Policy*. New Brunswick,
N.J.: Rutgers University Press, 1986. 268 pp.
       Examines New Jersey's experience regulating
Atlantic City casinos and provides a great deal of insight for
other jurisdictions. Lehne describes the state's Casino
Control Act and the two agencies charged with gaming
industry oversight. Licensing, casino operations, and
revenues are analyzed. The author concludes that licensing
has not been entirely effective in protecting the interests of
the public; casino operations oversight has been relaxed to
suit the industry; and little gaming revenue has gone into
redevelopment. Bibliographical references, index.

447.   Louisiana. House Legislative Services. *A Complete
Guide to Louisiana Gambling Law*. 2nd ed. Baton Rouge,
La.: Louisiana House of Representatives, House Legislative
Services, November 1994. Various pagings.
       Created to be a comprehensive gaming resource
guide for Louisiana state legislators. The work contains all
state statutory and constitutional provisions pertaining to
gaming. Also included are contact lists with addresses and
telephone numbers for each gaming regulatory board, the
Louisiana State Police, the Gaming Enforcement Division,
and the Attorney General's Gaming Division. Chapters
cover horse racing, riverboat gaming, land-based casinos,

charitable gaming, the lottery, video poker, and Indian gaming.

448.   Massachusetts. Senate Audit and Oversight Bureau. *Toward Gaming Regulation: Part II: Problem Gambling and Regulatory Matters.* Senate 1590. Boston, Mass.: Massachusetts Senate Audit and Oversight Bureau, March 1994. 47 pp.
　　　　Lists legislative recommendations on gambling regulation and problem gambling.   After noting that Massachusetts is an active participant in the gambling industry, the report states little has been done to address addictive behavior. A problem gambling prevalence survey has never been conducted, and no tax dollars are spent on teaching about or treating compulsive gambling. Recommendations include funding a comprehensive study to measure compulsive gambling; funding development of a statewide problem gambling education and treatment program out of five percent of the state lottery's advertising budget; and establishing a Massachusetts Gaming Policy Board and a State Gaming Commission.   Based on information and testimony from a 1993 public hearing series. Tables.

449.   Massachusetts. Senate Committee on Post Audit and Oversight. *Preliminary Report on Gaming in the Commonwealth.* Boston, Mass.: Massachusetts Senate Committee on Post Audit and Oversight, 6 July 1993. 23 pp.
　　　　Covers the legislative committee's public hearings on Massachusetts and the gaming industry. This group convened to analyze the state's role in the gaming industry; the role of gaming revenue in the state's revenue mix; the ramifications of expanding gaming; relevant security and regulatory issues; and the social costs of gaming. The first part of this report outlines regulatory issues, the second examines gaming in other states, and the third predicts four possible gaming scenarios that should be considered.

450.   McCabe, Michael H. *Gambling Fever: Odds Are, You've Got It*. Lombard, Ill.: Midwestern Legislative Conference of the Council of State Governments, April 1992. 25 pp.

Reviews legalization of gambling in twelve Midwestern states.   Sections on casinos focus on Deadwood, South Dakota, and the potential growth of riverboat gambling in Iowa, Missouri, and Illinois. While "state-sanctioned gambling has always been promoted as a potentially lucrative source of state revenues," state legislators and officials are warned to remain aware of its social consequences. Includes tables on gambling by state and type, and gambling and state revenues. Bibliographical references.

451.   McCarthy, John J. *Gambling Commissions*. LORL Inquiry No. 0284-91. Harrisburg, Penn.: Pennsylvania House of Representatives, Legislative Office for Research Liaison, 17 April 1991. Unpaged.

Contains sections on centralized gambling commissions from Nevada and New Jersey statutes. These excerpts cover gaming control board membership qualifications, appointments, terms, compensation, meetings and hearings, powers and duties, and regulations.

452.   Milan, Monica L. *Casino Gaming Legislation*. LORL Inquiry No. 0157-90. Harrisburg, Penn.: House of Representatives, Legislative Office for Research Liaison, 12 March 1990. Unpaged.

Summarizes casino gambling legislation in Iowa, Oregon, New York, Maryland, and Wisconsin.   This overview includes brief descriptions of legislative activity and includes pertinent excerpts from journal articles, agency regulations, legislative bills, and state laws.   Sections on Iowa and Illinois focus on riverboat casinos.

453.   Mills, John, and Thomas Doyle. "Money Laundering: New Challenges for Casino and Other Corporate Internal Auditors." *Management Accounting* 73 (January 1992): 31-33.

Describes how the Money Laundering Control Act of 1986 affects casino internal auditing practices. This law requires operators of businesses which deal with large amounts of cash to "establish internal controls designed to oversee, monitor, and review all money laundering type transactions." Currency Transaction Reports must be done for any cash transaction exceeding $10,000. The authors briefly cover how Nevada responded with regulations on reporting requirements for credit transactions and "players who cash out with gaming wins." They also explain how all casino departments must log by customer all transactions over $2,500 which happen within a twenty-four hour period. Includes discussion on how compliance requires employee training and how control testing is accomplished in casino cages and sports book areas. Bibliographical references.

454. Mills, John R. "Control Testing in the Gambling Industry." *CPA Journal* 61 (January 1991): 34-37.
Demonstrates why regulatory and auditing practices are critical in the gaming industry "where an infinite variety of fraud can be expected." Mills briefly covers the need for minimum levels of accounting and internal controls and then compares New Jersey and Nevada regulations. He concludes that states should emulate the way Nevada "standardized minimal internal and external control . . . with requirements for increased involvement of and reporting by external auditors" to minimize fraud and "major skimming."

455. Mitler, Ernest A. *Legal and Administrative Problems in the Control of Legalized Casino Gambling: A Comparative Study*. Ph.D. dissertation, Linacre College, Oxford University, 1986. University of Nevada, Las Vegas, Special Collections. 380 pp.
Argues the need for casino licensing reform, the need for the U.S. government to assume central responsibility for casino regulation nationwide, and the need for specialized governmental agencies to coordinate the interaction between large casino-resorts and the communities that surround them. The history of gaming in Nevada and Atlantic City, the limits

of gaming control, crime, and the use of casinos for redevelopment are discussed. Includes comparisons of gaming in the United States, Great Britain, and the rest of Europe. Bibliographical references.

456.   Montana.   Office   of   the   Legislative   Auditor. *Regulation and Monitoring of Video Gambling Machines.* Helena, Mont.: Montana Office of the Legislative Auditor, January 1994. 71 pp.

Contains recommendations on Montana's regulation and monitoring of video gambling machines. This lengthy report includes background information on the history of state gambling regulation, the use of video gambling machines, and the enforcement efforts of Montana's Gambling Control Division. Subsequent sections describe problems with taxation, reporting systems, compliance monitoring, and machine inspection. The conclusion states that the manual, labor-intensive system currently used is incapable of effectively and efficiently monitoring the 14,500 machines found in the state and urges implementation of an automated dial-up system. This would reduce staffing levels and improve industry integrity and accountability. Particularly useful for officials in other jurisdictions concerned with complex video gambling issues. Tables, charts.

457.   Moody, Eric N. "Nevada's Legalization of Casino Gambling in 1931: Purely a Business Proposition." *Nevada Historical Society Quarterly* 27 (Summer 1994): 79-100.

Explains why Nevada adopted its "nationally unique gambling law" in 1931. Support for this legislation came primarily from "gamblers and owners of gambling establishments who wished to expand their operations, and from business interests in the state who stood to benefit from the additional visitors and their spending." After providing background predating 1931, Moody describes in some detail the activities of that year's legislature and the efforts of individuals who either opposed or supported the enabling bill. He concludes that the law passed because "certain business interests in the state wanted it" and the "prevailing economic conditions" helped overcome opposition. Bibliographical references.

458.   Nevada. Gaming Control Board. Gaming Research. *Legalized Gambling in the State of Colorado.* Carson City, Nev.: Gaming Control Board, Gaming Research, 1991. 15 pp.
        Provides a detailed overview of gaming in Colorado, including charitable gaming, parimutuel wagering, the state lottery, and limited casino gaming. Regulations and licensing requirements will help business people interested in operating in Colorado. An economic and demographic profile of the state is also provided, and Indian gaming activities are mentioned.

459.   Nevada. Gaming Control Board. Gaming Research. *Legalized Gambling in the State of Montana.* Carson City, Nev.: Gaming Control Board, Gaming Research, 1990. 17 pp.
        Reviews gaming in Montana, including charitable gaming, bingo, keno and raffles, sports pools, card games, video gaming machines, parimutuel wagering, and the state lottery. Regulations and licensing requirements will help businesses considering operating in Montana. An economic and demographic profile of the state is provided, and Indian gaming activities are mentioned.

460.   Nevada. Gaming Control Board. Gaming Research. *Legalized Gambling in the State of South Dakota.* Carson City, Nev.: Gaming Control Board, Gaming Research, 1990. 15 pp.
        Highlights gaming in South Dakota, including charitable gaming, parimutuel wagering, the state lottery, and limited casino gaming in Deadwood. Regulations and licensing requirements will help businesses considering operating in South Dakota. An economic and demographic profile of the state is provided, and Indian gaming activities are mentioned.

461. *Nevada Gaming Law*. Las Vegas, Nev.: Lionel, Sawyer & Collins, 1991. 352 pp.

Gives a broad overview of gaming law which will be especially useful to casino managers and attorneys. The firm's lawyers have compiled information on regulatory agencies; licensing standards; corporate structures; casino employees; labor unions; contracts and debt collection; exclusion of persons; foreign gaming; gaming devices; taxation; accounting and cash reporting; disciplinary actions; and general casino operations. Lotteries and gaming crimes are also discussed. Index.

462. Nevada. Legislature. Legislative Commission. Subcommittee to Study Gaming. *Study of Gaming: Final Report*. Bulletin No. 93-4. Carson City, Nev.: Legislative Counsel Bureau, State of Nevada, 1992. 238 pp.

Explains Nevada gaming regulation and reports on gaming in other jurisdictions. Prepared for the Nevada Legislature, this report includes numerous recommendations. The Committee calls for continued effort to attract foreign visitors to Nevada; support for a national gaming symposium; support for amending the Indian Gaming Regulatory Act to make tribes more accountable to state authority; and continued opposition to a state lottery. Currently, state lotteries are prohibited by Nevada's Constitution.

463. New Jersey. Governor's Advisory Commission on Gambling. *Report and Recommendations of the Governor's Advisory Commission on Gambling*. Trenton, N.J.: The Commission, 1988. 229 pp.

Assesses gaming in New Jersey, including economic impact, crime, public policy, and compulsive gambling among adults and adolescents. The Commission finds that horse racing in New Jersey has been seriously hurt by casino gaming, and measures should be taken to ensure that industry's economic viability. It also calls for the establishment of an Office of Compulsive Gambling, redoubled efforts to control illegal gambling by juveniles, the allocation of revenues for a convention center, and a greater effort to curb crime associated with ancillary businesses and labor unions.

464.   Peterson, Scott C. *Changes to Limited Gaming in Deadwood*. Issue Memorandum 93-03. Pierre, S. Dak.: South Dakota Legislative Research Council, 17 May 1993. 4 pp.
       Reviews 1993 South Dakota legislation that made three significant changes to limited gaming in Deadwood, South Dakota. Upon passage, these senate bills allowed an increase in betting limits, an increase in the allowable number of gaming devices, and a revision of the distribution of tax revenues.

465.   Peterson, Scott C. *A Survey of Gambling in South Dakota*. Issue Memorandum 91-2. Pierre, S.Dak.: South Dakota Legislative Research Council, 19 November 1991. 10 pp.
       Reviews the history of gambling in South Dakota which was illegal until the 1933 Legislature approved betting on horse racing. This was expanded in 1949 to include dog racing. Games of chance sponsored by organizations for "public-spirited uses," including charities, and a state lottery were next. Legalization of video lottery games and on-line lotto games was then followed by the limited casino gaming now allowed in Deadwood. This chronology interestingly demonstrates how public acceptance of one form of gambling can lead to the subsequent legalization of other kinds.

466.   Rose, I. Nelson. *The Changing Law of Gambling Debts*. University of Nevada, Las Vegas, Special Collections. 1988. 12 pp.
       Outlines the development of gambling debt laws. Prior to Atlantic City's legalized gambling, casinos had little or no legal recourse in collecting gambling debts. Rose states, "if a player was willing to have his credit cut off and withstand harassing phone calls, he could stiff a casino." After legalization, New Jersey passed legislation that allowed casinos to collect on gaming debts. Other

jurisdictions, including Nevada, subsequently approved
similar legislation, and casinos may now take debtors to
court. A second development also emerged; gamblers are
suing casinos and winning, claiming their debts are due to
pathological gambling and therefore should not be col-
lectable.

467. Rose, I Nelson. *Gambling and the Law.* 1st ed.
Hollywood, Calif.: Gambling Times, 1986. 204 pp.
  Describes gambling law in a clear fashion intended
for the lay person. Rose provides legal information on
gaming licenses, card counting, casino blacklists,
bookmaking, casino debt collection, legal research, and a
host of other topics of interest to serious gamblers and
curious individuals. He also gives tax advice.

468. Rose, I. Nelson. "Gambling and the Law—Update
1993." *Hastings Communications and Entertainment Law
Journal (Comm/Ent.)* 15 (Fall 1992): 93-122.
  Reviews significant changes in U.S. gambling law in
1993. After identifying legal gambling as the "fastest
growing segment of the entertainment industry," Rose
provides a succinct overview of its history in this country.
He then covers the Indian Gaming Regulatory Act and
California v Cabazon Band of Mission Indians, gambling
debt collection, court cases benefitting casino operators,
taxation of winnings, gaming advertising, and video
lotteries. A concise, informative summary. Bibliographical
references.

469. Rothman, Michael, and Hollis Robbins.
"Government Regulation of Gambling Advertising:
Replacing Vice Prevention with Consumer Protection."
Journal of Gambling Studies 7 (Winter 1991): 337-360.
  Discusses the evolution of gambling advertising law.
The authors argue that present state laws should be reviewed
and a model statute should be developed. Numerous federal
laws and principal court cases are discussed.

470. Rychlak, Ronald J. "Video Gambling Devices." *UCLA Law Review* 37 (February 1990): 555-593.

Examines the history of gambling machines, the development of illegal video gambling devices, and the social problems caused by their widespread use. Illegal machines do not give payouts directly like their legal counterparts; instead, winnings are paid from separate sources such as nearby cash registers. These devices are now found nationwide because states have exerted little control over them; gambling statutes may be too old to address this more recent technology, for example, or law enforcement may have little concern because they think only small amounts of money are involved. "Most important, video gambling devices are difficult to differentiate from legal, amusement-only video games." The author stresses that states must establish laws preventing illegal video machines because they contribute to increases in crime, police corruption, and compulsive gambling. He includes sample language and useful information for state legislators who want to amend or establish state laws and regulations, including the important and necessary legal definition describing these machines. Bibliographical references.

471. South Dakota. Commission on Gaming. *Rules and Regulations for Limited Gaming*. Pierre, S. Dak.: South Dakota Commission on Gaming, 1993. 269 pp.

Provides text and citations for gaming laws and regulations in Deadwood, South Dakota. This includes general provisions and definitions of terms for license application; approval; authorized games; accounting regulations; foreclosures; security and surveillance; and exclusion lists.

472. Strate, Larry D. *Advertising Legalized Gambling: A Late Bloomer Under the First Amendment*. University of Nevada, Las Vegas, Special Collections. 1992. 29 pp.

Explores the legal restriction on gaming advertising, and discusses the case law and statutes which define it. *Edge Broadcasting Co. v U.S.*, the Charity Games Advertising Clarification Act, and the Indian Gaming Regulatory Act are identified as central to "the continuing attempt to balance the

interests of those seeking to advertise legalized gambling and
those seeking to reduce it."

473.   Vallen, Jerome J., ed. *Lionel, Sawyer & Collins
Nevada Gaming License Guide.* Las Vegas, Nev.: Lionel,
Sawyer & Collins, 1988. 175 pp.
        Documents the gaming license application process in
Nevada. Vallen explains "who needs to be licensed" and
compiles information on regulatory agencies, application
forms, licensing standards, applicant investigation, board
and commission hearings, judicial review, and the role of the
gaming attorney. Also includes tables of cases, statutes and
regulations, and biographical sketches of the firm's gaming
attorneys. Bibliographical references, index.

474.   Vince, Marian. *Nevada: Legislative History of
Gambling and Gaming Disputes.* University of Nevada, Las
Vegas, Special Collections, 1993. 61 pp.
        Provides a history of Nevada's Gaming Control
Board. Vince also explains the current dispute resolution
process and describes thirteen disputes which have gone to
judicial review since 1983. One involved a patron who
claimed to have won a $250,000 jackpot which the casino
refused to pay. The casino claimed the machine
malfunctioned, the Gaming Control Board supported the
casino, and eventually, the Nevada Supreme Court denied
the plaintiff's right to judicial review based on the issue of
jurisdiction. The Court decided that the Gaming Control
Board, not the Court, had jurisdiction in this dispute. The
patron did not get her money. Bibliographical references.

475.   Wendler, Kathryn A. *Legalized Low-Stakes
Gambling: "The Colorado Experience."* Master's thesis,
University of Nevada, Las Vegas, 1993. University of
Nevada, Las Vegas, Special Collections. 54 pp.
        Provides a legislative history and analysis of current
Colorado casino gaming. Gaming revenues, tax revenues,
the industry, and the towns hosting gaming operations are
discussed. Wendler concludes the amenities required to
transform Colorado gaming into something more than a

"boutique attraction" have yet to develop, and over-regulation has created more problems than it has solved. Includes a list of recommendations for other jurisdictions based on Colorado's experiences. Bibliographical references.

476. *What You Should Know! Limited Gaming Information Booklet.* Evergreen, Colo.: Grogan Report, 1991. 24 pp.

Highlights Colorado's Division of Gaming and the Limited Gaming Control Commission. Agency missions and agency members' biographical sketches comprise the bulk of this pamphlet. Gaming licenses are described, fees are posted, and a breakdown of the Division of Gaming budget is provided.

477. Zimmerman, Art. *Legal Gambling in Wisconsin.* Informational Paper No. 69. Madison, Wis.: Wisconsin Legislative Fiscal Bureau, January 1993. 45 pp.

Describes the 1992 creation of the Wisconsin Gaming Commission to coordinate and regulate the state-operated lottery, parimutuel wagering, and seventeen Indian-owned casinos. Also covers the Commission's purpose and structure; the development, operation, and regulation of legalized gambling in Wisconsin; and the enforcement responsibilities of the state's Gaming Commission and Department of Justice. Ten pages on Indian gaming provide a concise overview of pertinent federal law and court decisions, gaming compacts, procedures, requirements, and related contracts.

SUPPLEMENTAL MATERIALS

478. Alaska Department of Commerce and Economic Development. Games of Chance and Skill Section. *Statutes and Regulations: Games of Chance and Skill.* Juneau, Alaska: Alaska Department of Commerce and Economic Development, Games of Chance and Skill Section, January 1993. 50 pp.

479. *Alaska Statutes Governing Games of Chance and Skill (AS 05.15); Coin-Operated Devices and Punchboards (AS 43.15).* Juneau, Alaska: Alaska Department of Revenue, Charitable Gaming Division, August 1993. 32 pp.

480. Bergmeier, Dave. "Greyhound-Horse Owners Unite to Oppose Casinos in Kansas." *The Greyhound Review* 22 (December 1994): 13-14.

481. Bible, Paul A. "The Regulatory Structure of Gaming Control in Nevada: Suggestions for Reform." *Nevada Public Affairs Review* 2 (1986): 12-14.

482. Blakey, G. Robert. "Legal Regulation of Gambling Since 1950." *Annals of the Academy of Political and Social Sciences* 474 (1984): 12-22.

483. Cabot, Anthony. "Legal Highlights of 1993: Boring on the Surface, But Count Those Dollars." *Casino Journal* 7 (January 1994): 12.

484. Colorado. Senate. *Limited Gaming Act of 1991. An Act: Senate Bill 91-149 Concerning the Implementation of Section 9 of Article XVIII of the State Constitution With Respect to Limited Gaming, and in Connection Therewith, Making an Appropriation Therefore.* N.p., 1991. 73 pp.

485. Dao, James. "In Shift, Pataki Backs Legalized Casino Gambling to Aid Tourism." *New York Times* (8 December 1994): B16 (L).

486. Dao, James. "Legalizing of Casinos Gains in Albany: Opposition Weakens as Gambling Spreads Throughout the Nation." *New York Times* (7 February 1994): B5 (L).

487. Fagan, Neil. "Enforcement of Gaming Debts in Britain." *New York Law School Journal of International and Comparative Law* 8 (Winter 1986): 7-31.

488.   Faiss, Robert D., and Anthony N. Cabot. "Gaming on the High Seas." *New York Law School Journal of International and Comparative Law* 8 (Winter 1986): 105-107.

489.   *Focus on: Gambling Related Issues in Minnesota.* St. Paul, Minn.: DFL Caucus Research, Minnesota House of Representatives, March 27, 1991. 12 pp.

490.   "FRA Musters Forces to Fight Casino Gaming." *Nation's Restaurant News* 28 (8 August 1994): 1, 63. (Note: FRA stands for the Florida Restaurant Association.)

491.   "Gambling and Lotteries." *State Policy Reports* 10 (July 1992): 11-15.

492.   Grabenstein-Chandler, Jane. *The Evolution of Gambling in Nebraska: Amendments to Article 111 Section 24 of the Constitution.* Lincoln, Neb.: Nebraska Legislative Council, 1988. 36 pp.

493.   Greenberg, Pam. "Gambling on Casinos." *NCSL Legisbrief* 3 (February 1992): 1-2.

494.   Greenberg, Pam. "Most States Hold Off on Legalized Video Gambling Decisions." *Fiscal Letter* 15 (July/August 1993): 9-11.

495.   Illinois. General Assembly. *Metropolitan Entertainment District and Casino Gaming Regulatory Act.* N.p., 1992. 154 pp.

496.   "Indiana Court Ruling Allows State To Issue 11 Gambling Licenses." *Wall Street Journal* (22 November 1994): A3.

497.   Kelly, Joseph M. "British Gaming Act of 1968." *New York Law School Journal of International and Comparative Law* 8 (Winter 1986): 33-103.

498.   McMillen, Jan, and William R. Eadington. "The Evolution of Gambling Laws in Australia." *New York Law School Journal of International and Comparative Law* 8 (Winter 1986): 167-192.

499.   Minnesota. Department of Gaming. *Lawful Gambling: Chapter 349*. St. Paul, Minn.: Print Communication Division, 1990. 69 pp.

500.   Minnesota. Gaming Control Board. *Lawful Gambling Rules: Chapters 7861-7865*. St. Paul, Minn.: Print Communication Division, 1993. 50 pp.

501.   Mississippi. Legislature. *Mississippi Gaming Control Act. House Bill No. 2: (As Sent to the Governor): An Act to Provide for the Regulation, Licensing, and Taxation of Legal Gaming Within the State*. N.p., 1990. 119 pp.

502.   Nevada. Legislature. Legislative Commission. *Regulation of Gaming*. Bulletin No. 81-1. Carson City, Nev.: Legislative Commission of the Legislative Counsel Bureau, State of Nevada, 1980. 115 pp.

503.   New Jersey. Casino Control Commission. *Annual Report*. Trenton, N.J.: The Commission, 1979- . Annual. Various pagings.

504.   New Jersey. Department of Public Safety. *Annual Report*. Trenton, N.J.: The Department, 1963- . Annual. Various pagings.

505.   Ritsche, Daniel F. *The Evolution of Legalized Gambling in Wisconsin*. Research Bulletin 94-2. Madison, Wisc.: Wisconsin Legislative Reference Bureau, March 1994. 67 pp.

506.   Rose, Blaine Sullivan. "Constitutional Questions of Nevada Gaming Licensure: A Rights-Based Analysis." *Nevada Public Affairs Review* 2 (1986): 15-20.

507.   Rose, I. Nelson. "The Impact of American Laws on Foreign Legal Gambling." *New York Law School Journal of International and Comparative Law* 8 (Winter 1986): 129-165.

508.   Rose, I. Nelson. "Turning in the High Rollers: The Impact of the New Cash Regulations." *Nevada Public Affairs Review* 2 (1986): 21-26.

509.   Roske, Ralph J. "Gambling in Nevada: The Early Years, 1861-1931." *Nevada Historical Society Quarterly* 33 (Spring 1990): 28-40.

510.   Skola, Thomas J. "The Collection of Gaming Debts Outside the United States." *International Gaming and Wagering Business* 14 (15 September 1993): 78, 80-81.

511.   Thompson, William Norman. *Campaigns for Casinos*. 2nd ed. Las Vegas, Nev.: University of Nevada, Las Vegas, Center for Business and Economic Research, 1984. 57 pp.

512.   Todd, Nancy. "Legalizing Gambling and Doing it Right." *International Gaming and Wagering Business* 15 (5 May 1994): 75-76.

513.   "When Does a Tavern With a Few Video Poker Machines Become a Casino?" *From the State Capitals: Outlook From the State Capitals* 48 (9 May 1994): 1-4.

514.   Williams, John. *Charitable Gambling in Minnesota: An Information Brief on Legislative History, Rules and Regulations, and the Outlook for Charitable Gambling. House Research Information Brief.* Rev. ed. St. Paul, Minn: Minnesota House of Representatives, Research Department, June 1994. 17 pp.

515.   Williams, John. *Minimum Ages for Gambling in Minnesota.* House Research Information Brief. St. Paul,

Minn.: Minnesota House of Representatives, Research
Department, August 1993. 2 pp.

516.   Williams, John. *Minnesota Gambling: An Overview.*
House Research Information Brief.   St. Paul, Minn.:
Minnesota House of Representatives, Research Department,
July 1994. 4 pp.

517.   Wisconsin. Legislative Reference Bureau. *The
Evolution of Legalized Gambling in Wisconsin.* Research
Bulletin 94-2. Madison, Wisc.: Wisconsin Legislative
Reference Bureau, March 1994. 67 pp.

518.   Zazzali, James R., Kenneth D. Merin, and Barry H.
Evenchick. *Video Gaming.* Trenton, N.J.: New Jersey
Commission of Investigation, September 1991. 38 pp.

SECTION E

Casinos and Economic Development

Though seldom a first choice, casinos have long been used for economic development. The effectiveness of this policy has varied over the years and from jurisdiction to jurisdiction, and results have been interpreted in various ways. The costs and benefits of casinos are regularly challenged by those who either favor or oppose legalized gambling. This section of *Casino Gaming* presents a wealth of information and findings on the economics of casinos. Sources include government and private research reports, journal articles, business publications, and a variety of other materials.

519. Abell Foundation. *Casino Gambling: Should Baltimore Roll the Dice?* Baltimore: The Abell Foundation, 1994. 24 pp.
Evaluates the effects of casino gaming in Baltimore with a detailed overview of the possible social and economic benefits and costs. The Foundation, critical of gaming, suggests it could cost Baltimore residents $200 for every $40 it brings to the city. Bibliographical references, tables.

520. Adams, Michael, Julie Barker, and Charles Butler. "Let the Good Times Roll." *Successful Meetings* 40 (April 1991): 53-54, 57-58, 61-62.
Discusses "gaming destinations" as potential convention sites. Aimed at meeting planners, the article lists advantages and disadvantages of booking groups in Las Vegas, Reno, and Atlantic City. Conference costs in these areas are usually reasonable, and major hotel-casinos are increasingly interested in attracting conventions. Includes

brief descriptions of large hotels and their conference capacities and services.

521.   "American Survey: Rien ne va Plus." *Economist* 317 (15 December 1990): 23-24.
        Looks at the pros and cons of using legalized gambling to improve state economies. Some communities do not support legalization because religious leaders label it evil. There are also concerns about who benefits the most from gambling profits, citizens or casino owners. University of Nevada economics professor William Eadington says that it is as easy to "exaggerate the social costs of gambling" as it is to overestimate the financial rewards.

522.   Andersen, Kurt. "Las Vegas, U.S.A." *Time* 143 (10 January 1994): 42-51.
        Analyzes Las Vegas's rapid growth and transformation in a social and historical context, comparing the city's changes to those occurring nationwide. Once called "Sin City" because of its liberal laws and organized crime connections, Las Vegas is now a respectable, family-oriented vacation destination. For examples, Andersen looks at recently added elaborate theme-park hotel-casino attractions such as the Luxor, Treasure Island, and the MGM Grand, which provide "fun for the whole family." He compares these images to earlier ones and states that Las Vegas seems much less sensational now because it has "become Americanized, and even more, America has become Las Vegasized." While Las Vegas is still "vulgar," perceptions about it have changed because "Americans' collective tolerance for vulgarity has gone way, way up."

523.   Atlantic City Convention & Visitors Authority, and Longwoods Travel USA. *Atlantic City Research Program, July 1994: A Research Project of the Atlantic City Convention & Visitors Authority*. Atlantic City, N.J.: Longwoods Travel USA, 1994. 164 pp.
        Provides a thorough marketing study of Atlantic City, New Jersey. Includes discussion of visitor profiles

and trip characteristics; the importance of gaming and the emergence of other gaming venues; Atlantic City's image and advertising; and a long-term diversification strategy. This is an excellent example of how a marketing study for a tourist destination should look.

524.   Aztar Corp. *Atlantic City Market: 1994*. University of Nevada, Las Vegas, Special Collections. 1994. 26 pp.
        Analyzes the financial performance of Atlantic City casinos from 1978 to 1994 and argues that the casino industry is healthy and growing there. This report, issued to counter negative perceptions of Atlantic City, demonstrates that visitation trends are solid, operating profits are almost as good as Las Vegas, and additional hotel rooms are needed. The threat of riverboat casinos operating in Philadelphia is also addressed. Title on cover: *Atlantic City is Alive and Getting Better*.

525.   Caneday, Lowell. *Attitudes Toward Tourism in Deadwood, South Dakota, 1990*. University of Nevada, Las Vegas, Special Collections. 1990. 22 pp.
        Studies the effects of tourism policy changes on Deadwood, South Dakota. Attitudes towards tourism and gaming, perceptions of the change caused by gaming, and opinions concerning decisions made regarding tourism in South Dakota were surveyed. Local residents and business owners were polled separately. Majorities in both groups recognized that increased tourism and the introduction of gaming had significantly changed their community, and on the whole, they found this to be positive. Neither group would change present tourism policies or reduce efforts to attract tourists through gaming.

526.   *Casino Industry's Economic Impact on New Jersey*. Newark, N.J.: Touche Ross & Co., 20 October 1987. 64 pp.
        Reports results of a Touche Ross & Co. study, commissioned by the Atlantic City Casino Association, on the positive economic impacts of New Jersey's casino industry. Most of this is comprised of charts and tables

showing effects on employment, effects on tourism,
revenues from casinos, effects on property taxes, uses of
casino revenue funds, and costs of casino regulation. A
cover letter includes the following conclusions on the casino
industry: it is one of the state's major employers; it has
generated billions in revenues for state, county, city, and
federal coffers; much of these revenues have been used to
improve services for New Jersey's elderly and handicapped;
and projections about the economic impact of casinos were
far surpassed by actual performance. Charts, tables.

527.   Chicago. Mayor's Gaming Commission, Nicholas J.
Bua, Chair. *Report to the Mayor*. Chicago: The
Commission, 1992. 98 pp.
        Examines a proposed casino-entertainment center for
Chicago. The report identifies opportunities the project
would create, as well as issues and concerns such as
organized crime and effective public control. The
Commission supports the project and recommends thorough
regulation and firm oversight of the project as keys to
success. Other recommendations include selecting a site that
does not overburden the existing transportation infrastructure
and limiting hotel rooms for the project to 300 in order to
spread the benefits of the complex by encouraging visitors to
experience other Chicago amenities.

528.   Christiansen, Eugene Martin. *Legal Gambling in
New York City*. New York: Christiansen/Cummings
Associates, Inc., 1990. 10 pp.
        Addresses the prospects of legalized gaming in New
York City and briefly discusses lotteries, sports betting, and
casinos. Christiansen points out that casinos are very
popular with Americans, and casinos in two states win
nearly as much as the combined revenues of lotteries in
thirty-one states. However, he is quick to note that
Americans also lose considerable amounts of money in
casinos, and such businesses are expensive to regulate
adequately. He concludes that casinos would adversely
affect the state lottery, horse racing, and off-track betting
enterprises.

529.   Christiansen, Eugene Martin. *Legalized Gambling: Trends and Issues*. New York: Christiansen/Cummings Associates, 1991. 21 pp.

Explores the proliferation of gaming from a financial perspective. Christiansen identifies lotteries as the fastest growing form of legalized gaming during the 1980s, enjoying the largest market share, forty percent, of a $24 billion industry. Casinos followed with thirty-two percent, and parimutuels with fifteen percent. As a means of generating tax revenues, lotteries average a forty-nine percent return on dollars gambled, while casinos average eight percent nationwide. Christiansen argues that though lotteries raise more tax revenues, casinos offer economic benefits, such as capital investment, tourism stimulation, and jobs. Conversely, they also cause increased compulsive gambling, expensive regulation, reallocation of consumer spending, rising crime rates, and problems associated with growth. Because lotteries tend to mature and stagnate, Christiansen predicts that video lottery terminals (VLTs) and the conversion of on-line lottery ticket sales networks into on-line gaming device networks in the 1990s are likely trends.

530.   Clines, Francis X. "Gambling, Pariah No More, Is Booming Across America." *New York Times* (5 December 1993): 1, 32 (L).

Discusses the rapid growth and popularity of legalized gambling throughout the United States. Most Americans now view gambling as recreation or "mass entertainment," not as a sin or vice. The first state lotteries in the mid-1960s began changing America's moral stance on gambling, a shift accelerated by the increasing dependence of state and local governments on gaming revenues. Las Vegas's "futuristic casino-theme parks" are proof of gaming's mainstream stature, and in 1992, consumers spent $29.9 billion on gambling. Charts.

531.   Connecticut. Task Force to Study the Feasibility of Additional Casino Gambling in Connecticut. *Final Report:*

Casino Gambling. Hartford, Conn.: The Task Force, 1993.
47 pp.

Provides a majority report favoring urban casinos
and a minority report speaking against them.   The
conclusions of the majority were summed up succinctly in
the report's subtitle, "Jobs, Revenues and Entertainment."
The minority found such promises to be "fool's gold,"
complaining that as gambling has proliferated in Connecticut
the state has been diligent only at totaling up the revenues;
they have never properly accounted for the substantial social
and economic costs associated with gambling.

532.   Corelli, Rae. "Betting on Casinos." *Maclean's* 107
(30 May 1994): 26-29.

Looks at the spread of casino gambling in Canada
and the United States.   Corelli notes that "once-puritanical
Ontario, deficit-ridden and strapped for cash . . . is the third
province to conclude that yesterday's vice could well be
tomorrow's virtue."   Governments "have gone from
regulating gambling to promoting it"; Ontario officials, for
example, argued that casinos will increase tax revenues,
employment, economic development, and tourism. Many of
the province's customers come from northern Michigan and
Ohio, a pattern that will change dramatically if Detroit
legalizes casinos and attracts customers. Gambling issues
are the same on both sides of the border, and increasing
competition is a major concern.

533.   Deloitte & Touche. *Economic and Other Impacts of
Gaming, Entertainment & Hotel Facility Proposed for
Chicago, Illinois: Presentation to the City of Chicago
Gaming Commission.* Chicago: Deloitte & Touche, 1992.
20 pp.

Provides an economic assessment of a proposed
gaming-entertainment facility in Chicago.   The report
provides background on Chicago's economy and the gaming
industry as well as projections for incremental visitation;
employment impacts; sales/output impacts; fiscal impacts;
existing Illinois gaming; local product substitution; and
industrial park development.

534.   Derrick, Gabrielle.   "Wagering on the Profits of Casinos." *Business Review Weekly* 6 (11 April 1994): 54.

Reviews the promotion of legalized gambling in the United States to increase state revenues. This one-page article from an Australian journal succinctly covers the debate about gaming, the "hospitality industry's top growth sector," and notes that many American states have legalized it or are considering legalization. Proponents look at large casino profits, while opponents raise concerns about increased crime, regressive taxes, and compulsive gambling. The success of Indian operations like Connecticut's Foxwood High Stakes Bingo and Casino, however, helps persuade legislators to support legalization.

535.   Detroit, Michigan.   Casino Gaming Study Commission. *Final Report.*   Detroit, Mich.: The Commission, 1988. 114 pp.

Reports on the conclusions of an exhaustive casino impact study authorized by Detroit's mayor. Casinos may have significant potential for lowering Detroit's high unemployment rate. They could also generate $500 million in new state and local taxes and aid local area businesses. Revenues could be applied to education, law enforcement, anti-drug abuse programs, infrastructure repair and development, and a variety of other social programs. This study finds that casinos could even have positive effects on families, since unemployed members would find work. Tables.

536.   Diamond, Randy. "Atlantic City Seeks Life Beyond Gambling." *Christian Science Monitor* 86 (19 January 1994): 8.

Reports on Atlantic City's problems fifteen years after casino gambling was legalized. The author calls the city "a picture of urban America at its worst," where "slums by the sea sit next to shiny glass-and-steel casino towers." Now the state plans to spend $1.5 billion on redevelopment efforts which will include a convention center, a "non-casino" hotel, and "an entertainment-and-shopping complex to be built on an elevated boardwalk." While city officials

are optimistic about these changes, other people are
concerned about the future of the city's casinos as gambling
spreads throughout the country. Like Las Vegas, Atlantic
City wants to provide family entertainment so it can attract a
larger audience.

537.   Eadington, William R. *Recent National Trends in the
Casino Gaming Industry and Their Implications for the
Economy of Nevada*. University of Nevada, Las Vegas,
Special Collections. 1992. 14 pp.
     Recognizes the various ways casino-style gaming
operations are increasing throughout the United States and
identifies a number of implications for Nevada's gaming
industry. Eadington proposes that to remain competitive in
the face of video lottery terminals (VLTs), Indian gaming,
riverboat casinos, urban casinos, and mining town gaming,
Nevada's major destination resort cities must improve the
variety and quality of their recreation and entertainment
offerings. He also predicts that downtown Las Vegas
casinos and older Las Vegas Strip casinos will experience
high attrition, while Reno's fate will be determined by its
ability to attract capital for expansion and market itself.
Should California legalize VLTs or casinos, Nevada's
gaming industry could be seriously affected.

538.   Eadington, William R., comp. *Materials Pertaining
to Gaming in America*. Reno, Nev.: University of Nevada,
Reno. Bureau of Business and Economic Research, 1982.
301 pp.
     Provides a collection of articles on various aspects of
casino gaming, including corporate strategies, economic
trends, casino management, and organized crime.

539.   *Economic Impacts of Casino Gambling*. Memphis,
Tenn.: Promus Companies, 4 January 1994. 6 pp.
     Presents the gaming industry's perspective that
casino taxes greatly increase government revenues.
Supporting examples show these funds have been spent on
reforming gang members, building industrial parks,
improving police protection, and modernizing water

systems. Sometimes, however, fiscal expectations are not met, primarily because government officials make errors or incorrect assumptions. The report stresses that states and local communities should draft legislation to "help insure a commercially viable industry" that does not limit losses or wagers; evaluate prospective casinos thoroughly to determine if they are reputable; "require casino operators to pay for infrastructure improvements necessary for their casinos to operate"; develop leases that ensure all public monies used will be fully reimbursed; and "give preference to prospective casino operators who commit to using local labor, goods, and services." Casino operators, public officials, and private developers must work together.

540.   Economics Research Associates. *Economic Benefits of Gaming Sites in Chicago.* Chicago, Ill.: Economic Research Associates, 1994. 54 pp.
        Analyzes three possible sites and the potential visitor market for gaming activities in Chicago. Prepared for Metropolitan Structures and the Whitman Corporation, this economic benefit study concludes that the Illinois Center site is the most advantageous choice, because it would attract more tourists from greater distances. Visitors from more than 300 miles away would spend larger amounts of money on hotel rooms, off-site restaurants, stores, cultural facilities, and attractions, thus increasing the project's economic benefits. Tables.

541.   *Effects of Casino Gaming on State Lotteries.* Memphis, Tenn.: Promus Companies, 21 March 1994. 2 pp.
        Argues that casinos do not adversely affect lottery revenues. This brief industry-sponsored report cites statistics from five states to show how "lottery revenues have gone up, not down, since the introduction of casino gaming." Lotteries and casinos attract different people and "provide two different entertainment experiences"; casino customers participate for "social interaction and fun, not to get rich."

542.   *Final Report of the Commission on State Tax and Financing Policy.* Indianapolis, Ind.: Indiana Legislative Services Agency, November 1990. 5 pp.

Reports on findings of a legislative-appointed commission instructed to study and make recommendations on Indiana tax and revenue issues. The feasibility of casino gambling in Gary was part of this assignment. Commission members reviewed an earlier study on this subject and seriously questioned the accuracy of the enormous sums of money it projected. Rather than making conclusive recommendations, they expressed concern that limited staff and funding made it impossible to do the necessary in-depth research a valid conclusion requires.

543.   Florida. Department of Commerce. *Implications of Casino Gambling as an Economic Development Strategy.* N.p., 1994. University of Nevada, Las Vegas, Special Collections. 14 pp.

Addresses economic and social issues raised by the "Proposition for Limited Casinos" that was placed on Florida's November 1994 ballot. The Department determined that casino gambling would not be of economic benefit to the state. There is also sufficient evidence to suggest that gambling would harm the state's tourism industry and other development efforts. This study provides interesting comparisons between the tourism economies of Florida and Nevada and information on casino market saturation and the social costs of gambling.

544.   Florida. Executive Office of the Governor. *Casinos in Florida: An Analysis of the Economic and Social Impacts.* Tallahassee, Fla.: Office of Planning and Budget, 1994. 110 pp.

Discusses Florida's current gaming environment, potential tax revenues from land-based and riverboat casinos, and crime and social costs associated with casinos. According to this study, casino costs significantly outweigh the benefits of legalization. Social and crime costs for Florida citizens are estimated to be a minimum of $2.16

billion annually, while expected tax revenues are estimated at between $155 million and $276 million.

545.   Fox Consulting. *Casino Gambling in Harrison County: An Economic Feasibility Analysis.* Prepared by Fox Consulting for the Harrison County Development Commission. Reno, Nev.: Fox Consulting, 1992. 46 pp.
     Anticipates the economic impact of dockside casinos in Harrison County, Mississippi. The study has two main components, an assessment of impact on the private sector and of the financial impact on government. Costs and benefits are assessed in terms of new dollars injected into the economy, employment, convention business impact, revenue impact, the costs of regulation, and increased demand on public services and infrastructure.

546.   *Gambling & Taxes: It's Your Money.* Lakewood, Colo.: Riskman, 1993. 30 pp.
     Offers individuals information on how to report income and loss from gambling activities. General rules on income and taxes, gambling tax rules, and suggested methods of recording wagering activities are provided.

547.   Gold, Steven D. "It's Not a Miracle, It's a Mirage." *State Legislatures* 20 (February 1994): 28-31.
     Argues that relying on legalized gambling for revenues has become increasingly suspect. The author first stresses that expectations are greatly inflated and gambling does not add enough revenue to allow states to "reduce reliance on taxes." Moreover, the industry's success will greatly diminish as it spreads across the country because competition increases, since "casinos are most beneficial when they attract many residents from outside states." Gold then uses statistics on lottery revenues to illustrate how people are confused about state finances and the gains legal gambling promises. He concludes that the "potential revenue from gambling is relatively limited when viewed in the overall context of a state budget." Also, any benefits need to be "weighed against its regressivity and the social costs" that often result. Tables.

548.   Goodman, Robert. *Legalized Gambling as a Strategy for Economic Development*. Northampton, Mass.: United States Gambling Study, 1994. 222 pp.

Criticizes economic impact studies of gambling, because most studies grossly exaggerate gaming's benefits and understate its costs. Goodman laments a "critical lack of objective knowledge about the real economic and social costs and benefits of legalized gambling." He also fears that as states become dependent on gaming revenues, they will expand gaming and create a political spiral that will lead to lax regulation and control. Indian gaming, while seen as beneficial in the short term, faces serious legal challenges, and its long term viability is uncertain. Though sharply critical of how legal gambling is promoted, perceived, and managed, Goodman offers a list of recommendations to better control and regulate the industry. Bibliographical references.

549.   Greenberg, Pam. "Gambling: Some States Bet on Big Returns." *Fiscal Letter* 13 (November/December 1991): 9, 11.

Reports on how increasing numbers of states are turning to legalized gambling for revenues. Greenberg briefly outlines the revenues generated by state lotteries, casinos, parimutuel wagering, and charitable gambling, and a chart lists casino gambling taxes for nine states. Since competition for gambling dollars will continue to increase as more locations offer opportunities, Greenberg concludes that over time "gambling revenues likely will make only a limited contribution to state economies." Tables.

550.   Hantges, Tom, and Joseph D. Milanowski. *The Future of the Las Vegas Gaming Industry: Las Vegas '94*. Las Vegas, Nev.: USA Capital Management Group, 1993. 16 pp.

Evaluates how the proliferation of gaming in other jurisdictions will affect Las Vegas. Hantges and Milanowski expect Las Vegas to remain the world's largest gaming market, citing the opening of mega-resorts as a necessary development for broadening the appeal of the city. Premier properties and properties with a secure market niche are expected to fair well through the 1990s. The only dark cloud in this report is the idea that a general downturn in the economy could affect financing for continued development and stall the local economy. Bibliographical references.

551. Hayes, Jack. "Casino 'Meal Deals' Hurt Biloxi Operators." *Nation's Restaurant News* 28 (14 November 1994): 7, 89.
Discusses the negative effects of riverboat casinos on nearby Biloxi restaurants. Operators who supported legalization are now suffering financially from intense competition. Casinos, whose "profits subsidize food cost," offer the same meals at greatly reduced prices, and new restaurants, attracted to the area due to gambling-related growth, worsen the situation. Local restaurateurs "never anticipated that casino patrons would spend virtually all of their time indoors, well-fed and well-supplied with beverage." Staffing at local operations was also affected, because casinos offered restaurant workers higher salaries. A solution would have been "to limit the casinos' restaurant power"; in New Orleans, for example, the Louisiana Restaurant Association "was able to insert a clause into that state's casino law limiting the size and type of restaurants" in a land-based casino scheduled to open in 1996.

552. Hazel, Debra. "Betting on Nevada Is a Sure Thing." *Chain Store Age Executive* 68 (April 1992): 25-27.
Looks at the steady growth of retail trade in Las Vegas. Retail development continues to expand because the area's population continues to grow; many Californians are attracted to the area, for example, because of no state income or probate taxes, the lower cost of living, and the "continually growing hospitality industry." While some retailers are choosing neighborhood-based sites to attract nearby residents, other companies are planning major projects in areas aimed at tourists, since "tourism has not decreased substantially in Las Vegas, despite drops in travel overall." The city's recent emphasis on family activities has

helped keep tourism at the level retail market growth requires.

553.   Johnson, Cathy M., and Kenneth J. Meier. "The Wages of Sin: Taxing America's Legal Vices." *Western Political Quarterly* 43 (September 1990): 577-595.
        Studies state policies on taxing alcohol, tobacco, and gambling, so-called "sin taxes." After noting that such taxes have become increasingly important to public policy and politics, the authors examine how "sin-tax policies affect state revenues," how political forces and policy actions interact, and how such interactions affect consumption. Legislators may support sin taxes for many reasons. The "influence of citizens, however, was best seen through the influence of religious forces"; for example, a "large Catholic population was associated with legalized gambling and low alcohol taxes." Johnson and Meier also conclude that while such policy decisions as legalizing gambling do increase revenue, tax rates "do not directly affect policy outcomes (consumption of sin)." This interaction of politics and policy outcomes exemplifies the "complexities of the policy making process." Tables, bibliographical references.

554.   Johnson, David B., William Oakland, and Timothy P. Ryan. *Incremental Economic Impact of a Single Casino in New Orleans.* University of Nevada, Las Vegas, Special Collections. 1992. 26 pp.
        Quantifies the economic benefits and costs of casino and riverboat gaming in New Orleans. Information is provided in tabular form, with headings for casino win estimations, new visitors, tax revenues, direct casino employment, one-time construction impact, and crime-related costs. Tables.

555.   Kindt, John Warren. "The Economic Impacts of Legalized Gambling Activities." *Drake Law Review* 43 (1993-1994): 51-95.
        Examines how legalized gambling affects state and local economies. Kindt first argues that gaming industry officials narrowly focus on select aspects of local economies

which   distorts the benefits they "allegedly" bring to
communities and then reviews a 1992 proposal for a large
Chicago casino to illustrate his point.   He notes, for
example, that as criticism against the project increased, the
projected numbers of tourists and new jobs grew.
Following sections discuss the socio-economic costs of
legalized gambling; the "black hole of economics" in
Deadwood, South Dakota; the gaming industry's profit
margin advantages and operating strategies; and "a summary
of the unique social costs" gambling exacts. This article
clearly discusses most of the complex arguments made by
opponents of legalized gambling. Tables, bibliographical
references.

556.   Koselka, Rita. "Fantasyland." *Forbes* 151 (1 March
1993): 62, 63, 65.
      Investigates suspect politics and questionable
economic benefits surrounding a proposed New Orleans
casino project. Governor Edwin Edwards "rammed a bill
through the legislature," denying city and state residents a
vote on the issue, and then assured angry citizens that it
"would generate a minimum of $100 million a year in
revenues to help cover the state's $600 million annual
deficit." City Mayor Sidney Barthelemy expects additional
millions, both up front and annually, as well as the creation
of 5,000 jobs. Koselka, saying this "arithmetic is shaky,"
looks at the devious way Christopher Hemmeter and Caesars
World were chosen to develop the project and how their
projected revenue estimates are very inflated and unrealistic.
While Atlantic City and Las Vegas rely heavily on casinos to
attract tourists, New Orleans businesses are concerned that
this casino would take "big chunks out of the existing tourist
trade," a critical component of the city's economy.

557.   Koselka, Rita, and Christopher Palmeri. "Snake
Eyes." *Forbes* 151 (1 March 1993): 70-72.
      Covers problems caused by the recent growth of
legalized gambling across the country. In Central City,
Colorado, for example, tax revenues increased from
$350,000 to $6.5 million per year since legalization in 1991,

while debt increased from $500,000 to $20 million from costs accrued to support the industry. Gambling-related stocks have also proliferated, and their values have increased dramatically. More companies plan to go public. The authors stress that new tax revenues depend on attracting tourists from other areas, a task that gets much more difficult as gambling becomes increasingly available. They predict that "investors and lenders will realize that the gambling bubble is about to burst."

558. Lane, Randall. "Keeping the Money at Home." *Forbes* 152 (8 November 1993): 214, 216.

Looks at the possibility of opening casinos in "financially hard-pressed" Pennsylvania. Governor Robert Casey strongly opposed legalized gambling, but as his last term ends in 1994, plans for land and water-based casinos are being made. Major industry leaders are ready to move into the state. Lane labels an important and often-repeated argument, increasingly used to support legalized gambling, a "defense tactic: legalize it at home or the locals will go elsewhere to lose their money." In 1992, Philadelphia area gamblers lost almost $1 billion in Atlantic City, just sixty miles away. This tactic is a major reason gambling has proliferated so rapidly.

559. Leiper, Neil. "Tourism and Gambling." *GeoJournal* 19 (1989): 269-275.

Researches the relationship between gambling and tourism. Using New Zealand as an example, Leiper first notes that gambling promoters worldwide emphasize how casinos attract tourists and the economic benefits they bring. He briefly reviews research on gambling behavior which "can satisfy a basic need of life, to experience risk" in manageable doses. He then cites H.P. Gray's tourism model which divides travelers into two categories: "wanderlusters" who seek risk by venturing into unfamiliar territory, and "sunlusters" who vacation primarily for recreation and relaxation with little risk involved. After describing gambling in ten tourist destinations, including Monte Carlo, Macau, Kathmandu, and Nevada, the author states that "sunluster" tourists are more inclined to gamble because they "turn to contrived forms of risk" not provided elsewhere on their trips. Geography, or location, plays an important part because there is a "persistent link between political borders and casinos that attracts significant numbers" of gamblers from adjacent countries where gambling is illegal. Bibliographical references.

560.   Lester, David, Alan F. Arcuri, and Franklin Smith. "Impact of Casino Gambling at Two Institutions." *Community College Review* 12 (Winter 1984/1985): 51-56.
     Describes how two colleges in the Atlantic City area were affected by legalized gambling and the "economic boom" which followed. Atlantic Community College offers a two-year program, while Richard Stockton State College offers a four-year bachelor's degree. After describing the differences between two and four-year institutions in general, and these two in particular, the authors state that the colleges reacted very differently to the rapid changes casinos created. The community college began an "innovative experiment in vocational education: the Casino Career Institute," a program "targeted at specific management needs ranging from casino law and casino accounting to casino security." This curriculum is credited with stabilizing enrollments and increasing graduation rates, while providing "new vitality and favorable publicity." Stockton State College administration, however, was "strongly against offering courses specifically geared to the hotel or casino industry," and its curriculum did not change at all.

561.   Longman, Phillip. "The Tax Mirage." *Florida Trend* 37 (June 1994): 62-67.
     Explains why casino gaming would be bad for Florida. First, gambling is so widespread now that "its ability at any given location is less and less of a draw to outsiders." Longman then refutes the argument that fewer residents would lose money elsewhere; any revenue gains would be offset by social costs and the diversion of money from area businesses to casinos. Revenue promises by industry promoters may be highly inflated and based on

experiences in other states, and thus unrealistic for Florida. Casinos, for example, would adversely affect state lottery earnings, while causing increases in compulsive gambling and crime. People who gamble have less money to spend on those goods and services which raise sale or excise taxes. He concludes that "states cannot build economic strengths on the mental weaknesses and anti-capitalist urges of their citizens." Bibliographical references.

562.   MacIsaac, Merle. "Winner Take Nothing." *Canadian Business* 67 (May 1994): 36-39, 42.
        Examines the growth of gambling in Canada and the United States. MacIsaac argues that casinos, promoted to increase revenues dramatically, "accomplish their supposed miracles by sucking money out of other areas of the economy." After looking at the initial success and "spectacular popularity" of a Montreal casino, he stresses that "just because casinos are popular doesn't mean they are a good idea." For example, casino jobs are usually taken from other entertainment providers; increasing competition threatens the industry's future on both sides of the border; and dependence on taxes from casinos makes "government a prisoner to the gambling industry." He finally compares governments to compulsive gamblers because the pattern is the same. After an initially large win, losses occur and the addict keeps returning to recoup the money, only to lose more and more. Includes sidebars on Quebec's Casino de Montreal, legalized gambling in four Canadian provinces, and problem gamblers in Alberta.

563.   Madden, Michael K. *Economic and Fiscal Impacts Associated with Gaming: Deadwood, South Dakota.* Commissioned by the South Dakota Commission on Gaming and the Deadwood Economic Development Corporation. Pierre, S. Dak.: South Dakota Commission on Gaming, 1992. Various pagings.
        Details expenditure, employment, and earnings trends and assesses their fiscal impact one year after gaming was legalized in Deadwood, South Dakota. In 1991, total visitor spending in Lawrence County was estimated at

$45,492,000, up substantially from the pre-gaming, 1989 estimate of $17,601,000. While county spending increased by $141,000 (twenty-six percent), tax revenues generated by gaming and tourism increased by $385,654. Employment has also increased markedly along with earnings.

564.   McCabe, Michael H. *Gambling Fever: Odds Are, You've Got It.* Lombard, Ill.: Midwestern Legislative Conference of the Council of State Governments, April 1992. 25 pp.
   Traces legalization of gambling in the Midwest. McCabe first looks at lotteries, casinos, riverboat gambling, parimutuel wagering, and Indian gaming in Illinois, Indiana, Iowa, Kansas, Michigan, Minnesota, Missouri, Nebraska, North Dakota, South Dakota, and Wisconsin. For "financially strapped states struggling to make ends meet, gambling proceeds remain attractive," and such states are "riding their luck as far as it will take them." After discussing gambling revenues, he identifies issues that supporters and opponents debate. While initial earnings and added employment figures may be impressive, opponents argue that these revenues are not necessarily "used for their intended purposes," and most industry jobs pay little more than minimum wage and tips. Competition between states and "various segments of the gaming industry" itself continues to grow, and earnings can be "elusive in a crowded market-place." Social issues include concerns about increased crime and corruption, subversion of the work ethic, and compulsive gambling. Morally, some wonder if govern-ments should support activities set up to make people lose. McCabe concludes that as "the gambling field becomes more crowded in the years ahead, lawmakers and gaming officials will have to learn to read the warning signs and adjust to competition in order to protect their gambling proceeds." Tables, bibliographical references.

565.   Mobile, Alabama. Gaming Task Force. *Gaming Task Force Report to the City of Mobile.* Prepared by Hunter Interests, Inc., and the Gaming and Economic

Development Institute, 1993. University of Nevada, Las Vegas, Special Collections. 24 pp.

Lists primary findings, conclusions, and recommendations on gaming development opportunities in Mobile, Alabama. The existing tourism base will help support casino development in Mobile, and Hunter and GEDI believe that Mobile could prosper in the competitive gaming environment, establishing itself as a major destination for casino gaming in the Southeast. Demand is expected to bring between 2.8 and 4.0 million visitors to a downtown location, which would support a 45,000 to 60,000 square foot, high quality casino as part of a new convention facility. Economic benefits from tax revenues, tourist dollars, and employment are expected to be substantial. The Task Force also offers advice on how to invest tax revenues, implement the plan, and select from preferred developers/operators.

566.   Mooney, Bill. "Racing & Casinos in New Jersey." *Blood-Horse* 118 (5 December 1992): 5529-5534.

Describes the relationship between Atlantic City casinos and the area's horse racetracks. The Atlantic City Race Course, once one of the East Coast's best, literally shrunk in size because track acreage was sold for development. Wagering there is "barely a third" of the over $1.5 million bet everyday during the early 1960s. According to one study, New Jersey's lottery and casinos have caused a "56.8% loss in 'real dollars'" for the state's racing industry. This decrease, however, may be due to the ongoing decline in racing throughout the country. Now racetracks are recouping these losses by "slightly more than half" because of money made from simulcasting races to casinos for wagering there. Tables.

567.   Nevada. State Gaming Control Board. *Nevada Gaming Abstract*. Carson City, Nev.: The Board, 1972- . Annual publication.

Contains the combined financial information reported by nonrestricted Nevada gaming licensees grossing $1 million or more in revenue. In the 1994 edition (over 150 pages long), information is presented in the following sequence: combined balance sheets; combined income statements, both summary and in detail, for casino departments, room departments, food departments, and beverage departments; average numbers of employees; rates of room occupancy; per room per day statistics; gaming revenues per square foot; and ratios. Sections are broken down geographically; for example, in the second section, Clark County figures are divided into categories for the Las Vegas Strip, downtown Las Vegas, Laughlin, Boulder Strip, and the balance of the county.

568. New York City Council. Committee on Economic Development. *Exploring Legalized Casino Gambling and a Local Lottery for New York City, March 16, 1990: Report of the Committee on Economic Development.* Prepared by the Office of Policy and Research. New York: Council of the City of New York, 1990. 101 pp.

Studies the feasibility of introducing casino gaming and a New York City Lottery to raise badly needed revenues. Having analyzed revenues, tourism, marketing, employment, regulatory structure, crime, and social issues, the Commission concluded that casinos would be a desirable way to address the city's fiscal problems, and "gambling appears to be an idea whose time has come." A lottery is seen as a relatively inexpensive operation without the crime associated with casinos.

569. Parker, Robert E. *Job Creation and the Gaming Economic Development Strategy.* Prepared for the South West Social Science Association, New Orleans, Louisiana, 17-20 March 1993. University of Nevada, Las Vegas, Special Collections. 35 pp.

Examines the increased use of legalized gambling as a strategy for economic development and job creation and describes the economic impact gaming has had on Las Vegas. Types of jobs created by casino operations and salaries are discussed, along with some of the human and social consequences of gaming. Parker voices a cautionary note to communities considering gaming as a means of development. Bibliographical references.

570.   Peat, Marwick, Mitchell & Co. *Economic Impact of Legalized Casino Gambling in New York State and its Impact on Existing Forms of Gambling.* New York: Peat, Marwick, Mitchell & Co., 1981. 217 pp.

Analyzes the potential impacts of legalized casino gaming on the State of New York, including job creation, gaming revenues generated from residents and visitors, and the amount of tax revenues that the state could expect from such operations. The study concludes that the net impact of statewide casino gaming would be modest in total. Positive economic impact includes increased employment, taxes, and construction. The study also anticipates that horse racing, off track betting, the lottery, and Manhattan theaters would suffer from the presence of casinos.

571.   Phillips-Hymel, Sherry. *Louisiana Gaming: A State Budget Perspective.* Baton Rouge, La.: Louisiana Senate, Office of Fiscal Affairs and Policy Development, 13 May 1994. 150 pp.

Answers frequent questions about legalized gambling in Louisiana. The report begins with an introduction to the gaming industry in the United States and Louisiana; following sections separately cover casinos, Indian gaming, lotteries, riverboat gaming, and video poker. Each section first provides a nationwide perspective on the activity and then detailed information on how it operates in and affects Louisiana. The chapter on riverboats, for example, has tables which compare how different states regulate and tax riverboat casinos; the Louisiana portion looks at the state's regulations, licensing, and operating fees, disposition of those fees, and a variety of related statistics. The combination of United States comparisons and detailed Louisiana information makes this a very useful publication; it succinctly contains a wealth of valuable, well-presented information. Tables, maps, bibliographical references.

572.   Plein, Bill, comp. *Colorado Gaming Statistics: Central City, Black Hawk, Cripple Creek, October 1991-July 1993.* Denver, Colo.: Moore Commercial, 1993. Unpaged.

Compiles statistics from the Colorado Department of Revenue, Division of Gaming Monthly Statistics. Adjusted gross proceeds from casinos and individual games are graphed over a thirty-one month period. The number of casinos operating in each area and the market share of each municipality are also tracked. Copies of newspaper articles that discuss gaming in Colorado and provide tourism figures for Denver are also provided. Tables.

573.   Popkin, James, and Katia Hetter. "America's Gambling Craze." *U.S. News & World Report* 116 (14 March 1994): 42-43, 46.

Examines the rapid growth of legalized gambling in the United States. The authors first discuss how attitudes towards gambling have changed dramatically since Nevada first legalized it in 1931 and note that "Americans legally wagered $330 billion in 1992—a 1,800 percent increase over 1976." They argue that governments supporting gambling as an economic development tool may discover revenues will not be nearly as large as expected. In one project, a researcher analyzed the economic impact studies fourteen government agencies "relied upon before deciding to embrace casino gambling . . . most were written with a pro-industry spin and only four were balanced and factored in gambling's hidden costs." Casinos, for example, take money from other parts of local economies, and their profits decrease dramatically when competition appears in nearby areas. Sidebars provide some statistics showing how gambling is "invading the nation" and how casinos stack the odds.

574.   Raimondo, Henry J. *Economics of State and Local Government*. New York: Praeger, 1992. 271 pp.

Explains why states and local governments implement user charges and gambling to increase revenues. In chapter 11, pages 205-217, Nontax Revenues: User Charges and Gambling Revenues, the author states that nontax revenues gained popularity because of "the success of the tax limitation movement" and the ten-year decline in federal aid to local governments. In the section on gambling, he looks at the growth of legalization, profiles gambling revenues, and covers the pros and cons of state-sponsored lotteries. His conclusion notes that some think gambling is a "painless tax" while others "see the claim of abundant gambling revenues as overblown," particularly when administrative costs are considered. Also, "equity takes a blow" because gambling revenues are regressive. Tables, bibliographical references, index.

575.   Reed, Betsy. "America's New Addiction: How the Gaming Industry Is Seducing the States." *Dollars and Sense* 194 (July 1994): 18-21, 41-42.

Argues that industry promoters greatly exaggerate the economic benefits of legalized gambling. Using Atlantic City as an example, Reed highlights the negative effects gambling can have on communities. She notes, for example, that casinos there did little for the city's unemployment rate because workers moved in from other areas. Casinos took business from other tourist-oriented establishments, "a phenomenon economists call 'cannibalization.'" Money local residents spend on gambling is money not spent on other goods and services, which is one of several negative multiplier effects. Also, developers seldom address the costs incurred by the related increases in crime and compulsive gambling. Reed concludes that legalization creates an instant dependency when governments rely on it for revenue; opponents fear that the "gambling industry lobby, formidable even before legalization, will become virtually invincible once such dependence is in place." Includes a sidebar on the growth of Indian gaming.

576.   Restrepo, John. "Fiscal Impact Analysis: Assessing the Public Cost of Casino Development." *Casino Journal* 7 (November 1994): 38.

Describes how Fiscal Impact Analysis (FIA) is an important factor for jurisdictions considering gaming. FIAs focus on assessing public service costs associated with casino operations. Public service providers include municipalities, library districts, school districts, and utility districts.

577.   Restrepo, John, and Norman A. Kur.   "Assessing the Economic Impact of a Casino Resort." *Casino Journal* 7 (October 1994): 30, 67.

Explains how Economic Impact Analysis (EIA) works and how important EIA reports are in opening gaming in new jurisdictions. EIAs assess the construction and operational phases of a casino project. A good EIA will illuminate the full economic benefit of a casino project, making it more attractive to host jurisdictions.

578.   Rich, Wilbur C. "The Politics of Casino Gambling Detroit Style." *Urban Affairs Quarterly* 26 (December 1990): 274-298.

Investigates the success of Detroit's 1988 anti-casino campaign and its implications for the city. After a review of studies on gambling as an economic development tool, Rich describes Detroit's economy and high unemployment rates and why casinos were considered an attractive solution. Opponents, organized early in the campaign, objected on moral grounds and, citing Atlantic City's experience, stressed concerns about how casinos would ruin Detroit's image and cause increases in organized crime. An analysis of voting behavior and patterns indicates that for religious and economic reasons, the city's working class were instrumental in this defeat because they viewed "themselves as defenders of social norms." Tables, bibliographical references.

579.   Roehl, W.S. "Gambling as a Tourist Attraction: Trends and Issues for the 21st Century." In *Tourism: The State of the Art*, edited by A. V. Seaton. Chichester, England and New York: John Wiley & Sons, 1994. 867 pp.

Analyzes the relationship between casinos and tourism. In "Gambling as a Tourist Attraction: Trends and Issues for the 21st Century," chapter 16, pages 156-168, Roehl first notes "gambling has long been recognized as a tourist attraction." He then looks at how casinos spread, particularly in Australia and the United States, describes how European and American approaches to casinos and tourism differ and identifies why tourists gamble. The section on the social costs of gambling looks at crime, the "equity of casino taxes on residents," underage gambling, and the "impact of casino tourism on the host community." Included are results of a study that compared the social effects of tourism in Florida and Nevada. He concludes that "tourism researchers have not considered casino tourism part of the field" and stresses that the following issues need to be addressed: taxation equity issues; social impacts; economic impacts; casino tourism and "traveler decision making"; public policy; and competition. Citations in the text and bibliography refer to important works researchers should consult and are as useful as the information the chapter contains. Tables, bibliographical references.

580.   Ryan, Timothy P., Patricia J. Connor, and Janet F. Speyrer, Division of Business and Economic Research, University of New Orleans. *The Impact of Casino Gambling in New Orleans*. N.p., 1990. University of Nevada, Las Vegas, Special Collections. 105 pp.
        Predicts the social and economic impact of casino gambling on the New Orleans area. This study looks at the possible implications of three different casino scenarios: one European-style casino (limited to table games only, no slot machines or video poker); one 100,000 square foot state-owned and privately operated Las Vegas-style casino; and unlimited casino gaming similar to what exists in Las Vegas and Atlantic City. The authors conclude that the benefits of casino gaming include jobs, increased spending, and increased tax revenues. Costs are not easy to quantify, but include increased crime, deterioration of the business climate, increased compulsive gambling, increased prostitution, increased transience, increased political corruption, and exposure of the young to unsavory practices. Additionally, many of the new jobs created could go to outsiders.

581.   Santos, Hubert J. and Hope C. Seeley. *Casino Gambling in Connecticut: Jobs, Revenue and Entertainment: Report to the Casino Gambling Task Force*. Hartford, Conn.: Santos, Peck & Smith, 1992. Various pagings.

Contains transcripts from the Connecticut Casino Task Force Invitational Forum where industry officials from major gaming concerns, government regulators and economists, mental health officials, and others spoke on the economic benefits and social costs of urban casinos. The report also includes drawings of casinos proposed by Mirage Resorts and Harrah's, salary and other labor information, a report on organized crime, and a summary of Nevada's and New Jersey's casino regulatory systems.

582. Schaeffer, Glenn. *How Does Nevada Compete?* University of Nevada, Las Vegas, Special Collections. 1991. 10 pp.

Provides the text of Schaeffer's speech to the Nevada Interim Legislative Committee on Gaming, October 1991. He states that Las Vegas enjoys a competitive advantage over other tourist destinations for the following reasons: location and proximity to Los Angeles and the Pacific Rim, efficient government regulation of the casino industry, low taxes, an increased appetite for entertainment as a consumer category, and the competitive price of the Las Vegas experience. Since Schaeffer is president of Circus Circus Enterprises, Inc., the text provides insight into this highly successful company's strategic focus.

583. Shonkwiler, J.S. "Assessing the Impact of Atlantic City Casinos on Nevada Gaming Revenues." *Atlantic Economic Journal* 21 (June 1993): 50-61.

Uses a "dynamic unobserved components time series model" to investigate how Atlantic City casinos have affected Nevada's gross taxable gaming revenues. After noting how heavily Nevada depends on gaming, Shonkwiler adds that industry prospects there are uncertain due to the recent proliferation of legalized gambling elsewhere. He provides background information on both areas and then explains that his research is "focused on constructing a variable to account for gambling expenditures foregone in Nevada" because people can now gamble in New Jersey. This article includes "modeling considerations" and an empirical model for the research. He concludes that "by 1985 the impact of Atlantic

City casinos reached an apparently stable level of reducing Nevada gaming revenues by about 10 to 12 percent," and "interregional effects are not necessarily proportional to distance nor spread contiguously." Charts, bibliographical references.

584.   Simurda, Stephen J. "When Gambling Comes to Town." *Columbia Journalism Review* 32 (January 1994): 36-38.
        Instructs journalists on how to write about legalized gambling. After reviewing the industry's rapid growth and calling it "one of the biggest local stories of the decade," Simurda says that writing about gambling may be very confusing and difficult. Most journalists lack the "technical expertise" required, and issues are complicated and usually exaggerated. He urges reporters to thoroughly research gambling proposals, obtain a "variety of opinions," identify "financial conflicts," evaluate the "economic benefits" and "social costs," and, finally, understand regulatory needs and processes. He stresses that "journalists should not forget that they may be the only ones able to cast a skeptical eye" on plans to implement gambling.

585.   Sternleib, George, and James W. Hughs. *The Atlantic City Gamble.* Cambridge, Mass.: Harvard University Press, 1983. 215 pp.
        Looks at the promise and reality of casino gaming activities in Atlantic City. Sternleib and Hughs illuminate the social and economic problems that betray the hopes for a revitalized community. Since the introduction of gaming, crime has exploded, tax revenues have been swallowed by the industry's need for municipal services and regulation, housing costs have increased beyond the means of the residents, and jobs have gone to people living outside the city. At the conclusion of this thorough analysis, the authors give detailed suggestions on how other jurisdictions might benefit from Atlantic City's experience. Bibliographical references, index.

586.   Stokowski, Patricia A. "The Colorado Gambling Boom: An Experiment in Rural Community Development." *Small Town* 22 (May-June 1992): 12-19.

Describes how implementing gambling for economic development affected two small adjacent Colorado communities. Central City and Black Hawk were two of the state's oldest mining towns, and "history has shown that eventual decline and hard times are an inseparable part of resource-dependent" areas, because the "resource runs out." After turning to gambling, change happened rapidly; massive construction projects and a real estate boom occurred before the first casinos opened. While revenues, job opportunities, and tourism dramatically increased, town residents agree that these gains "have come at the expense of the county's quality of life." There are now more crimes, traffic, and alcohol-related deaths, and many residents left the area. Stokowski wonders if small communities really benefit from such changes; also, can they "maintain enough stability during this period of rapid growth to provide a coherent vision and planning agenda" when the ever expanding gambling industry asserts its force? Chart, illustrations.

587.   Stokowski, Patricia A. "Undesirable Lag Effects in Tourist Destination Development: A Colorado Case Study." *Journal of Travel Research* 32 (Fall 1993): 35-41.

Explains how tourism's benefits do not always follow expected time frames. Stokowski "introduces the term 'lag effects' to describe outcomes of community tourism development processes that lag behind anticipated goals." The implementation of casinos in two small Colorado towns, Central City and Black Hawk, illustrates how this development affected the "social and institutional organization of community life." After reviewing the literature on tourism planning and describing these towns, Stokowski lists the chronology of events from the initial proposal to the one-year anniversary of opened casinos. Suggestions on how to reduce negative lag effects follows, and she concludes that they "are likely to appear in social and human services, which trail economic benefits." She finally urges everyone involved in such development to carefully plan and manage "the temporal problems of growth impacts." Tables, bibliographical references.

588.   Sutphen, Sandra, Ronald M. Grant, and Barbara Ball. "Upping the Ante: Gambling as a Revenue Source for Local Governments." *Southeastern Political Review* 22 (March 1994): 77-95.
        Examines effects of California poker clubs on area revenues and crime rates. The authors first note that many cities are either exploring or implementing various forms of legalized gambling to raise revenues; California law, for example, allows municipalities to establish poker card clubs. They studied these clubs in five Los Angeles County cities over a ten-year period to determine if this revenue is stable or if it grows and if they cause increased crime. While results indicate that the clubs are "a relatively recession-proof source of income," their data does not prove that "revenues are stable and predictable" and increase at regular and expected rates. There was no correlation between poker clubs and increasing crime rates. Also interesting is the brief description of motivations for such gambling; poker combines chance and skill, and since it takes place "in groups, gamblers develop a social world which provides support, friendship and stability" in a neighborhood setting. Tables, bibliographical references.

589.   Taylor, Gary. "Gaming Industry a Legal Jackpot." *National Law Journal* 16 (28 February 1994): 1, 38-39.
        Explains how the growth of the gaming industry benefits lawyers. Taylor reviews the rapid growth of gambling throughout the United States, particularly in the Southeast, and interviews several attorneys who have established lucrative practices representing industry companies. One lawyer, for example, "parlayed his knowledge of administrative law into a gaming practice." Since casino operators "encounter a fair share of litigation during all phases of development," there is also an "an ongoing, steady volume of work" for attorneys who challenge industry operators on such issues as labor relations

and environmental matters. This article describes how the benefits of economic development can spread.

590. Thompson, William Norman. *Gambling as a Growth Industry in Tourism: A Nevada Perspective.* University of Nevada, Las Vegas, Special Collections. 1992. 11 pp.

Considers Nevada's disappearing casino monopoly vis-à-vis the rise of Indian gaming, riverboats, video lottery terminals, Canadian developments, and limited stakes casinos licensed by Colorado and South Dakota. Thompson uses the precipitous decline of Detroit and the American automobile industry as a model for examining Nevada's vulnerability to external competition, concluding that the "challenges of competition can be met" and that "certainly Nevada is not doomed to become another Detroit." Ironically, Detroit may become another Las Vegas with its recent venture into casino gaming.

591. Thompson, William Norman. *Legalized Gambling, Tourism, Economic Development: Inputs and Outputs, Stupid.* University of Nevada, Las Vegas, Special Collections. 1993. 33 pp.

Explores factors that have had a positive influence on recent gambling legalization campaigns in the United States. The single most important factor in the proliferation of gaming is the economic downturn of the late 1980s and concomitant budgetary problems experienced by state and local governments. Thompson anticipates that casinos will "be in every corner of the land" by the end of the century.

592. U.S. Congress. House. Committee on Small Business. *The National Impact of Casino Gambling: Hearing Before the Committee on Small Business.* 103rd Cong., 2nd sess., 21 September 1994. 165 pp.

Covers testimony from the House Committee on Small Business hearing on how casinos are affecting the United States. Citing a *New York Times Magazine* cover story on gambling's recent, amazing growth (see entry 38), Chair John LaFalce explained that the committee would examine the benefits and costs to both individual communities and the country as a whole. After stating "there is no question that casinos generate revenue, not only for casino owners but for local and state government," he notes that they will focus on four major areas of interest: gaming's impact on small businesses; the economic well-being of communities nationwide; gambling addiction; and crime. The following witnesses provided a wide variety of testimony: Nevada Representative James Bilbray; Webster Franklin, director, Chamber of Commerce, Tunica County, Mississippi; Robert Goodman, director of the U.S. Gambling Study; Earl Grinols, Economics professor from the University of Illinois; and Valerie Lorenz, director of the Compulsive Gambling Center, Baltimore, Maryland. The appendices include prepared statements by these individuals and letters from a diverse group of people involved with the industry in some way, including Indian gaming.

593.   *Wagering in Illinois: A Report Updating the Economic Impact of Gambling Activities.* Springfield, Ill.: Illinois Economic and Fiscal Commission, January 1994. 35 pp.

Covers the economic effects of gambling in Illinois. Separate chapters look at the impact of competition, horse racing, the lottery, and riverboat gambling. The riverboat section has a map outline showing operation locations followed by text, charts, and tables with statistics on each boat's state and local share of wagering and admission taxes for 1992 and 1993 and related eating and drinking sales taxes for site locations. Appendix B has more detailed charts for each riverboat that list monthly admissions, adjusted gross receipts, state shares of revenue, local shares of revenue, and table, slot, and total drop figures from December 1991, through July 1993. The Commission concludes that revenue from gaming will probably increase in the short term as riverboat gambling becomes fully implemented. As Illinois reaches its saturation point, however, these revenues will likely slow and level off due to competition among various forms of gambling and gambling opportunities in surrounding states. See entry 641 for the first edition of this report. Charts, tables.

594.   Walkoff, Neil E. *The Impact of Legalized Casino Gambling on Regional Economic Development: The Case of Atlantic City*. Master's thesis, University of Nevada, Las Vegas, 1993. University of Nevada, Las Vegas, Special Collections. 50 pp.

    Illustrates the economic benefits and costs that are associated with the introduction of casinos into a community. Walkoff shows that casino gaming in Atlantic City was hugely successful in fiscal terms and that every goal set by the city was surpassed, including 65,000 new jobs, $5 billion invested, hundreds of millions of dollars in tax revenues, and over $200 million in revenues for the aged and disabled. However, social costs have been severe, including the dislocation of residents and small businesses due to skyrocketing real estate values. As a result, apart from the casinos, Atlantic City remains largely abandoned or condemned.

595.   Warker, Kimberly J. *Casino Gambling as Urban Development: A Case Study of the Political Economy of Atlantic City, New Jersey*. Ph.D. dissertation, University of Delaware, 1988. University of Nevada, Las Vegas, Special Collections. 341 pp.

    Analyzes the impact gaming has had on Atlantic City and New Jersey. Fiscally, casinos have been a windfall for the state treasury and local coffers, and New Jersey residents seem to favor continuation of the state gaming policy. However, the distribution of casino benefits does not include Atlantic City's residential base. New jobs went to outsiders, a quarter of Atlantic City's residents were forced to move by rising property values, and one-third of the community's housing stock has been demolished. There are more vacant stores than before gaming was introduced, and serious crime has doubled.

596. Worsnop, Richard L. "Lucrative Lure of Lotteries and Gambling." *Editorial Research Reports* 1 (9 November 1990): 634-647.

Examines both sides of the debate on implementing government-sanctioned legalized gambling to raise revenues. The author explains why it is popularly considered a "voluntary tax," how it historically goes through cycles of acceptance and prohibition, why it may not be a reliable revenue source, and how it can adversely affect the poor and result in problem gamblers. Worsnop's discussion includes Indian gaming, riverboat gaming, the computerization of gambling equipment, and the possibility of a national lottery to reduce the federal deficit. Tables, bibliographical references.

SUPPLEMENTAL MATERIALS

597. Barron, James. "States Sell Chances for Gold as a Rush Turns to Stampede." *New York Times* (28 May 1989): 1, 24 (L).

598. Barrows, Jim. "Welcome to Las Vegas, the 'Family' Entertainment Capital of the World!" *Nevada Business Journal* 8 (November/December 1993): 8-11.

599. Boulard, Garry. "New Orleans Decides to Take Casino Route to Get in the Black." *Christian Science Monitor* 86 (22 July 1994): 3.

600. Bradley, Ann. "Gambling Project Proposed in Chicago To Help Generate Capital for Schools." *Education Week* 12 (9 June 1993): 22.

601. Bryan, Richard H. "Gaming and Diversification: Forces That Will Shape Nevada's Future." *Nevada Public Affairs Review* 2 (1986): 4-6.

602. Busse, Tim. "Casinos: The Impact on Tourism Still Unclear." *Minnesota Cities* 79 (March 1994): 13.

603.   Campbell, Jenny. "Endless Gaming Thrives in Atlantic City." *Hotel & Motel Management* 208 (16 August 1993): 28, 35.

604.   Chicago. Mayor's Gaming Commission, Nicholas J. Bua, Chair. *Summary of Report to the Mayor.* Chicago: The Commission, 1992. 24 pp.

605.   Coleman, Calmetta. "Is Casino Gambling in West Baden, Ind., Answer to a Prayer?" *Wall Street Journal* (26 August 1994): A1.

606.   Cooper, Helene. "Mixed Blessing: Southern Town's Past Haunts Golden Future From Gambling Riches." *Wall Street Journal* (22 June 1994): A1.

607.   Dao, James. "Comptroller's Report Questions Benefits From Casino Gambling." *New York Times* (3 April 1994): 24 (L).

608.   Eadington, William R. "Casinos Are No Economic Cure-All." *New York Times* (13 June 1993): F13 (L).

609.   Eadington, William R., and John Rosecrance. "Betting on the Future: Gambling in Nevada and Elsewhere." *Nevada Public Affairs Review* 2 (1986): 1-3.

610.   Francis, David R. "States May Not Find Jackpot in Gambling." *Christian Science Monitor* 86 (11 March 1994): 11.

611.   "Gambling Stirs Rhode Island Debate." *New York Times* (16 November 1992): A13 (L).

612.   Glastris, Paul, and Andrew Bates. "The Fool's Gold in Gambling: States Learn How Hard It Is to Control Gaming." *U.S. News & World Report* 110 (1 April 1991): 22-23.

613.   Greenberg, Pam. "Gambling: Some States Bet on Big Returns." *Fiscal Letter* 13 (November/December 1991): 9-11.

614.   Hansen, Karen, and Megan Seacord. "A 20th Century Gold Rush." *State Legislatures* 17 (March 1991): 14-16, 18, 20.

615.   Hayes, Jack. "Restaurateurs Credited With Win as Gaming Bills Go Bust." *Nation's Restaurant News* 28 (21 November 1994): 1, 4.

616.   Judson, George. "Rowland Says a Casino Will Revive Bridgeport." *New York Times* (7 December 1994): B7 (L).

617.   Katz, Jeffrey L. "Raising the Stakes on Legal Gambling." *Governing* 3 (February 1991): 17, 19-20.

618.   King, Wayne. "Casinos' Unkept Promise Turns 15: Atlantic City Wants to Stop Being Gambling's Bad Example." *New York Times* (22 June 1993): B1, B5 (L).

619.   Madden, Michael K. *Economic and Fiscal Impacts Associated with the First Year of Gaming: Deadwood, South Dakota.* Commissioned by the South Dakota Commission on Gaming. Pierre, S. Dak.: South Dakota Commission on Gaming, 1992. 48 pp.

620.   McGowan, Richard. *State Lotteries and Legalized Gambling: Painless Revenue or Painful Mirage.* Westport, Conn.: Praeger, 1994. 171 pp.

621.   New Jersey. Atlantic County Division of Economic Development, and G.M. Slusher. *The Casino Gaming Industry and its Impact on Southern New Jersey.* Atlantic City, N.J., 1991. 31 pp.

622.   Nordheimer, Jon. "Atlantic City Seeks to Lure Non-Gamblers: Casinos Feeling Threat of Rivals in Region." *New York Times* (10 April 1994): 37, 44 (L).

623.   Nordheimer, Jon. "In the Shadows of the Casinos: After Streak of Prosperity, Brigantine, N.J., Hits a Slump." *New York Times* (27 January 1994): B6 (L).

624.   Oleck, Joan. "Are They Gambling With Your Future?" *Restaurant Business* 91 (20 November 1992): 110, 112-114, 119-120.

625.   Passell, Peter. "The False Promise of Development by Casino." *New York Times* (12 June 1994): sec. 3, p. 5 (L).

626.   Peirce, Neal R. "Casinos—Urban America's Last Resort? Gaming, Which Siphons Off Nearly $300 Billion of Americans' Wealth and Potential Savings Each Year, Has Come to the Cities." *National Journal* 24 (1 August 1992): 1798.

627.   Perlman, Ellen. "A Taxing Problem: New Orleans Fails To Find New Revenue." *City & State* (6 December 1993): 3, 21.

628.   "Rolling Dice for Taxes." *Christian Science Monitor* 86 (12 April 1994): 18.

629.   Ross, Elizabeth. "Connecticut Links Casino Proposal to State Revenues, Job Creation." *Christian Science Monitor* 85 (26 January 1993): 9.

630.   Rubenstein, Joseph. "Casino Gambling in Atlantic City: Issues of Development and Redevelopment." *Annals of the American Academy of Political and Social Science* 474 (July 1986): 61-71.

631.   Rychlak, Ronald J. "Lotteries, Revenues and Social Costs: A Historical Examination of State-Sponsored

Gambling." *Boston College Law Review* 34 (December 1992): 11-81.

632.   Salomon, Alan. "Gambling Is Winner for Mississippi." *Advertising Age* 65 (18 July 1994): 10.

633.   Serwer, Andrew E. "Welcome to the New Las Vegas." *Fortune* 129 (24 January 1994): 105.

634.   Shear, Jeff. "States Hope to Reap Even Bigger Kitties." *Insight* 7 (23 September 1991): 22-24.

635.   Smith, James F. "Las Vegas East? Atlantic City Ten Years After the Referendum." *Nevada Public Affairs Review* 2 (1986): 50-55.

636.   "States Are Cashing in on the Wages of Sin . . . Cigarettes, Drugs, and Gambling." *From the State Capitals: The Outlook.* 48 (11 April 1994): 1-4.

637.   Sylvester, Kathleen. "Casinomania: Jackpot Fever." *Governing* 6 (December 1992): 22-26.

638.   Sympson, Ron. "Place Your Bets: Casino Gambling Is on Such a Roll That Some Towns Figure They'll Have to Okay It Just to Remain Competitive." *Restaurant Business* 93 (1 November 1994): 54-67.

639.   Teske, Paul, and Bela Sur. "Winners and Losers: Politics, Casino Gambling, and Development in Atlantic City." *Policy Studies Review* 10 (Spring/Summer 1991): 130-137.

640.   U.S. Congress. House. Committee on Small Business. Subcommittee on Procurement, Tourism, and Rural Development. *The Impact of Economic Growth on Small Businesses in Las Vegas: Hearing Before the Subcommittee on Procurement, Tourism and Rural Development of the Committee on Small Business, House of*

Representatives. 102 Cong., 1st sess., Las Vegas, Nevada, 17 June 1991. 111 pp.

641. *Wagering in Illinois: A Report on the Economic Impact of Existing and Proposed Forms of Gambling.* Springfield, Ill.: Illinois Economic and Fiscal Commission, June 1992. 115 pp.

642. Walkup, Carolyn. "Casinos Trump Operators in Gaming Towns: Jackpot Hopes Bottom Out as Diners Flock to Gambling Venues." *Nation's Restaurant News* 28 (8 August 1994): 1, 63.

643. Witcher, Gregory. "Would Casinos Reinvigorate Detroit or Ruin It? Mayor and Some of His Strongest Backers Split." *Wall Street Journal* (23 May 1988): 42.

644. Zeller, Laurie Hirschfield. "Distressed Cities Increasingly Bank on Casino Gambling." *National Civic Review* 82 (Summer 1993): 302-304.

645. Zimmerman, Kevin. "Iowa Gambles on Showbiz Future." *Variety* 343 (3 June 1991): 65, 68.

SECTION F

Casinos and American Society

Gambling and casinos are phenomena rooted in the American experience, and their proliferation has sparked considerable study and debate. Moral and ethical concerns, values, quality of life issues, mental health considerations, and a host of other factors crowd the discussion on casinos in American society. This section covers the history of gambling and casinos and the social issues raised by casinos and legalized gambling. Among the materials listed are books and journal articles written by social scientists, historians, mental health professionals, and theologians.

646. Aasved, Mikal J. *Don't Bet the Farm: The Expansion of Legalized Gambling and Growing Bankruptcy Rates in Minnesota: Is there a Link?* St. Paul, Minn.: M.J. Aasved, 1991. 41 pp.
    Traces the development of legal gaming activities in Minnesota as a possible explanation for steadily increasing bankruptcy rates. Though unable to establish a direct statistical correlation, interviews with consumer credit counselors, bankruptcy attorneys, and other professionals suggest that there is a relationship. Aasved also finds that gambling-related financial problems are not restricted to the lower socioeconomic class and that most reported gambling problems are related to pulltabs.

647. Aasved, Mikal J., and James M. Schaefer. *Deal Me In! Gambling and its Impacts in a Central Minnesota Vacation Community.* St. Paul, Minn.: Minnesota Department of Human Services, Mental Health Division, August 1992. 87 pp.

Reports on a study conducted to identify the effects of legalized gambling on Brainerd, Baxter, and Willmar, Minnesota. This analysis covers research methods, types and sites of available gambling, players' preferences, economic and social effects, and community attitudes. Recommendations stress that the public should be informed of the amounts of gambling losses; Indian casinos should voluntarily publicize their profits; sources of money such as cash machines should be limited near gambling sites; problem gambling awareness and prevention efforts should receive publicity and support; and compulsive gamblers should have ready access to groups or activities that can help them with their problems. Tables, bibliographical references.

648. Abbott, Douglas A., and Sheran L. Cramer. "Gambling Attitudes and Participation: A Midwestern Survey." *Journal of Gambling Studies* 9 (Fall 1993): 247-263.

Investigates the extent of gambling in Nebraska and assesses "differences in gambling attitudes and behavior between men and women, in various income groups, living in rural and urban areas." The study's results indicate that "gambling was pervasive in all segments of this Midwestern sample; however, men spent more than women and urban residents wagered more than rural residents." Although most respondents viewed gambling as a harmless form of recreation, it was determined that the poor spent the largest percentage of their incomes on it. A tenth of the gamblers questioned reported family problems caused by gambling.

649. Abt, Vicki, and Douglas J. McDowell. "Does the Press Cover Gambling Issues Poorly? Evidence From a Newspaper Content Analysis." *Sociology and Social Research* 71 (April 1987): 193-197.

Argues that newspapers shape "public perceptions of gambling, often in misleading ways." Abt and McDowell first look at the growth of commercial gambling and explain how "all modern campaigns for gambling legalization have been played out in the press." They state that newspapers do not adequately cover gambling and complete a content analysis of all 1985 issues of the *Philadelphia Inquirer* as evidence. The newspaper, one of the country's largest and most respected, hardly covered gambling at all, although Philadelphia is close to Atlantic City casinos which were having a record-breaking year. They conclude that newspaper coverage of gambling "is characterized by inconsistencies, superficial focal points, and much incomplete and missing information." The resulting public confusion adversely affects the formation of sound public policy. Tables, bibliographical references.

650.   Abt, Vicki, James F. Smith, and Eugene Martin Christiansen. *The Business of Risk: Commercial Gambling in Mainstream America*. Lawrence, Kans.: University Press of Kansas, 1985. 286 pp.

Examines the history and sociological, psychological, economic, and political structures of legalized, commercial gambling in the United States. Chapters cover such topics as the controversy surrounding gambling; a discussion on state lotteries, casinos, and racetrack betting; an "explanation of gambling behavior"; and an analysis of gambling as a social institution and its relationship to American values. Gambling is a "major American leisure industry" comprised of private corporations and state governments which have a "guaranteed advantage" over the players; odds always favor the operators. As it spreads, gambling is "being changed into routine behaviors that serve economic ends for the operators and the state, rather than leisure purposes for the individual." By not addressing this inequity, public policy seriously ignores the needs of the "public good." Tables, bibliographical references, index.

651.   Abt, Vicki, and Martin C. McGurrin. "Commercial Gambling and Values in American Society: The Social Construction of Risk." *Journal of Gambling Studies* 8 (Winter 1992): 413-420.

Argues that public policy should consider gambling as a "culturally defined and socially managed form of risk-taking behavior," or recreational play, which alleviates everyday stress. Positive and negative perceptions of gambling are based on the cultural or "social construction of reality" and reflect "conflicts in American values." This sociological analysis shows how gambling fits into American culture and is a "caricature" of deep-seated values, concepts little explored in other discussions on the subject. Bibliographical references.

652.   Abt, Vicki, Martin C. McGurrin, and James F. Smith. "Gambling: The Misunderstood Art." *Leisure Sciences* 6 (1984): 205-220.
        Proposes that gambling shares elements found in "acceptable" sports, including established rules, regulatory commissions, standardized equipment, and sociability. The authors use psychological and sociological principles to analyze the social functions of casino and racetrack gambling. Arguing that this framework achieves objective results, they conclude that gambling is not a socially deviant activity, a view commonly held by social scientists; instead, it provides recreation for players and generally reflects this country's mainstream culture.

653.   Alcamo, John. *Atlantic City: Behind the Tables.* Grand Rapids, Mich.: Gollehon, 1991. 233 pp.
        Gives an insider's account of the action in Atlantic City, rich with the fun and excitement that attracts so many people to casinos. A professional musician and industry employee, Alcamo recounts stories of high rollers, big deals, casino executives, dealers, and some very interesting players. Light reading.

654.   Arcuri, Alan F., David Lester, and Franklin O. Smith. "Shaping Adolescent Gambling Behavior." *Adolescence* 20 (Winter 1985): 935-938.
        Reports survey results which found that sixty-four percent of the student body at one Atlantic City high school have gambled in the city's casinos. Some students were regular customers who used allowances, shoplifting, and drug sales proceeds to fund their gambling. The authors stress that compulsive gambling is a major threat to these

teenagers and question the "extent to which society encourages and facilitates pathological behaviors." Bibliographical references.

655.   Asbury, Herbert. *Sucker's Progress: An Informal History of Gambling in America from the Colonies to Canfield.* New York: Dodd, Mead, 1938. 493 pp.

Reflects on the development of commercial gambling halls and riverboat gambling in the United States from 18th-century New Orleans to early 20th-century New York. The eras of John Morrissey (1831-78), politician and "boss of gambling in New York," and Richard A. Canfield (1855-1914), "the richest professional gambler in all history," are highlighted. This classic work also provides historical background and how-to-play and how-to-cheat information on many popular games, including faro, poker, craps, policy, roulette, loo, keno, pitch, three-card monte, chuck-a-luck, and banco. Bibliographical references, index.

656.   Atkins, Joe. "The States' Bad Bet." *Christianity Today* 35 (25 November 1991): 16-18.

Traces recent spread of legalized gambling to improve local economies. While quoting proponents' and opponents' viewpoints, the author notes that there is "only one outcome guaranteed: someone will lose." Shortfalls in lottery revenues, for example, adversely affected educational funding in California and Florida; other negatives include increased political corruption, crime, and competition for gamblers' dollars. More importantly, perhaps, states are forcing people to be "losers," and as one Christian leader says, it is a "moral problem that is unconscionable."

657.   Beare, Margaret E., Wanda Jamieson, and Anne Gilmore. *Legalized Gaming in Canada.* N.p., 1988. University of Nevada, Las Vegas, Special Collections. 357 pp.

Provides a province-by-province history and assessment of contemporary gambling in Canada. Gaming operations, regulatory structures, and lotteries are covered.

The authors' concerns include insufficient regulation, lack of authority, and weak auditing requirements.

658. Bell, Raymond C. *Moral Views of Gambling Promulgated by Major American Religious Bodies.* Prepared for the Commission on the Review of the National Policy Toward Gambling. N.p., 1974. University of Nevada, Las Vegas, Special Collections. 85 pp.

Offers a preliminary study of the ethical aspects of gambling intended to lend direction to further study, particularly as it applies to the issue of legalization. Bell concludes that while Roman Catholic, Jewish, and Eastern Orthodox religious bodies have relaxed attitudes towards gambling, Protestant opposition to gambling is strong and rooted in moral principle. As the largest of the religious bodies in the nation, the Protestant perspective carries considerable weight.

659. Berg, Charles A. "Gaming and Cities." *Minnesota Cities* 76 (November 1991): 6-11.

Presents a state legislator's views on legalizing gambling in Minnesota's cities. He urges communities opposing gambling to prevent it by law with a city council vote under *Minnesota Statutes* 349.213. Areas favoring gambling "should integrate it into the city's economic strategy," and may "enact more stringent regulation . . . than the state currently requires." After briefly discussing 1991 Minnesota legislation which clarified how the state's cities can regulate gambling, and gambling's beneficial and negative impacts, the author looks at the positive relationship between one town and a nearby Indian casino which made both groups winners.

660. Bergler, Edmund. *The Psychology of Gambling.* New York: Hill and Wang, 1957. Reprint. New York: International Universities Press, 1985. 224 pp.

Explores the psyche of the "neurotic sucker-gambler." The author's premise is that the compulsive gambler is a "neurotic with an unconscious wish to lose." It is a concept that Bergler pioneered in "The Psychology of the Gambler," *Imago* 22 (1936): 409-441 and attempts to substantiate here with clinical proof. Bergler is one of the most frequently cited psychoanalysts of all time. Index.

661. "Bet on It! How Americans Feel About Casino Gaming and Other Wagering." *Casino Journal* 7 (September 1994): 40-41.

Identifies public attitudes on gaming. This survey, conducted in 1994 for *Casino Journal* by Fabrizio, McLaughlin and Associates, breaks down results by age, race, sex, political affiliation, income, education, and religious affiliation. While 53.7 percent of all Americans approve of casino gaming, over 66 percent of younger respondents favor casinos. "Those most in favor of gaming overall were high-income, well-educated, Catholic males, under 65." Graphs.

662. Better Government Association. *The Better Government Association's Concurring Report on Speaker Madigan's Casino Gambling Task Force.* Chicago, Ill.: Better Government Association, 1993. 11 pp.

Calls for a state-wide referendum on whether or not to permit the opening of a casino in Chicago. This report provides commentary on revenue, crime, social costs, jobs, and organized criminal activity projections associated with the proposed Chicago casino-entertainment complex. Includes "The Incremental Economic Impact of Casino Gambling in Chicago" by Timothy P. Ryan.

663. *Better Government Association Staff White Paper: Casino Gambling in Chicago.* Chicago, Ill.: Better Government Association, October 1992. 126 pp. plus 18 appendices.

Argues that state and city officials are not considering the social and economic concerns a proposed Chicago casino raises. Association President William Lear and Executive Director J. Terrance Brunner state that the group cannot support the 1992 proposal because established city planning procedures were bypassed and important social issues are "not being addressed." The sections on social effects cover such topics as compulsive gambling, underage gambling and drinking, regressive taxation, and increasing crime and homelessness. Economic issues include casino taxation, employment, competition, market saturation, and the actual costs of the social problems listed above. The paper's text and several appendices contain a useful collection of statistics and information supporting the Association's position. Tables, bibliographical references.

664.   Bogert, Carroll. "Fool's Gold in Black Hawk?" *Newsweek* 123 (28 March 1994): 22-24.
        Analyzes the effects of casinos on Black Hawk, Colorado. One of three rural areas in Colorado with casinos, the town found legalized gambling caused many unexpected consequences. While Black Hawk now has "more money than it knows what to do with," crime, congestion, and noise pollution have greatly increased, and the town's atmosphere has dramatically changed. Powerful casinos' adverse effects on local government's autonomy and potential competition from casinos in nearby Central City are other major issues.

665.   Borg, Mary O., Paul M. Mason, and Stephen L. Shapiro. "The Incidence of Taxes on Casino Gambling: Exploiting the Tired and Poor." *American Journal of Economics and Sociology* 50 (July 1991): 323-332.
        Surveys "equity of taxes on casino gambling" using sample data from people who "either live in or have traveled to Las Vegas and Atlantic City." This article's data, equations, and variables correlate how much people spend on gambling to their income size. The authors conclude that such taxes are regressive because those with lower incomes gamble larger percentages of their incomes than individuals with higher incomes. When debating legalizing gambling, policy makers should understand that these taxes "place a proportionately heavier burden on low income groups." Tables, bibliographical references.

666.   Bybee, Shannon. "Problem Gambling: One View from the Gaming Industry Side." *Journal of Gambling Behavior* 4 (Winter 1988): 301-308.

Argues that the medical-based disease model using the label "compulsive gambling" denies individuals responsibility for their actions and places undue blame on casino operators. After noting that many "commercialized" activities, such as smoking and drinking, cause problems for some people, the author argues that casinos should not "bear the ultimate legal or moral responsibility" for this problem. Understanding that casino profits benefit the "public good" more than they benefit casino operators creates a better framework for analyzing this issue. He urges people concerned with problem gambling to work with a wide variety of other groups, including casino operators, to help find solutions. Bibliographical references.

667.   Cabot, Anthony. "Does Casino Gambling Have a Place in Society?" *Casino Journal* 7 (December 1994): 14.

Addresses the philosophical debate over gaming's place in society. Cabot readily concedes that casinos produce no useful product and serve merely as adult recreation. Gambling is an enjoyable pursuit that involves controlled risk that is unrelated to productive activity. It is similar to other recreational activities such as skiing, sky diving, or racing, with the exception that risk involved in gambling is economic, not physical. "The gaming industry is a responsible citizen if its customers leave after a few days of play, having experienced a pleasurable experience at a fair price."

668.   Callaway, Andrew, et al. *Assessing the Social Impacts of Gambling, as Perceived by Local Government and Agency Officials, on Permanent Residents of Black Hawk, Colorado.* Boulder, Colo.: Tourism Management Program, University of Colorado at Boulder, 1992. 34 pp.

Uses personal interviews and questionnaires to assess the social impacts of gambling in Black Hawk, Colorado. The study finds that with the disappearance of traditional gathering places and the conversion of the few existing local businesses into casinos, the small-town life of Black Hawk has vanished. Due to the growth of year-round tourism, the "residents' attitudes have quickly plummeted from euphoria to antagonism."

669.   Campbell, Collin S., and John Lowman, eds. *Gambling in Canada: Golden Goose or Trojan Horse? A Report from the First National Symposium on Lotteries and Gambling, May 1988.* Burnaby, B.C.: Simon Frasier University, School of Criminology, 1989. 417 pp.

Covers trends in gambling around the world, the history of regulatory agencies in Canada, gambling law and law enforcement, gambling behavior, casino development models, a comparison between gambling in Canada and Australia, and the potential social and economic benefits and costs of gambling. William Eadington, William Thompson, and John Dombrink are among the contributors to this volume. Bibliographical references.

670.   Caneday, Lowell, and Jeffrey Zeiger. "The Social, Economic, and Environmental Costs of Tourism to a Gaming Community as Perceived by Its Residents." *Journal of Travel Research* 30 (Fall 1991): 45-49.

Analyzes attitudes on tourism and its effects on Deadwood, South Dakota soon after casinos were legalized. The survey, which included people living within the city limits and people operating businesses in the area's historic district, assessed a wide variety of perceptions on such social, economic, and environmental topics as real estate availability and cost, traffic conditions, recreation availability and accessibility, police protection, air quality, and incidence of crime, alcoholism, and drug abuse. The authors found that a community's "character and reputation" change with "tourism generated by gambling"; individual attitudes vary depending on how personal lives are affected by such changes, either positive or negative; and "economic activity tends to be concentrated in the geographic vicinity of the gambling district." Tables, bibliographical references.

671.   Caro, Peter, et al. *Assessing the Social Impacts of Gambling, as Perceived by Local Government and Agency Officials, on Permanent Residents of Cripple Creek, Colorado.* Boulder, Colo.: Tourism Management Program, University of Colorado at Boulder, 1992. 34 pp.

Uses personal interviews and questionnaires to assess the social impacts of gambling in Cripple Creek, Colorado. The study suggests that gambling has provided a boost to the local economy, but traffic congestion, the loss of local services, and a more transient population have caused the sense of community to disappear. Year-round tourism was seen as beneficial; the study, however, was conducted before the residents had experienced a summer season with gaming.

672.   "Casinos Continue to Spread, Touted as 'Entertainment.'" *Bottom Line on Alcohol in Society* 15 (Summer 1994): 56-63.

Covers recent reports on the rapid growth and widespread acceptance of legalized gambling and the increase of addictive gambling in the United States. Increasing numbers of high school students are developing this problem due to the availability of gambling opportunities and peer pressure to participate. Casinos use many ploys to encourage customers frequently to spend more than intended. Such enticements as free drinks for gamblers exacerbate the problem since there appears to be a link between addictive behavior and alcoholism. The article argues that governments legalizing casinos have little regard for people destroyed by compulsive gambling.

673.   Chafetz, Henry. *Play the Devil: A History of Gambling in the United States from 1492 to 1955.* New York: Bonanza Books, 1960. 475 pp.

Recounts the tale of gambling in America and substantiates the notion that Americans will bet on anything. In exposing the nation's love-hate fascination with gambling, Chafetz provides the reader with an enjoyable experience and a wealth of information. *Play the Devil* covers gambling in America from the arrival of Columbus through the western expansion to the middle of this century. Bibliographical references, index.

674.   City of Vancouver, British Columbia. *City of Vancouver Casino Review: A Discussion Paper.* N.p., 1994.   University of Nevada, Las Vegas, Special Collections. 42 pp.

Responds to the March 1994 Vancouver City Council decision to consider introducing a major casino to the city's central waterfront. This paper was prepared to help citizens understand how a major casino may affect their community by addressing issues such as the city's image, business and tourism, jobs, problem gambling, crime, housing and real estate values, existing gaming, and municipal revenues and expenses. A list of gaming experts provided here is fraught with incorrect address information.

675.   Coggins, Ross, ed.   *The Gambling Menace.* Nashville, Tenn.: Broadman Press, 1966. 128 pp.

Identifies gambling as a "social evil," defines the Christian citizen's responsibility toward it, and suggests a plan of action to confront the menace. While strongly anti-gambling with religious overtones, contributions to this text are well written and researched. Bibliographical references.

676.   Connecticut. Task Force on Casino Gambling. *Final Report—Casino Gambling.* Hartford, Conn.: Connecticut General Assembly, Finance, Revenues and Bonding Committee, January 1993. Various pagings.

Presents results of legislative analysis on possible implementation of casino gambling in Connecticut. The majority report endorses casino gaming because it will create employment opportunities and boost state and local revenues. It also states that problems associated with casinos are exaggerated; crime and compulsive gambling, for example, can be controlled through effective planning. The opposing minority report stresses that a thorough, objective, and professional study must be done because many issues should be resolved, including the long-term impact of casinos, the effect of competition from the regional proliferation of casinos, the negative effects on existing businesses, the net effects on employment and the value of casino jobs, and the inherent costs of crime and problem gambling. Accompanying exhibits include a survey of business' attitudes towards gambling, discussion of related regulatory issues, and a 1989 New Jersey Gaming Enforcement Annual Report. Tables, bibliographical references.

677. Custer, Robert L., and Harry Milt. *When Luck Runs Out*. New York: Facts on File, 1985. 239 pp.
Offers a thorough examination of compulsive gambling and its treatment, describing the disorder, symptoms, stages of the disease, and how to treat it. A chapter on the female compulsive gambler is also provided. This work is highly useful to the compulsive gambler and his or her family, as well as the mental health professional. Custer, a psychiatrist, is among the most respected authorities on compulsive gambling in the world. Index.

678. Domestic and Foreign Ministry Society. *The Social, Economic and Environmental Consequences of Casino Gambling*. New York: Domestic and Foreign Ministry Society, 1994. 88 pp.
Provides an edited transcript of the Under the Glitz Conference, Four Queens Hotel, Las Vegas, Nevada, 1994. Nearly thirty presenters from academia, the environmental movement, industry, public service, and the clergy address key public policy issues from various perspectives. At issue is "whether revenue generated by the spread of legalized gambling is worth the social cost."

679. Dostoyevsky, Fyodor. *The Gambler*. Translated by Constance Garnett. New York: Heritage Press, 1967. 187 pp.
Paints a tragic picture of a young compulsive gambler. This novel, a self-portrait of the author, offers a deep and personal image of the afflicted that has been studied by Freud and many other social scientists interested in compulsive disorders.

680.   Drinan, Robert F. "Should Gambling Be Curbed?"
In *The Fractured Dream: America's Divisive Moral Choices.*
New York: Crossroad, 1991. 217 pp.
    Analyzes how legalized gambling creates a moral
conflict between American churches and government policy.
This chapter, pages 117-125, looks at the issue from a
religious viewpoint and stresses that governments are
exploiting citizens to increase revenues. After covering the
history of legalized lotteries, the author argues that the recent
growth in gambling legalization has occurred with little
comment from church leaders. He states that "the surge of
gambling may create such problems of addiction and
government hypocrisy that religious leaders may re-enter the
field." Index.

681.   Eadington, William R. "Impact of Casino Gambling
on the Community: Comment on Pizam and Poleka." *Annals
of Tourism Research* 13 (1986): 279-282.
    Responds to the Pizam and Poleka study, cited
below (see entry 738), praising the authors for creating a
foundation for how jurisdictions should "examine casinos as
a potential tool for economic development or revitalization."
Eadington stresses, however, that the study's focus on two
Massachusetts communities, where gambling would be
limited to a single complex in each town, does not reflect
locations where industry growth is expected and
encouraged. He also questions if surveys of area residents
are wholly valid, since public opinion tends to sensationalize
casinos and responses will be based on whether participants
believe the industry's impacts will directly "improve or
deteriorate one's present quality of life in that community."
He states that this is a very complicated issue which should
involve evaluation of a variety of information; citizen
surveys are just one important component. Bibliographical
references.

682.   Eadington, William R. *The Political Economy of the
Legal Casino Gaming Industry in the United States.* Paper
no. 84-1. Reno, Nev.: University of Nevada, Reno. Bureau
of Business and Economic Research, 1984. 27 pp.

Reports on the economic characteristics and social legitimacy of the casino industry in the United States. Pricing, marketing, and management strategies for casinos in Nevada and New Jersey are discussed. Social problems that can intensify as a result of gaming operations include political corruption, compulsive gambling, organized crime activity, prostitution, and loansharking. Eadington concludes that excess profitability allows for the extreme growth and expansion of the casino industry in Atlantic City and Nevada and that the sheer size of the industry in those jurisdictions creates substantial social costs. He suggests that locations interested in introducing casino gaming consider limiting the growth, profit potential, and marketing activities of casinos as a way to limit negative social side effects.

683. Eadington, William R., ed. *Gambling and Society: Interdisciplinary Studies on the Subject of Gambling.* Springfield, Ill.: Thomas, 1976. 466 pp.

Examines gambling, games, gamblers, gaming markets, and gambling history in a collection of articles by thirty-three contributors. The book is divided into five sections by discipline: The Legalization of Gambling; The Economics of Gambling; The Sociology of Gambling; The Psychology of Gambling; and The Mathematics of Gambling. Contributors include economists, sociologists, psychologists, mathematicians, and industry officials.

684. Eadington, William R., ed. *Gambling Research: Proceedings of the Seventh International Conference on Gambling and Risk Taking, 1987.* 5 vols. Reno, Nev.: Bureau of Business and Economic Research, College of Business Administration, University of Nevada, Reno, 1988.

Explores myriad aspects of gambling and risk taking. These five volumes focus on world-wide public policy, business and economic studies, gamblers and gambling behavior, quantitative analysis, and pathological gambling. Bibliographical references.

685.   Eadington, William R., and Judy A. Cornelius, eds. *Gambling Behavior and Problem Gambling*. Reno, Nev.: Institute for the Study of Gambling and Commercial Gaming, College of Business Administration, University of Nevada, Reno, 1993. 678 pp.

Responds to an increased interest in gambling behavior and compulsive gambling that is accompanying the rapid proliferation of gaming. Eadington and Cornelius have compiled forty articles written by psychologists and sociologists from Europe and the United States. The seven sections of this anthology are Gambling Behavior Attributes and Observations; Studies in Compulsive and Pathological Gambling Behavior; Theories on Addiction; Pathological Gambling: Studies of [Gambling's] Prevalence in Society; Gambling and Youth; Gambling and Crime; and Approaches to Treatment of Problem Gambling. Articles are scholarly and provide numerous references for additional reading. Bibliographical references.

686.   Edwards, Jerome E. "From Back Alley to Main Street: Nevada's Acceptance of Gambling." *Nevada Historical Society Quarterly* 33 (Spring 1990): 16-27.

Traces the evolution of gambling in Nevada since legalization in 1931, an event which placed the state's "reputation under a thick cloud of moral criticism for many years." Edwards identifies several characteristics which made this landmark legislation possible, including the lack of financial "resources necessary for economic viability," the very small population predominated by men, and the low statistics for church membership. The bill, which generated little discussion when introduced, was easily passed and approved. Further analysis shows that Nevada's tremendous population growth since 1940 is "directly attributable to the expansion of gambling and of its supporting services." This industry's growth and acceptance in Nevada has directly led to its acceptance and recent and rapid expansion throughout the country. Bibliographical references.

687.   Elger, Heidi, et al. *Assessing the Social Impacts of Gambling, as Perceived by Local Government and Agency Officials, on Permanent Residents of Central City, Colorado.* Boulder, Colo.: Tourism Management Program, University of Colorado at Boulder, 1992. 35 pp.
     Uses personal interviews and questionnaires to assess the social impacts of gambling in Central City, Colorado. Conducted seven months after the introduction of gaming, this study suggests that the lives of residents have been disrupted due to rising property values and "loud and crowded" conditions. Though the plentiful jobs and an improved economy are appreciated, the overwhelming sentiment of Central City's residents is that the quality of life has declined since casinos opened. Another concern is the devaluation of the town's historical significance with the gutting and renovation of many downtown buildings.

688.   Epstein, Rebecca L. *Meaning in the Mirage: The Domestication of Vice in a Late 20th Century Las Vegas Strip Resort.* Honors thesis, University of Michigan, 1993. University of Nevada, Las Vegas, Special Collections. 80 pp.
     Identifies Las Vegas as the hub of changing American values. The Mirage Resort pioneered the concept of Las Vegas as a mainstream, family entertainment center, and since its 1990 opening, the city has been tremendously successful at distancing itself from its "Green Felt Jungle, Sin City" past. Indeed, with the opening of several other megaresorts on the Las Vegas Strip, the city has become a respectable, family recreation center.

689.   Fabian, Ann Vincent. *Card Sharps, Dream Books, & Bucket Shops: Gambling in 19th Century America.* Ithaca, N.Y.: Cornell University Press, 1990. 250 pp.
     Provides a narrative that weaves the many forms of gambling and speculation typical of 19th-century America into a cultural tapestry. Though gambling ran counter to the morals of the time, it permeated the growing capitalist economy. Fabian explores the tension between forms of speculation that were acceptable and forms that were not,

noting that by the end of the century "investors" who had grown wealthy from trading in risky stocks and commodities were representing themselves as upstanding citizens. Bibliographical references, index.

690.   Findlay, John M. *People of Chance: Frontiers of Gambling and Society from Jamestown to Las Vegas.* New York: Oxford University Press, 1986. 272 pp.

Traces gambling in America from colonial times through the period of western expansion, concluding with the "New Frontiersmen" of contemporary Las Vegas. Findlay finds an affinity between the wide-open risk-taking of frontier society and the lifestyles that are manifest in contemporary Las Vegas. He maintains that "Southern Nevadans experience the same transience, the same lack of permanent commitment, the same fortune seeking, and the same tensions and shortages that typified previous settlements of westering Americans." Life in America's playground, boomtown, or last frontier is vividly captured. Bibliographical references and index.

691.   Findlay, John M. "Suckers and Escapists? Interpreting Las Vegas and Post-War America." *Nevada Historical Society Quarterly* 33 (Spring 1990): 1-15.

Argues that Las Vegas's popularity and population growth represent significant but little-analyzed cultural changes during the post-war era. While many view this period as conservative, conventional, and bland, the city represented glamour, luxury, and excitement "which had never before been both so accessible and so acceptable." Tourism there reflected the nationwide availability of "economic abundance, increased leisure and convenience, greater mastery over nature, and expanded personal freedom." Related cultural shifts include such innovations as the Apollo rocket, the McDonald's restaurant chain, the interstate highway system, international airline service, and "theme parks, shopping malls, and redeveloped downtowns." Bibliographical references.

692.   Frank, Michael L. "Underage Gambling in Atlantic City Casinos." *Psychological Reports* 67 (1990): 907-912.
Surveys casino gambling behavior of underage students at a college near Atlantic City from 1986 through 1988. Findings included the following: over half of the student body had gambled within the preceding year; gambling behavior changed little from year to year; age did not affect gambling behavior; and there were no correlations between the "subjects' sex, their family size, or parental marital status." The author did find relationships between gambling and other risk-taking behavior and gambling and increased drinking. Also, the sample reveals a potential for problem gambling that is higher than that of the general population, and like other gamblers, these students remember wins more than losses. Casino admission controls are obviously ineffective since these students had such easy access. Bibliographical references.

693.   Gallas, Walter W., et al. *The Political Dimension of Urban Tourism: Land-Based Casino Gaming, City Leadership, and Changing Attitudes Toward Tourism Management in New Orleans.* New Orleans, La.: University of New Orleans, College of Urban and Public Affairs, 1994. 17 pp.
Contains a "Paper presented at 'Quality Management in Urban Tourism: Balancing Business and Environment.' University of Victoria, Victoria, British Columbia, November 1994." Recounts the political process by which New Orleans introduced land-based casinos and explains the concerns of various community interest groups. The authors suggest that the introduction of casinos was the product of a "bigger is better" mentality that does not provide for a sound tourism management policy. Gallas and his coauthors fear that unrestricted tourism development could destroy the character and flavor of New Orleans. Bibliographical references.

694.   Gallup Organization. *New Jersey Residents' Attitudes and Behavior Regarding Gambling.* Prepared for

the Council on Compulsive Gambling of New Jersey, Inc. Princeton, N.J.: Gallup Organization, 1993. 90 pp.

Reports on the results of a telephone survey of 1,016 adults living throughout New Jersey. According to the survey, ninety-six percent of New Jersey residents have gambled, with a majority having done so in the past year. Lotteries were the most common activity (82 percent), followed by slot machines (75 percent) and casino gambling (74 percent). Far fewer people bet on horses or played bingo. On average, the largest amount ever gambled in one day was $403, with the majority of respondents (53 percent) never gambling more than $100. Only thirteen percent had ever gambled over $500 in one day.

695.   Galski, Thomas, ed. *The Handbook of Pathological Gambling.* Springfield, Ill.: Charles C. Thomas, 1987. 211 pp.

Explains how clinicians, mental health professionals, social workers, and others can aid in the diagnosis, treatment, and rehabilitation of compulsive gamblers. Includes a survey of the literature, and numerous references. Bibliographical references, index.

696.   "Gambling in the U.S.: Public Finance or Public Problem." *The Journal of Social Issues* 35 (Summer 1979): 1-185.

Features eleven articles edited by Maureen Kallick-Kaufmann and Peter Reuter that discuss gambling from the perspectives of various disciplines, including law, economics, political science, history, and psychology. Several articles discuss gambling behavior and attitudes, the number of people in the United States who gamble, and the potential consequences of widespread legalized gaming. Other articles examine gaming as a source of public revenue, the challenges inherent in gaming regulation, and public opinion regarding changing gambling laws.

697.   Geisler, Norman L., and Thomas A. Howe. *Gambling: A Bad Bet.* Old Tappan, N.J.: F.H. Revell, 1990. 156 pp.

Attacks all forms of gambling as psychologically, morally, and socially damaging. Geisler and Howe cite numerous cases that show that gambling ruins lives. From a Fundamentalist Christian perspective, the authors refute myriad gamblers' fallacies, such as "it's just entertainment" and "I'll quit when I get ahead." They firmly oppose such seemingly innocuous and widespread practices as church-sponsored bingo.

698.   Geyer, Canon Edward B. *The Atlantic City Experience: Gaming and the Church.* Atlantic City, N.J.: Diocese of New Jersey, Atlantic City Mission, 1993. 10 pp.

Discusses the moral aspects of gaming. Gaming, as opposed to gambling, is defined as "the wagering of one's discretionary or recreational income. As such, it does not impact, or put in jeopardy a person's individual economic status. On the other hand, gambling, the risk of one's livelihood, e.g. home mortgage payments, and/or, rent for lodgings, educational expenses. . . , is considered sinful." Geyer sees gaming as a legitimate pastime that has biblical origins and a fact of life in American culture.

699.   Grant, Ocean, and Garry J. Smith. "Social Reward, Conflict, and Commitment: A Theoretical Model of Gambling Behavior." *Journal of Gambling Studies* 9 (Winter 1993): 321-339.

Introduces a model of gambling behavior which "examines the linkage between regular gamblers, the gambling institution, and outside society. This model is based on participant observation in an urban casino and a review of the related literature. The intention is to explore the structural and cultural factors operating both in society at large and in a gambling institution and to connect them with the personal characteristics of avid regular gamblers to explain their gambling behavior and its consequences." They conclude that the social rewards offered by casinos attract gamblers and shape their subsequent gambling entanglement.

700.   Greenberg, Pam. "Not Quite the Pot of Gold." *State Legislatures* 18 (December 1992): 24-27.
        Discusses possible outcomes from decisions on state-legalized gambling. Full understanding of the pros, cons, and inherent risks is critical. While casinos bring money and jobs to communities, they can also cause revenue destabilization and increased property taxes, traffic, crime, pollution, and compulsive gambling. Suppressing gambling, when a neighboring state legalizes it, can cause a migration of financial resources to locations that allow it. Greenberg includes positive and negative examples from Deadwood, South Dakota and three rural Colorado communities.

701.   Gros, Roger. "Do the Right Thing: Nancy Todd Steers Gaming Campaigns Along the Straight and Narrow." *Casino Journal* 7 (September 1994): 35-36.
        Examines failed 1994 casino campaigns and offers advice on how the industry can maximize its chances for success in the future. This article is based on an interview with Nancy Todd, president of the Todd Company, a nationally recognized firm for planning and running gaming campaigns. By "getting the legal issues out of the way first," Todd stresses that many problematic situations will not arise later. She also recommends designating casino sites in the enabling legislation to ease residents' concerns about locations. Giving revenues to local governments for allocation is preferable to getting entangled in revenue designations where everyone gets a piece of the action.

702.   Halliday, Jon, and Peter Fuller. *The Psychology of Gambling.* London: Allen Lane, 1974. 310 pp.
        Brings together several seminal texts on the psychology of gambling, including Freud's study of Dostoyevsky and works by Ralph Greenson and Robert M. Lindner. In a lengthy introduction, Peter Fuller investigates the relationship between gambling, religion, capitalism, and pornography. Bibliographical references, index.

703.   Haubrich-Casperson, Jane, and Doug Van Nispen. *Coping with Teenage Gambling.* New York: Rosen Publishing Group, 1993. 147 pp.
        Provides an overview of compulsive gambling among juveniles. Speaking to teenagers directly, this book "offers them the opportunity to assess their own behavior for signs of addiction." The authors are nationally certified gambling counselors. Bibliographical references, index.

704.   Haythorn, J. Denny. "Compulsive Gambling: A Selected, Annotated Bibliography." *Law Library Journal* 82 (Winter 1990): 147-160.
        Contains over 110 briefly annotated citations for "readily available" books and periodical articles on the medical and legal aspects of problem gambling. In his introduction, Haythorn says that while the concept of compulsive gambling increasingly appears in criminal cases, "courts have not been inclined to allow this defense." In his concise literature review, he notes that most materials focus on the psychology and sociology of gambling, not the legal ramifications of gambling as addictive behavior.

705.   Herman, Robert D. *Gamblers and Gambling: Motives, Institutions, and Controls.* Lexington, Mass.: Lexington Books, 1976. 142 pp.
        Provides a social context for gambling by uncovering relationships between gambling and other practices and institutions. Herman looks at types of games, gambling and money, horse racing, compulsive gambling, gambling rackets, law enforcement, and organized crime. Bibliographical references, index.

706.   Herman, Robert D., ed. *Gambling.* New York: Harper & Row, 1969. 264 pp.
        Explores the social and psychological meanings of gambling and the public policy debate it has inspired. Though written over twenty-five years ago, these essays are still pertinent to the gambling policy issues. Contributors include Edmund Bergler, Thorstein Veblen, William F. Whyte, Leo Rosten, and Robert F. Kennedy.

707.   Hodge, James. "Big Easy Bishops Bitten by Burg's Betting Bug." *National Catholic Reporter* 28 (July 3 1992): 3.

Reports that most Catholic leaders were not involved in New Orleans' heated casino debate. In this short article, Hodge notes that he current archbishop said little about the issue, and retired Archbishop Philip Hannan spoke against legalization without much visibility, perhaps because the "church itself relies heavily on bingo and other games of chance to raise revenue." Hannan did write a letter to the City Council denouncing the social problems casinos cause while endorsing bingo as a recreational activity that funds Catholic schools.

708.   Hulse, James W. *Forty Years in the Wilderness: Impressions of Nevada, 1940-1980*.   Reno, Nev.: University of Nevada Press, 1986. 141 pp.

Provides an interpretive history of Nevada, drawing attention to the state's unstable population, limited resources, and dependence on gaming for revenue. Hulse investigates "the industry's stimulation of the whole fabric of community life" and suggests that Nevadans are "prisoners of the 'industry' that they had tolerated." Despite fantastic profits for gaming companies and substantial revenues for the state, the author finds Nevada's record in welfare, human rights, and education profoundly disturbing. Bibliographical references, index.

709.   Jackson, Richard, and Lloyd Hudman. "Border Towns, Gambling, and the Mormon Culture Region." *Journal of Cultural Geography* 8 (1987): 35-48.

Discusses relationships between Nevada's border towns of West Wendover, Jackpot, and Mesquite and adjacent areas in Utah and Idaho. A brief history examines the influence of the Mormon religion on Nevada's history and the growth of gambling in the state. The authors then examine population and casino industry growth in these communities and state that "Nevada's border towns are reliant on the population of the Mormon culture region" for casino patronage. This may seem ironic since Utah, one of only two states which prohibits any form of gambling, suppresses it due to Mormon opposition. The Church's stand on the issue, however, may seem ambivalent since Nevada casinos have advertised on "the Mormon Church-owned radio and television station KSL." Since gambling will probably never be legal in Utah, that state's population will continue to take money out of Utah to gamble in adjacent Nevada communities. Maps, bibliographical references.

710. Johnson, Steven L. "Kin and Casinos: Changing Family Networks in Atlantic City." *Current Anthropology* 26 (June 1985): 397-399.

Explains how people moving to urban areas for economic advantages rely on family ties to help with the often difficult transition. "Relatives living in the cities provide potential migrants with information about jobs and actual migrants with lodging, contacts (for employment), and a ready-made social network," causing kinship networks to change and grow. The author surveyed a sample of Atlantic City residents in 1981 and 1982 and discovered that many respondents were recently acquainted with previously little-known relatives interested in Atlantic City's job opportunities. Family relationships are important for this kind of migration to urban centers worldwide, and as Atlantic City continues to grow, kinship networks there will continue to change and expand. Bibliographical references.

711. Kaplan, H. Roy, and William R. Blount. "The Impact of the Daily Lottery on the Numbers Game: Does Legalization Make a Difference." *Journal of Gambling Studies* 6 (Fall 1990): 263-274.

Uses data obtained in a Florida police raid to demonstrate that legal lotteries do not divert funds from illegal numbers games. "The records ranged over a thirteen week period encompassing five weeks prior to the inception of Florida's legal daily numbers and lotto games and seven weeks afterward. While there was a seventeen percent decline of monies wagered on the illegal games during the first week of the legal games, illegal wagers quickly rebounded to pre-legalization levels."

712.   Kinnel, Lillian. *Research Response: Effects of Casino Gambling on Welfare Costs.* Springfield, Ill.: Illinois General Assembly, Legislative Research Unit, 19 October 1992. 8 pp.
        Reviews relationship between casino gambling and welfare costs in Deadwood, South Dakota and Atlantic City, New Jersey before and after gambling legalization. Limited data from various research projects show that the number of Aid to Families with Dependent Children (AFDC) and food stamp recipients did not increase; declines actually occurred in many areas, attributable in part to changes in federal eligibility requirements. Nevada, best known for legal gambling, has the lowest percentage of its population on AFDC among four comparable states in its region. These findings refute the belief that the casino industry attracts people who can least afford to gamble and turn to public assistance for support. Tables, bibliographical references.

713.   Klein, Howard J. "Tired Brains...Tired Games: Casinos Could Learn a Lot From Video Arcades." *International Gaming and Wagering Business* 13 (15 July 1992): 14, 15.
        Compares the decline in table game revenues to the tremendous popularity of slot machines. While Klein attributes this decline to changing lifestyles, the recession, and age demographics, he stresses that the major factor is the technological innovation and marketing that have reinvented slot machines. He argues that similar approaches to table games could dramatically increase their popularity as well.

714.   Kusyszyn, Igor, ed. *Studies in the Psychology of Gambling.* New York: Simon and Schuster, 1972. 172 pp.
        Examines several aspects of gambling behavior including compulsive gambling. This collection of scholarly papers addresses why people gamble and attempts to draw distinctions between professional, compulsive, and recreational gamblers. Contributions with varying levels of

sophistication make this volume useful for professionals, psychology students, and interested laypersons.

715.   Ladouceur, Robert, et al.   "Social Cost of Pathological Gambling." *Journal of Gambling Studies* 10 (Winter 1994): 399-409.
      Assesses the financial burdens created by pathological gambling of Gamblers Anonymous participants. "Results show that important debts, loss of productivity at work, and legal problems are associated with pathological gambling. Discussion is formulated in terms of the social cost of adopting a liberal attitude toward the legalization of various gambling activities."

716.   Larson, Cynthia R. *Compulsive Gambling: An Exploratory Study.* Master's thesis, University of Nevada, Las Vegas, 1993.   University of Nevada, Las Vegas, Special Collections. 81 pp.
      Provides a comprehensive overview of the literature on the nature and extent of gambling addiction in the United States. Larson concludes that the devastation caused by compulsive gambling is far worse than what is widely acknowledged, that it is a disease that is very difficult to treat, and that further research is badly needed as legalized gambling continues to proliferate.   Bibliographical references.

717.   Learock, John B. *A Lecture on Gambling, and the Delinquency of the City Authorities: Delivered in the Melodeon, Boston, February 24, 1862.* Boston: Printed by Richard L. Daley, 1862.
      Decries the proliferation of gambling houses in Boston, charging that there never has been a worse class of men on the face of the earth than that of the professional gambler. Learock goes on to chastise public officials for refusing to suppress gambling activities.   This is an interesting piece, not only for its historical importance, but for its flaming rhetoric and insight into corruption.

718.   Lesieur, Henry R. *The Chase: Career of the Compulsive Gambler.* Cambridge, Mass.: Schenkman Pub. Co., 1984. 323 pp.
      Provides a broad sociological study of the pathological gambler. Lesieur examines the "spiral of options and involvement" associated with compulsive gambling, abstinence-and-relapse cycles, the gambler's family life, and criminal and other fund-raising activities employed by compulsive gamblers to support their addiction.

719.   Lester, David. "Access to Gambling Opportunities and Compulsive Gambling." *International Journal of Addictions* 29 (1994): 1611-1616.
      Compares the availability of gambling opportunities to participation in Gamblers Anonymous chapters. In 1991, Lester compared the number of Gamblers Anonymous chapters to the opportunities for legal gambling in the contiguous United States. His study did not consider the number of problem gamblers who do not participate in this group or the number of people who cross state lines to gamble. This basic comparison, however, indicates that "the total number of forms of gambling available in a state was associated with the density of Gamblers Anonymous chapters," results that certainly warrant further research. Tables, bibliographical references.

720.   Lester, David, ed. *Gambling Today.* Springfield, Ill.: Thomas, 1979. 148 pp.
      Investigates several major social issues that arise from gambling and gambling behavior in the United States and Great Britain. Chapters by nine contributors cover the impact of casino gaming on Atlantic City, the economic aspects of gambling, illegal gambling, gamblers, why people gamble, treatment of compulsive gambling, Gamblers Anonymous, and gambling in Great Britain. Index.

721.   Lester, David, and Donald Jason. "Suicides at the Casino." *Psychological Reports* 64 (February 1989): 337-338.

Studies suicides occurring in Atlantic City casinos from 1982 to 1986. This brief article notes that eleven suicides took place during this period: four were casino employees, two were casino visitors, and five were casino hotel guests. Available information on six of these showed that three people killed "themselves after losing large sums of money" while gambling. Bibliographic references.

722. Long, Patrick, Jo Clark, and Derek Liston. *Win, Lose or Draw? Gambling With America's Small Towns.* Washington, DC: Aspen Institute, 1994. 97 pp.
Explores the effect gaming has had on Black Hawk, Central City, and Cripple Creek, Colorado and Deadwood, South Dakota. The intent of this report is to help other jurisdictions learn from the Colorado and South Dakota experiences and plan for the possible introduction of limited-stakes casino gaming. Current policy and practice, regulation, revenue collection and distribution, economic development assistance, social consequences, and planning are covered. Bibliographical references.

723. Madden, Michael K. "Gaming in South Dakota: A Statistical Description and Analysis of Its Socioeconomic Impacts." In *Gaming in South Dakota.* Vermillion, S.Dak.: University of South Dakota, Business Research Bureau, November, 1991. 83 pp.
Identifies economic and social effects of gaming activities in South Dakota. In his economic analysis, Madden discusses such topics as the development of gaming in the state, the kinds of gaming available, the amounts of money spent on gambling, and its influence on employment, income, and business formations. The social analysis looks at legalized gambling's effects on public welfare, child abuse and neglect, divorce, bankruptcy, child support enforce-ment, and real estate foreclosures. The study's methodology and statistical analysis provide a useful framework for people who want to conduct similar studies in other locations. Charts, tables, bibliographical references.

724.   Mangalmurti, Sandeep, and Robert Allan Cooke.
State Lotteries: Seducing the Less Fortunate? A Heartland
Policy Study, no. 35. Chicago, Ill.: Heartland Institute, 23
April 1991. 38 pp.

Compares the benefits and costs of state-run
lotteries. While this work does not address casinos, its
discussion of the positive and negative effects of lotteries
apply to other forms of legalized gambling. The authors ask
if lotteries are an unfair tax on the disadvantaged, if lottery
advertising is misleading and hurts the underclass, and if
lotteries contribute to increases in problem gambling and
crime. They conclude: "the analysis of playing trends and
advertising procedures does indeed support many of the
claims that state lotteries exploit the vulnerabilities of the
weakest populations of our society," and these costs far
outweigh any economic benefits. Indeed, the state becomes a
"predator," not a "protector," of its citizens. Includes
sidebars on lottery operations in Illinois, Michigan,
Missouri, and Wisconsin. Tables, bibliographical
references.

725.   Martinez, Tomas M. *The Gambling Scene: Why
People Gamble.* Springfield, Ill.: Charles C. Thomas,
1983. 231 pp.

Provides a thorough review of gambling theories and
explores the sociology of compulsive gambling. Martinez
also expounds upon the social cost of compulsive gambling,
the roles of government and the media in promoting
gambling, and gambling and the criminal justice system.
Index.

726.   Maryland. Governor's Task Force to Study
Gambling. *Final Report of the Governor's Task Force to
Study Gambling.* Baltimore, Md.: The Task Force, 1994.
16 pp.

Provides a thorough overview of gambling in
Maryland, including types of state-regulated activities and
illegal gambling. The social aspects of gaming and the
competition between charitable gaming and private business
are discussed. While several bills authorizing riverboat

gaming in Maryland were defeated, the 1993 Legislature approved one piece of legislation allowing cruise ships visiting Maryland ports of call to continue casino gaming operations while in Maryland waters. Maryland also permits slot machines and casino gaming for charitable purposes, a state lottery, and horse racing.

727. Mascarenhas, Oswald A.J. "An Empirical Methodology for the Ethical Assessment of Marketing Phenomena Such as Casino Gambling." *Journal of Marketing Science* 18 (Summer 1990): 209-220.

Analyzes results of a study conducted in a large midwestern city where legalized casino gambling was being considered. Gambling, a very controversial issue, was selected to show how psychometric measures can be used to assess the ethical beliefs of consumers. The article includes a brief introduction on methodologies for evaluating marketing ethics; measurement problems in ethical assessments; a brief review of the literature on gambling; ethical assessment methodology; and explanations of the sample's design and data collection. Heads of households were asked open-ended questions about the positive and negative effects of casinos, and the author concludes, as he expected, that "casino gamblers and gamers obtained higher pro-gambling scores than non-gamblers." Tables, bibliographical references.

728. Mason, Paul M., Stephen L. Shapiro, and Mary O. Borg. "Gaming Tax Incidence for Three Groups of Las Vegas Gamblers." *Applied Economics* 21 (September 1989): 1267-1277.

Studies three groups of Las Vegas gamblers to determine if casino gambling taxes are equitably distributed. These groups were residents of Clark County (which includes Las Vegas), residents from other parts of Nevada, and visitors from out-of-state. The authors first look at previous research on gambling taxes and then explain their methodology and the data they collected. They found that these "three groups are very different, and consequently, so too are the implications for tax equitability" and that gambling taxes were most regressive for local residents, followed in order by out-of-state visitors and residents from elsewhere in Nevada. The state's policy makers may want to consider prohibiting casino employees from gambling and correlate game preference to income level, adjusting "the relative taxes on those games accordingly." Tables, bibliographical references.

729.   Medley, Keith Weldon. "Big Gamble in the Big Easy." *Historic Preservation* 46 (1 July 1994): 26-31, 92, 94.
        Examines the potentially destructive effects of casino and riverboat gaming on New Orleans. Selected sites are very close to the French Quarter, the city's oldest neighborhood and the country's second oldest historical district. After noting that New Orleans is one of the "poorest cities in the nation" and susceptible to the economic promises of legalized gambling, Medley reviews the area's history and long-standing preservation efforts. Unfortunately, in spite of those efforts, the French Quarter has been changing to lure tourists, and city residents fear that casino gambling will destroy the area. "New Orleans's charm will be lost and there will be few genuine tourist draws left." He finally asks if the "historic fabric and character of the city" will survive the influx of ever-growing numbers of tourists.

730.   Misrach, Richard. "Las Vegas Runs Dry." *Audubon* 94 (July 1992): 56-63.
        Illustrates how rapid growth in Las Vegas affects water use and supply. This pictorial essay of seven photographs vividly shows this area's use of water means "less for ranching, agriculture, and the delicate species of the Southwest desert." Subjects include a casino's large outside fountain, a desert landscape, and a rural road.

731.   Mok, Waiman P., and Joseph Hraba. "Age and Gambling Behavior: A Declining and Shifting Pattern of Participation." *Journal of Gambling Studies* 7 (Winter 1991): 313-335.

Finds that chronological age is negatively related to gambling behavior and that within that trend, people of different ages are engaged in different types of gambling. The authors offer several explanations for these phenomena.

732.   Moody, Gordon E. *Quit Compulsive Gambling: The Action Plan for Gamblers and Their Families.* Wellingborough, Northhampton: Thorsons, 1990. 144 pp.
Provides a self-help guide for compulsive gamblers, their families, and friends. Much of this information is based on the author's twenty-four-year relationship with Gamblers Anonymous and Gam-Anon. This work is also useful for mental health professionals. Bibliographical references, index.

733.   Nassir, Diane E. "Nevada Welfare Assistance Caseloads and Gaming: A Cautionary Tale." *Nevada Historical Society Quarterly* 37 (Summer 1994): 115-141.
Investigates the relationship between growth in Nevada's gaming industry and increases in state welfare assistance caseloads. While caseloads normally decrease during periods of economic growth, Nevada experienced the opposite effect. It "led the nation in the number of newly created jobs between 1988 and 1990," and simultaneously welfare caseloads "rose dramatically." The state has the country's highest percentage of service employment because of its tourist economy that mainly consists of "jobs which are low in wages, marginal in benefits and always vulnerable to seasonal layoffs." In addition to her statistical analysis, the author includes a brief history of gambling and public assistance in Nevada and explains how the State Welfare Division makes projections using an employment variable labeled "hotels, gaming, and recreation." She concludes that other areas considering legalized gambling should look at Nevada's "cautionary tale of impoverishment behind a veil of glitter." Tables, bibliographical references.

734.   Newmark, David L. *Covert Religious Aspects of Gambling.* Ph.D. dissertation, The Professional School of

Psychology, San Francisco, 1989. University of Nevada, Las Vegas, Special Collections. 85 pp.

Explains the relationship between covert religious impulses and gambling through three case studies involving compulsive and recreational gamblers. This study also explores major differences between compulsive gamblers who undiminishingly crave the intense high of gambling action and recreational gamblers who experience this high in a subdued form that diminishes over time. Newmark observes that recreational gamblers set appropriate limits, exercise more diligence, patience, and tolerance for hard work, and lead fuller lives. On the other hand, compulsive gamblers live in a dream world of self-delusion, experiencing altered states similar to religious ecstatic states. Compulsive gamblers were found to be either depressed or exhibitionistic. Their behavior is a "misguided attempt to experience and integrate spiritual transcendence as a way of transforming the self."

735.   Padavan, Frank. *Rolling the Dice: Why Casino Gambling is a Bad Bet for New York . . . a Legislative Report.* N.p., 21 April 1994. 35 pp.

Presents four major reasons why casino gambling would be bad for New York. State Senator Padavan argues that casinos are not a reliable source for state revenue, are not an economic development program, cause increases in crime, and create more victims than winners. Supporting evidence is grouped in chapters titled The Economy, Crime, and Social Costs, which contain statistics and experts' opinions from a variety of sources. He concludes that a comptroller's projected annual revenue gain of $410 million, still used as an estimate, is too high because it is based on an outdated 1978 study which did not consider competition from the growth of legalized gambling or the possible effects of federal gambling taxation. Bibliographical references.

736.   Painton, Priscilla. "Boardwalk of Broken Dreams." *Time* 134 (25 September 1989): 64-69.

Discusses how casino gaming affected Atlantic City. Eleven years after legalization, the city has lost population and services like movie theaters and supermarkets, while experiencing increased crime, pollution, welfare assistance, and homelessness. "Life in Atlantic City is paradoxical to the point of perversity." Little goodwill exists between casino officials and city residents because of their "completely different visions." Donald Trump, for example, wants to turn it "into a giant nonresidential entertainment park." Little is being done to correct these problems, because everyone blames them on other people or groups. The casinos have not always kept their promises, perhaps in part because profits are down, and many residents have moved elsewhere.

737. Perdue, Richard R., Patrick T. Long, and Lawrence Allen. "Rural Resident Tourism Perceptions and Attitudes." *Annals of Tourism Research* 14 (1987): 420-429.

Examines tourism as a "regional economic development tool." While this Colorado-based study of tourism, rural areas, and outdoor recreation does not include casinos, the authors' survey methodology and questions could be readily modified to determine local attitudes and perceptions on legalized gambling. This article will be valuable to a variety of researchers. Tables, bibliographical references.

738. Pizam, Abraham, and Julianne Pokela. "The Perceived Impacts of Casino Gambling on a Community." *Annals of Tourism Research* 12 (1985): 147-165.

Investigates public attitudes towards casino gambling in rural Adams and Hull, Massachusetts. The authors conducted a telephone survey of 400 area residents to determine how they thought a single hotel casino would affect their communities. After reviewing previous research, they describe their sampling methodology, which included telephone surveys, in-depth interviews, and focus groups. Perceived impacts were grouped into political, economic, and social categories. Their findings "show little consensus as to the positive impacts, but much greater agreement over the negative impacts that a hotel casino might have in the respondents' towns." Concerns included how the enterprise would affect their community's character, crime rates, standard of living, and job availability and the effectiveness of state regulation. Tables, bibliographical references.

739.   Plume, Janet. "Casinos Rattle the Historic Rafters: Preservation Versus Economic Development in Southern Casino Towns." *Casino Journal* 7 (October 1994): 38-39.
         Reports on the battles between historic preservationists and casino developers in New Orleans and Natchez, Mississippi. Preservationists argue that casinos cause overdevelopment, which threatens the unique charm and historical character of these old cities. The destruction of buildings, severe traffic congestion, and overcrowding are major areas of concern.

740.   Politzer, Robert M., Charles E. Yesalis, and Clark J. Hudak, Jr. "The Epidemiologic Model and the Risks of Legalized Gambling: Where Are We Headed?" *Health Values* 16 (March/April 1992): 20-27.
         Questions how professionals currently assess the public health risks of compulsive gambling. The authors briefly review the epidemiologic model, which "weighs equally the contributions of societal behaviors by considering," in this case, the interaction of the gambler or the host, the action of gambling or the agent, and the environment, which includes "community and culture." The frequent focus on how the environment affects the individual, and decisions about legalization based on concern about increased rates of problem gamblers, are "not as effective as employing strategies that are aimed at those at the highest risk." This emphasis also places undue blame on the gaming industry or "producer of the agent," which limits the industry's participation in finding solutions. Tables, bibliographical references.

741.   Pollock, Michael. *Hostage of Fortune: Atlantic City and Casino Gambling.* Princeton, N.J.: Center for Analysis of Public Issues, 1987. 204 pp.
         Provides a political, social, and economic history of Atlantic City from the early 1960s through 1986. This work

conveys the stark contrast between wealth and poverty in Atlantic City while pointing a finger at regulatory agencies and state and local governments for mismanaging a potential fiscal miracle. Pollock cautions other jurisdictions interested in casino gaming to insulate regulatory apparatus from the whims of individual politicians, separate regulation from development functions, anticipate and cushion the social upheavals that casinos will cause, and train unskilled workers to take advantage of new opportunities. It is also important to understand that casinos can wield considerable political power and to limit their lobbying activities; to take advantage of the spin-off effects of gaming such as conventions and tourism; and to understand the nature of the casino industry itself, which takes in a great deal of money and parcels out a portion of it to a lucky few.

742.   Powell, Stephen. *A Gambling Bibliography Based on the Collection at the University of Nevada, Las Vegas.* Las Vegas, Nev.: University of Nevada, Las Vegas, Special Collections, 1972. 162 pp.

Lists 1,754 citations arranged alphabetically in thirteen subject areas including casino games, law, casino operations, gambling around the world, and moral and religious literature, all located in Special Collections, University of Nevada, Las Vegas. Although not annotated, this work is a valuable guide to gambling literature published prior to 1972 and a guide to the holdings of one of the world's great gambling collections. Bibliography.

743.   *The Proliferation of Legalized Gaming in Nevada.* Faculty: William Eadington, I. Nelson Rose, George Olesinski; sponsored by the University of Nevada, Reno, Division of Continuing Education and the Institute for the Study of Gambling and Commercial Gaming, College of Business Administration. Reno, Nev.: University of Nevada, Reno, 1992. Various pagings.

Provides a collection of papers presented at the Hotel/Gaming Management Program. The authors address the phenomenal proliferation of gaming in America and the challenges it presents to regulation and public policy.

Gaming in various jurisdictions is discussed, and revenue data is provided. The legal aspects of gaming, case law, and legislation are also covered.

744.   Ravitz, Mel. "Community Development: Salvation or Suicide?" *Social Policy* 19 (Fall 1988): 17-21.

Analyzes economic and community development efforts in Detroit, Michigan. The author, a City Council member, argues that economic development is the current "catchword" and discusses the failures of specific projects in Detroit and how they adversely affected residents in a variety of ways. One proposed project would establish casino gambling, which he states "represents the economics of utter desperation." The projected 50,000 jobs will not materialize, and gambling could cause the increased crime and destruction of small businesses that Atlantic City experienced. Ravitz concludes that public officials must change their development policies, which look outward for solutions, and instead focus directly on their cities' residents and infrastructure, linking business to neighborhoods and supporting improved public services, schools, and crime prevention.

745.   Reeling, Glenn E. *A Five Year Comparison (1980-85) of Attitudes New Jersey Residents Have Regarding Gambling, Especially in Atlantic City.* Jersey City, N.J.: Jersey City State College, 1986. 90 pp.

Assesses public attitudes toward gambling shortly after the introduction of casinos in Atlantic City and then five years later. Topics discussed include morality and victims of gambling, financial benefits of gambling, education and gambling, traits associated with gamblers, and law and gambling. The prevailing attitude that gambling is not immoral did not change in five years. However, a strong sense developed that people who could not afford to do so were gambling, and fewer people believed that revenues from gambling would help education and senior citizens, or revitalize the economy, as promised. While respondents in 1980 believed that government should pay to treat compulsive gamblers, by 1985, more people believed that the casinos should bear that responsibility. Unchanged, a third of the respondents still utilized the services of bookies, even though legal gambling was available.

746.   Rose, I. Nelson. "Compulsive Gambling and the Law: From Sin to Vice to Disease." *Journal of Gambling Behavior* 4 (Winter 1988): 240-260.
    Examines how viewing compulsive gambling as a mental disorder conflicts with the "dominant legal view in the law that gambling is a vice." This conflict began in 1980 when the American Psychiatric Association recognized "'pathological gambling' as an official mental disease or disorder." Before, the responsibility for gambling was placed on individuals, acting on free will, who were seen as weak and punishable, the view currently held by the U.S. court system. The concept of free will is negated when compulsive gambling is perceived as an illness beyond the individual's control. Rose looks at specific cases dealing with insanity defenses and tax, bankruptcy, and family law; he also discusses casino efforts to recover the debts compulsive gamblers have accrued. He concludes that the courts will have to decide who bears the "legal responsibilities for the damages caused by compulsive gamblers." Bibliographical references.

747.   Rosecrance, John D. *Gambling Without Guilt: The Legitimation of an American Pastime*. Pacific Grove, Calif.: Brooks/Cole Pub. Co., 1988. 174 pp.
    Provides a historical overview of gambling in the United States. Rosecrance recognizes the mainstreaming that gaming has experienced over the past two decades and addresses attendant social issues including the social worlds of gambling, gambling behavior, illegal gambling, compulsive gambling, and coping with loss. Chapters on the future of gambling and the international scene are also provided. Index.

748.   Ross, Gary. *No Limit: The Incredible Obsession of Brian Molony*. New York: William Morrow, 1987. 301 pp.

Originally published as *Stung* (Stoddard Publishing Co. Ltd., 1987). Describes the amazing odyssey of Brian Molony, a quiet, unassuming, hard-working young banker and compulsive gambler. To support his addiction, Molony defrauded a Canadian bank of nearly ten million dollars through a trail of bogus loans. In one four-month period, he won $450 million, but lost $457 million. Casinos in Atlantic City loved him.

749.   Saad, Lydia. *Americans Losing Appetite for Gambling*. Gallup Poll News Service, vol. 67, no. 29. Princeton, N.J.: Gallup Poll News Service, 1992. 5 pp.

Finds that the American public may be losing its enthusiasm for expanding legalized gambling. Acceptance for all of the various forms of legalized gambling is down, with sports betting hardest hit at a thirty-three percent approval rating. State lotteries are the most acceptable form of gambling with a seventy-five percent approval rating, while riverboat gaming is approved by sixty percent, Las Vegas and Atlantic City are approved by fifty-one percent, the introduction of urban casinos is approved by forty percent, and Indian Gaming is approved by fifty-one percent. Opinions on arguments for and against gaming are also analyzed.

750.   Shaffer, Howard J., Sharon A. Stein, Blase Gambino, and Thomas N. Cummings, eds. *Compulsive Gambling: Theory, Research, and Practice*. Lexington, Mass.: Lexington Books, 1989. 350 pp.

Provides an overview of compulsive gambling for the mental health professional. This book addresses theories on compulsive gambling, models of treatment, public policy implications, and current research. Bibliographical references, index.

751.   Skolnick, Jerome H. *House of Cards: Legalization and Control of Casino Gambling*. Boston: Little, Brown, 1978. 382 pp.

Explores the imperfect phenomenon of casino gaming. Skolnick wonders how regulators are able to cage

the tiger and control an industry with so much cash running
through it, especially when the industry is seen by many
Americans as being built on vice. He views gambling
regulation and control as an uncertain and precarious
enterprise, and this book illustrates why this opinion is
valid. Bibliographical references.

752.   Skolnick, Jerome H. "A Zoning Merit Model for
Casino Gambling." *Annals of the American Academy of
Political and Social Science* 474 (1984): 48-60.
       Argues that locations considering casino gambling
should not follow Nevada or Atlantic City examples.
Nevada's economy, for example, is so dependent on the
gaming industry that it "dominates politics at every level."
Atlantic City experienced serious problems with increased
crime and housing costs and "displacement of the elderly and
poor"; also, casinos provided little employment to residents.
After discussing the social problems casinos cause, Skolnick
looks at regulatory procedures and problems in New Jersey,
Nevada, and Great Britain. He then proposes a "zoning
merit model" for casino location and regulation. The use of
zoning means that "a state would first have to determine the
ideal number of casinos to be in that state, where they would
be located, and what likely impact they would have on
surrounding communities." Merit means that an operation
applying for a casino license would submit a detailed and
rigorously reviewed proposal and "would have to prove its
qualifications competitively and would have to be willing to
be investigated." This approach allows states to have a great
deal of control over the "location and character" of the casino
industry from the beginning. Bibliographical references.

753.   Sloan, Jim. *Nevada: True Tales From the Neon
Wilderness.* Salt Lake City, Utah: University of Utah Press,
1993. 209 pp.
       Contains eleven interesting essays on people and
experiences unique to Nevada. Written by a Reno journalist,
this highly praised collection contains two chapters related to
casinos. The Natural is about Ross Durham, "a bashful,
gawky genius who grows up in the underworld of Las

Vegas, where cheating is a legitimate profession" to become one of the best slot machine cheats ever. The article covers his long career, arrest, and rehabilitation making "'training films' to be used by casinos and gaming agents in spotting a cheat." In Team Player, a woman spends time at casinos looking for a cocktail waitress job and finds brief employment playing slot machines for a high roller, who gets the $172,000 jackpot she "wins" for him. Other essays look at prostitution, wild mustangs, and "frontier justice."

754. Smith, James Frederick. *Conflicting Images of Gambling in American Culture.* University of Nevada, Las Vegas, Special Collections. 1992. 24 pp.

   Observes that the changing perceptions of gaming and its legitimation as a recreational activity are consistent with fundamental changes in mass cultural values. Smith concludes that gambling today manifests a propensity for "un-abashed public display of wealth" and conspicuous consumption, which are signs of a civilization in decline. Gambling is now mass-marketed to a bored consumer with great expectations but low motivation. To Smith, the American middle class is sadly "looking for new diversions and the proverbial quick fix." Bibliographical references.

755. Spanier, David. *Inside the Gambler's Mind.* The Gambling Studies Series. Reno, Nev.: University of Nevada Press, 1994. 240 pp.

   Examines the psychology of professional gamblers. In his foreword, Spanier states that "gambling is good for you," and his book embraces the sociological perspective that it is acceptable social, recreational, and risk-taking behavior. He discusses how gambling provides excitement, how people set up systems to help themselves win, how gambling can be addictive, and how casino environments are created to attract customers. The author includes the "perspectives of gamblers, casino operators, academic researchers, and regulators," and his analysis of the exciting physical sensations casino gamblers experience is particularly interesting. Index.

756.   Spanier, David. *Welcome to the Pleasuredome: Inside Las Vegas.* Reno, Nev.: University of Nevada Press, 1992. 275 pp.

Traces the development of Las Vegas from its dusty past as a railroad town, through the glitz and glamour of the fifties, to its present status as the world's largest theme park. Spanier knows and loves Las Vegas like few others and tells his story of wealth, crime, excitement, the casino business, visionaries, brothels, and terribly bad taste, as an astute insider. Includes biographical information on many prominent Las Vegans, including Steve Wynn, the Binions, and Bugsy Siegel. Index.

757.   "States Are Cashing in on the Wages of Sin . . . Cigarettes, Drugs, and Gambling." *From the State Capitals: The Outlook* 48 (11 April 1994): 1-4.

Reports on the increasing importance of "sin taxes" which bring "millions of dollars" to state revenues. After noting that "states can actually hike these taxes without fear of public censure," the article briefly covers video slot profits in South Dakota and possible tax increases on video poker in Louisiana. Also, Montana's state legislature may allow the Wolf Point tribe to offer more casino games on their reservation "in return for giving the state a cut of the profits."

758.   Stubbles, Russell. "The Deadwood Tradition: Putting Gambling Before Planning in South Dakota." *Small Town* 21 (November-December 1990): 20-27.

Investigates the consequences of casino gambling in Deadwood, South Dakota. After discussing the town's past and development of its casinos, Stubbles looks at the amount of money gambling and tourism generate. While there have been major increases in revenues, there is also more traffic and noise and "the loss of certain community-oriented retail businesses and a change in the community's social fabric." City officials have identified historic preservation and city planning goals they want to meet by the year 2000. Other communities considering casinos must understand both the positive and negative effects of legalized gambling so they can plan for, and in turn direct, the changes that result.

759.   Svendsen, Roger, and Tom Griffin. *Gambling Choices and Guidelines.* St. Paul, Minn.: Minnesota Department of Human Services and the Minnesota Institute of Public Health, 1993. 15 pp.
       Issued as a public service pamphlet for those seeking social guidance and information on gambling. Svendsen and Griffin discuss gambling as a recreational activity that requires a moderate approach and one which, for some people, can get out of hand. They also advise the reader on what to say to someone who may have a gambling problem.

760.   Taira, Ricky. *Legal Gambling Among Japanese Americans.* Master's thesis, California State University, Long Beach, 1993. University of Nevada, Las Vegas, Special Collections. 79 pp.
       Explores the prevalence of gambling among Japanese Americans and examines "demographic and economic factors among Japanese Americans who gamble." Results "indicate that gambling is a popular pastime . . . however, gambling does not appear to be a problem in a clinical sense." The author states that public officials, such as social workers, should understand that gambling is an important, culture-based recreational activity for many Japanese Americans. Bibliographical references.

761.   Thompson, Hunter S. *Fear and Loathing in Las Vegas: A Savage Journey to the Heart of the American Dream.* New York: Random House, 1971. 206 pp.
       Offers an original in Gonzo journalism that no casino gaming bibliography should ignore; this first appeared in *Rolling Stone* magazine 95 (11 Nov. 1971) and 96 (25 Nov. 1971). Thompson blows into Las Vegas on a cloud of marijuana smoke and narcotic vapors and whirls around town like a stoned tornado on speed. His thought was to "buy a fat notebook and record the whole thing, as it happened, without editing," but he somehow fell short. Of his visit to Circus Circus Thompson observes, "what the

whole hep world would be doing on Saturday Night if the
Nazis had won the war." Thompson lends a very unique
perspective to a very unique city.

762.   Thompson, William N., R. Keith Schwer, Richard
Hoyt, and Dolores Brosnan. "Not in My Backyard: Las
Vegas Residents Protest Casino." *Journal of Gambling
Studies* 9 (Spring 1993): 47-62.
      Surveys Las Vegas-area residents to determine
attitudes about casinos in their neighborhoods. After
discussing Nevada casinos since legalization, the authors
briefly review 1989 state legislation which created "Gaming
Enterprise Districts" in counties whose populations exceed
400,000; casinos which want to locate outside of these
districts can not obtain gaming licenses unless they
successfully petition the appropriate officials for approval.
This petition must address such issues as the availability of
roads, water, and sanitation and the casino's effect on the
neighborhood's "quality of life." Data, gathered randomly
from 967 households which had "purchased a home within
the last two years," showed that the "proximity to a casino is
of some importance to home purchasers." More important
concerns included industrial plants, crime, and "potential
nuclear waste route locations"; less important were the
locations of fast food restaurants and shopping centers. The
authors conclude that a community's residents and their
concerns about casino locations should be considered in
areas where gambling is legalized.

763.   Thompson, William Norman. *If You Embrace
Gambling, You Better Love Gambling*. University of
Nevada, Las Vegas, Special Collections. 1993. 47 pp.
      Continues Thompson's ongoing study of campaigns
to legalize casino gaming. The author recognizes that the
poor economy of the 1980s, pressures from the gaming
industry, and the proliferation of state lotteries, which he
believes have caused a softening of the perception of
gambling as vice, have all contributed to the spread of casino
gaming. However, Thompson's tone is highly cautionary as
he urges communities to take a timid approach to gaming and

to really know what they are getting into, before they embrace casinos. Includes appendices: European and American Casino Gaming Compared, Casinos Without Crime, is it Possible? and The Politically Acceptable Model of Casino Gaming.

764.   Thompson, William Norman. *Legalized Gambling: A Reference Handbook.* ABC-CLIO Series on Contemporary World Issues. Santa Barbara, Calif.: ABC-CLIO, 1994. 209 pp.
        Provides an exceptionally useful reference tool for understanding key aspects of gambling in the United States and Canada. Essays on gambling history, government involvement, why people gamble, and the pros and cons of legalized gambling are complemented by several directories and bibliographies, as well as coverage of important legislation and biographical sketches. A reference work that is this well organized and provides such excellent coverage of its topic would be useful in any field. With the lack of reference tools for studying gambling, this handbook is indispensable. Bibliography, index.

765.   Thompson, William Norman. "Machismo: Manifestations of a Cultural Value in the Latin American Casino." *Journal of Gambling Studies* 7 (Spring 1991): 143-164.
        Explores the concept of *machismo* as it manifests itself in Latin American casinos. Sections of this paper address charismatic authority structures, violence, honor, national integrity, gender roles, and the games *machos* play.

766.   Todd, Nancy. "The Bad Seed: How Louisiana, Past and Present, Threatens the Integrity of the Gaming Industry." *Casino Journal* 7 (October 1994): 19.
        Warns that Louisiana is setting itself up for a major gaming scandal. Todd claims that the free-wheeling politics of Louisiana that allowed lawmakers to approve gaming without public input could spell disaster for the industry. Provides a concise history of gambling in Louisiana.

767.   Turner, Wallace. *Gamblers' Money: The New Force in American Life*. Boston: Houghton Mifflin, 1965. 306 pp.
      Examines legalized gambling in Nevada as a social experiment gone awry. Writing when gangsters were fully vested in Las Vegas, Turner paints a picture of corruption that no amount of regulation could curb. Thirty years ago, the author feared that casino operators would ultimately use their wealth, political power, and natural instinct for applying leverage to expand their destructive activities beyond Nevada's borders. Index.

768.   *Underage Gaming*. Memphis, Tenn.: Promus Companies, 11 November 1993. 6 pp.
      Presents the gaming industry's perspective on underage gambling. This report briefly reviews adolescent gambling behavior and states that it is a serious problem because it is illegal for both individuals and casinos. Also, research shows that many compulsive gamblers start during their teens.   State laws identifying where minors are permitted in casinos vary throughout the country; a listing of these restrictions for ten states are included. "Young people, their parents, and casino employees" must work together to help lessen this problem; casinos, for example, "must create a corporate culture or ethos that does not tolerate underage gaming."   Other suggestions for prevention include community awareness programs, casino signage, and employee training programs.

769.   United States. Commission on the Review of the National Policy Toward Gambling. *Gambling in America*: *Final Report*. Washington, D.C.: GPO, 1976. 192 pp.
      Concludes three years of research and hearings on a wide variety of gambling issues. Finds that eighty percent of the American public approve of gambling and that prohibiting it is impossible. The Commission recommends that all fifty state governments and the federal government cooperate to regulate gambling and that casino-style gaming operations should not be viewed as a financial panacea for states facing revenue problems. The report also looks at federal gambling statutes, the national policy towards

gambling, state and local gambling enforcement, American attitudes and behaviors toward gambling, casinos, pari-mutuel wagering, lotteries, bingo, and illegal gambling.

770.   United States. Commission on the Review of the National Policy Toward Gambling. *Gambling in America*: *Final Report, Appendices 1-3*. 3 vols. Washington, D.C.: GPO, 1976.
        Provides a compendium of expert opinions on a wide variety of gambling topics, including moral and religious aspects, law enforcement, state policies, foreign experiences, and federal taxation. Volume two offers a survey of American attitudes and behavior, and volume three summarizes the thousands of pages of Commission hearings. Bibliographical references.

771.   Volberg, Rachel A. *Gambling and Problem Gambling Among Adolescents in Washington State: Report to the Washington State Lottery*. Albany, N.Y.: Gemini Research, 1993. 41 pp.
        Surveys 1,054 Washington State teenagers between the ages of thirteen and seventeen to determine gambling activities, losses, and possible associations with other risk-taking behaviors including drug and alcohol abuse. Key findings include: eighty-three percent of the respondents had gambled; those who had gambled tended to be males with a weekly income; raffles, sports events, cards, dice, and board games were the most common forms of gambling; the mean age at which respondents began to gamble was twelve years old; one percent were rated as problem gamblers, while nine percent were determined to be at risk; and problem gamblers were significantly more likely to have used tobacco, alcohol, and drugs than non-problem gamblers.

772.   Volberg, Rachel A. *Gambling and Problem Gambling in Washington State: Report to the Washington State Lottery*. Albany, N.Y.: Gemini Research, 1993. 34 pp.
        Surveys 1,502 Washington State residents over the age of eighteen to determine gambling activities, losses, and

problems which may have resulted from such activities. Key findings include: ninety-one percent of the respondents had gambled sometime in their lives; gamblers tended to be white, over the age of thirty, and high school graduates with an annual household income over $25,000 per year; 1.9 percent of the population are considered compulsive gamblers; problem gamblers tend to be male, under thirty years old, non-white, and unmarried; sports wagering, non-Indian bingo, and the lottery's Daily Game are more closely associated with problem gambling than other gambling activities; and forty-nine percent of the group who were rated as lifetime problem or possible problem gamblers did not have a current problem, suggesting that with the lack of treatment programs they were able to overcome their difficulties on their own.

773. Volberg, Rachel A. "The Prevalence and Demographics of Pathological Gamblers: Implications for Public Health." *American Journal of Public Health* 84 (February 1994): 237-214.
Argues that the recent and rapid spread of legalized gambling raises "serious public health concerns" about the related increase of compulsive gambling. For her study, Volberg collected epidemiological data to "determine the prevalence of probable pathological gambling in the general population" and demographics "from pathological gamblers entering treatment programs" in five states. She concludes that while gambling availability and participation differ in these locations, "the demographics of pathological gamblers" are similar; minorities, children, and women are identified as "specific at-risk groups." Policy and program officials must seriously consider these research implications where legalized gambling is proposed or implemented. Tables, bibliographical references.

774. Volberg, Rachel A., and Randall M. Stuefen. "Gambling and Problem Gambling in South Dakota." In *Gaming in South Dakota*. Vermillion, S. Dak.: University of South Dakota, Business Research Bureau, 12 November 1991. 27 pp.

Presents survey results of "gambling involvement and gambling problems" in South Dakota. The authors' findings include: the state's rate of problem and pathological gambling is lower than that of the Northeast but higher than Minnesota and Iowa; South Dakota has more female problem gamblers than any other state; and the "greatest monthly expenditures on gambling are for video lottery and slot machines." They urge educators, addiction treatment professionals, state agencies, and gaming industry officials to take whatever steps necessary to develop "prevention, education, and treatment services." Tables, charts, bibliographical references.

775.   Wagenaar, Willem Albert. *Paradoxes of Gambling Behaviour*. Essays in Cognitive Psychology. Hillsdale, N.J.: Erlbaum, 1988. 126 pp.

Studies the approaches gamblers take in playing such games as blackjack, roulette, and lotteries. Wagenaar concludes that the biggest paradox of gambling is that it exists at all, since his studies show that most gamblers know that they will not win in the long run. He attributes the paradox to the gamblers' isolation of the next round of gambling from the inevitable long term outcome; they believe that they will be lucky the next time. "People find it difficult to appreciate the true nature of roulette wheels, dice, cards and the drawing of lots. The difficulty is made worse by the clever design of casino games and lotteries." Bibliographical references, index.

776.   Wolf, John D. "Taking a Gamble on the Casino Industry." *Christian Century* 107 (17 January 1990): 36, 38.

Reports on the controversy surrounding casino gambling in Gary, Indiana. Proponents cite increased employment for this economically-depressed area. Opponents, led by over 200 local church groups, are concerned about this issue's morality and argue that most jobs would not go to area residents; "those that did would be low-paying menial positions." Moreover, based on Atlantic City's experience, casinos would cause "increased crime, prostitution, corruption, and drug trafficking," offsetting any economic benefits. One gaming analyst said that the best locations for casinos are economically depressed areas, while others respond that this attitude reflects a "racial overtone in the industry's thrust" since such areas are usually comprised predominantly of minorities. A brief overview on gambling in Indiana is included.

777.   Worsnop, Richard L. "Gambling Boom: Will the Gaming Industry's Growth Hurt Society?" *CQ Researcher* 4 (November 1994): 241-264.
        Contrasts the explosive economic growth of legalized gaming with potential social drawbacks. Americans wagered a record $329.9 billion in 1992, losing $29.9 billion, and the author questions whether this extraordinary activity will result in increased compulsive gambling, the corruption of professional sports, problems for states saddled with Indian gaming operations, or other problems.

SUPPLEMENTAL MATERIALS

778.   Aasved, Mikal J., and J. Clark Laundergan. *You Betcha: Gambling and Its Impacts in a Northern Minnesota Community.* St. Paul, Minn.: M.J. Aasved, J.M. Schaefer, 1992. 87 pp.

779.   Aasved, Mikal J., and James M. Schaefer. *Who Needs Las Vegas? Gambling and its Impacts in a Southwestern Minnesota Agricultural Community.* St. Paul, Minn.: Minnesota Department of Human Services, Mental Health Division, August 1992. 63 pp.

780.   Barron, James. "Has the Growth of Gambling Made Society the Loser in the Long Run?" *New York Times* (31 May 1989): A18 (L).

781.   Becker, Gary S. "Economic Viewpoint: Higher 'Sin' Taxes: A Low Blow to the Poor." *Business Week* 3108 (5 June 1989): 23.

782.   Berman, Linda, and Mary-Ellen Siegel. *Behind the 8-Ball: A Guide for Families of Gamblers*. New York: Simon & Schuster, 1992. 285 pp.

783.   Blair, Gwenda. "Betting Against the Odds: Addiction to Gambling Destroys Lives and Ruins Businesses." *New York Times Magazine II: The Business World* (25 September 1988): 57, 76, 78, 80-81.

784.   Blume, Sheila B.   "Pathological Gambling and Switching Addictions: Report of a Case." *Journal of Gambling Studies* 10 (Spring 1994): 87-98.

785.   Borg, Mary O., Paul M. Mason, and Stephen L. Shapiro. "An Economic Comparison of Gambling Behavior in Atlantic City and Las Vegas." *Public Finance Quarterly* 18 (July 1990): 291-312.

786.   Braidfoot, Larry. "Gambling: Why Christians Must Say No." *Fundamentalist Journal* (1987): 20, 22, 61.

787.   British Columbia. Gaming Commission. *Report to the Attorney General By the Gaming Commission on the Status of Gaming in British Columbia.*   Victoria, B.C.: Queen's Printer for British Columbia, 1988. 32 pp.

788.   Brown, Basil R. "The Selective Adaption of the Alcoholics Anonymous by Gamblers Anonymous." *Journal of Gambling Studies* 7 (Fall 1991): 187-205.

789.   Bruce, A.C., and J.E.V. Johnson.   "Male and Female Betting Behavior: New Perspectives." *Journal of Gambling Studies* 10 (Summer 1994): 183-198.

790.   Carlton, Peter L., and Paul Manowitz. "Factors Determining the Severity of Pathological Gambling in Males." *Journal of Gambling Studies* 10 (Summer 1994): 147-158.

791. Chavira, Ricardo. "The Rise of Teenage Gambling." *Time* 137 (25 February 1991): 78.

792. Ciarrocchi, Joseph. "Severity of Impairment in Dually Addicted Gamblers." *Journal of Gambling Studies* 3 (1987): 16-26.

793. Citizens' Research Education Network. *The Other Side of the Coin: A Casino's Impact on Hartford.* Hartford, Conn.: Citizens' Research Education Network, 1992. 6 pp.

794. Conlin, Joseph. "When Christians Meet in Sin City." *Successful Meetings* 37 (December 1988): 67-69.

795. Coulombe, Andrée, Robert Ladouceur, Raymond Desharnais, and Jean Jobin. "Erroneous Perceptions and Arousal Among Regular and Occasional Video Poker Players." *Journal of Gambling Studies* 8 (Fall 1992): 235-244.

796. Cummings, Thomas N., and Blase Gambino. "Perceptions by Treatment Staff of Critical Tasks in the Treatment of the Compulsive Gambler." *Journal of Gambling Studies* 8 (Summer 1992): 181-200.

797. David, Florence Nightingale. *Games, Gods and Gambling: The Origins and History of Probability and Statistical Ideas from the Earliest Times to the Newtonian Era.* New York: Hafner, 1962. 275 pp.

798. DeParle, Jason. "Casinos Became Big Players in the Overhaul of Welfare." *New York Times* (9 May 1994): A1, A9 (L).

799. Dickerson, M. "Gambling: Dependence Without a Drug." *International Review of Psychiatry* 1 (1989): 157-172.

800. Elia, Christopher, and Durand F. Jacobs. "The Incidence of Pathological Gambling Among Native

Americans Treated for Alcohol Dependence." *International Journal of Addictions* 28 (July 1993): 659-666.

801.   Fabian, Ann Vincent. *Rascals and Gentlemen: The Meaning of American Gambling, 1820-1890.* Ph.D. dissertation, Yale University. Ann Arbor, Mich.: University Microfilms, 1983. 383 pp.

802.   Fisher, Sue. "Gambling and Pathological Gambling in Adolescents." *Journal of Gambling Studies* 9 (Fall 1993): 277-288.

803.   Frank, Michael L., David Lester, and Arnold Wexler. "Suicidal Behavior Among Members of Gamblers Anonymous." *Journal of Gambling Studies* 7 (Fall 1991): 249-254.

804.   Frey, James H. "Gambling: A Sociological Review." *Annals of the American Academy of Political and Social Science* 474 (July 1984): 107-121.

805.   Gabriel, Trip. "From Vice to Nice: The Suburbanization of Las Vegas." *New York Times Magazine* (1 December 1991): 68-71, 79, 80-81, 84.

806.   Galski, Thomas. *Handbook of Pathological Gambling.* Springfield, Ill.: C.C. Thomas, 1987. 211 pp.

807.   *Gambling: Crime or Recreation?* The Information Series on Current Topics.   1992 ed. Wylie, Tex.: Information Plus, 1992. 88pp.

808.   Heineman, Mary. "Compulsive Gambling: Structured Family Intervention." *Journal of Gambling Studies* 10 (Spring 1994): 67-76.

809.   Holmstrom, David. "Casino Gambling Surges in U.S., Tempting More Teenagers." *Christian Science Monitor* 86 (17 February 1994): 3.

810.   Holmstrom, David. "U.S. Is Gambling as Never Before." *Christian Science Monitor* 85 (26 January 1993): 8.

811.   Kearney, Christopher A., and Ronald S. Drabman. "Risk-Taking/Gambling-Like Behavior in Preschool Children." *Journal of Gambling Studies* 8 (Fall 1992): 287-298.

812.   Keren, Gideon, and Charles Lewis. "The Two Fallacies of Gamblers: Type I and Type II." *Organizational Behavior & Human Decision Processes* 60 (October 1994): 75-89.

813.   Knapp, T.J., and B.C. Lech. "Pathological Gambling: A Review With Recommendations." *Advances in Behavior Research and Therapy* 9 (1987): 21-49.

814.   Lesieur, Henry R., and Richard J. Rosenthal. "Pathological Gambling: A Review of the Literature." *Journal of Gambling Studies* 7 (Spring 1991): 5-39.

815.   Lesieur, Henry R., and Robert Klein. "Pathological Gambling Among High School Students." *Addictive Behaviors* 12 (1987): 129-135.

816.   Levine, Art. "Playing the Adolescent Odds." *U.S. News & World Report* 108 (18 June 1990): 51.

817.   Marriott, Michel. "Fervid Debate on Gambling: Disease or Moral Weakness?" *New York Times* (21 November 1992): 1, 22 (L).

818.   Mascarenhas, Oswald A.J. "Spousal Ethical Justifications of Casino Gambling: A Psychometric Analysis." *Journal of Consumer Affairs* 25 (Summer 1991): 122-143.

819.   Meier, Barry. "A Confusion of Competition Cools Florida's Casino Fever." *New York Times* (8 August 1994): B6 (L).

820.   Minnesota. Institute of Public Health. *Gambling Facts: Minnesota Gambling Background Information.* St. Paul, Minn.: Minnesota. Institute of Public Health, 1993. 16 pp.

821.   Mobilia, Pamela. "Gambling as a Rational Addiction." *Journal of Gambling Studies* 9 (Summer 1993): 121-152.

822.   Murray, John B. "Review of Research on Pathological Gambling." *Psychological Reports* 72 (June 1993): 791-810.

823.   *Overview of Problem Gambling Research.* Memphis, Tenn.: Promus Companies, 1994. 20 pp.

824.   Ploscowe, Morris, and Edwin J. Lukas. *Gambling.* Philadelphia: American Academy of Political and Social Science, 1950. 209 pp.

825.   Rachlin, Howard. "Why Do People Gamble and Keep Gambling Despite Heavy Losses?" *Psychological Science* 1 (September 1990): 294-297.

826.   Rosecrance, John. "The Sociology of Casino Gamblers." *Nevada Public Affairs Review* 2 (1986): 27-31.

827.   Rosecrance, John. "Why Regular Gamblers Don't Quit: A Sociological Perspective." *Sociological Perspectives* 29 (July 1986): 357-378.

828.   Rosenthal, R.J. "Pathological Gambling." *Psychiatric Annals* 22 (1992): 72-78.

829.   Ross, Elizabeth. "Critics Worry About Gambling Consequences in New England." *Christian Science Monitor* 86 (31 March 1994): 3.

830.   Smith, James F., and Vicki Abt. "Gambling as Play." *The Annals of the American Academy of Political and Social Science* 474 (July 1984): 122-132.

831.   Taber, Julian I., John L. Collachi, and Edward J. Lynn. "Pathological Gambling: Possibilities for Treatment in Northern Nevada." *Nevada Public Affairs Review* 2 (1986): 39-42.

832.   Templar, Donald I., Jackie Moten, and George Kaiser. "Casino Gaming Offense Inmates: What Are These Men Like?" *Journal of Gambling Studies* 10 (Fall 1994): 237-246.

833.   Thompson, William Norman. "Patterns of Public Response to Lottery, Horserace, and Casino Gambling Issues." *Nevada Review of Business & Economics* 9 (Spring 1985): 12-22.

834.   Volberg, Rachel A., and Henry J. Steadman. "Accurately Depicting Pathological Gamblers: Policy and Treatment Implications." *Journal of Gambling Studies* 8 (Winter 1992): 401-412.

835.   Wagenaar, Willem Albert. *Paradoxes of Gambling Behavior*. Essays in Cognitive Psychology. Hillsdale, N.J.: Erlbaum, 1988. 126 pp.

836.   Walker, Michael B. "Irrational Thinking Among Slot Machine Players." *Journal of Gambling Studies* 8 (Fall 1992): 245-261.

837.   Walker, Michael B. *The Psychology of Gambling*. International Series in Experimental Social Psychology. New York, N.Y.: Pergamon Press, 1992. 262 pp.

838.   Walters, Glenn D. "The Gambling Lifestyle: I. Theory." *Journal of Gambling Studies* 10 (Summer 1994): 159-182.

839.   Walters, Glenn D. "The Gambling Lifestyle: II. Treatment." *Journal of Gambling Studies* 10 (Fall 1994): 219-235.

840.   Welles, Chris. "America's Gambling Fever: Everybody Wants a Piece of the Action—But Is it Good for Us?" *Business Week* 3102 (24 April 1989): 112-115, 118, 120.

841.   Will, George F. "In the Grip of Gambling." *Newsweek* 113 (8 May 1989): 78.

842.   Wolff, Phyllis. *Lifestyles of a High Roller.* Grand Rapids, Mich.: Gollehon, 1991. 247 pp.

SECTION G

Casinos and Crime

Casinos have long been linked to crime and criminals. Part myth, part history, and part reality, this association often becomes the center of debate when the pros and cons of casinos are weighed. The literature in this section explores the possible relationship between casinos and various types of criminal activity, from street crime and gang violence to political corruption and infiltration of the industry by organized crime. A variety of studies and reports provide interesting, though often contradictory, testimony.

843.   Albanese, Jay S. "The Effect of Casino Gambling on Crime." *Federal Probation* 49 (June 1985): 39-44.
Argues that increasing crime rates in Atlantic City are not caused by casinos. This study correlated the number of crimes, changes in police manpower, changes in the city's average daily population, increases in the number of buildings and businesses, and crimes reported elsewhere in New Jersey. The author concludes that increases in crime may occur in any city that experiences the kind of growth Atlantic City did after gambling was legalized; casinos, however, are not solely responsible. Also, "the lack of any direct casino-crime link" may be the result of the New Jersey's Casino Control Act's "intensive crime prevention" provisions. Tables, bibliographical references.

844.   Buck, Andrew J., and Simon Hakim. "Does Crime Affect Property Values?" *The Canadian Appraiser* 33 (Winter 1989): 23-27.
Reports on a case study which found that Atlantic City's casinos caused higher crime rates which consequently

resulted in decreased property values.   The study's
theoretical background, data and research methods, and an
analysis of its empirical results are included. The summary
states that increases in crimes were directly related to
casinos; also, "crime levels in accessible areas diminish with
distance from Atlantic City" and "all crimes but larcenies
adversely affect land values."   Tables, bibliographical
references.

845.   Buck, Andrew J., Joseph Deutsch, Simon Hakim,
Uriel Spiegel, and J. Weinblatt. "A Von Thunen Model of
Crime, Casinos and Property Values in New Jersey." *Urban
Studies* 28 (1991): 673-686.
        Analyzes the relationship between Atlantic City
casinos, increased crime rates, and lowered land values
using J.H. Von Thunen's 1826 agricultural land-use model.
The article covers the model's theoretical background, data
description, methodology, and analysis of variables.
Findings suggest that gaming's economic advantages were
offset by the adverse effects of increased crime rates that
lowered property values. Tables, bibliographical references.

846.   Buck, Andrew J., Simon Hakim, and Uriel Spiegel.
"Casinos, Crime, and Real Estate Values: Do They Relate?"
Journal of Research in Crime and Delinquency 28 (August
1991): 288-303.
        Examines study results which determined that
legalized gaming in Atlantic City increased crime rates,
resulting in lowered property values. The article includes the
study's theoretical background, data, research methods, and
an analysis of the results. According to the authors, the cost
of crime is substantial and negates the economic benefits of
legalized gaming. Tables, bibliographical references.

847.   *The Casino/Street Crime Connection.* Memphis,
Tenn.: Promus Companies, 1 January 1993. 8 pp.
        Presents the gaming industry's argument that casinos
do not increase crime. After noting that several academic
researchers focused solely on Atlantic City to prove this
correlation, the report states that such studies did not

consider several other relevant factors; crime rates, for
example, in the state increased simultaneously suggesting
that Atlantic City's crime rates were "just a reflection of a
general increase in crime." Also, since the daily population
of residents and visitors grew after the arrival of casinos,
"crime may have gone up just because there were more
people around to be perpetrators and victims." Since crime
in a sample of riverboat gaming sites in Illinois, Mississippi,
and Iowa has not increased, concerns about this supposed
correlation should not affect decisions about legalizing
gaming.

848.   Chicago Crime Commission. *An Analysis of Key
Issues Involved in the Proposed Chicago Casino Gambling
Project.* Chicago, Ill.: Chicago Crime Commission, 1990.
27 pp.
        Looks at projected increases in jobs, organized
crime, ambient crime, and cost estimates of a proposed
Chicago casino-entertainment complex. This Commission
concludes that 15-20,000 new jobs will be created, albeit at
the low end of the wage scale. There is little doubt that
organized crime will attempt to infiltrate casino operations
and ancillary services, and keeping it out will be an ongoing
battle. The potential for public and union corruption is high;
street crime, illegal gambling, loan sharking, and law
enforcement costs will all rise significantly. The report also
concludes that tax revenues estimated by project promoters
are greatly exaggerated.

849.   Chiricos, Ted. *Casinos and Crime: An Assessment
of the Evidence.* University of Nevada, Las Vegas, Special
Collections, 1994. 12 pp.
        Analyzes "the available evidence concerning possible
links between casinos and crime." Chiricos, a professor at
Florida State University's School of Criminology and
Criminal Justice, concludes that casinos do not cause crime.
"When population is adjusted for tourists and other visitors,
crime rates in Atlantic City, Las Vegas, and Reno are lower
than the major tourist cities in Florida." Bibliographical
references, tables, graphs.

850.   Curran, Daniel, and Frank Scarpitti. "Crime in
Atlantic City: Do Casinos Make a Difference?" *Deviant
Behavior: An Interdisciplinary Journal* 12 (1991): 431-449.
        Argues that using FBI crime figures to correlate
Atlantic City casinos and increased crime rates may be
erroneous. While these figures show significant growth in
crime, "they do not differentiate crime that occurs in the
community and that which occurs in the casinos" and do not
consider the city's many tourists. By analyzing community-
based crimes and crimes in casinos separately, the authors
conclude that increases in crime were not significantly related
to gaming. Tables, bibliographic references.

851.   Demaris, Ovid. *How Greed, Corruption and the
Mafia Turned Atlantic City into the Boardwalk Jungle.* New
York: Bantam Books, 1986. 436 pp.
        Exposes the crime, political corruption, and Mafia
infiltration of Atlantic City casinos. Written by the author of
the *Green Felt Jungle*, this book paints a vivid picture of a
city consumed by greed and ruthless exploitation. Attention
is given to top *Mafiosi*, corrupt government officials, and
each boardwalk casino. Index.

852.   Dombrink, John Dennis. *Outlaw Businessmen:
Organized Crime and the Legalization of Casino Gambling.*
Ph.D. dissertation, University of California, Berkeley,
1981.   University of Nevada, Las Vegas, Special
Collections. 362 pp.
        Argues that ambivalent attitudes toward gambling in
the United States have caused a powerful underground
economy and a legal gambling industry that has taken many
forms. Dombrink investigated two referendums to legalize
casino gambling in the 1970s, one in New Jersey that passed
and one in Florida that failed.   He concludes that if
influential politicians and powerful economic interests view
gambling as a threat, the initiative will fail. Conversely, if
they see it as a benefit, it will pass even when the industry is
stigmatized. Bibliographical references.

853.   Dombrink, John, and William Norman Thompson. "The Report of the 1986 Commission on Organized Crime and Its Implications for Commercial Gaming in America." *Nevada Public Affairs Review* 2 (1986): 70-75.
Discusses the report filed by the President's Commission on Organized Crime and a paper which was drafted by consultants Dombrink and Thompson. In their paper, the authors call for a moratorium on legal gambling until research on public policy issues can be completed. They also propose a federal-state partnership approach to control gambling.

854.   Florida. Department of Law Enforcement. *The Question of Casinos in Florida: Increased Crime, Is It Worth the Gamble?* Draft. Florida Department of Law Enforcement, 1994. 9 pp.
Presents the Department's strong opposition to casinos in Florida. Reasons to reject casinos include the likelihood of increased index crime rates, juvenile gambling, drunk driving, and infiltration by traditional and non-traditional organized crime groups.

855.   Florida Sheriffs Association, Florida Police Chiefs Association, and the Florida Department of Law Enforcement. *Casinos and Crime, Is it Worth the Gamble? A Summary Report and Position Paper.* Tallahassee, Fla.: Florida Sheriffs Association, 1994. 15 pp.
Presents the position of three Florida law enforcement groups on the introduction of casino gaming in the state. The Florida Sheriffs Association, the Florida Police Chiefs Association, and the Florida Department of Law Enforcement are all strongly opposed to any expansion of legalized gambling in Florida. Of primary concern is the explosive increase in crime that occurred in Atlantic City and Gulfport, Mississippi following the introduction of casinos and the fear that similar increases would probably happen in Florida. This report, released just prior to the 1994 ballot initiative on gambling, compares crime statistics from Atlantic City, Gulfport, and various Florida cities.

856. Friedman, Joseph, Simon Hakim, and J. Weinblatt. "Casino Gambling as a 'Growth Pole' Strategy and Its Effects on Crime." *Journal of Regional Science* 29 (November 1989): 615-623.

Presents results of a study which correlates casinos and crime rates in sixty-four "localities with a population of over 1,000" next to or near Atlantic City; it did not include the city itself because the high number of visitors made it "difficult to define appropriate crime rates." Since major increases occurred in violent crimes, burglary, and car theft in areas thirty miles or less from the city, the authors conclude that the social costs of legalized gambling may "outweigh" the economic advantages, particularly in adjacent locales which receive little or no economic benefit. Tables, map, bibliographical references.

857. Giacopassi, David, and B. Grant Stitt. "Assessing the Impact of Casino Gambling on Crime in Mississippi." *American Journal of Criminal Justice* 18 (1993): 117-131.

Analyzes Biloxi, Mississippi's crime rates before and after the advent of casinos. The article includes a lengthy literature review and explanation of the study's methodology and results. The authors determined that only larceny and car theft statistics showed significant growth. They conclude, though, that "24-hour a day casino operations" do change communities, particularly in areas adjacent to the casinos, making more police and "more court and correctional capacity" mandatory. Tables, bibliographical references.

858. Hadjian, Ciran Marie. *Tourism and Crime in Las Vegas: Content Analysis of Components of Tourism and Crime in Las Vegas from Newspaper Articles.* Master's thesis, California State Polytechnic University, Pomona, 1992. University of Nevada, Las Vegas, Special Collections. 192 pp.

Explores the relationship between crime and tourism and tests the assumption that tourism negatively affects the "socio-cultural components" of a community. Hadjian concludes that tourism has negative and positive effects that cause stress and conflict, and she urges planners to take this into consideration. Casino cities, in particular, suffer higher crime rates than most metropolitan areas, and the author makes recommendations for controlling the problem. Bibliographical references.

859. Hakim, Simon. *The Impact of Casino Gambling on Crime in Atlantic City and Its Region.* University of Nevada, Las Vegas, Special Collections, 1985. Various pagings.

Illustrates, with dozens of charts and graphs, the effect casinos have had on a host of criminal activities in Atlantic City and vicinity. The increase in crime since the introduction of casino gaming in 1979 is partially attributed to the increased opportunity for criminal action that is associated with the introduction of any economic stimulus into an economically-depressed region. Hakim also concludes that the crime rate associated with Atlantic City casinos is significantly higher than what would have resulted from an alternative economic enterprise. Charts.

860. Hakim, Simon, and Andrew J. Buck. "Do Casinos Enhance Crime?" *Journal of Criminal Justice* 17 (1989): 409-416.

Investigates the relationship between crime and casinos in Atlantic City. The study's economic model includes a "before and after analysis . . . to separate the casino effect from the natural accretion of crime"; findings show significant increases in crime in both the city and nearby areas readily accessible to it. The authors stress that locales considering casino gaming must consider this correlation and the "anticipated costs of interjurisdictional crime spillover" in adjacent areas unaffected by the economic benefits casinos bring. Tables, bibliographical references.

861. Illinois. Criminal Justice Information Authority. *Casino Gambling and Crime in Chicago: The Impact of the Proposed Casino Complex on the Chicago, Cook County, and Selected State and Federal Criminal Justice Agencies.* Chicago, Ill.: Illinois Criminal Justice Information Authority, 1992. 63 pp.

Explores the impact of a proposed Chicago casino-entertainment complex on Cook County's criminal justice system costs. With this complex, Cook County index crime figures are expected to increase from 2.4 percent to 5.8 percent. System expenditures could rise from $42 million to $100 million annually. Non-index crimes such as drunk driving, fraud, extortion, embezzlement, prostitution, and drug offenses have not been quantified in this study but are also expected to significantly increase system costs. Regulating casinos, and their ancillary services and industries, to minimize penetration by organized crime is projected to cost an estimated $31 million to $53.2 million per year.

862.   Illinois. Criminal Justice Information Authority. *Riverboat Gambling and Crime in Illinois: Preliminary Report on Riverboat Gambling in Joliet, Impact on Criminal Activity and Law Enforcement Workloads.* Chicago, Ill.: Illinois Criminal Justice Information Authority, 1994. 33 pp.
Investigates the potential impact riverboat casinos might have on crime and law enforcement activities. Preliminary findings suggest that riverboat casinos afford a highly controlled and secure setting. There has not been a substantial increase in criminal activity as a result of riverboat gaming operations in Joliet, Illinois, and city officials and law enforcement administrators there have a very positive view of the enterprise. Charts.

863.   King, Rufus. *Gambling and Organized Crime.* Washington, D.C.: Public Affairs Press, 1969. 239 pp.
Investigates legal and illegal gambling, law enforcement, casino licensing, political corruption, and the state as gambling promoter. An excellent overview of the Mob's infiltration of Nevada casinos is accompanied by recommendations on how to curtail illegal gambling operations. In this classic work, King urges America to fight the proliferation of legal gaming beyond Nevada's borders. Bibliographical references, index.

864.   Kinnee, Kevin B. *Practical Gambling Investigation Techniques*. Elsevier Series in Practical Aspects of Criminal and Forensic Investigation. New York: Elsevier, 1992. 228 pp.

Explains how to conduct criminal investigations of illegal gambling operations and is written for practicing law enforcement personnel. While this title does not relate directly to legalized casino gambling, it provides useful information on how money is laundered, how background checks are conducted, and how probable cause is determined. A history of illegal gambling and its relationship to organized crime is also included. Bibliographical references, index.

865.   "Las Vegas Casinos Respond to Rash of LA 'Gang Member' Robberies." *Hotel/Motel Security and Safety Management* 12 (October 1994): 1-3.

Covers armed robberies at casinos in or near Las Vegas during 1993 and 1994, many purportedly done by Los Angeles gang members. Casinos are targeted because they contain large amounts of easily-obtained cash. Physical security measures, such as bars around cashier cages, have been minimal because most operators want their casinos to be aesthetically "user-friendly" rather than forbidding. Many casino officials are now modifying cashiers' areas with artistically-placed bars and plexiglass to prevent access, increasing security staff, and training other personnel on what to do in such situations.

866.   Margolis, Jeremy D. *Preliminary Report to the City of Chicago Gaming Commission: The Crime Issue*. Chicago, Ill.: Altheimer & Gray, 1992. 47 pp.

Studies the potential impact of a proposed Chicago casino-entertainment complex on street crime and public corruption. This report also discusses the need to safeguard casinos and ancillary services from infiltration by organized crime. Margolis, who was contracted to do the study by Caesars World, Hilton Hotels, and Circus Circus, concludes that cooperation with police, development of a sound regulatory framework, solid internal casino security, and open dialogue with community groups would keep the crime issue from ruling out the casino project.

867.   Massachusetts. Senate. Committee on Post Audit and Oversight. *Toward Gaming Regulation: Part I: Crime.* Boston, Mass., January 1994. 35 pp.
       Examines the relationship between legalized gaming in a community and crime rates there and in nearby areas. The Committee reviewed crime data compiled nationwide and from several metropolitan areas which have casinos; they found few statistical patterns or trends directly relating crime to casinos. This report, done by the Senate Committee on Post Audit and Oversight, includes two recommend-ations. Regulation of any Massachusetts casino industry should include oversight of gaming license holders and all businesses contracting with those state-regulated facilities. Enabling legislation should include language apportioning the various responsibilities and functions of policy development and implementation among a wide array of individuals and concerns; this will minimize the overall impact of possible corruption by any one individual. Tables, bibliographical references.

868.   New Jersey. Commission of Investigation. *Video Gambling.* Renton, N.J.: The Commission, 1991. 38 pp.
       Examines the problem of organized criminals illegally using video gambling devices in New Jersey and offers possible solutions. Thousands of machines are in urban areas where they are played by people who can least afford to lose money. The Commission calls for better licensing practices, stronger enforcement with harsher penalties, the banning of devices that are easily converted to illegal purposes, and more frequent machine inspections. They caution against liberalizing gaming laws or introducing new forms of gambling as a hedge against illegal gambling activity.

869.   Ochrym, Ronald George. "Street Crime, Tourism and Casinos: An Empirical Comparison." *Journal of Gambling Studies* 6 (Summer 1990): 127-138.

Examines "crime rates in several New Jersey tourist areas and non-tourist areas to determine if crime is statistically different in Atlantic City." The article contains a brief literature review, an explanation of the study's model, data, and methodology, and an analysis of crime rates. The author concludes that "tourist destinations" have mean crime rates higher than other areas, and crime rates grow due to increased tourism, whether or not casinos are present. Tables, bibliographical references.

870. Pennsylvania. Crime Commission. *An Investigation into the Conduct of Lackawanna County District Attorney, Attorney General Ernest D. Preate, Jr.* Conshohocken, Pa.: The Commission, 1994. 189 pp.

Investigates the campaign activities of Pennsylvania Attorney General Ernest D. Preate, Jr. The investigation was done in response to allegations that Preate sought campaign contributions from operators of illegal video poker machines in exchange for a "hands off" non-enforcement policy. The Commission concludes that there is enough evidence to warrant the assignment of a special prosecutor to further examine the case, and sufficient basis for the Elections Commission to investigate violations of the Election Code.

871. Reid, Ed, and Ovid Demaris. *The Green Felt Jungle.* New York: Trident Press, 1963. 242 pp.

Exposes the Mafia's domination of Las Vegas in the 1950s and early 1960s. This book portrays a city that is awash in graft, greed, and depravity and controlled by ruthless mobsters, crooked politicians, and tainted bureaucrats. Though it has been thirty-two years since *The Green Felt Jungle* was published, a less flattering view of Las Vegas and the casino industry has yet to be written.

872. U.S. President's Commission on Organized Crime. *Organized Crime and Gambling: Record of Hearing VII, June 24-26, 1985, New York.* Washington, D.C.: GPO, 1985. 866 pp.

Reviews the connection between organized crime and legal and illegal gambling. Hundreds of billions of dollars are wagered each year by Americans, and a significant portion of this money ultimately becomes the profits of organized crime groups. Over three days, thirty-six witnesses testified on illegal gambling prosecution in Chicago, federal gambling law enforcement policy, corruption in casino licensing, college basketball, boxing, and the infiltration of casinos by traditional organized crime groups. The roles Nevada and New Jersey regulatory agencies play in "hardening" casinos against infiltration are also discussed.

873.   Woolner, Ann. *Washed in Gold: The Story Behind the Biggest Money-Laundering Investigation in U.S. History*. New York: Simon & Schuster, 1994. 391 pp.
Investigates the elaborate money-laundering operations of the Medellín drug cartel and the U.S. Drug Enforcement Agency's efforts to stop them. While these events are not associated with legalized gambling, casinos have been tied to alleged money-laundering activities; this book provides detailed information on how money laundering works. Index.

874.   Zendzian, Craig A. *In the Shadows: The Vulnerability of Casino Ancillary Services to Racketeering*. Ph.D. dissertation, City University of New York, 1990. University of Nevada, Las Vegas, Special Collections. 220 pp.
Explains how organized crime can exploit the potential ineffectiveness of laws that fail to protect casinos from racketeers. Zendzian cautions that the window of greatest vulnerability is where vending registration occurs, and he urges changes in casino law which will intensify the scrutiny of vending license applicants. Bibliographical references.

875.   Zendzian, Craig A. *Who Pays? Casino Gambling, Hidden Interests, and Organized Crime*. New York: Harrow and Heston, 1993. 149 pp.

Argues that organized crime has always been associated with casinos in the United States. After a brief history of legalized gambling, particularly in Nevada, Zendzian traces its development in the Bahamas and New Jersey. While federal and state enabling legislation has tried to prevent organized crime's infiltration, "there is too much cash money involved in casino gambling and there are too many ways to be corrupt." Vending registration, not licensing, is now the "weakest of all casino controls." The author states that it is necessary for the gaming industry to be very active in establishing regulations to eliminate criminal involvement, and Indian gaming is now especially susceptible to such corruption. Bibliographical references, index.

SUPPLEMENTAL MATERIALS

876.   Buck, Andrew J., Simon Hakim, and Uriel Spiegel. "The National Rate of Crime by Type of Community." *Review of Social Economy* 43 (1985): 245-259.

877.   Casey, Steven C., and Connecticut. State Legislature. Public Safety Committee. *The Negative Impact of Casino Gambling.* Hartford, Conn.: Public Safety Committee, 1981. 15 pp.

878.   Johnson, Craig R. "Gov't as Pit Boss: Should States Embrace Casino Gaming?" *International Gaming and Wagering Business* 15 (5 July 1994): 26-27.

879.   Kroeber, Hans-Ludwig. "Roulette Gamblers and Gamblers at Electronic Game Machines: Where Are the Differences." *Journal of Gambling Studies* 8 (Spring 1992): 79-92.

880.   McGurrin, Martin C., and Vicki Abt. "Overview of Public Policy and Commercial Gambling." *Journal of Gambling Studies* 8 (Winter 1992): 325-329.

881.   Meyer, Gerhard, and Thomas Fabian. "Delinquency Among Pathological Gamblers: A Casual Approach." *Journal of Gambling Studies* 8 (Spring 1992): 61-78.

882.   Peterson, Iver. "Casino Cheating 101: Police and Other Officials Learn to Spot Those Who Break the Rules of the Game." *New York Times* (4 May 1994): B1, B4 (L).

883.   U.S. Congress. Senate. Committee on Governmental Affairs. Permanent Subcommittee on Investigations. *Illegal Use of Video Gambling Machines: Hearing Before the Permanent Subcommittee on Investigations of the Committee on Governmental Affairs.* 98th Cong., 2nd sess., 1 October 1984.   115 pp.

884.   Weinstein, Adam K. "Note: Prosecuting Attorneys for Money Laundering: A New and Questionable Weapon in the War on Crime." *Law and Contemporary Problems* 51 (Winter 1988): 369-386.

CHAPTER 4

Government Agencies and Indian Gaming Locations: A State-by-State Breakdown

This chapter provides directory listings for federal and state agencies involved in gaming regulation and oversight and Indian gaming locations for tribes with gaming compacts. Since most legalization occurs on the state level, this section also includes telephone numbers for state legislative information and directory listings for state legislative research libraries which can provide assistance. These listings were compiled and verified by telephone, Spring 1995. Since directory information can change rapidly, some of this may be out of date before publication. The following listings, however, will remain useful as a guide on how regulatory agencies are organized. It is helpful to know, for example, that Louisiana gaming enforcement is maintained by the State Police, and Iowa's gaming department is in the Division of Investigation, Department of Public Safety. Many libraries have a variety of standard directories which offer current information of this kind. Also, most state library reference desks will provide information on their state's governmental agencies.

FEDERAL AGENCIES

Indian Gaming Management Staff
Bureau of Indian Affairs
U.S. Department of The Interior
1849 C St. NW

Mail Stop 2070, MIB
Washington, DC 20240
Phone: (202) 219-4068
Fax: (202) 273-3153

National Indian Gaming
Commission
1850 M St. NW
Washington, DC 20036
Phone: (202) 632-7003

Senate Select Committee
on Indian Affairs
Hart Senate Office Building,

Rm. SH838
Washington, DC 20510
Phone: (202) 224-2251

U.S. Travel Data Center
1100 New York Ave. NW
Suite 450
Washington, DC 20005-3934
Phone: (202)408-1832

STATE AGENCIES

Alabama

LEGISLATIVE INFORMATION
House: (205) 242-7627
Senate: (205) 242-7826

LEGISLATIVE LIBRARIES

Legislative Reference
Service
613 State House
Montgomery, AL 36130
Phone: (242) 334-7560
         (334) 242-7579
Fax: (334) 242-4358

Alaska

LEGISLATIVE INFORMATION
(907) 465-4648

LEGISLATIVE LIBRARIES

Reference Library
Legislative Affairs Agency
130 Steward St., Suite 400
Juneau, AK 99801-2105
Phone: (907) 465-3808
Fax: (907) 465-2029
(907) 465-4844

REGULATORY AGENCIES

Division of
Charitable Gaming
Department of Revenue
P.O. Box 110440
Juneau, AK 99811-0440
Phone: (907) 465-2581

Arizona

LEGISLATIVE INFORMATION
House: (602) 542-4221
Senate: (602) 542-3559

LEGISLATIVE LIBRARIES

Department of Library Archives and Public Records
Research Division, Rm. 300
1700 West Washington
State Capitol
Phoenix, AZ 85007
Phone: (602) 542-3701
Fax: (602) 542-4400

Senate Research
1700 West Washington, Rm. 2-B
Phoenix, AZ 85007
Phone: (602) 542-3171
Fax: (602) 542-4400

REGULATORY AGENCIES

Arizona Lottery
4740 East University Dr.
Phoenix, AZ 85034
Phone: (602) 921-4400

Department of Racing
15 South 15th Ave., Suite 100
Phoenix, AZ 85007
Phone: (602) 542-5151

Arizona State Gaming Agency
15 South 15th Ave., Suite 100
Phoenix, AZ 85007
Phone: (602) 542-5151

Bingo Section
Arizona Department of Revenue
1600 West Monroe
Phoenix, AZ 85007

Phone: (602) 542-3227

INDIAN GAMING

Chin Indian Community
Route 2, Box 27
Maricopa, AZ 85007
Phone: (602) 569-2618
Chairman: Martin J. Antone
Compact approved 3/19/93; published 3/31/93. Superseded by compact approved 7/30/93; published 8/18/93. Gaming Devices/ Keno/ Lottery/ Off-Track Pari-Mutuel Wagering/ Pari-Mutuel Wagering on Horse Racing/ Pari-Mutuel Wagering on Dog Racing

Cocopah Tribe of Arizona
Bin G
Somerton, AZ 85350
Phone: (602) 627-2102
Chairman: Dale Phillips
Compact approved 8/17/92; published 8/24/92. Superseded by compact approved 7/30/93; published 8/18/93. Gaming Devices/ Keno/ Lottery/ Off-Track Pari-Mutuel Wagering/ Pari-Mutuel Wagering on Horse Racing/ Pari-Mutuel Wagering on Dog Racing

Colorado River Indian Tribes
Route 1, Box 23-B
Parker, AZ 85344
Phone: (602) 669-5271
Compact approved 7/29/94; published 8/9/94. Gaming Devices/ Keno/ Lottery/ Off-Track Pari-

Mutuel Wagering/ Pari-Mutuel
Wagering on Horse Racing/ Pari-
Mutuel Wagering on Dog Racing

**Fort McDowell Mohave-
Apache Indian Community**
P.O. Box 17779
Fountain Hills, AZ 85269
Phone: (602) 990-0995
President: Clinton Pattea
Compact approved 12/23/92 pub-
lished 12/30/92. Superseded by
Compact approved 7/30/93; pub-
lished 8/18/93. Gaming Devices/
Keno/ Lottery/ Off-Track Pari-
Mutuel Wagering/ Pari-Mutuel
Wagering on Horse Racing/ Pari-
Mutuel Wagering on Dog Racing

Fort Mojave Indian Tribe
500 Merriman
Needles, CA 92363
Phone: (619) 326-4591
Chairperson: Patricia Madueno
Compact approved 10/22/93;;
published 11/10/93. Gaming De-
vices/ Keno/ Lottery/ Off-Track
Pari-Mutuel Wagering/ Pari-
Mutuel Wagering on Horse Rac-
ing/ Pari-Mutuel Wagering on
Dog Racing

**Gila River Indian
Community**
P.O. Box 97
Sacaton, AZ 85247
Phone: (602) 562-3311
Governor: Thomas R. White
Compact approved 8/1/93;
published 8/18/93. Gaming

Devices/ Keno/ Lottery/ Off-
Track Pari-Mutuel Wagering/
Pari-Mutuel Wagering on Horse
Racing/ Pari-Mutuel Wagering
on Dog Racing

Haulapai Tribe
P.O. Box 179
Peach Springs, AZ 86434
Phone: (602) 769-2216
Compact approved 4/15/94; pub-
lished 4/26/94. Gaming Devices/
Keno/ Lottery/ Off-Track Pari-
Mutuel Wagering/ Pari-Mutuel
Wagering on Horse Racing/ Pari-
Mutuel Wagering on Dog Racing

Kaibab Paiute Tribe
Tribal Affairs Building
Pipe Spring, AZ 86022
Phone: (602) 643-7245
Compact approved 4/8/94; pub-
lished 4/26/94. Gaming Devices/
Keno/ Lottery/ Off-Track Pari-
Mutuel Wagering/ Pari-Mutuel
Wagering on Horse Racing/ Pari-
Mutuel Wagering on Dog Racing

Pascua Yaqui Tribe
7474 South Camino De Oeste
Tucson, AZ 85746
Phone: (602) 883-2838
Chairman: Albert Garcia
Compact approved 7/30/93; pub-
lished 8/18/94. Gaming Devices/
Keno/ Lottery/ Off-Track Pari-
Mutuel Wagering/ Pari-Mutuel
Wagering on Horse Racing/ Pari-
Mutuel Wagering on Dog Racing

Quechan Indian Tribe
P.O. Box 11352
Yuma, AZ 85364
Phone: (619) 572-0213
President: Fritz E. Brown
Gaming Devices/ Keno/ Lottery/
Off-Track Pari-Mutuel Wagering/
Pari-Mutuel Wagering on Horse
Racing/ Pari-Mutuel Wagering
on Dog Racing

San Carlos Apache Tribe
P.O. Box O
San Carols, AZ 85550
Phone: (602) 475-2361
Chairman: Harrison Talgo
Compact approved 10/25/93;
published 11/10/93. Gaming Devices/ Keno/ Lottery/ Off-Track
Pari-Mutuel Wagering/ Pari-Mutuel Wagering on Horse Racing/ Pari-Mutuel Wagering on
Dog Racing

Tohono O'Odham Tribe
P.O. Box 837
Sells, AZ 85634
Phone: (602) 383-2221
Chairman: Sylvester Listo
Compact approved 7/30/93; published 8/18/93. Gaming Devices/
Keno/ Lottery/ Off-Track Pari-Mutuel Wagering/ Pari-Mutuel
Wagering on Horse Racing/ Pari-Mutuel Wagering on Dog Racing

Tonto Apache Tribe
Tonto Reservation Number 30
Payson, AZ 85541
Phone: (602) 474-5000

Chairperson: Jeri Johnson
Compact approved 8/11/93; published 8/18/93. Gaming Devices/
Keno/ Lottery/ Off-Track Pari-Mutuel Wagering/ Pari-Mutuel
Wagering on Horse Racing/ Pari-Mutuel Wagering on Dog Racing

White Mountain Apache Tribe
P.O. Box 700
Whiteriver, AZ 85941
Phone: (602) 338-4346
Chairman: Ronnie Lupe
Compact approved 7/30/93; published 8/18/93. Gaming Devices/
Keno/ Lottery/ Off-Track Pari-Mutuel Wagering/ Pari-Mutuel
Wagering on Horse Racing/ Pari-Mutuel Wagering on Dog Racing

Yavapai-Apache Indian Community
P.O. Box 1188
Camp Verde, AZ 86322
Phone: (602) 567-3649
Gaming Devices/ Keno/ Lottery/
Off-Track Pari-Mutuel Wagering/
Pari-Mutuel Wagering on Horse
Racing/ Pari-Mutuel Wagering
on Dog Racing

Yavapai-Prescott Tribe
530 East Merritt St.
Prescott, AZ 86301-2038
Phone: (602) 445-8790
President: Patricia McGee
Compact approved 7/15/92; published 7/21/92. Gaming Devices/
Keno/ Lottery/ Off-Track Pari-

Mutuel Wagering/ Pari-Mutuel
Wagering on Horse Racing/ Pari-
Mutuel Wagering on Dog Racing

Arkansas

LEGISLATIVE INFORMATION
House: (501) 375-7771
Senate: (501) 682-6107

LEGISLATIVE LIBRARIES

**Bureau of Legislative
Research**
State Capitol, Rm. 315
Little Rock, AR 72201
Phone: (501) 682-1937
Fax: (501) 682-1936

REGULATORY AGENCIES

**Arkansas Racing
Commission**
P.O. Box 3076
Little Rock, AR 72203
Phone: (501) 682-1467

California

LEGISLATIVE INFORMATION
House: (916) 445-3614
Senate: (916) 445-4251
Bill copies: (916) 445-2323

LEGISLATIVE LIBRARIES

**Office of the Legislative
Counsel**
Bureau Library
925 L St., Lower Level
Sacramento, CA 95814-3772
Phone: (916) 445-2609
Fax: (916) 322-4721

Capitol Office
Phone: (916) 445-3551
Fax: (916) 324-0454

REGULATORY AGENCIES

**Gaming Registration
Program**
Bureau of Investigation,
Division of Law Enforcement
California Department of Justice
P.O. Box 163029
Sacramento, CA 95816
Phone: (916) 227-4246

California State Lottery
600 North 10th St.
Sacramento, CA 95814
Phone: (916) 323-7095

**California Horse Racing
Board**
1010 Hurley Way, Suite 190
Sacramento, CA 95825
Phone: (916) 263-6000

INDIAN GAMING

**Barona Band of the Capitan
Grande of Diegueno
Mission Indians**
1095 Barona Rd.

Gtype

OVERNMENT AGENCIES

Lakeside, CA 92040
Phone: (619) 443-6612
Chairman: Clifford La Chappa
Compact approved 6/23/92; published 7/21/92. Pari-Mutuel Wagering on Horse Racing

Cabazon Band of Cahuilla Mission Indians
84-235 Indio Spring Dr.
Indio, CA 92201
Phone: (619) 342-2593
Chairman: John A. James
Compact approved 3/27/90; published 4/2/90. Pari-Mutuel Wagering on Horse Racing

San Manuel Band of Serrano Mission Indians
5438 North Victoria Ave.
Highland, CA 92346
Phone: (714) 862-8509
Chairman: Henry Duro
Compact approved 3/26/91; published 4/2/91. Pari-Mutuel Wagering on Horse Racing

Sycuan Band of Diegueno Mission Indians
5459 Dehesa Rd.
El Cajon, CA 92021
Phone: (619) 445-2613
Spokesperson: Anna Sandoval
Compact approved 10/10/90; published 10/18/90. Pari-Mutuel Wagering on Horse Racing

Viejas Group of Capitan Grande Band of Diegueno Mission Indians

P.O. Box 908
Alpine, CA 92201
Phone: (619) 445-3810
Compact approved 6/25/90; published 6/29/90. Pari-Mutuel Wagering on Horse Racing

Colorado

LEGISLATIVE INFORMATION
Btw. sessions: (303) 866-3521
During sessions: (303) 866-3055

LEGISLATIVE LIBRARIES

Legislative Council
State Capitol, Rm. 048
Denver, CO 80203
Phone: (303) 866-4799
Fax: (303) 866-3855

REGULATORY AGENCIES

Colorado Limited Gaming Control Commission
Division of Gaming
720 South Colorado Blvd., Suite 540-S
Denver, CO 80222
Phone: (303) 757-7555

Colorado Racing Commission
1560 Broadway, Suite 1540
Denver, CO 80202
Phone: (303) 894-2990

Colorado Lottery
201 West 8th, Suite 600

Pueblo, CO 81003,
Phone: (719) 546-2400

**Licensing and
Elections Division**
Office of the Secretary of State
1560 Broadway, Suite 200
Denver, CO 80202
Phone: (303) 894-2251

INDIAN GAMING

Southern Ute Indian Tribe
P.O. Box 737
Ignacio, CO 81137
Phone: (303) 563-4033
Chairman: Leonard C. Burch
Compact approved 10/1/92;
published 10/8/92. Slot Machines/ Blackjack/ Racing/ Off-track Betting/ Keno/ Lottery

Ute Mountain Ute Tribe
Towaoc, CO 81334
Phone: (303) 565-3571
Chairperson: Judy Knoght-Frank
Compact approved 7/6/92; published 7/10/92. Slot Machines/
Blackjack/ Keno/ Poker

Connecticut

LEGISLATIVE INFORMATION
(203) 566-5736

LEGISLATIVE LIBRARIES

Legislative Library

Legislative Office Building,
Rm. 5400
Hartford, CT 06106
Phone: (203) 240-8881
Fax: (203) 240-8881

**Law and Legislative
Reference Unit**
State Library
231 Capitol Ave.
Hartford, CT 06106
Phone: (203) 566-4601
Fax: (203) 566-2133

REGULATORY AGENCIES

Charitable Games
Connecticut Division of
Special Revenue
85 Alumni Rd.
Newington, CT 06111
Phone: (203) 667-5023

Off-Track Betting
Connecticut Division of
Special Revenue
P.O. Box 11424
Newington, CT 06111
Phone: (203) 566-3949

Gambling Regulation
Connecticut Division of
Special Revenue
P.O. Box 11424
Newington, CT 06111
Phone: (203) 566-3949

Connecticut State Lottery
Division of Special Revenue
P.O. Box 11424

Newington, CT 06111
Phone: (203) 566-2912

INDIAN GAMING

Mashantucket Pequot Tribe
Box 160 Indiantown Rd.
Ledyard, CT 06339
Phone: (203) 536-2681
Chairman: Richard A. Hayward
Compact approved 5/24/91; published 5/31/91. Blackjack/ Poker/ Dice/ Money-Wheels/ Roulette/ Baccarat/ Chuck-A-Luck/ Pan Game/ Over and Under/ Horse Race Game/ Acey-Deucey/ Beat the Dealer/ Bouncing Ball/ Lottery/ Pari-Mutuel Wagering, Animal Races/ Off Track Simulcasting on Reservation by Telephone/ Pari-Mutuel Wagering, Jai Alai/ Video Facsimiles, any Game of Chance

Mohegan Indian Tribe
27 Church Ln.
Uncaseville, CT 06382
Phone: (203) 848-9252
Compact approved 5/17/94; published 12/16/94. Blackjack/ Poker/ Dice/ Money-Wheels/ Roulette/ Baccarat/ Chuck-A-Luck/ Pan Game/ Over and Under/ Horse Race Game/ Acey-Deucey/ Beat the Dealer/ Bouncing Ball/ Lottery/ Off Track Pari-Mutuel Betting, Animal Races/ Pari-Mutuel Betting thru Simulcasting on Animal Races/ Pari-Mutuel Wagering, Jai Alai/ Pari-Mutuel Betting, Dog Racing/ Pari-Mutuel Betting, Horse Racing/ Video Facsimiles, any Game of Chance/ Telephone Betting on any Lottery Game/ Off Track Pari-Mutuel Telephone Betting on Animal Races

Delaware

LEGISLATIVE INFORMATION
(302) 739-4114

LEGISLATIVE LIBRARIES

Legislative Council
Legislative Hall
Dover, DE 19903
Phone: (302) 739-5808
Fax: (302) 739-3895

REGULATORY AGENCIES

Delaware Gaming Control Commission
Department of
Administrative Service
Division of Professional
Regulation
P.O. Box 1401
Cannon Building, Suite 203
Dover, DE 19903
Phone: (302) 739-4522

Delaware Thoroughbred Racing Commission
Department of Agriculture
2320 South Dupont Hwy.

Dover, DE 19901
Phone: (302) 739-4811

**Delaware Harness Racing
Commission**
Department of Agriculture
2320 Dupont Highway
Dover, DE 19901-5515
Phone: (302) 739-4811

Delaware State Lottery
McKee Business Park,
Suite 102
1575 McKee Rd.
Dover, DE 19901
Phone: (302) 739-5291

District of Columbia

REGULATORY AGENCIES

**Lottery and Charitable
Games Control Board
(Charitable Games)**
2101 Martin Luther King Jr.
Ave. SE, Fourth Floor
Washington, DC 20020
Phone: (202) 645-8000

**Lottery and Charitable
Games Control Board
(Lottery)**
2101 Martin Luther King Jr.
Ave. SE, Fifth Floor
Washington, DC 20020
Phone: (202) 645-8071

Florida

LEGISLATIVE INFORMATION
(904) 488-4371

LEGISLATIVE LIBRARIES

**Division of Legislative
Library Services**
701 Capitol
Tallahassee, FL 32399-1400
Phone: (904) 488-2812
Fax: (904) 488-9879

REGULATORY AGENCIES

**Pari-Mutuel
Wagering Division**
Florida Department of
Business Regulation
1940 Monroe, Northwood Court
Tallahassee, FL 32399-1036
Phone: (904) 488-9125

**Florida Department of
the Lottery**
Capitol Complex
Tallahassee, FL 32399
Phone: (904) 487-7725

Georgia

LEGISLATIVE INFORMATION
House: (404) 656-5015
Senate: (404) 565-5040

LEGISLATIVE LIBRARIES

**Office of
Legislative Counsel**
316 State Capitol
Atlanta, GA 30334
Phone: (404) 656-5000
Fax: (404) 651-9292

House Research Office
Legislative Office Building
18 Capitol Square
Atlanta, GA 30334
Phone: (404) 656-3206
Fax: (404) 657-8449

Senate Research Office
204 Legislative Office Building
18 Capitol Square
Atlanta, GA 30334
Phone: (404) 656-0015
Fax: (404) 651-8503

REGULATORY AGENCIES

**Georgia Bureau of
Investigation**
P.O. Box 370808
Decatur, GA 30037-0808
Phone: (404) 244-2561

Hawaii

Note: Hawaii has no legalized
gambling.

LEGISLATIVE INFORMATION
(808) 587-0700

LEGISLATIVE LIBRARIES

**Legislative
Reference Bureau**
Capitol Center Basement
1177 Alakea St.
Honolulu, HI 96813
Phone: (808) 587-0690
Fax: (808) 587-0699

Idaho

LEGISLATIVE INFORMATION
(208) 334-3175

LEGISLATIVE LIBRARIES

Legislative Services Office
State Capitol
East Wing, Lower Level
Boise, ID 83720
Phone: (208) 334-2475
(208) 334-4822
Fax: (208) 334-2125

REGULATORY AGENCIES

Idaho Lottery
P.O. Box 6537
Boise, ID 83707
Phone: (208) 334-2600

**Idaho State Racing
Commission**
Department of Law Enforcement
P.O. Box 700
Meridian, ID 83680-0070
Phone: (208) 884-7080

INDIAN GAMING

Coeur D'Alene Tribe
Tribal Headquarters
Plummer, ID 83851
Phone: (208) 274-3101
Chairman: Ernest Stensgar
Compact approved 2/5/93; published 2/12/93. Lottery/ Pari-Mutuel Wagering on Horses, Dogs, Mules/ Simulcast of Racing

Kootenai Tribe
P.O. Box 1269
Bonners Ferry, ID 83805-1269
Phone: (208) 267-3519
Chairperson: Velma A. Bahe
Compact approved 10/29/93; published 11/10/93. Lottery/ Pari-Mutuel Wagering on Horses, Dogs, Mules/ Simulcasting of Racing

Illinois

LEGISLATIVE INFORMATION
(217) 782-3944

LEGISLATIVE LIBRARIES

Legislative Research Bureau
112 State Capitol
Springfield, IL 62706
Phone: (217) 782-6625
Fax: (217) 785-4583

Legislative Research Unit
222 South College
Third Floor, Suite 301
Springfield, IL 62704
Phone: (217) 782-6851
Fax: (217) 785-7572

REGULATORY AGENCIES

Illinois Gaming Board
P.O. Box 19474
Springfield, IL 62794-9474
Phone: (217) 524-0226
Responsible for professional and occupational liscensing in the gaming industry

Office of Bingo and Charitable Games
Illinois Department of Revenue
P.O. Box 19480
Springfield, IL 62794-9840
Phone: (217) 524-4164

Illinois Racing Board
State of Illinois Center
100 West Randolph St., Suite 11-100
Chicago, IL 60601
Phone: (312) 814-2600

Illinois State Lottery
Department of the Lottery
201 East Madison
Springfield, IL 62702
Phone: (217) 524-5155

Indiana

LEGISLATIVE INFORMATION
(317) 232-9856

LEGISLATIVE LIBRARIES

**Legislative
Information Bureau**
302 State House
Indianapolis, IN 46204
Phone: (317) 232-9856
Fax: (317) 232-2554

REGULATORY AGENCIES

**Indiana Horse Racing
Commission**
Ista Center, Suite 412
150 West Market St.
Indianapolis, IN 46204
Phone: (317) 233-3119

Hoosier Lottery
Tan Am Plaza, Suite 1100
201 South Capitol Ave.
Indianapolis, IN 46225
Phone: (317) 264-4800

Iowa

LEGISLATIVE INFORMATION
(515) 281-5129

LEGISLATIVE LIBRARIES

Legislative Service Bureau
State House

Des Moines, IA 50319
Phone: (515) 281-3312
    (515) 281-4800
Fax: (515) 281-8027

State Law Library of Iowa
State House
Des Moines, IA 50319
Phone: (515) 281-5124
Fax: (515) 281-5405

REGULATORY AGENCIES

**Iowa Racing and Gaming
Commission**
Department of
Inspections and Appeals
Lucas State Office Bldg., 2nd Fl.
Des Moines, IA 50319
Phone: (515) 281-7352
Responsible for professional and
occupational licensing in the
gaming industry.

Iowa Lottery Board
Department of
Revenue and Finance
2015 Grand Ave.
Des Moines, IA 50312
Phone: (515) 281-7900

**Iowa Division of
Inspections**
Department of Inspections
and Appeals
Lucas State Office Building
Des Moines, IA 50319
Phone: (515) 281-7357

Gaming Department
Iowa Division of
Criminal Investigation
Department of Public Safety
Wallace State Office Bldg.
502 East 9th
Des Moines, IA 50319
Phone: (515) 281-5138

INDIAN GAMING

Omaha Tribe of Nebraska
P.O. Box 368
Macy, NE 68039
Phone: (402) 837-5391
Chairman: Doran L. Morris, Sr.
Compact approved 2/24/92; published 2/28/92. Dice Games/ Slot Machines/ Video Games of Chance/ Wheel Games/ Simulcasting/ Card Games/ Sports Betting Pools & Sports Betting/ Lotteries/ Parlor Games

Sac and Fox Tribe of Mississippi in Iowa
Route 2, Box 56-C
Tama, IA 52339
Phone: (515) 484-4678
Chief: Keith C. Davenport
Compact approved 4/24/92; published 4/30/92. Dice Games/ Slot Machines/ Video Games of Chance/ Wheel Games/ Card Games/ Sports Betting Pools/ Sports Betting/ Parlay Cards/ Lotteries/ Keno

Winnebago Tribe of Nebraska

Winnebago, NE 68701
Phone: (402) 878-2272
Chairman: Louis LaRose
Compact approved 4/22/92; published 4/30/92. Lotteries/ Keno/ Pari-Mutuel Betting on Simulcast Horse or Dog Races/ Video Games of Chance/ Slot Machines/ Twenty-One/ Red Dog/ Roulette/ Big Six/ Craps/ Poker/ Sports Betting Pools/ Sports Betting/ Parlay Cards

Kansas

LEGISLATIVE INFORMATION
(913) 296-3296

LEGISLATIVE LIBRARIES

Kansas State Library
Legislative Reference
Third Floor, Statehouse
Topeka, KS 66612
Phone: (913) 296-3296
Fax: (913) 296-6650

REGULATORY AGENCIES

Bingo Enforcement
Kansas Department of Revenue
Division of
Alcoholic Beverage Control
4 Townsite Plaza, Suite 210
200 Southeast Sixth St.
Topeka, KS 66603-3512
Phone: (913) 296-3825

**Kansas Racing
Commission**
3400 Southwest Van Buren
Topeka, KS 66611-2228
Phone: (913) 296-5800

Kansas Lottery
128 North Kansas Ave.
Topeka, KS 66603
Phone: (913) 296-5700

Kentucky

LEGISLATIVE INFORMATION
(502) 564-8100
(502) 564-2500

LEGISLATIVE LIBRARIES

**Legislative Research
Commission**
State Capitol, 4th Fl.
Frankfort, KY 40601
Phone: (502) 564-8100
Fax: (502) 223-5094

REGULATORY AGENCIES

**Kentucky
Racing Commission**
4063 Ironworks Pk.,
Bldg. B
Lexington, KY 40511
Phone: (606) 255-2448

**Kentucky
Lottery Corporation**
6040 Dutchman's Ln.,

Suite 400
Louisville, KY 40205
Phone: (502) 473-2200

Louisiana

LEGISLATIVE INFORMATION
During sessions: (504) 342-2456
Btw. sessions: (504) 342-2431

LEGISLATIVE LIBRARIES

**Legislative Research
Library**
House Legislative Services
P.O. Box 94012
Baton Rouge, LA 70804
Phone: (504) 342-2434
Fax: (504) 342-0768

Senate Law Library
P.O. Box 94183
State Capitol
Baton Rouge, LA 70804
Phone: (504) 342-2414
Fax: (504) 342-0369

REGULATORY AGENCIES

Video Gaming Division
Department of
Public Safety and Corrections
Office of State Police,
Gaming Enforcement
P.O. Box 66614
Baton Rouge, LA 70896
Phone: (504) 925-1900

**Gaming Enforcement
Division**
Department of
Public Safety and Corrections
Office of State Police
265 South Foster
Baton Rouge, LA 70806
Phone: (504) 925-4799

**Charitable Gaming
Division**
Department of
Public Safety and Corrections
Office of State Police,
Gaming Enforcement
P.O. Box 66614
Baton Rouge, LA 70896
Phone: (504) 925-1835

Louisiana Lottery
P.O. Box 90008
Baton Rouge, LA 70879
Phone: (504) 297-2000

**Louisiana State Racing
Commission**
320 North Carrollton Ave.,
Suite 2-B
New Orleans, LA 70119
Phone: (504) 483-4000

INDIAN GAMING

**Chitimacha Tribe
of Louisiana**
Tribal Center
P.O. Box 661
Charenton, LA 70523
Phone: (318) 923-4973
Chairman: Ralph Darden

Compact approved 10/29/92;
published 7/6/93. Amended
6/3/94; published 6/14/94. Electronic Games of Chance/ Black-
jack/ Roulette/ Craps/ Poker/
Mini-Baccarat/ Keno

**Coushatta Tribe
of Louisiana**
P.O. Box 818
Elton, LA 70532
Phone: (318) 584-2209
Chairman: Lovelin Poncho
Compact approved 10/29/92;
published 11/4/92. Amended
2/21/95; published 3/1/95. Elec-
tronic Games of Chance/ Bac-
carat/ Mini-Baccarat/ Blackjack/
Roulette/ Craps/ Poker/ Keno

**Tunica-Biloxi
Tribe of Louisiana**
P.O. Box 311
Mansura, LA 71351
Phone: (318) 253-9767
Chairman: Earl Barbry, Sr.
Compact approved 11/10/92;
published 11/19/92. Electronic
Games of Chance/ Blackjack/
Roulette/ Craps/ Poker/ Baccarat/
Mini-Baccarat/ Keno

Maine

LEGISLATIVE INFORMATION
(207) 289-1692

LEGISLATIVE LIBRARIES

Law and Legislative Reference Library
State House, Station 43
Augusta, ME 04333
Phone: (207) 287-1600
Fax: (207) 287-6467

REGULATORY AGENCIES

Maine State Police Licensing Division
Department of Public Safety
State House, Station #164
Augusta, ME 04333
Phone: (207) 624-8775

Maine Harness Racing Commission
Department of Agriculture
State House, Station #28
Augusta, ME 04333
Phone: (207) 287-3221

Maine State Lottery
Bureau of Alcoholic Beverages
and Lottery Operations
State House, Station #8
Augusta, ME 04333
Phone: (207) 624-6700

Maryland

LEGISLATIVE INFORMATION
(410) 841-3810

LEGISLATIVE LIBRARIES

Library and Information Services
Department of
Legislative Reference
90 State Cir.
Annapolis, MD 21401
Phone: (410) 841-3810
Fax: (410) 848-3850
(410) 841-3850

REGULATORY AGENCIES

Maryland Racing Commission
Department of
Licensing and Regulation
501 St. Paul Place, 10th Fl.
Baltimore, MD 21202
Phone: (410) 333-6267

Maryland State Lottery
Plaza Office Center, Suite 204
6776 Reisterstown Rd.
Baltimore, MD 21215
Phone: (410) 764-5700

Massachusetts

LEGISLATIVE INFORMATION
(617) 727-7030

LEGISLATIVE LIBRARIES

Legislative Reference
State Library
341 State House

Boston, MA 02133
Phone: (617) 727-2590
Fax: (617) 727-5819

REGULATORY AGENCIES

Massachusetts Office of the Attorney General
Public Protection Bureau
1 Ashburton Pl.
Boston, MA 02108
Phone: (617) 727-2200

Massachusetts State Lottery
60 Columbian St.
Braintree, MA 02184
Phone: (617) 849-5555

Massachusetts State Racing Commission
Department of Consumer Affairs
and Business Regulation
1 Ashburton Pl., Rm. 1313
Boston, MA 02108
Phone: (617) 727-2581

Michigan

LEGISLATIVE INFORMATION
(517) 373-0170

LEGISLATIVE LIBRARIES

Legislative Service Bureau
P.O. Box 30036
Lansing, MI 48909-7536
Phone: (517) 373-0472

Fax: (517) 373-0171

Policy Library
House Democratic Policy Staff
Roosevelt Building, 7th Fl.
Lansing, MI 48909
Phone: (517) 373-9868
Fax: (517) 373-5966

REGULATORY AGENCIES

Michigan Bureau of State Lottery
Department of Treasury
101 East Hillsdale
Lansing, MI 48909
Phone: (517) 335-5600

Charitable Gaming Division
Michigan Bureau of State Lottery
Department of Treasury
101 East Hillsdale
Lansing, MI 48909
Phone: (517) 335-5780

Michigan Office of Racing Commissioner
Department of Agriculture
37650 Professional Center Dr.,
Suite 105-A
Livonia, MI 48154-1100
Phone: (313) 462-2400

INDIAN GAMING

Bay Hills Indian Community
Route 1
Brimley, MI 49715

Phone: (906) 248-3241
Chairman: Jeff Parker
Compact approved 11/19/93;
published 11/30/93. Craps/ Dice
Games/ Wheel Games/ Roulette/
Banking Card Games/ Electronic
Games of Chance/ Keno

Grand Traverse Band
of Ottawa and Chippewa
Indians
Route 1, Box 135
Suttons Bay, MI 49682
Phone: (616) 271-3538
Chairman: Joseph C. Raphael
Compact approved 11/19/93;
published 11/30/93. Craps/ Dice
Games/ Wheel Games/ Roulette/
Banking Card Games/ Electronic
Games of Chance/ Keno

Hannahville Indian
Community
N14911 Hannahville Rd.
Wilson, MI 49896-9728
Phone: (906) 466-2342
Chairman: Kenneth Meshiguad
Compact approved 11/19/93;
published 11/30/93. Craps/ Dice
Games/ Wheel Games/ Roulette/
Banking Card Games/ Electronic
Games of Chance/ Keno

Keweenaw Bay Indian
Colony
Center Building
Route 1, Box 45
Baraga, MI 49908
Phone: (906) 353-6623
Chairman: Frederick Dakota

Compact approved 11/19/93;
published 11/30/93. Craps/ Dice
Games/ Wheel Games/ Roulette/
Banking Card Games/ Electronic
Games of Chance/ Keno

Lac Vieux Desert
Band of Lake Superior
Chippewa Indians
P.O. Box 446
Watersmeet, MI 49969
Phone: (906) 358-4577
Chairman: John McGeshick
Compact approved 11/19/93;
published 11/30/93. Craps/ Dice
Games/ Wheel Games/ Roulette/
Banking Card Games/ Electronic
Games of Chance/ Keno

Saginaw Chippewa Indian
Tribe
7070 East Broadway Rd.
Mount Pleasant, MI 48858
Phone: (517) 772-5700
Chief: Ronald Falcon
Compact approved 11/19/93;
published 11/30/93. Craps/ Dice
Games/ Wheel Games/ Roulette/
Banking Card Games/ Electronic
Games of Chance/ Keno

Saulte Ste. Marie Tribe of
Chippewa
206 Greenough St.
Sault Ste. Marie, MI 49783
Phone: (906) 635-6050
Chairperson: Bernard Bouschor
Compact approved 11/19/93;
published 11/30/93. Craps/ Dice
Games/ Wheel Games/ Roulette/

Banking Card Games/ Electronic
Games of Chance/ Keno

Minnesota

LEGISLATIVE INFORMATION
House: (612) 296-6646
Senate: (612) 296-2887

LEGISLATIVE LIBRARIES

**Legislative
Reference Library**
645 State Office Building
St. Paul, MN 55155
Phone: (612) 296-8338
        (612) 296-7661
Fax: (612) 296-9731

REGULATORY AGENCIES

**Minnesota
Gambling Control Board**
1711 West County Rd. B,
Suite 300 South
Roseville, MN 55113
Phone: (612) 639-4000

Minnesota State Lottery
2645 Long Lake Rd.
Roseville, MN 55113
Phone: (612) 635-8100

**Minnesota Racing
Commission**
7825 Washington Ave. South,
Suite 800
Bloomington, MN 55439

Phone: (612) 341-7555

INDIAN GAMING

Note: Indian gaming sites in
Minnesota have individual compacts for specific types of games.

**Bois Forte Band
of Minnesota Chippewa
(Nett Lake)**
P.O. Box 16
Nett Lake, MN 55722
Phone: (218) 757-3261
Chairman: Eugene Boshey, Sr.
Compact, Video Games of
Chance approved 3/27/90; pub-
lished 4/2/90. Compact, Black-
jack approved 9/29/91; published
10/3/91

**Fond Du Lac Band
of Minnesota Chippewa**
105 University Rd.
Cloquet, Minnesota 55720
Phone: (218) 879-4593
Chairman: Robert Peacock
Compact, Video Games of
Chance approved 3/27/90; published 4/2/90. Compact, Blackjack approved 9/25/91; published
10/3/91

**Grand Portage Band
of Minnesota Chippewa**
P.O. Box 428
Grand Portage, MN 55605
Phone: (218) 475-2279
Chairman: James Hendrickson

Compact, Video Games of
Chance approved 3/27/90; published 4/2/90. Compact, Blackjack approved 9/25/91; published
10/3/91

**Leech Lake Band
of Minnesota Chippewa**
Route 3, Box 100
Cass Lake, MN 56633
Phone: (218) 335-8200
Chairman: Alfred Pemberton
Compact, Video Games of
Chance approved 3/27/90; pub-
lished 4/2/90. Compact, Black-
jack approved 9/25/91; published
10/3/91

**Lower Sioux
Indian Community**
Rural Route 1, Box 308
Morton, MN 56270
Phone: (507) 697-6185
President: Joseph Goodthunder
Compact, Video Games of
Chance approved 3/27/90; pub-
lished 4/2/90. Compact, Black-
jack approved 9/25/91; published
10/3/91

**Mille Lacs Band
of Minnesota Chippewa**
Star Route HRC 67, Box 194
Onamia, MN 56359
Phone: (612) 532-4181
Chairperson: Margaret Anderson
Compact, Video Games of
Chance approved 6/25/90; pub-
lished 6/29/90. Compact, Black-

jack approved 9/25/91; published
10/3/91

**Prairie Island Community
of the Minnesota
Mdewakanton Sioux**
1158 Island Blvd.
Welch, MN 55089
Phone: (612) 385-2554
President: Dale Childs
Compact, Video Games of
Chance approved 3/27/90; pub-
lished 4/2/90. Amended 4/27/91;
published 4/30/91. Compact,
Blackjack approved 9/25/91;
published 10/3/91

**Red Lake Band
of Chippewa Indians**
P.O. Box 550
Red Lake, Minnesota 56671
Phone: (218) 679-3341
Chairman: Gerald Brun
Compact, Video Games of
Chance approved 8/2/91; pub-
lished 8/9/91. Amended 9/9/92;
published 9/16/92. Compact,
Blackjack approved 9/25/91;
published 10/3/91. Amended
9/9/92; published 9/16/92

**Shakopee Mdewakanton
Sioux Community**
2330 Sioux Trail, N.W.
Prior Lake, MN 55372
Phone: (612) 445-8900
Chairman: Leonard Prescott
Compact, Video Games of
Chance approved 3/27/90; pub-
lished 4/2/90. Compact, Black-

jack approved 9/25/91; published
10/3/91

**Upper Sioux
Indian Community**
P.O. Box 147
Granite Falls, MN 56241
Phone: (612) 564-2360
Chairperson: Dean Blue
Compact, Video Games of
Chance approved 11/16/90.
Amended 4/21/91; published
4/30/91. Compact, Blackjack ap-
proved 9/25/91; published
10/3/91

**White Earth Band
of Minnesota Chippewa**
P.O. Box 418
White Earth, MN 56591
Phone: (218) 983-3185
Chairman: Darrell Wadena
Compact, Video Games of
Chance approved 11/8/91; pub-
lished 11/13/91. Compact, Black-
jack approved 9/25/91; published
10/3/91

Mississippi

LEGISLATIVE INFORMATION
During sessions: (601) 359-3719
Senate (Btw. sessions):
(601) 359-3229
House (Btw. sessions):
(601) 359-3358

LEGISLATIVE LIBRARIES

**Legislative
Reference Bureau**
P.O. Box 1018
Jackson, MS 39215-1018
Phone: (601) 359-3135
Fax: (601) 359-3728

REGULATORY AGENCIES

**Mississippi
Gaming Commision**
P.O. Box 23577
Jackson, MS 39225-3577
Phone: (601) 961-4400

INDIAN GAMING

**Mississippi Band
of Choctaw Indians**
P.O. Box 6010
Philadelphia, MS 39350
Phone: (601) 656-5251
Tribal Chief: Phillip Martin
Compact approved 1/15/93; pub-
lished 1/29/93. Amended
10/29/94; published 11/9/94.
Craps/ Roulette/ Blackjack/
Poker/ Baccarat-Chemin De Fer/
Slot Machines

Missouri

LEGISLATIVE INFORMATION
(314) 751-4633

LEGISLATIVE LIBRARIES

**Committee
on Legislative Research**
Legislative Library
State Capitol, 117-A
Jefferson City, MO 65101
Phone: (314) 751-4633
Fax: (314) 751-0130

Senate Research
c/o Senate Post Office
State Capitol
Jefferson City, MO 65101
Phone: (314) 751-4666
Fax: (314) 751-2745

REGULATORY AGENCIES

Bingo Division
Missouri Gaming Commission
1616 Industry Dr.
Jefferson City, MO 65109
Phone: (314) 526-5370

Riverboat Division
Missouri Gaming Commission
1616 Industry Dr.
Jefferson City, MO 65109
Phone: (314) 526-4080

Missouri Lottery
1900 Craigshire Rd.
St. Louis, MO 63146
Phone: (314) 579-0900

Montana

LEGISLATIVE INFORMATION
During sessions: (406) 444-4853
Btw. sessions: (406) 444-3064

LEGISLATIVE LIBRARIES

Legislative Council
State Capitol, Rm. 102
Helena, MT 59620-1706
Phone: (406) 444-3598
Fax: (406) 444-2588

REGULATORY AGENCIES

**Gambling Control
Division**
Montana Department of Justice
P.O. Box 201424
Helena, MT 59620-1424
Phone: (406) 444-1971

Montana State Lottery
2525 North Montana Ave.
Helena, MT 59601
Phone: (406) 444-5825

**Montana Board of
Horseracing**
P.O. Box 200512
Helena, MT 59620-0512
Phone: (406) 444-4287

INDIAN GAMING

**Assiniboine and Sioux
Tribes of the
Fort Peck Reservation**

P.O. Box 1027
Poplar, MT 59244
Phone: (406) 768-5155
Chairman: Caleb Shields
Compact approved 6/24/92; published 6/30/92. Amended 9/1/92; published 9/8/92. Amended 4/7/93; published 4/14/93. Video Machines for Keno, Poker, and Bingo/ Simulcast Racing/ Lottery Games

Chippewa-Cree Tribe of the Rocky Boy's Reservation
Rocky Boy Route, Box 544
Box Elder, MT 59521
Phone: (406) 395-4282
Chairman: John Sunchild, Sr.
Compact approved 10/1/93; published 10/20/93. Video Gambling Machines for Bingo, Draw Poker, and Keno/ Simulcast Racing/ Calcutta Pools/ Fantasy Sports Leagues/ Fishing Derbies and Betting on Natural Occurrences/ Lotteries/ Shake-a-Day and Shaking for Music or a Drink/ Raffles/ Live Keno/ Sports Pools and Sports/ Tab Games

Crow Tribe
P.O. Box 159
Crow Agency, MT 59022
Phone: (406) 638-2601
Chairman: Clara Nomee
Compact approved 6/30/93; published 9/28/93. Amendment approved 9/19/93; published 9/28/93. 2nd Amendment approved 11/5/93; published 11/30/93. Video Gaming Machines/ Simulcast Racing/ Calcutta Pools/ Fantasy Sports Leagues/ Lotteries/ Fishing Derbies/ Betting on Natural Occurences/ Shake-a-Day/ Raffles/ Live Keno/ Sports Pools/ Tab Games

Northern Cheyenne Tribe
P.O. Box 128
Lame Deer, MT 59043
Phone: (406) 477-8283
President: Llevando Fisher
Compact approved 4/15/93; published 5/3/93. Correction to Notice 5/14/93; published 6/3/93. Superseded by compact approved 12/13/93; published 12/27/93. Video Gaming Machines/ Simulcast Racing/ Calcutta Pools/ Fantasy Sports Leagues/ Lotteries/ Fishing Derbies/ Betting on Natural Occurences/ Shake-a-Day/ Raffles/ Live Keno/ Sports Pools/ Sports Tab Games

Nebraska

LEGISLATIVE INFORMATION
During sessions: (402) 471-2709
Btw. sessions: (402) 471-2271

LEGISLATIVE LIBRARIES

**Legislative
Reference Library**
State Capitol, Rm. 1201
P.O. Box 94945
Lincoln, NE 68509
Phone: (402) 471-0075
        (402) 471-0076
Fax: (402) 471-2126

**Nebraska
Library Commission**
1200 N St., Suite 120
Lincoln, NE 68509-2023
Phone: (402) 471-4015
        (402) 471-4017
Fax: (402) 471-2083
        (402) 471-4028

REGULATORY AGENCIES

**Division of
Charitable Gaming**
Nebraska Department of Revenue
P.O. Box 94818
Lincoln, NE 68509
Phone: (402) 471-5937

Nebraska Lottery
Nebraska Department of Revenue
P.O. Box 98901
Lincoln, NE 68509-8901
Phone: (402) 471-6102

**Nebraska
Horse Racing Commission**
P.O. Box 95014
Lincoln, NE 68509
Phone: (402) 471-4155

INDIAN GAMING

Omaha Tribe of Nebraska
P.O. Box 368
Macy, NE 68039
Phone: (402) 837-5391
Chairman: Doran L. Morris, Sr.
Compact approved 3/27/90; published 4/20/90. Casino Type
Gaming

Nevada

LEGISLATIVE INFORMATION
During sessions: (702) 678-5545
Btw. sessions: (702) 697-5160

LEGISLATIVE LIBRARIES

**Legislative
Counsel Bureau**
Legislative Building
Capitol Complex
Carson City, NV 89710
Phone: (702) 687-6827
Fax: (702) 687-3048

REGULATORY AGENCIES

**Nevada State
Gaming Control Board**
1150 East William St.
Carson City, NV 89710
Phone: (702) 687-6500
Responsible for key professional
and occupational licensing in the
gaming industry. Other casino

employees must obtain work permits.

Nevada Gaming Commission
1150 East William St.
Carson City, NV 89710
Phone: (702) 687-6530

Nevada Gaming Policy Committee
c/o Governor's Office
Capitol Building
Carson City, NV 89710
Phone: (702) 687-5670

Gaming Division
Attorney General's Office
198 South Carson St.
Carson City, NV 89710

INDIAN GAMING

Fort Mojave Tribal Council
500 Merriman Ave.
Needles, CA 92363
Phone: (619) 326-4591
Chairperson: Nora Garcia
Compact approved 9/9/94; published 9/21/94. Casino Type Gaming

Moapa Band of Payute Indians
Box 340
Moapa, NV 89025
Phone: (702) 865-2787
Chairperson: Rosalyn Mike

Compact approved 12/9/94; published 12/22/94. Slots Only

New Hampshire

LEGISLATIVE INFORMATION
(603) 271-2239

LEGISLATIVE LIBRARIES

Office of Legislative Services
109 State House
Concord, NH 03301
(603) 271-3435
Fax: (603) 271-6607

REGULATORY AGENCIES

New Hampshire Bureau of Gaming Enforcement
Department of Safety,
Division of Enforcement
10 Hazen Dr.
Concord, NH 03305
Phone: (603) 271-3354

New Hampshire Lottery
Box 1208
Concord, NH 03302
Phone: (603) 271-3391

New Hampshire Racing Commission
Carrigan Commons
244 North Main St., Third Fl.
Concord, NH 03301-5041
Phone: (603) 271-2158

New Jersey

LEGISLATIVE LIBRARIES

Office of Legislative Services Library
140 East Front St., CN 068
Trenton, NJ 08625-0068
Phone: (609) 984-4321
Fax: (609) 984-4321

State Government Information Services
140 East Front St., CN520
Trenton, NJ 08625
Phone: (609) 292-6210
Fax: (609) 984-7901

Government Reference Section
Phone: (609) 292-6220
Fax: (609) 984-7900

Government Law Section
Phone: (609) 292-6230
Fax: (609) 984-7901

New Jersey Government Publication Section
Phone: (609) 292-6294
Fax: (609) 984-7900

REGULATORY AGENCIES

New Jersey Casino Control Commission
Tennessee Ave. & The Boardwalk
Atlantic City, NJ 08401
Phone: (609) 441-3422
Responsible for professional and occupational licensing in the gaming industry.

Division of Gaming Enforcement
New Jersey Department of
Law and Public Safety
140 East Front St., CN 047
Trenton, NJ 08625
Phone: (609) 292-9394

New Jersey Racing Commission
Department of
Law and Public Safety
140 East Front St., CN 088
Trenton, NJ 08625
Phone: (609) 292-0613

New Jersey State Lottery
140 East Front St., CN 041
Trenton, NJ 08625-0041
Phone: (609) 599-5800

Legalized Games of Chance Control Commission
Division of Consumer Affairs
New Jersey Department of
Law and Public Safety
P.O. Box 46000
Newark, NJ 07101
Phone: (201) 648-2710

New Mexico

LEGISLATIVE INFORMATION
(505) 986-4600

LEGISLATIVE LIBRARIES

**Legislative
Counsel Services**
State Capitol, Rm. 311
Santa Fe, NM 87503
Phone: (505) 986-4600
Fax: (505) 986-4610

REGULATORY AGENCIES

**Division of
Alcohol and Gaming**
New Mexico Department of
Regulation and Licensing
P.O. Box 25101
Santa Fe, NM 87504-5101
Phone: (505) 827-7066
Fax: (505) 827-7068

**New Mexico
Racing Commission**
Highland Station
P.O. Box 8576
Albuquerque, NM 87198
Phone: (505) 841-6400

INDIAN GAMING

Jicarilla Apache Tribe
P.O.Box 507
Dulce, NM 87528
Phone: (505) 759-3242

Compact approved 3/15/95; published 3/22/95. Any or all Class III games that, as of the date of this compact, are permitted within the State of New Mexico for any purpose

Mescalero Apache Tribe
P.O. Box 176
Mescalero, NM 88340
Phone: (505) 671-4495
Compact approved 3/15/95; published 3/22/95. Any or all Class III games that, as of the date of this compact, are permitted within the State of New Mexico for any purpose

Pueblo of Isleta
P.O. Box 1270
Isleta, NM 87022
Phone: (505) 869-3111
Compact approved 3/15/95; published 3/22/95. Any or all Class III games that, as of the date of this compact, are permitted within the State of New Mexico for any purpose

Pueblo of San Felipe
P.O. Box 4339
San Felipe Pueblo, NM 87001
Phone: (505) 867-3381
Compact approved 3/15/95; published 3/22/95. Any or all Class III games that, as of the date of this compact, are permitted within the State of New Mexico for any purpose

Pueblo of San Juan
P.O. Box 1099
San Juan Pueblo, NM 87599
Phone: (505) 852-4400
Compact approved 3/15/95; published 3/22/95. Any or all Class III games that, as of the date of this compact, are permitted within the State of New Mexico for any purpose

Pueblo of Sandia
Box 6008
Bernalillo, NM 87004
Phone: (505) 867-3317
Compact approved 3/15/95; published 3/22/95. Any or all Class III games that, as of the date of this compact, are permitted within the State of New Mexico for any purpose

Pueblo of Santa Ana
2 Dove Rd.
Bernalillo, NM 87004
Phone: (505) 867-3301
Compact approved 3/15/95; published 3/22/95. Any or all Class III games that, as of the date of this compact, are permitted within the State of New Mexico for any purpose

Pueblo of Santa Clara
P.O. Box 580
Espanola, NM 87532
Phone: (505) 753-7326
Compact approved 3/15/95; published 3/22/95. Any or all Class III games that, as of the date of

this compact, are permitted within the State of New Mexico for any purpose

Pueblo of Taos
P.O. Box 1846
Taos, NM 87571
Phone: (505) 758-9593
Compact approved 3/15/95; published 3/22/95. Any or all Class III games that, as of the date of this compact, are permitted within the State of New Mexico for any purpose

Pueblo of Tesuque
Route 5, Box 360-T
Santa Fe, NM 87501
Phone: (505) 983-2667
Compact approved 3/15/95; published 3/22/95. Any or all Class III games that, as of the date of this compact, are permitted within the State of New Mexico for any purpose

New York

LEGISLATIVE INFORMATION
(518) 455-7545

LEGISLATIVE LIBRARIES

Legislative Library
337 State Capitol
Albany, NY 12224
Phone: (518) 455-4000
Fax: (518) 463-0218

**Legislative
Tax Study Commission**
Empire State Plaza
Albany, NY 12248
Phone: (518) 455-4785
Fax: (518) 455-5396

Senate Research Service
777 New York State Senate
Senate Chambers
Albany, NY 12247
Phone: (518) 455-3355
Fax: (518) 455-3552

REGULATORY AGENCIES

**New York State Racing
and Wagering Board**
120 Broadway, 13th Fl.
New York, NY 10271
Phone: (212) 417-4200

New York State Lottery
Division of the Lottery
1 Broadway Center
P.O. Box 7500
Schenectady, NY 12301-7500
Phone: (518) 388-3300

INDIAN GAMING:

Oneida Indian Nation
P.O. Box 1, West Rd.
Oneida, NY 13421
Phone: (315) 697-8251
Head Chief: L. David Jacobs
Compact approved 6/4/93; published 6/15/93. Baccarat/ Bang/ Beat the Dealer/ Bell Jars/ Best Poker Hand/ Big Nine/ Big Six/

Blackjack/ Card Wheel/ Chuck-a-Luck/ Color Wheel/ Craps/ The Fruit Wheel/ Hazard/ Horse Race Game/ Horse Race Wheel/ Joker Seven/ Keno/ Merchandise Wheels/ Mini Baccarat/ Money Wheel/ Pai Gow/ Red Dog/ Acey-Deucey/ Roulette/ Super Pan Game/ Under & Over Seven

St. Regis Mohawk Tribe
Community Building
Hogansburg, NY 13655
Phone: (518) 358-2272
Compact approved 12/6/93; published 12/13/93. Amended 1/19/95; published 1/30/95. Baccarat/Bang/ Beat the Dealer/ Bell Jars/ Best Poker Hand/ Big Nine/ Big Six/ Blackjack/ Card Wheel/ Chuck-a-Luck/ Color Wheel/ Craps/ The Fruit Wheel/ Hazard/ Horse Race Game/ Horse Race Wheel/ Joker Seven/ Keno/ Merchandise Wheels/ Mini Baccarat/ Money-Wheel/ Pai Gow/ Red Dog/ Acey-Duecey/ Roulette/ Super Pan Game/ Under & Over Seven

North Carolina

LEGISLATIVE INFORMATION
(919) 733-7779

LEGISLATIVE LIBRARIES

Legislative Library

Legislative Office Building
300 North Salsbury St.
Raleigh, NC 27603
Phone: (919) 733-9390
Fax: (919) 733-3113

Institute of Government Library
CB Number 3330 Knapp Bldg.
University of North Carolina
Chapel Hill, NC 27599-3330
Phone: (919) 966-4172
Fax: (919) 966-4762

REGULATORY AGENCIES

North Carolina Department of Human Resources
Facilities Service Division
701 Barbour Dr.
P.O. Box 29530
Raleigh, NC 27626-0530
Phone: (919) 733-3029

INDIAN GAMING

Eastern Band of Cherokee Indians
Qualla Boundary
P.O. Box 455
Cherokee, NC 28719
Phone: (704) 497-2771
Compact approved 9/22/94; published 10/3/94. Raffles/ Video Games of Chance

North Dakota

LEGISLATIVE INFORMATION
(701) 224-2916, (701) 224-2000

LEGISLATIVE LIBRARIES

Legislative Council
State Capitol
600 East Blvd.
Bismark, ND 58505
Phone: (701) 328-4900
Fax: (701) 328-3615

REGULATORY AGENCIES

North Dakota Gaming Section
Office of the Attorney General
600 East Blvd.
Bismarck, ND 58505-0040
Phone: (701) 224-4848

INDIAN GAMING

Devils Lake Sioux Tribe
P.O. Box 359
Fort Totten, ND 58335
Phone: (701) 766-4221
Chairman: Peter Belgarde
Compact approved 12/17/92; published 12/30/92. Pari-Mutuel Racing Addendum approved 8/3/93; published 8/18/93. Slot Machines/ Video Lottery Terminals/ Blackjack/ Poker/ Pari-Mutuel/ Sports & Calcutta Pools/ Pull-tabs/ Raffles/ Keno/

Punchboard & Jars/ Paddle-wheels/ Craps/ Indian Dice

Sisseton-Wahpeton Sioux Tribe

Route 2, Agency Village
Sisseton, SD 57262
Phone: (605) 698-3911
Chairman: Russell Hawkins
Compact approved 1/25/93; published 2/3/93. Amended 7/1/94; published 7/13/94. Slot Machines/ Paddlewheels/ Blackjack/ Poker/ Keno/ Sports & Calcutta Pools/ Pari-Mutuel & Simulcast Betting/ Raffles/ Punchboards/ Craps/ Indian Dice

Standing Rock Sioux Tribe

P.O. Box D
Fort Yates, ND 58538
Phone: (701) 854-7231
Chairman: Charles W. Murphy
Compact approved 12/8/92; published 12/21/92. Video Lottery Terminal/ Slot Machines/ Paddlewheel/ Blackjack/ Poker/ Keno/ Sports & Calcutta Pools/ Pari-Mutuel

Three Affiliated Tribes of Fort Berthold

P.O. Box 220
New Town, ND 58763
Phone: (701) 627-4781
Chairman: Wiblur D. Wilkison
Compact approved 12/3/92; published 12/11/92. Addendum approved 3/1/94; published 3/10/94. Video Lottery/ Slot Ma-chines/ Blackjack/ Poker/ Keno/ Punchboards/ Paddlewheels/ Craps/ Indian Dice/ Pari-Mutuel Wagering on Horse Racing

Turtle Mountain Band of Chippewa Indians

Belcourt, ND 58316
Phone: (701) 477-6451
Compact approved 11/27/92; published 12/3/92. Pari-mutuel Racing Addendum approved 7/14/93; published 7/29/93. Video Lottery/Slot Machines/ Blackjack/ Poker/ Keno/ Punchboards/ Paddlewheels/ Craps/ Indian Dice/ Pari-Mutuel Wagering on Horse Racing

Ohio

LEGISLATIVE INFORMATION
(614) 466-8842

LEGISLATIVE LIBRARIES

Legislative Service Commission

77 South High St., 9th Fl.
Columbus, OH 43266-0342
Phone: (614) 466-7434

REGULATORY AGENCIES

Ohio Racing Commission

77 South High St., 18th Fl.
Columbus, OH 43266-0416
Phone: (614) 466-2757

Ohio Lottery Commission
615 West Superior Ave. NW
Cleveland, OH 44113
Phone: (216) 787-3200

**Charitable Foundations
Section**
Ohio Office of the
Attorney General
101 East Town, 4th Fl.
Columbus, OH 43215-5148
Phone: (614) 466-3180

Oklahoma

LEGISLATIVE INFORMATION
(405) 521-5642

LEGISLATIVE LIBRARIES

**Legislative Reference
Division**
Department of Libraries
Rm. 109, State Capitol
Oklahoma City, OK 73105
Phone: (405) 521-2753

**Oklahoma Publications
Clearing House**
Department of Libraries
200 Northeast 18th St.
Oklahoma City, OK 73105

REGULATORY AGENCIES

**Oklahoma
Horse Racing Commission**
6501 North Broadway,

Suite 100
Oklahoma City, OK 73116
Phone: (405) 848-0404

INDIAN GAMING

**Tonkawa Tribe of
Oklahoma**
P.O. Box 70
Tonkawa, OK 74653
Phone: (405) 628-2561
Compact approved 10/28/94;
published 11/9/94. Off-Track
Pari-Mutuel Simulcast Horse
Wagering

Oregon

LEGISLATIVE INFORMATION
(503) 378-8551

LEGISLATIVE LIBRARIES

Legislative Library
Rm. 347, State Capitol
Salem, OR 97310
Phone: (503) 986-1668
Fax: (503) 986-1684

REGULATORY AGENCIES

**Oregon Racing
Commission**
800 NE Oregon St., #11
Portland, OR 97232
Phone: (503) 299-5820

Oregon State Lottery
P.O. Box 12649
Salem, OR 97309
Phone: (503) 373-0202

**Charitable Activities
Section**
Gaming Unit, Oregon
Department of Justice
1515 Southwest 5th Ave.,
Suite 410
Portland, OR 97201
Phone: (503) 229-5725

INDIAN GAMING

**Confederated Tribes of
Coos, Lower Umpqua and
Siuslaw Indians**
455 South 4th
Coos Bay, OR 97420
Phone: (503) 267-5454
Compact approved 2/3/95; published 2/16/95. Video Lottery/ Keno/ Off-Race Course Mutuel Wagering

**Confederated Tribes of the
Grand Ronde Community**
P.O. Box 638
Grand Ronde, OR 97347
Phone: (503) 879-5211
Compact approved 6/10/94; published 6/17/94. Amended 2/21/95; published 3/1/95. Video Lottery/Keno/ Off-Race Course Mutuel Wagering

**Confederated Tribes of
Siletz Indians of Oregon**

P.O. Box 549
Siletz, OR 97380
Phone: (503) 444-2532
Compact approved 3/14/95; published 3/22/95. Video Lottery/ Keno/ Off-Race Course Mutuel Wagering

**Confederated Tribes of the
Warm Springs Reservation
of Oregon**
P.O. Box C
Warm Springs, OR 97761
Phone: (503) 553-1161
Compact approved 3/6/95; published 3/13/95. Video Lottery/ Keno/ Off-Race Course Mutuel Wagering

Coquille Indian Tribe
P.O. Box 1435
Coos Bay, OR 97420
Phone: (503) 267-4587
Compact approved 2/1/95; published 2/16/95. Video Lottery/ Keno/ Off-Race Course Mutuel Wagering

**Cow Creek Band of
Umpqua Tribe of Indians**
2400 Stewart Pkwy., Suite 300
Roseburg, OR 97470
Phone: (503) 672-9405
Chairman: Sue M. Shaffer
Compact approved 11/20/92; published 11/30/92. Amended 1/17/95; published 1/30/95. Video Lottery/ Keno

Klamath Tribes
P.O. Box 436
Chiloquin, OR 97624
Phone: (503) 783-2029
Compact approved 2/13/95; published 2/24/95. Video Lottery/ Keno/ Off-Race Course Mutuel Wagering

Umatilla Indian Tribe
P.O. Box 638
Pendleton, OR 97801
Phone: (503) 276-3165
Chairman: Elwood H. Patawa
Compact approved 2/2/94; published 2/15/94. Amended 10/6/94; published 10/18/94. Video Lottery/ Keno/ Off-Race Course Mutuel Wagering

Pennsylvania

LEGISLATIVE INFORMATION
(717) 787-2342

LEGISLATIVE LIBRARIES

Legislative Reference Bureau
Rm. 641, Main Capitol Building
Harrisburg, PA 17120-0033
Phone: (717) 787-4816
Fax: (717) 783-2396

Senate Library
157 Main Capitol Building
Harrisburg, PA 17120-6120
Phone: (717) 787-6120

Fax: (717) 783-5021
Joint State Government Commission
Finance Building, Rm. G-16
Harrisburg, PA 17120
Phone: (717) 787-6803
Fax: (717) 787-7020

REGULATORY AGENCIES

Pennsylvania Racing Commission
Department of Agriculture
2301 North Cameron St., Rm. 304
Harrisburg, PA 17110
Phone: (717) 787-1942

Pennsylvania State Lottery
Department of Revenue
2850 Turnpike Industrial Dr.
Middletown, PA 17057
Phone: (717) 986-4052

Bureau of Business Trust Fund Taxes
Pennsylvania Department of Revenue
Department 280901
Fourth and Walnut St.
Harrisburg, PA 17128-0901
Phone: (717) 787-8275

Rhode Island

LEGISLATIVE INFORMATION
(401) 751-8833

LEGISLATIVE LIBRARIES

Research Office
Legislative Council
Rm. 101, State House
Providence, RI 02903
Phone: (401) 277-3757
Fax: (401) 277-6065

REGULATORY AGENCIES

Games of Chance
Rhode Island State Police
311 Danielson Pk.
North Scituate, RI 02857
Phone: (401) 444-1000

**Division of Racing
and Athletics**
Rhode Island Department of
Business Regulation
233 Richmond St., Suite 234
Providence, RI 02903
Phone: (401) 277-6541

Rhode Island Lottery
1425 Pontiac Ave.
Cranston, RI 02920
Phone: (401) 463-6500

INDIAN GAMING

Narragansett Indian Tribe
P.O. Box 268
Charlestown, RI 02813
Phone: (401) 364-1100
Compact approved 8/29/94;
published 12/16/94. Blackjack/
Poker/ Carribean Poker/ Pai

Gow/ Dice/ Money-Wheel/
Roulette/ Baccarat/ Chuck-a-
Luck/ Pan Game/ Over & Under/
Horse Race Game/ Acey-Deucey/
Beat the Dealer/ Bouncing Ball/
Sic Bo/ Red Dog/ Any Game of
Chance authorized in New Jersey,
Nevada, and Connecticut/ Any
Lottery Game including Keno,
Numbers, and Lotto/ Off-Track
Pari-Mutuel Betting on Animal
Races/ Pari-Mutuel Betting thru
Simulcasting on Animal Races/
Pari-Mutuel Betting on Jai-Alai/
Pari-Mutuel Betting on Dog Rac-
ing/ Pari-Mutuel Betting on
Horse Racing/ Video Facsimiles
of any Game of Chance/ Slot
Machines/ Telephone Betting on
any Lottery Game/ Off-Track
Pari-Mutuel Telephone Betting
on Animal Races

South Carolina

LEGISLATIVE INFORMATION
(803) 734-2060

LEGISLATIVE LIBRARIES

Legislative Council
State House
P.O. Box 11489
Columbia, SC 29211
Phone: (803) 734-2425
Fax: (803) 734-2145

REGULATORY AGENCIES

South Carolina Department of Revenue
P.O. Box 125
Columbia, SC 29214
Phone: (803) 737-4767

South Dakota

LEGISLATIVE INFORMATION
(605) 773-4498

LEGISLATIVE LIBRARIES

Legislative Research Council
State Capitol
500 East Capitol Ave.
Pierre, SD 57501-5070
Phone: (605) 773-4498
Fax: (605) 773-4576

REGULATORY AGENCIES

South Dakota Commission of Gaming
118 East Missouri
Pierre, SD 57501
Phone: (605) 773-6050

South Dakota Lottery
207 East Capitol Ave.
Pierre, SD 57501
Phone: (605) 773-5770

Special Tax Division
South Dakota

Department of Revenue
700 Governor's Dr.
Pierre, SD 57501-2291
Phone: (605) 773-3311

Criminal Investigation Division
South Dakota
Attorney General's Office
East Highway 31
Pierre, SD 57501
Phone: (605) 773-3215

INDIAN GAMING

Cheyenne River Sioux Tribe
P.O. Box 590
Eagle Butte, SD 57625
Phone: (605) 964-4155
Chairman: Greg Bourland
Compact approved 11/19/93; published 12/3/93. Blackjack/ Poker/ Slot Machines

Crow Creek Sioux Tribe
P.O. Box 658
Fort Thompson, SD 57339
Phone: (605) 245-2221
Chairman: Nelson Blaine, Jr.
Compact approved 4/9/92; published 4/15/92. Amended 4/8/93. Blackjack/ Poker/ Slot Machines

Flandreau Santee Sioux Tribe
P.O. Box 283
Flandreau, SD 57028
Phone: (605) 997-3891

Compact approved 7/30/90; published 8/2/90. Blackjack/ Poker/ Slot Machines

Lower Brule Sioux Tribe
Lower Brule, SD 57548
Phone: (605) 473-5561
Compact approved 9/4/91; published 9/17/91. Amended 4/7/92; published 4/14/92. Blackjack/ Poker/ Slot Machines

Oglala Sioux Tribe
Pine Ridge, SD 57770
Phone: (605) 867-5659
Compact approved 10/14/93; published 10/28/93. Blackjack/ Poker/ Slot Machines

Rosebud Sioux Tribe
Rosebud, SD 57570
Phone: (605) 747-2381
Compact approved 4/6/93; published 4/14/93. Blackjack/ Poker/ Slot Machines

Sisseton-Wahpeton Sioux Tribe
Route 2 Agency Village
Sisseton, SD 57262
Phone: (605) 698-3911
Compact, Slot Machines approved 3/25/91; published 4/1/91. Amended 9/24/93; published 10/7/93. Amended 1/26/95; published 2/16/95. Compact, Video Lottery approved 11/26/91; published 12/4/91

Standing Rock Sioux Tribe
P.O. Box D
Fort Yates, ND 58538
Phone: (701) 854-7231
Compact approved 12/8/92; published 12/21/92. Blackjack/ Poker/ Slot Machines

Yankton Sioux Tribe of South Dakota
P.O Box 248
Marty, SD 57361
Phone: (605) 384-3641
Compact approved 6/13/91; published 6/19/91. Blackjack/ Poker/ Slot Machines

Tennessee

LEGISLATIVE INFORMATION
(615) 741-3511

LEGISLATIVE LIBRARIES

Office of Legal Services
G-16 War Memorial Building
Nashville, TN 37243-0059
Phone: (615) 741-3091
Fax: (615) 741-1146

REGULATORY AGENCIES

Tennessee State Racing Commission
Volunteer Plaza, Suite 635
500 James Robertson Pkwy.
Nashville, TN 37243-1138
Phone: (615) 741-1952

Texas

LEGISLATIVE INFORMATION
(512) 463-1252, (512) 463-4630

LEGISLATIVE LIBRARIES

**Legislative
Reference Library**
P.O. Box 12488
Austin, TX 78711
Phone: (512) 463-1252
Fax: (512) 475-4626

REGULATORY AGENCIES

Texas Racing Commission
9420 Research Echelon 3,
Suite 200
Austin, TX 78759
Phone: (512) 794-8461

Bingo Division
P.O. Box 16630
Austin, TX 78761-6630
Phone: (512) 323-3700

Lottery Division
P.O. Box 16630
Austin, TX 78761-6630
Phone: (512) 323-3700
(800) 375-6886

Utah

Note: there is no legalized
gambling in Utah.

LEGISLATIVE INFORMATION
Senate: (801) 538-1029
House: (801) 538-1035

LEGISLATIVE LIBRARIES

**Office of Legislative
Research and
General Counsel**
436 State Capitol
Salt Lake, UT 84114
Phone: (801) 538-1032
Fax: (801) 538-1712

Vermont

LEGISLATIVE INFORMATION
(802) 828-2231

LEGISLATIVE LIBRARIES

Legislative Council
115 State St., Drawer 33
Montpelier, VT 05633-5301
Phone: (802) 828-2231
Fax: (802) 828-2424

**Reference and Law
Services**
Vermont Department of Libraries
Montpelier, VT 05609
Phone: (802) 828-3268
Fax: (802) 828-2199

REGULATORY AGENCIES

**Vermont
Racing Commission**

State Office Building
120 State St.
Rutland, VT 05602
Phone: (802) 786-5050

**Vermont
Lottery Commission**
P.O. Box 420
South Barre, VT 05670
Phone: (802) 479-5686

Virginia

LEGISLATIVE INFORMATION
(804) 786-6530

LEGISLATIVE LIBRARIES

**Division of
Legislative Services**
Legislative Reference Library
910 Capitol St.
General Assembly Building,
Second Floor
Richmond, VA 23219
Phone: (804) 786-3591
Fax: (804) 371-0169

REGULATORY AGENCIES

**Virginia
Racing Commission**
Department of
Commerce and Trade
P.O. Box 1123
Richmond, VA 23208
Phone: (804) 371-7363

Virginia State Lottery
900 E. Main St.
Richmond, VA 23219
Phone: (804) 692-7000

Washington

LEGISLATIVE INFORMATION
(206) 786-7573

LEGISLATIVE LIBRARIES

State Library
P.O. Box 42460
Olympia, WA 98504-2460
Phone: (206) 753-4027
Fax: (206) 586-7575

REGULATORY AGENCIES

**Washington
Horse Racing Commission**
7912 Martin Way, Suite D
Olympia, WA 98506
Phone: (206) 459-6462

Washington State Lottery
814 4th Ave.
Olympia, WA 98506
Phone: (206) 753-1412

**Washington State
Gambling Commission**
P.O. Box 42400
Olympia, WA 98504-2400
Phone: (206) 438-7685

Responsible for professional and occupational licensing in the gaming industry.

INDIAN GAMING

Confederated Tribes of the Chehalis Reservation

P.O. Box 536
Oakville, WA 98568
Phone: (206) 273-5911
Compact approved 2/22/93; published 3/4/93. Blackjack/ Money-Wheel/ Roulette/ Baccarat/ Chuck-a-Luck/ Pai Gow/ Chemin De Fer/ Craps/ 4-5-6/ Ship-Captain-Crew/ Horses/ Beat the Dealer/ Over-Under Seven/ Beat My Shake/ Horse Race/ Sweet Sixteen/ Sport Pools/ Sic-Bo/ Carribean Stud Poker/ Lottery/ Keno/ Instant Tickets/ Punch Boards/ Pull-Tabs

Jamestown S'Klallam Tribe of Washington

305 Old Blyn Highway
Sequim, WA 98382
Phone: (206) 452-8471
Compact approved 4/20/93; published 5/3/93. Amended 3/10/95; published 3/22/95. Blackjack/Carribean Stud/ Baccarat/ Chemin de Fer/ Red Dog/ Pai Gow/ Moneywheel/ Chuck-a-Luck/ Craps/ 4-5-6/ Ship-Captain-Crew/ Horse (stop dice)/ Beat the Dealer/ Over-Under Seven/ Horse Race/ Single & Double Zero Roulette/ Beat My Shake/

Sweet Sixteen/ Sic-Bo/ Sports Pools/ Other Table Games/ Lottery type games/ Punch Boards/ Pull-Tabs

Lower Elwha Klallam Tribe

1666 Lower Elwha Rd.
Port Angeles, WA
Phone: (206) 452-8471
Compact approved 2/11/93; published 2/19/93. Blackjack/ Money-Wheel/ Roulette/ Baccarat/ Chuck-a-Luck/ Pai Gow/ Chemin de Fer/ Craps Blackjack/ 4-5-6/ Ship-Captain-Crew/ Horse/ Beat the Dealer/ Over-Under Seven/ Beat My Shake/ Horse Race/ Sweet Sixteen/ Sports Pools/ Sic-Bo/ Caribbean Stud Poker/ Lottery/ Keno Instant Tickets/ Punch Boards/ Pull-Tabs

Muckleshoot Indian Tribe

39015 172nd Ave., SE
Auburn, WA 98002
Phone: (206) 939-3311
Compact approved 4/23/93; published 5/6/93. Baccarat/ Beat My shake/ Beat the Dealer/ Blackjack/ Chemin De Fer/ Chuck-a-Luck/ Craps/ 4-5-6/ Horse/ Horse Race/ Money-Wheel/ Over-Under Seven/ Pai Gow/ Poker/ Red Dog/ Roulette/ Satellite (off-track) wagering on horses/ Ship-Captain-Crew/ Sic-Bo/ Sports Pools/ Sweet Sixteen/ Punchboards/ Washington State Lottery

Nooksack Indian Tribe of Washington

P.O. Box 157
Deming, WA 98224
Phone: (206) 592-5176
Compact approved 4/23/93; published 6/23/93. Amendment approved 7/11/94; published 7/20/94. Blackjack/Money-Wheel/ Roulette/ Baccarat/ Chuck-a-Luck/ Pai Gow/ Red Dog/ Chemin de Fer/ Craps/ 4-5-6/ Ship-Captain-Crew/ Horse (stop dice)/ Beat the Dealer/ Over-Under Seven/ Beat My Shake/ Horse Race/ Sweet Sixteen/ Sports Pools/ Sic-Bo/ Poker/ Any table games authorized for play in Nevada/ Punch Boards/ Pull-Tabs

Quileute Tribal Council

P.O. Box 279
La Push, WA 98350-0279
Phone: (206)374-6163
Compact approved 2/13/95; published 2/24/95. Blackjack/ Money-Wheel/ Roulette/ Baccarat/ Chuck-a-Luck/ Pai Gow/ Red Dog/ Chemin de Fer/ Craps/ 4-5-6/ Ship-Captain-Crew/ Horse (stop dice)/ Beat the Dealer/ Over-Under Seven/ Beat My Shake/ Horse Race/ Sweet Sixteen/ Sports Pools/ Sic-Bo/ Poker/ Any table games authorized for play in Washington/ Punch Boards/ Pull-Tabs

Squaxin Island Indian Tribe

Southeast 70 Squaxin Ln.
Shelton, WA 99040
Phone: (206) 426-3442
Compact approved 9/ 17/93; published 10/7/93. Baccarat/ Beat My Shake/ Beat the Dealer/ Blackjack/ Chemin De Fer/ Chuck-a-Luck/ Craps/ 4-5-6/ Horse (stop dice)/ Horse Race/ Money-Wheel/ Satellite(off-track) wagering on horse/ Roulette/ Over-Under Seven/ Pai Gow/ Red Dog/ Ship-Captain-Crew/ Sic-Bo/ Sweet Sixteen/ Punchboards/ Pull-Tabs

Swinomish Indian Tribal Community

P.O. Box 817
La Conner, WA 98257
Phone: (206) 466-3163
Compact approved 2/11/93; published 2/19/93. Blackjack/ Money-Wheel/ Roulette/ Baccarat/ Chuck-a-Luck/ Pai-Gow/ Red Dog/ Chemin de Fer/ Craps/ 4-5-6/ Ship-Captain-Crew/ Horse/ Beat the Dealer/ Over-Under Seven/ Beat My Shake/ Horse Race/ Sweet Sixteen/ Sic-Bo/ Sports Pools/ Other table games authorized by the State/ Tribal Lottery/ Horse Racing/ Punch Boards/ Pull-Tabs

Tulalip Tribes of Washington

6700 Totem Beach Rd.

Marysville, WA
Phone: (206) 653-4585
Compact approved 9/25/91; published 10/3/91. Amended 7/20/92; published 12/20/93. Amended 12/7/93; published 12/20/93. Blackjack/ Money-Wheel/ Roulette/ Baccarat/ Chuck-a-Luck/ Pai Gow/ Red Dog/ Chemin de Fer/ Craps/ 4-5-6/ Ship-Captain-Crew/ Horse (stop dice)/ Beat the Dealer/ Over-Under Seven/ Beat My Shake/ Horse Race/ Sweet Sixteen/ Sports Pools/ Sic-Bo/ Poker/ Any other table game authorized for play in the state of Nevada/ Punch Boards/ Pull-Tabs

Upper Skagit Indian Tribe
2284 Community Plaza
Sedro Woolley, WA 98284
Phone: (206) 856-5501
Compact approved 2/19/93; published 3/4/93. Blackjack/ Money-Wheel/ Roulette/ Baccarat/ Chuck-a-Luck/ Pai Gow/ Chemin de Fer/ Craps/ 4-5-6/ Ship-Captain-Crew/ Horse/ Beat the Dealer/ Over-Under Seven/ Beat My Shake/ Horse Race/ Sweet Sixteen/ Sports Pools/ Sic-Bo/ Keno/ Instant Tickets/ On-Line Games/ Lottery/ Punch Boards/ Pull-Tabs/ Other Authorized Table Games

West Virginia

LEGISLATIVE INFORMATION
(304) 348-8905

LEGISLATIVE LIBRARIES

**Legislative
Reference Library**
State Capitol, Rm. MB-27
Charleston, WV 25305
Phone: (304) 347-4830
Fax: (304) 347-4825

REGULATORY AGENCIES

**West Virginia
Racing Commission**
P.O. Box 3327
Charleston, WV 25333
Phone: (304) 558-2150

West Virginia Lottery
Department of Tax and Revenue
P.O. Box 2067
Charleston, WV 25327
Phone: (304) 558-0500

Wisconsin

LEGISLATIVE INFORMATION
(608) 266-9960

LEGISLATIVE LIBRARIES

**Legislative Research
Bureau**

100 North Hamilton St.
P.O. Box 2037
Madison, WI 53701-2037
Phone: (608) 266-0341
Fax: (608) 266-5648

REGULATORY AGENCIES

**Wisconsin
Gaming Commission**
1802 West Beltline Hwy.
P.O. Box 8941
Madison, WI 53708-8941
Phone: (608) 266-7777

Office of Indian Gaming
Wisconsin Gaming Commission
P.O. Box 8941
Madison, WI 53708-8941
Phone: (608) 261-8800

INDIAN GAMING

**Bad River Band of Lake
Superior Tribe of
Chippewa Indians**
P.O. Box 39
Odanah, WI 54861
Phone: (715) 682-7111
Compact aproved 3/30/92; pub-
lished 4/3/92. Electronic Games
of Chance/ Blackjack/ Pull-Tabs

**Forest County
Potawatomi Community**
P.O. Box 346
Crandon, WI 54520
Phone: (715) 478-2093

Compact approved 8/4/92; published 8/10/92. Electronic Games
of Chance/ Blackjack/ Pull-Tabs

**Lac Courte Oreilles Band
of Lake Superior Chippewa**
Route 2, Box 2700
Hayward, WI 54843
Phone: (415) 634-8934
Compact and first amendment ap-
proved 4/13/92; published
4/20/92. Electronic Games of
Chance/ Blackjack/ Pull-Tabs

**Lac du Flambeau Band of
Lake Superior Chippewa**
P.O. Box 67
Lac du Flambeau, WI 54538
Phone: (715) 588-3303
Compact approved 6/23/92; pub-
lished 7/1/92. Electronic Games
of Chance/ Blackjack/ Pull-Tabs

**Menominee Indian Tribe of
Wisconsin**
P.O. Box 397
Keshena, WI 54135
Phone: (715) 799-5100
Compact approved 8/3/92; pub-
lished 8/10/92. Electronic Games
of Chance/ Blackjack/ Pull-Tabs

**Oneida Tribe of
Indians of Wisconsin**
N7210 Seminary Rd.
Oneida, WI 54155
Phone: (414) 869-2772
Compact approved 1/24/92; pub-
lished 1/30/92. Electronic Games
of Chance/ Blackjack/ Pull-Tabs

Red Cliff Band of Lake Superior Chippewa
P.O. Box 529
Bayfied, WI 54814
Phone: (715) 779-3701
Compact approved 3/4/92; published 3/10/92. Electronic Games of Chance/ Blackjack/ Pull-Tabs

St. Croix Chippewa Indians of Wisconsin
P.O. Box 287
Hertel, WI 54845
Phone: (715) 349-2195
Compact approved 3/4/92; published 3/10/92. Electronic Games of Chance/ Blackjack/ Pull-Tabs

Sokoagan Chippewa Community
Route 1, Box 625
Crandon, WI 54520
Phone: (715) 478-2604
Compact approved 2/6/92; published 2/13/92. Electronic Games of Chance/ Blackjack/ Pull-Tabs

Stockbridge-Munsee Community of Mohican Indians of Wisconsin
Route 1
Bowler, WI 54416
Phone: (715) 793-4111
Compact approved 4/15/92; published 4/23/92. Electronic Games of Chance/ Blackjack/ Pull-Tabs

Wisconsin Winnebago Indian Tribe
P.O. Box 667

Black River Falls, WI 54615
Phone: (715) 284-9343
Compact approved 7/30/92; published 8/5/92. Electronic Games of Chance/ Blackjack/ Pull-Tabs

Wyoming

LEGISLATIVE INFORMATION

House Sessions: (307) 777-7765
Senate Sessions: (307) 777-6185
Btw. Sessions: (307) 777-7881

LEGISLATIVE LIBRARIES

Legislative Service Office
State Capitol, Rm. 213
Cheyenne, WY 82002
Phone: (307) 777-7881
Fax: (307) 777-5466

Wyoming State Law Library
Supreme Court and
State Library Building
Cheyenne, WY 82002
Phone: (307) 777-7609
Fax: (307) 777-7240

REGULATORY AGENCIES

Wyoming Pari-Mutuel Wagering Commission
Barrett Building, #210
Cheyenne, WY 82002
Phone: (307) 777-5887

CHAPTER 5

Associations, Organizations, Experts, & Consultants

This chapter provides information on associations, organizations, experts, and consultants with specialized knowledge of gambling or the casino gaming industry. These associations and organizations represent a broad range of interests including public policy and administration, regulation, public health, education, and the gaming industry. Experts and consultants were selected based on their substantial contributions to the literature and to public discussion on gaming and gambling. Information was collected via questionnaire, Spring 1995. Due to space limitations, the knowledge and activities of these groups and individuals are only briefly described in the entries that follow.

ASSOCIATIONS & ORGANIZATIONS

American Gaming Association
Frank Fahrenkopf, Jr., Pres.
William F. Sittman, Exec. V.P.
555 13th St. NW
Washington, DC 20004
Phone: (202) 637-5676
Represents the gaming industry in Washington, D.C.; monitors legislation and acts as an education center to raise public aware- ness of gaming as a legitimate and thriving industry.

Canadian Foundation on Compulsive Gambling
505 Consumers Rd., #605
Willowdale, Ontario
Canada M2J4V8
Phone: (416) 499-9800
Provides support for the study of compulsive gambling and lobbies

for government support for
research and treatment programs.

Center for the Study
of the States
Rockefeller Institute
411 State St.
Albany, NY 12203-1003
Phone: (518) 443-5285
Supports research activities and
promotes public awareness of
pressing social issues such as the
proliferation of casinos.

Council on Compulsive
Gambling of Nevada
4535 West Sahara Ave.
Las Vegas, NV 89102
Phone: (702) 364-2625
Acts as a public health and awareness service to educate the public
on compulsive gambling and
encourage support for treatment
programs. The council is one of
the most active state affiliates of
the National Council on
Compulsive Gambling.

Council on Compulsive
Gambling of New Jersey
1315 West State St.
Trenton, NJ 08418
Phone: (609) 599-3299
Fax: (609) 599-5383
Provides health and awareness
services that educate the public
on compulsive gambling and
encourages support for treatment
programs. The council is one of
the most active state affiliates of

the National Council on
Compulsive Gambling.

Gam-Anon International
Service Office
P.O. Box 157
Whitestone, NY 11357
Phone: (718) 352-1671
Gives relatives and close friends
of compulsive gamblers a support group and provides ways to
better understand and help the recovering compulsive gambler.
Holds national conferences and
quarterly local symposia and has
hundreds of chapters worldwide.
Publications: *Gam-A-News* (quarterly); various pamphlets and information sheets.

Gamblers Anonymous
P.O. Box 17173
Los Angeles, CA 90010
Phone: (213) 386-8789
Fax: (213) 386-0030
Consists of problem gamblers
joined together to quit gambling.
This association is patterned after
Alcoholics Anonymous. Holds
semi-annual conferences and has
hundreds of local chapters worldwide. Publications: *Annual
Directory; A New Beginning* (irregular); *Lifelines Bulletin*
(monthly); *Sharing Recovery
with Gamblers Anonymous* (irregular pamphlets).

Gaming and Economic Development Institute

1800 Diagonal Rd., Suite 600
Alexandria, VA 22314
(703) 684-4433

Conducts research, workshops, and conferences on gambling and economic development.

Gaming Resource Center

Susan Jarvis, Dir.
University of Nevada, Las Vegas,
James Dickinson Library
4505 South Maryland Pkwy.
Las Vegas, NV 89154-7010
Phone: (702) 895-3252

Holds one of the world's largest collections of monographs, periodicals, books, photographs, and other materials related to gaming. Provides general library reference services for gaming-related topics.

Institute for the Study of Gambling and Commercial Gaming

William Eadington, Dir.
Judy Cornelius, Assoc. Dir.
College of Business
Administration
University of Nevada, Reno
Reno, NV 89557-0901
Phone: (702) 784-1477

Sponsors major international gaming conferences and conducts seminars for the gaming industry. Publications: *Journal of Gambling Studies* (quarterly), co-published with the National Council on Problem Gambling; annual conference proceedings.

International Association of Gaming Attorneys

Judy Klein, Exec. Dir.
2600 West Oakey
Las Vegas, NV 89104
Phone: (702) 382-3840
Fax: (702) 382-8135

Acts as a referral service providing information on gaming attorneys and regulatory bodies nationwide.

International Gaming Institute

Vincent Eade, Dir.
University of Nevada, Las Vegas
4505 South Maryland Pkwy.
Las Vegas, NV 89154-6037
(702) 895-3966
(702) 895-4109

Provides a setting in which to study, analyze, and evaluate the gaming and casino entertainment industry. Educators, business leaders, government representatives, policymakers, and students come to gain a basic orientation to the industry or to pursue advanced study. Publications: *Gaming Research and Review Journal* (semi-annual).

National Center for American Indian Enterprise Development

9650 Flair Dr., #303
El Monte, CA 91731
Phone: (818) 442-3701

Promotes employment and self-sufficiency by assisting Native Americans in starting and expanding business enterprises, including gaming.

National Council on Problem Gambling

John Jay College of
Criminal Justice
445 West 59th St., Room 1521
New York, NY 10019
Phone: (212) 765-3833
Fax: (212) 541-9752

Seeks to increase awareness of and concern for problem gambling. This organization includes professionals in health, education, and law, and recovering gamblers, their families, and supporters. Conducts professional training seminars and information programs, sponsors annual conferences, and maintains a speakers bureau. A good source for statistical information. Publications: *Journal of Gambling Studies* (quarterly), co-published with the Institute for the Study of Gambling and Commercial Gaming; *National Council on Problem Gambling: Newsletter* (quarterly).

National Indian Gaming Association

Timothy Wapato, Exec. Dir.
904 Pennsylvania Ave. SE
Washington, D.C. 20003
(202) 546-7711
(202) 546-1755

Serves as an information clearinghouse for Indian gaming issues and tribal community development; works with tribes, policymakers, and the public. Publications: *Indian Gaming Magazine* (monthly).

National Indian Policy Center

George Washington University
2136 Pennsylvania Ave. NW
Washington, D.C. 20052
Phone: (202) 994-1446
Fax: (202) 994-4404

Provides information on myriad policy issues to over 500 U.S. Indian tribes and Alaska Native Villages. Established by Congressional initiative, the center supports research and policy analysis, serves as an information clearinghouse, and sponsors conferences and seminars on issues concerning American Indians and Alaska Natives. Publications: various research and policy papers.

Nevada Pari-Mutuel Association

300 South Fourth St.
Las Vegas, NV 89101

Phone: (702) 387-2021
Assists casinos with the negotiation of pari-mutuel contacts and
acts as a lobbyist for the casino
industry at all levels of government.

Nevada Resort Association
2300 W. Sahara, Suite 440-32
Las Vegas, NV 89102
Phone: (702) 362-2472
Fax: (702) 362-9278
Represents approximately forty-
three members, monitors federal,
state, and local legislation, and
acts as a lobbyist for the casino
industry at all levels of government.

**North American Gaming
Regulators Association**
P.O. Box 21886
Lincoln, NE 68542-1886
Phone: (402) 474-4261
Studies gaming regulation and
conducts seminars for gaming
regulators and industry officials.
Publications: *NAGRA News-
letter* (monthly).

**Public Gaming Research
Institute**
15825 Shady Grove Rd.,
Suite 130
Rockville, MD 20850

Phone: (301) 330-7600
Conducts seminars and trade
shows for the gaming industry.
Publications: *Gaming Technolo-
gies* (monthly); *Public Gaming
International* (monthly); *Indian
Gaming Magazine*, co-published
by the National Indian Gaming
Association (monthly).

United Jewish Appeal
Federation of Jewish
Philanthropies of New York
Task Force on
Compulsive Gambling
130 East 59th St.
New York, NY 10022
Phone: (212) 980-1000
Encourages gambling addiction
organizations, community programs, social services, and
synagogues which address compulsive gambling. Gamblers,
professionals, and concerned
individuals illuminate problems
and develop services for and
through the Jewish community.
Holds periodic conferences, and
maintains a speakers bureau.
Publications: *Bulletin* (monthly),
conference proceedings.

EXPERTS & CONSULTANTS

Vicki Abt, Prof.
Sociology Dept.
Penn State University
Woodland Rd.
Abington, PA 19001
Phone: (215) 881-7335
Fax: (215) 881-7317
Knowledge: gambling legalization campaigns, sociology of leisure, risk taking behavior, social psychology of addiction, gambling and social policy. Consulting: National Council on Problem Gambling; expert testimony provided to state legislatures; cited by the President's Commission on Organized Crime.

Ken Adams,
Consultant and Historian
Ken Adams & Associates
5170 Point View Way
Sparks, NV 89431
(702) 331-6201
Knowledge: casino operations, history and development of casino management. Former casino operations director, casino manager, keno department manager. Chair, University of Nevada Reno, Hotel Gaming Program Advisory Committee. Consulting: executive management, strategic planning, new casino development, personnel recruiting

and training, market and operational analysis, customer development and marketing, regulatory development. Publications: *Nevada Gaming Almanac* (annual); *Nevada Gaming Directory* (annual); *Adams Report* (monthly).

Jason N. Ader, V.P.
Research Division
Smith Barney
388 Greenwich, 30th Fl.
New York, NY 10013
Phone: (212) 816-3803
Fax: (212) 816-8558
Knowledge: Las Vegas and Atlantic City casino/hotel operators and emerging market participants. Slot manufacturers, route operators, racetrack owners, Native American gaming management companies and gaming-related manufacturers and distributors. Publications: *Global Gaming Almanac* (annual); *Gaming Industry Consolidation Watch; Smith Barney Weekly Gaming Update;* monthly state-gaming updates for Louisiana, Illinois, Mississippi.

David Anders, Analyst
Raymond James & Associates
880 Carillon Pkwy.
St. Petersburg, FL 33716-1102

Phone: (813) 573-8954
Fax: (813) 573-8095
Knowledge: gaming and lottery equipment suppliers and respective market sizes. In-depth research conducted on Las Vegas-based gaming operations and emerging operations. Publications: regularly publishes detailed reports on various aspects of gaming, including riverboat gaming and Indian gaming.

Yale Braunstein
School of Library &
Information Science
University of
California, Berkeley
Berkeley, CA 94720-4600
Phone: (510) 642-2235
Fax: (510) 642-5814
E-mail:
YMBLIS@CMSA.berkeley.edu
Knowledge: economics of the information, communications, and entertainment industries. Financial and economic impact of gaming operations. Consulting: economic and financial models, cost/benefit analysis, regulatory analysis.

Kathleen P. Brewer,
Assoc. Prof.
College of Hotel Administration
University of Nevada, Las Vegas
4505 South Maryland Pkwy.
Las Vegas, NV 89154-6021
Phone: (702) 895-3643
Fax: (702) 895-4872

E-mail: pearl@nevada.edu
Knowledge: gaming technology and gaming systems, mathematics of casino games. Consulting: numerous speaking engagements on computers and their applications to gaming such as management information systems and slot tracking.

Anthony N. Cabot, Partner
Lionel, Sawyer & Collins
Bank of America Plaza
300 South 4th St., Suite 1700
Las Vegas, NV 89101
Phone: (702) 383-8840
Fax: (702) 383-8845
Knowledge: gaming licensing and regulation, Nevada gaming, gaming policy, credit and collection law, patron disputes, and international gaming law. Representative clients: Caesars Palace, Las Vegas Hilton, Sheraton-Desert Inn, Anchor Gaming, Casino Athens Consortium, MGM Grand, Shufflemaster, Inc., Pelican Gaming, Tropicana Hotel & Casino, Nevada Pari-mutuel Association, Nevada Resort Association.

Lowell Caneday, Dir.
School of HPEL
Oklahoma State University
Colvin Center
Stillwater, OK 74078
Phone: (405) 744-5493
Fax: (405) 744-6507

E-mail:
Lowell@uml.ucc.okstate.ed
Knowledge: gambling in historic western towns, gambling as a leisure pursuit, historic preservation. Consulting: Deadwood, South Dakota.

Thomas F. Cargill, Prof.
Bureau of Business
and Economic Research
University of Nevada, Reno
Reno, NV 89557-0901
Phone: (702) 784-6812
Fax: (702) 784-4337
Knowledge: regional analysis, regional modeling, macro economic performance and gaming policy. Publications: *Nevada Business and Economic Indicators* (annual), *Quarterly Report on the Nevada Economy* (quarterly), *Reno/Sparks Business Attitude Survey* (semi-annual) .

Christopher Chadbourne,
Pres.
Christopher Chadbourne
& Associates
131 Mt. Auburn St.
Cambridge, MA 02138
Phone: (617) 547-5330
Fax: (617) 547-2877
Knowledge: leveraging of assets, waterfront and downtown development, tourism plans, regulatory tools including zoning and design review, infrastructure impact assessment, urban design, and comprehensive planning.

Consulting: gaming/riverfront plans for Natchez, Shreveport, Houston, Vicksburg, D'Iberville, and other cities.

Eugene M. Christiansen,
Pres.
Christiansen/Cummings
Associates Inc.
145 Madison Ave, 3rd Fl.
New York, NY 10016
Phone: (212) 779-9797
Fax: (212) 779-9809
Knowledge: an independent consulting and financial services firm serving the gaming, communications, and entertainment industries, as well as government agencies that regulate these industries. Specific activities include representation in financial acquisitions, securing financing for recapitalization, advising on new market ventures, and corporation and market analysis. Consulting: findings have been presented to numerous groups, conferences, and organizations. Mr. Christiansen's testimony has been sought by the U.S. Congress and state and local governments. His advice is often solicited by business, banks and other financial institutions, by counsel in legal proceedings, and the news media.

Christopher Craig, Associate
Center for State Policy Research
11 Dupont Circle

Washington, DC 20036
Phone: (202) 328-9393
Fax: (202) 328-9337
Knowledge: legislative, regulatory systems and processes, and political intelligence gathering, analysis, and dissemination. Consulting: media advisor, television, print, and radio, for all aspects of gaming. Advises financial investors about current and likely political developments and fulfills the role of general counsel. Publications: *State Gaming Issues Reports* (annual); legislative intelligence reports.

John R. Cross, Assoc. Prof.
Sociology Dept., CLB 033
Oklahoma State University
Stillwater, OK 74078-0395
Phone: (405) 744-6121
Fax: (405) 744-5780
E-mail:
JRC@mus.ucc.okstate.edu
Knowledge: problem gambling, Indian gaming, economic development, Indian law.

Lawrence Dandurand, Prof.
Marketing Dept.
University of Nevada, Las Vegas
4505 South Maryland Pkwy.
Las Vegas, NV 89154-6010
Phone: (702) 895-3591
Fax: (702) 895-4854
E-mail: lorenzo@nevada.edu
Knowledge: market strategy and planning, international marketing, market research, marketing

technology, casino gaming markets. Consulting: marketing research, marketing strategy and planning.

Howard Dickstein, Atty.
Dickstein and Merin
2001 P St., Suite 100
Sacramento, CA 95814
Phone: (916) 443-6911
Fax: (916) 447-8336
Knowledge: all aspects of federal Indian law from Indian gaming to Indian health. Consulting: legal representation of Indian tribes and investors with an interest in economic development on Indian lands.

Vincent Eade, Dir.
International Gaming Institute
University of Nevada, Las Vegas
4505 South Maryland Pkwy.
Las Vegas, NV 89154-6037
Phone: (702) 895-3966
Fax: (702) 895-4109
Knowledge: human resources management in the gaming industry. Development of gaming curricula for two and four-year educational institutions. Consulting: seminars for national and international gaming operators, educators, and regulators. Publications: *Gaming Research and Review Journal* (semi-annual).

Ann Fabian,
Assoc. Prof.
American Studies

Yale University
P.O. Box 208236, Yale Station
New Haven, CT 06520
Phone: (203) 432-1188
Fax: (203) 432-4493
E-mail: afabian@minerva.cis.yale
Knowledge: history of gambling
and the opposition to gambling.
Publications: *Card Sharps,
Dream Books, & Bucket Shops:
Gambling in 19th-Century
America* (Ithaca, N.Y.: Cornell
University Press, 1990).

John M. Findlay,
Assoc. Prof.
Dept. of History
University of Washington
Seattle, WA 98195
Phone: (206) 543-5790
Knowledge: history of gambling
in the "successive American
west," including Las Vegas
before 1965. Publications:
*People of Chance: Gambling in
American Society from
Jamestown to Las Vegas* (New
York: Oxford University Press,
1986).

Brian R. Ford,
National Director of Gaming
Industry Services
Ernst & Young LLP
2 Commerce Square
2001 Market St.
Philadelphia, PA 19103-7096
Phone: (215) 448-5010
Fax: (215) 448-4069

Knowledge: all aspects of casino
accounting, auditing, and tax related services as well as financial
advisory and management consulting. Litigation support and
dispute resolution, human resources consulting and information technology services including systems planning, design,
and integration. Consulting: pre-
licensing and pre-opening
services including market
demand, financial feasibility, and
economic impact and cost
segregation studies. Assistance
with license applications, design
and implementation of systems
of internal control, operational
reviews, and financial analyses.
Due diligence reviews, valuation
services, corporate finance
assistance with acquisitions
divesture, reorganizations, and
bankruptcy. Publications:
Compilation of Gaming Data
(annual); *Compilation of Casino
Financial Accounting Disclosures*
(annual); *Tax Issues in the
Gaming Industry* (annual).

E. Malcolm Greenlees,
Jackson Prof. of Business
Dept. of Economics and Business
Linfield College
McMinnville, OR 97128
Phone: (503) 434-2403
Knowledge: Certified Public Ac-
countant with expertise in casino
accounting and financial man-
agement and lodging and gaming

systems. Publications: *Casino Accounting and Financial Management* (Reno, Nev.: University of Nevada Press, 1988). Consulting: consultant on gaming and litigation matters with a variety of organizations.

Simon Hakim, Prof.
Economics Dept.
Temple University
Cecil B. Moore and Broad St.
Philadelphia, PA 19122
Phone: (215) 204-5037
Fax: (215) 204-8173
BITNET: V555TE@Templevm
Knowledge: local and regional impact of casinos, feasibility studies for new casinos, and the effect of casinos on regional crime. Consulting: impact and feasibility consulting for companies and government agencies, casino operations in Atlantic City, and horse betting. Grants from the National Institute of Justice to study the impact of casino gambling.

Kenneth Harrison,
Assoc. Prof.
Economics Dept.
Stockton State College
Pomona, NJ 08240
Phone: (609) 652-4435
Fax: (609) 748-5559
E-mail:
IAPROD255@stockton.edu
Knowledge: New Jersey gaming, economic development, and tax

policy. Consulting: economic impact of casino gaming.

Jeremy Hawes,
Gaming Analyst
Moody's Investors Service
99 Church St.
New York, NY 10007
Phone: (212) 553-0300
Fax: (212) 553-4700
Knowledge: Moody's assigns credit ratings to virtually all public debt issues for casinos and gaming-related companies worldwide. Publications: Moody's reports and industry commentaries.

George Ignatin,
Assoc. Prof.
Economics Dept.
School of Business
University of Alabama,
Birmingham
1150 Tenth Ave. South
Birmingham, AL 35294-4460
Phone: (205) 934-8830
Fax: (205) 975-6234
Knowledge: economics of gambling, sports betting, forecasting, economic impacts, cost/benefit analysis, public policy, labor economics and wage productivity, and probability and odds/line making. Consulting: economic impacts of greyhound tracks, casinos, keno, and lotteries. Provided a response to the Alabama Family Alliance's opposition to casinos. Acts as an

expert witness in a wide variety of lawsuits.

Bruce Elliott Johansen, Prof.
Dept. of Communication
University of Nebraska at Omaha
Omaha, NE 68182
Phone: (402) 554-4851
Fax: (402) 554-3296
E-mail:
johansen@cwis.unomaha.edu
Knowledge: Native American studies. Publications: *Life and Death in Mohawk Country* (Golden, Colo.: North American Press, 1993). Consulting: consultant to the Akwesasne Mohawk Tribe.

Craig R. Johnson
Gaming Development
International
200 West Madison St.,
Suite 3630
Chicago, IL 60606
Phone: (312) 407-6992
Fax: (312) 407-6990
Knowledge: riverboat gaming, emerging gaming markets, international gaming, technology, communications applications, interactive gaming, regulatory planning. Consulting: new venue development, market analysis, and strategic planning.

Jim Kilby,
Boyd Prof. of Gaming
Hotel Management Dept.
University of Nevada, Las Vegas
4505 South Maryland Pkwy.
Las Vegas, NV 89154-6021
Phone: (702) 436-7954
Fax: (702) 436-7964
Knowledge: twenty-five years of experience in all phases of casino operations. Consulting: consultant to many of the largest gaming companies in Asia, Australia, Korea, Nevada, Atlantic City, and the Caribbean.

Ray Koon, Pres.
Associated Gaming Consultants
3721 South Highland, Suite 705a
Las Vegas, NV 89109-1051
Phone: (702) 735-2550
Fax: (702) 735-1877
Knowledge: thirty-six years of law enforcement and corporate experience in gaming operations, regulatory compliance, gaming statutes and regulations, investigative and licensure functions, multifaceted training programs. Consulting: operational risk analysis, gaming laws and regulations, building and casino security, assets protection, and overall operational integrity. Expert witness in federal and state courts and before legislatures. Guest lecturer. Publications: *Ray Koon's GAMING/GRAM.*

Paul E. Larsen, Atty.
Lionel Sawyer & Collins
Bank of America Plaza
300 South 4th St., Suite 1700

Las Vegas, NV 89101
Phone: (702) 383-8819
Fax: (702) 383-8845
Knowledge: federal and state cash reporting and money laundering regulations for casinos, state and local gaming licensing of persons and organizations, new games and gaming devices, and taxation. Consulting: on behalf of clients, worked closely with the United States Treasury Department, United States Congress, and the Nevada Gaming Control Board to develop legislation and regulations regarding cash reporting for casinos.

Sam A. Le Blanc, Atty.
Gaming Practice Group
Adams & Reese Law Firm
4500 One Shell Square
New Orleans, LA 70139
Phone: (504) 585-3234
Fax: (504) 566-0210
Knowledge: gaming litigation of all types, including administrative, constitutional, regulatory, financial, zoning, political, neighborhood class actions, labor, and commercial. Consulting: all aspects of gaming.

Patrick T. Long,
Assoc. Prof.
College of Business and Administration
University of Colorado at Boulder
Campus Box 419, Room 403
Boulder, CO 80309

Phone: (303) 492-2381
Fax: (303) 492-5962
E-mail:
Patrick.Long@Colorado.edu
Knowledge: state and community gaming policies, community-based casino gaming, limited-stakes gaming, economic and social impacts of gaming on community life, residents' attitudes regarding gaming development, rural economic development, tourism planning and development. Presentations for National Conference for State Legislatures, National Association of State Development Agencies, United States Travel and Tourism Administration, International Traveler Services Association, Travel and Tourism Research Association, plus numerous print, radio, and TV interviews.

Michael K. Madden, Prof.
Business Dept.
University of South Dakota
P.O. Box 220
Box Elder, SD 57719
Phone: (605) 348-2498
Fax: (605) 348-2498
Knowledge: economic impact analyses, market research, feasibility studies, statistical analysis, survey analysis. Consulting: various aspects of casino gaming.

Heidi McNeil, Atty.
Indian Law Practice Group
Snell & Wilmer Law Firm

400 East Van Buren
Phoenix, AZ 85004-0001
Phone: (602) 382-6366
Fax: (602) 382-6070
Knowledge: represents persons and companies dealing with Indian tribes both on and off the reservation as well as tribes, tribal enterprises, and individual Indians. Pro bono representation of Indians and Indian interests, including support of Indian economic development and self-sufficiency programs. Practice includes Bureau of Indian Affairs and National Indian Gaming Commission regulation, Department of Interior Affairs, licensing, preparing, and negotiating management contracts and collateral agreements, preparation of ordinances/ resolutions, gaming crime, lobbying Arizona legislature on behalf of clients, forecast of positive and negative economic and crime impact of gaming upon reservations, financing, leasing, taxation, real property and labor issues relating to Indian Gaming. Offices in Phoenix, Salt Lake City, and Tucson.

Wayne Mehl,
Government Relations
Consultant
Nevada Resort Association
2725 Carter Farm Court
Alexandria, VA 22306
Phone: (703) 780-1025
Fax: (703) 799-9404

Knowledge: casino gaming, United States Congress, regulatory structure. Consulting: consultant to the Nevada casino industry on federal government actions. Lobbyist.

Joe Milanowski,
Director of Research
USA Capital
3900 South Paradise Rd.,
Suite 263
Las Vegas, NV 89109
Phone: (702) 734-1737
Fax: (702) 734-7868
Knowledge: gaming industry and gaming finance. Consulting: gaming finance.

John R. Mills, Prof.
Accounting and CIS Dept.
University of Nevada, Reno
Mail Stop 26
Reno, NV 89557-0016
Phone: (702) 784-6884
Fax: (702) 784-1769
Knowledge: Financial analysis, accounting controls, U.S.C. Title 31 (REG 6A) and proposal analysis. Consulting: New Orleans Rivergate Project, Windsor Casino Project, Houston Gaming Study. Provides Casino Control & U.S.C. Title 31 (REG 6A) training.

Rodney L. Murray,
Chief Inspector
Tribal Gaming Agency
Tulalip Tribes of Washington

6410 33rd Ave. NE
Marysville, WA 98271
Phone: (360) 651-1111, ext. 241
Knowledge: casino security and
industrial security. Consulting:
counsels gaming inspectors, directors, business committees, and
commissioners on all aspects of
casino security. Writes training
manuals in casino security, lodging and restaurant security, and
tribal gaming commission/
agency operations.

James J. Murren,
Managing Dir.
Dept. of Research
CJ Lawrence/Deutsche Bank
1290 Ave. of The Americas
New York, NY 10104-0101
Phone: (212) 468-5487
Fax: (212) 468-5222
Knowledge: financial analysis,
corporate finance, securities anal-
ysis, market analysis. Consult-
ing: consultant to casino and ho-
tel executives, gaming commis-
sions, and Indian tribes. Publica-
tions: *CJ Lawrence Gaming
Daily*, *Gaming Weekly*.

Albert C. Ovedovitz,
Assoc. Prof.
Quantitative Analysis Dept.
College of Business
Administration
St. John's University
Grand Central and Utopia Pkwys.
Jamaica, NY 11439
Phone: (516) 667-1768

Fax: (718) 990-1868
E-mail: VFPC47A@prodigy.com
Knowledge: probability/statistics,
economic impact studies, economic forecasts of revenues, modeling, and forensic economics.
Consulting: all of the above.

Robert E. Parker,
Assoc. Prof.
Dept. of Sociology
University of Nevada, Las Vegas
4505 South Maryland Pkwy.
Las Vegas, NV 89154-5033
Phone: (702) 895-0263
Fax: (702) 895-4800
E-mail: bobp@nevada.edu
Knowledge: use of casinos as an
economic development strategy,
Indian gaming, lotteries, jobs
created by gaming, trends in the
evolution of legalized gaming.

James Reiter, Chairman
Tribal Gaming
Menominee Tribal Gaming Corp.
P.O. Box 760
Keshena, WI 54135
Phone: (715) 799-3600
Fax: (715) 799-4051
Knowledge: Indian gaming is-
sues, tribal-state compacts, gam-
ing operations, and vendors.
Bingo, casino, restaurant, and ho-
tel operations as a total package.

I. Nelson Rose, Prof.
Ross McCollum Law Center
Whittier Law School
5353 West 3rd St.

Los Angeles, CA 90020
Phone: (213) 938-3621 ext. 213
Fax: (213) 938-3460
E-mail: nrose@law.whittier.edu
Knowledge: gambling law, compulsive gambling and the law, and Indian gaming. Consulting: extensive government, industry, and international legal consulting. Expert witness in administrative, civil, and criminal trials. Publications: over 100 articles on gaming law and a nationally syndicated column *Gambling and the Law*, published in leading gaming publications.

Joseph Rubenstein,
Prof. of Anthropology, SOBL
Richard Stockton College of
New Jersey
Pomona, NJ 08241
Phone: (609) 652-4512
Fax: (609) 748-5559
E-mail:
IAPROD490@VAX003.Stockton
Knowledge: gambling and development and applied medical anthropology. Consulting: Project Administrator for the Community Health Assessment Project of Southeast New Jersey.

Arnold C. Schrader, D.P.E.,
Pres. & CEO
A. C. Schrader Development
Corp., International
3124 Harborside Drive
Las Vegas, NV 89117
Phone: (702) 254-7000

Fax: (702) 254-9850
Knowledge: development of hotels and hotel-casinos nationally and internationally. All stages of development, including design, construction, operations, and training of operational personnel. A.C. Schrader has constructed 158 hotels of which thirty-seven are design built. Consulting: West Europe, Pacific Rim, and South America. Offices in Germany, Italy, and South Africa.

Howard Schwartz
Marketing and Research Director
The Gambler's Book Shop
630 South 11th St.
Las Vegas, NV 89101
Phone: (702) 382-7555
(800) 522-1777
Fax: (702) 382-7594
Knowledge: modern publications on gambling, gaming research, and probability studies. Gambler's Book Club offers one of the largest collections of gambling books in the world. Consulting: assists writers, film makers, industry officials, and others in gaming-related research. Publications: retail book catalog.

Charles A. Stansfield, Prof.
Dept. of Anthropology and
Geography
Rowan College of New Jersey
201 Mullica Hill Rd.
Glassboro, NJ 08028

Phone: (609) 256-4500 ext. 3978 Knowledge: casino gaming as an urban revitalization tool, urban resort development, Indian gaming, Atlantic City gaming industry's prospects in an era of intensifying competition.

Frederick K. Steiner, Jr.,
Partner
Indian Law Practice Group
Snell & Wilmer Law Firm
One Arizona Center
Phoenix, AZ 85004-0001
Phone: (602) 382-6228
Fax: (602) 382-6070
Knowledge: Indian law, arbitration and bankruptcy. Represents businesses in their dealings with Indian tribes and personnel-related matters. Offices in Phoenix, Salt Lake City, and Tucson.

Larry A. Strate,
Assoc. Prof.
Finance/Business Law Dept.
University of Nevada, Las Vegas
4505 S. Maryland Pkwy.
Las Vegas, NV 89154-6008
Phone: (702) 895-3010
Fax: (702) 895-4650
Knowledge: gaming advertising, minors and debt collection, Indian gaming, and judicial selection. Consulting: consultant to attorneys and judges.

William N. Thompson, Prof.
Public Administration Dept.
University of Nevada Las Vegas
4505 South Maryland Pkwy.
Las Vegas, NV 89154-6026
Phone: (702) 895-3319
Fax: (702) 895-3606
E-mail: wthompson@nevada.edu
Knowledge: legalization of gambling, Indian gaming, socio-economic impacts of the gambling industry. Consulting: gaming consultant to the President's Commission on Organized Crime, several government gaming study organizations, Indian nations, and commercial casinos.

Nancy Todd, Pres.
The Todd Company, Ltd.
5713 Superior Drive, Suite B1
Baton Rouge, LA 70816
Phone: (504) 293-5788
Fax: (504) 293-7078
Knowledge: gaming legalization process, structuring of bills, obtaining voter approval of gaming initiatives. Consulting: associated with 130 political campaigns in thirty-four states. Worked with candidates and projects in national, state, and local campaigns. Counseled states, office holders, and casinos. Speaker and commentator, both nationally and internationally.

Roger Alan Walton
12550 West 2nd Dr.
Lakewood, CO 80228-5012
Phone: (303) 988-5580
Fax: (303) 988-5580
Knowledge: Colorado government, politics, mediation, and public affairs. Consulting: public affairs and political consultant. Mediator in Colorado.

Jeffrey Zeiger,
Assoc. Prof. of Tourism
Business Dept.
Black Hills State University
Spearfish, SD 57799-9674
Phone: (605) 642-6341
Fax: (605) 642-6214
E-mail:
JZeiger@ mystic.bhsu.edu
Knowledge: marketing research, visitor intercept studies, and casino feasibility. Consulting: marketing research, visitor intercept studies, and feasibility studies.

APPENDIX A

Gaming Periodicals & Investment Companies

This appendix selectively lists current journals, magazines, newsletters, and trade publications relating to the casino gaming industry. Gaming publications can be hard to find and transitory in nature. Since most of these titles are not represented in such standard periodical directories as *Ulrich's International Periodicals Directory,* full addresses and phone numbers have been provided. As with any group of print materials, prices change and quality varies. Readers are advised to contact publishers directly for current order information and sample issues before placing subscriptions.

Atlantic City Action. Glasco Associates, Inc., 33 South Presbyterian Ave., Atlantic City, NJ 08404 (609) 347-1225. 1978- . Monthly. $125/year.

Provides a wealth of financial information on New Jersey's casino industry, including gross winnings by individual property, type of game, casino size, number of slots, market share, and table holdings. Factors affecting casino profitability, such as regulations and tour-bus traffic, are also monitored.

Atlantic City Magazine. ABARTA Metro Publishing, 1000 West Washington Ave., Pleasantville, NJ 08232 (609) 272-7900. 1977- . Monthly. $19.95/year.

Features articles on how to play various casino games and offers information on what to do, where to stay, and where to dine in Atlantic City. This glossy publication also covers local events and new services for tourists.

Blackjack Forum. RGE Publishing, 414 Santa Clara Ave., Berkeley, CA 94610 (510) 465-6452. 1984- . Quarterly. $40/year.

Covers the game of blackjack for very serious or professional players. Articles address such subjects as the fundamentals of shuffle tracking and other technical aspects of the game, including cheating techniques employed by unscrupulous casinos and players. Regular updates on blackjack action around the world are also provided.

Blackjack Review. Spur of the Moment Publishing, P.O. Box 541967, Merritt Island, FL 32954-1967 (407) 452-2957. 1992- . Quarterly. $25/year.

Reviews new blackjack products, books, and important news stories. Similar to *Blackjack Forum*'s highly advanced, technical approach to the game.

Card Player. Card Player, Inc., 3140 South Polaris Ave., Las Vegas, NV 89102 (702) 871-1720. 1988- . Monthly. $39/year.

Promotes poker and other card games. Spiced with articles on gamblers of the old West and the best shows in Las Vegas, this magazine is for the gaming enthusiast and is comprised mostly of advertisements sponsored by Nevada casinos and California Indian gaming operations.

Casino Chronicle. Casino Chronicle, Inc., 1412 Chanticleer, Cherry Hill, NJ 08003 (609) 751-8620. 1983- Weekly newsletter. $155/year.

Tracks legislative and regulatory developments around the United States and spotlights key gaming executives and major business deals. Detailed revenue statistics for Atlantic City are regularly provided.

Casino Journal. Casino Journal of Nevada, 3100 W. Sahara Ave., Suite 209, Las Vegas, NV 89102 (702) 253-6230. 1992- . Monthly. $36/year.

Offers regular columns on casino revenue, gaming technology, gaming law, stock reviews, politics, and marketing. The "What's New" column tracks all developments relevant to gaming in jurisdictions throughout the United States.

Casino Journal's National Gaming Summary. Casino Journal of Nevada, 3100 W. Sahara Ave., Suite 209, Las Vegas, NV 89102 (702) 253-6230. 1993- . Weekly. $298/year.

Provides a state-by-state update of gaming issues and trends with some international coverage. Emphases are on political, regulatory, and legal environments, including legislation, law suits, and other developments that affect gaming operations. Also includes a weekly stock report.

Casino Magazine. Casino Magazine, 15 South Fifth St., Suite 900, Minneapolis, MN 55402 (800) 950-9467 (612) 376-8959. 1991- . Monthly. $15/year.

Features regular columns on gaming stocks, table games and slots, and gaming tournaments. Articles critique gaming venues around the world.

Casino Player. Casino Journal Publishing Group, 2524 Arctic Ave., Atlantic City, NJ 08401 (609) 344-9000. 1991- . Monthly. $24/year.

Features articles such as "The Hottest New Table Games" and "Taking the Mystery Out of Craps." This glossy publication for the gaming enthusiast contains many full-page color advertisements for major casinos nationwide and "how to play" information. The smiling faces of happy winners abound.

Casino Securities Watch. Rouge et Noir, Inc., P.O. Box 1146, Midlothian, VA 23113 Telephone number unavailable. 1990- . Weekly newsletter. $520/year.

Provides up-to-date news and financial information on casinos and the casino industry and analysis of such external market conditions as monetary exchange rates and inflation. Its masthead reads "a newsletter devoted to management consulting reports on publicly traded hotel/casinos."

Casinos: The International Casino Guide. B.D.I.T.,
Inc., P.O. Box 1405, Port Washington, NY 11050 (516)
944-5508. 1990- . Annual. $25/year.

Provides directory information on the world's legally
operating casinos. Coverage of North America is current
and thorough, and includes Indian and non-Indian casino
operations in twenty-one U.S. states, Canada, and the
Caribbean. Includes address and location information,
population of the nearest town, number and type of games
offered, casino size, ownership, hotel facilities and rates,
amenities, and nearby recreational opportunities.
Bibliographical references.

Current Blackjack News. Pi Yee Press, 7910
Ivanhoe Ave., #34, La Jolla, CA 92037-4511 (619) 456-
4080. 1979- . Weekly looseleaf. $95/year.

Contains current information on establishments
offering blackjack, including the latest house rules. The Lake
Tahoe Harvey's, for example, paid 10:1 odds on Valentine's
Day for blackjack hands with the king and queen of hearts.
For the enthusiast.

*From the State Capitals. Lottery, Parimutuel and
Casino Regulation.* Wakeman-Walworth, Inc., 300 North
Washington St., Alexandria, VA 22314 (703) 549-8606
1990- . Weekly newsletter. $295/year.

Tracks gaming-related legislation and litigation in the
United States. Primarily for industry and government
officials.

Gaming Products and Services. RCM Enterprises,
Inc., Twelve Oaks Center, Suite 922, Wayzata, MN 55391
(612) 473-5088. 1993- . Monthly. $36/year.

Showcases the world of gaming technology from on-
line keno systems to swing-out slot machine seats. Provides
timely articles on industry developments from around the
country, including riverboats and Indian reservations.
Aspects of casino design and architecture are also discussed.

Gaming Research and Review Journal. International Gaming Institute, William F. Harrah College of Hotel Administration, University of Nevada, Las Vegas, Las Vegas, NV 89154-6037 (702) 895-3412. 1994- . Semi-annual. $76/year.

Features articles on gaming management and practices. Topics include industry and social trends, legal and administrative issues, government policy, and research studies on casino marketing, human resources, finance, and administration. Contributors are leading scholars and experts in the field.

Gaming Today. Gaming Today, P.O. Box 93116, Las Vegas, NV 89193 (702) 798-1151. 1994- . Weekly tabloid. $115/year.

Tracks Las Vegas's casino industry and offers extensive coverage of sports betting. Also announces special events in Las Vegas.

Grogan Report. S.P. Grogan, 30746 Bryant Drive, P.O. Box 249, Evergreen, CO 80439 (303) 670-0808. 1991- . Monthly. $80/year.

Claims to be "the authoritative source for casino gaming." Stephen Grogan is an industry insider, and his report features interviews with important industry figures and regulators. He also covers noteworthy industry leaders, revenue figures, and casino openings.

Indian Gaming. Public Gaming Research Institute, 15825 Shady Grove Rd., Suite 130, Rockville, MD 20850 (301) 330-7600. 1990- . Monthly. $40/year.

Provides national coverage on Indian gaming, including current news stories, regulations, court cases, and listings of all tribal operations. Also offers insight on Indian culture and how gaming revenues improve the lives of Native Americans.

Indian Gaming News. BMT Communications, 7 Penn Plaza, New York, NY 10001-3900 (800) 223-9638 (212) 594-4120. 1995- . Bi-weekly. $295/year.

Reports on legal, regulatory, and commercial developments in Indian gaming.

International Gaming & Wagering Business. BMT Communications, 7 Penn Plaza, New York, NY 10001-3900 (800) 223-9638 (212) 594-4120. 1990- . Monthly. $72/year.

Provides an insider's perspective on the gaming industry, from acquisitions and mergers to business failures, regulation, riverboats, Indian gaming, and foreign gaming. Widely considered the single most important trade publication in the field and frequently quoted in other sources.

Journal of Gambling Studies. Human Sciences Press, 233 Spring St., New York, NY 10013-1578 (212) 620-8000. 1985- . Quarterly. $160/year.

Studies the phenomenon of gambling as a social, economic, legal, psychological, pathological, and recreational activity in society. Contributors are professionals and academics representing all social sciences. The official journal of the National Council on Problem Gambling, co-sponsored by the Institute for the Study of Gambling and Commercial Gaming.

Las Vegas Review Journal. Donrey Media Group, 1111 West Bonanza, Las Vegas, NV 89106 (702) 383-0211. Daily. $195/year.

Provides daily coverage of the gaming industry. The business section of this newspaper covers gaming stories worldwide. Major gaming events such as casino openings and the passage of gaming legislation are frequently front-page news.

Louisiana Gaming Industry News. Gaming Industry Research Institute of the South, P.O. Box 2250, New Orleans, LA 70176 (504) 523-5514. 1993- . Weekly newsletter. $250/year.

Provides detailed revenue figures and timely information on Louisiana and Mississippi gaming operations. Riverboat sailing schedules, Louisiana lottery sales, pari-mutuel betting, and local gaming stock performances are also covered.

Midwest Players. RCM Enterprises, Inc., Twelve Oaks Center, Suite 922, Wayzata, MN 55391 (612) 473-5088. 1993- . Bi-weekly tabloid. $48/year.

Offers "how-to-play" information, a directory of gaming establishments, relevant book reviews, and more. This tabloid is an enthusiast's guide to gaming action and a useful resource for tracking the rapidly expanding Midwest gaming market.

Nevada Magazine. Nevada Magazine, 1800 Highway 50 East, Suite 200, Carson City, Nevada 89710 (702) 687-5416. Subscriptions: P.O. Box 1942, Marian, Ohio 43305 (800) 669-1002. 1975- . Bi-monthly. $14.95/year.

Contains articles focusing on historical and contemporary Nevada. Sponsored by the Nevada Commission on Tourism, each issue contains a detailed events section which lists a wide variety of activities arranged geographically for Las Vegas, Reno-Tahoe, and the state's rural areas. Casino extravaganzas and promotions are regularly listed. Also includes previews and reviews of casino shows and performers. For residents and tourists. Subtitled "The Magazine of the Real West." Formerly *Nevada Highways and Parks.*

New Jersey Casino Journal. Casino Journal Publishing Group, Bayport One, Suite 470, West Atlantic City, NJ 08232 (609) 484 8866. 1986- . Monthly. $36/year.

Surveys the gaming industry and provides political and economic analysis of gaming initiatives. Regularly provides coverage of complete U.S. casino gaming revenues, company profiles, casino stock reports, people in the news, and articles on gaming technology and products.

Passenger Vessel News. Pearson Publishing Co., P.O. Box 8662, Metairie, LA 70011 (504) 455-9758. 1989- . Bi-monthly. $95/year. Subscription price includes *Riverboat Gaming Report.*

Covers gambling boats with some information on charter boats, ferries, and sightseeing vessels. Includes current events and activities of specific gaming companies and operations. The publication's considerable amount of advertising is placed by ship builders, marine engine manufacturers, restaurant equipment suppliers, interior designers, and casino suppliers.

Ray Koon's Gaming/Gram. Ray Koon's Gaming/Gram, 3271 South Highland, Suite 705A, Las Vegas, NV 89109-1051 (702) 735-2550. 1985- . Weekly newsletter. $600/year.

Provides "a professional overview of international gaming." Publisher Ray Koon was Chief of the Nevada Gaming Control Board's Investigations Division for eighteen years, and this newsletter focuses on licensing and regulatory activity in Nevada. Also covers national and international gaming developments, new gaming devices, and other topics of interest to executives, attorneys, regulators, and industry officials.

Riverboat Gaming News. BMT Communications, 7 Penn Plaza, New York, NY 10001-3900 (800) 223-9638 (212) 594-4120. 1995- . Bi-weekly. $295/year.

Tracks legal, regulatory, and commercial developments in riverboat gaming.

Riverboat Gaming Report. Pearson Publishing Co., P.O. Box 8662, Metairie, LA 70011 (504) 455-9758. 1989- . Monthly. $95/year. Subscription price includes *Passenger Vessel News.*

Provides industry updates on excursion and dockside riverboat casino operations. Each report includes tabular data on boats operating in Iowa, Illinois, Missouri, Mississippi, and Louisiana, including size of the vessel, number of gaming positions, slots and table games, passengers, and winnings.

Rouge et Noir Resort Management Report. Rouge et Noir, Inc., P.O. Box 1146, Midlothian, VA 23113 Telephone number unavailable. 1984- . Monthly newsletter series containing four reports: *Rouge et Noir Resort Management Report. Nevada Report. New Jersey Report. Capsule Summary.* $595/year.

Provides timely, detailed charts and tables of casino revenues by individual property and by geographic location.

World Gaming Directories. World Gaming Directories, Inc., 3601 Vegas Plaza Dr., Las Vegas, NV 89109 (702) 735-6338. 1992- . Annual. Looseleaf or computer file. $495/year.

Provides directory information on casinos worldwide, including riverboats, cruise ships, and Indian gaming, and regulatory agencies, equipment manufacturers, and supply companies.

World Gaming Report. Shaw & Hardin, The Chapel House, 121 Plymouth St., Carver, MA 02330 (508) 866-4981. 1980- . Monthly newsletter. $100/year.

Provides a "roving reporter's view" of the gaming industry with narrative accounts of current events and developments at gaming locales nationwide. Issues showcase destinations such as Mesquite, Nevada, and Connecticut's Foxwoods High Stakes Bingo and Casino. Also covers business deals and career moves of industry people. A calendar of gaming events, such as industry expositions, is regularly featured.

INVESTMENT FIRMS PRODUCING GAMING INDUSTRY STUDIES & REPORTS

The following companies regularly provide gaming industry analysis. Many of their reports are compiled in *Investext*, a CD-ROM database produced by Information Access Company, which may be available in larger libraries.

Bear Stearns Companies Ltd.
245 Park Avenue
New York, NY 10167-0002
Phone: (212) 272-2000

CJ Lawrence / Deutsche Bank Securities Corp.
1290 Avenue of The Americas
New York, NY 10104-0101
Phone: (212) 468-5487
Fax: (212) 468-5222

Dean Witter Reynolds
Two World Trade Center
New York, NY 10048-0203
Phone: (212) 392-2222

Moody's Investors Service
99 Church Street
New York, NY 10007
Phone: (212) 553-0300
Fax: (212) 553-4700

Oppenheimer & Co. Ltd.
Oppenheimer Tower
World Financial Center
New York, NY 10281
Phone: (212) 667-7000

Raymond James & Associates
880 Carillon Parkway
St. Petersburg, FL 33716-1102
Phone: (813) 573-8954
Fax: (813) 573-8095

Smith Barney Holdings, Inc.
1345 Avenue of the Americas
New York, NY 10105
Phone: (212) 399-6000

Standard & Poor's Corp.
25 Broadway
New York, NY 10004
Phone: (800) 233-2310
              (212) 208-8000
Fax: (212) 412-0459

Wertheim Schroder & Co., Inc.
787 7th Avenue, 5th Floor
New York, NY 10019
Phone: (212) 492-6000
Fax: (212) 492-6295

APPENDIX B

"How-To-Gamble" Books

This section lists twenty-four how-to-play titles recommended by Howard Schwartz, Marketing Director, Gambler's Book Shop, Las Vegas. Mr. Schwartz is a recognized authority on popular gaming literature, and his selections are considered the best selling and most authoritative works of their kind. They are arranged, at his suggestion, by subject.

BACCARAT

Hebert, Byron F. *Power Baccarat.* Wynadotte, Mich.: Hebert and Associates, 1993. 241 pp. Paperbound, $19.95

BIG SIX MONEY WHEEL

Cohen, R. Carl. *Beating the Casinos' Big Six Money Wheel.* Philadelphia: Carl R. Cohen, 1987. 34 pp. Paperbound, $4.95

BLACKJACK

Griffin, Peter A. *The Theory of Blackjack.* Las Vegas, Nev.: Huntington Press, 1979. 254 pp. Paperbound, $18.95

Revere, Lawrence. *Playing Blackjack as a Business.* New York: Carol Publishing, 1969. 176 pp. Paperbound, $14.95

Thorp, Edward O. *Beat the Dealer.* New York: Random House, 1962. 220 pp. Paperbound, $9.95

Uston, Ken. *Million Dollar Blackjack.* Van Nuys, Calif.: Gambling Times, 1981. 330 pp. Paperbound, $18.95

Wong, Stanford. *Professional Blackjack.* La Jolla, Calif.: Pi Yee Press, 1975. 352 pp. Paperbound, $19.95

CRAPS

Grafstein, Sam. *The Dice Doctor.* Las Vegas, Nev.: GBC Press, 1981. 146 pp. Paperbound, $14.95

Midgley, Thomas. *Craps: A Smart Shooter's Guide.* Las Vegas, Nev.: GBC Press, 1980. 219 pp. Paperbound, $12.95

Scarne, John. *Scarne on Dice.* Hollywood, Calif.: Wilshire Press, 1980. 496 pp. Paperbound, $15.95

KENO

McClure, Wayne. *Lottery and Keno Winning Strategies.* Las Vegas, Nev.: GBC Press, 1991. 174 pp. Paperbound, $14.95

PAI GOW

Zender, Bill. *Pai Gow Without Tears.* Las Vegas, Nev.: Bill Zender, 1989. 80 pp. Paperbound, $24.95

POKER

Brunson, Doyle. *Super Systems.* Las Vegas, Nev.: B&G Publishing, 1978. 605 pp. Hardbound, $50.00

Sklansky, David. *The Theory of Poker*. Las Vegas, Nev.: Two Plus Two Publishing, 1987. 276 pp. Paperbound, $29.95

Sklansky, David, and Mason Malmuth. *Hold 'Em Poker for Advanced Players*. Las Vegas, Nev.: Two Plus Two Publishing, 1988. 212 pp. Paperbound, $29.95

Sklansky, David, and Mason Malmuth. *Seven Card Stud for Advanced Players*. Las Vegas, Nev.: Two Plus Two Publishing, 1989. 220 pp. Paperbound, $29.95

PROBABILITY

Epstein, Richard. *The Theory of Gambling and Statistical Logic*. San Diego, Calif.: Academic Press, 1977. 450 pp. Paperbound, $29.95; hardbound, $72.00

Orkin, Mike. *Can You Win?* New York: W.H. Freeman Co., 1991. 181 pp. Paperbound, $11.95

Packel, Edward. *The Mathematics of Games and Gambling*. Washington, D.C.: The Mathematical Association of America, 1991. 141 pp. Paperbound, $16.00

ROULETTE

Barnhart, Russell T. *Beating the Wheel*. New York: Carol Publishing, 1992. 216 pp. Paperbound, $12.95

Shelley, Ron. *Roulette Wheel Study*. Atlantic City, N.J.: Ron Shelley, 1987. 124 pp. Paperbound, $50.00

Squire, Norman. *How To Win at Roulette*. London: Old Castle Books, 1968. 221 pp. Paperbound, $12.95

VIDEO POKER

Frome, Lenny. *Expert Video Poker for Las Vegas.* Las Vegas, Nev.: Compu-Flyers, 1994. 34 pp. Paperbound, $9.95

Paymar, Dan. *Video Poker Precision Play.* Las Vegas, Nev.: Dan Paymar, 1992. 68 pp. Paperbound, $12.95

These materials can be ordered through local bookstores or from the Gambler's Book Shop, 630 South Eleventh Street, Las Vegas, NV 89101 (800) 522-1777 Fax (702) 382-7594. The Gambler's Book Shop is the largest bookstore of its kind in the world and offers a free catalog listing over 1,000 gambling titles.

APPENDIX C

Public Gaming Companies

This appendix is a directory of public companies that provide gaming-related goods or services and are traded on major United States stock exchanges. Entries include the company's name, address, telephone number, and a brief description of its activities. This information was gathered by telephone, May 1995. Current information on these companies can be found in such standard library resources as *Compact Disclosure, Dun's Million Dollar Directory,* Moody's manuals, *Standard and Poor's Register,* and *Ward's Business Directory.*

Comprehensive lists of gaming companies are difficult to compile because there are no standard industrial classification (SIC) codes for gaming activities. SIC Codes are classification numbers the United States Department of Commerce uses to identify and group providers of specific types of goods or services. They are an excellent tool for pulling together companies that are in the same type of business. Gaming-related companies, however, are typically classified under broader SIC codes such as Hotels and Motels (7011), Coin-Operated Amusement Devices (7993), Holding Companies Not Elsewhere Classified (6719), Manufacturers Not Elsewhere Classified (3999), and Computer-Related Services Not Elsewhere Classified (7379). These groups bring together diverse companies involved in varying activities that do not precisely fit into other code categories.

PUBLIC GAMING COMPANIES

Acres Gaming Inc.
3229 W. Tompkins Ave.
Las Vegas, NV 89103
(702) 795-8962
Gaming equipment manufacturer

**American Casino
Enterprises Inc.**
6243 Industrial Rd.
Las Vegas, NV 89118
(702) 896-8888
Indian gaming facilities
managment

**American Gaming &
Entertainment Ltd.**
Bayport One
Yacht Club Dr., Suite 300
West Atlantic City, NJ 08232
(609) 272-7700
Indian gaming development and
services

Ameristar Casinos Inc.
P.O. Box 508
Jackpot, NV 89825
(702) 755-6011
Hotel/casino operator

Anchor Gaming
815 Pilot Rd., Suite G
Las Vegas, NV 89119
(702) 896-7568
Gaming route and casino operator

Argosy Gaming Co.
219 Piasa St.
Alton, IL 62002

(618) 474-7500
Riverboat casino operator

Autotote Corp.
888 7th Ave., Suite 1808
New York, NY 10106
(212) 541-6440
Racetrack betting machine
manufacturer

Aztar Corp.
2390 E. Camelback Rd.,#400
Phoenix, AZ 85016
(602) 381-4100
Hotel/casino operator

Bally Entertainment Corp.
8700 W. Bryn Mawr Ave.
Chicago, IL 60631
(312) 399-1300
Hotel/casino operator

**Bally Gaming International
Inc.**
6601 S. Bermuda Rd.
Las Vegas, NV 89119
(702) 896-7700
Gaming equipment manufacturer

**Bally's Casino Holdings
Inc.**
8700 W. Bryn Mawr Ave.
Chicago, IL 60631
(312) 399-1300
Holding Company

Bally's Grand Inc.
3645 Las Vegas Blvd. South

Las Vegas, NV 89109
(702) 739-4848
Hotel/casino operator

Bally's Park Place Inc.
Park Place and the Boardwalk
Atlantic City, NJ 08401
Hotel/casino operator

Bass PLC
20 North Audley St.
London W1Y 1WE
England
071-409-1919
Gaming equipment manufacturer,
betting shop and club operator

Becker Gaming Inc.
740 S. Decatur Blvd.
Las Vegas, NV 89107
(702) 258-5200
Casino and gaming route holding
company

**Black Hawk Gaming and
Development Co. Inc.**
2060 Broadway, #400
Boulder, CO 80302
(303) 444-0240
Casino operator

Boardwalk Casino Inc.
3734 Las Vegas Blvd. South
Las Vegas, NV 89109
(702) 739-8481
Hotel/casino operator

Boomtown Inc.
P.O. Box 399
Verdi, NV 89439
(702) 345-6000
Hotel/casino operator

Boyd Gaming Corp.
2950 S. Industrial Rd.
Las Vegas, NV 89109
(702) 792-7200
Hotel/casino operator

Caesars World Inc.
1801 Century Park East,
Suite 2600
Los Angeles, CA 90067
(310) 552-2711
Hotel/casino operator

**Capital Gaming
International Inc.**
Bayport One, Suite 250
8025 Black Horse Pike
West Atlantic City, NJ 08232
(609) 383-3333
Riverboat gaming and Indian
gaming management operations

Casino America Inc.
2200 Corporate Blvd. NW,
Suite 310
Boca Raton, FL 33431
(407) 995-6660
Hotel/casino operator

**Casino and Credit
Services Inc.**
1100 E. Hector St., Suite 400
Conshohocken, PA 19428
(610) 834-8710
Debt collection and credit
reporting agency

Casino Data Systems
3265 W. Tompkins Ave.
Las Vegas, NV 89103
(702) 891-8925
Slot accounting and player-
tracking equipment manufacturer

Casino Magic Corp.
711 Casino Magic Dr.
Bay St. Louis, MS 39520
(601) 467-9257
Casino operator

Casino Resource Corp.
850 N. Wisconsin St.
Elkhorn, WI 53121
(414) 723-6660
Gaming industry marketing
consultants

Circus Circus Enterprises Inc.
2880 Las Vegas Blvd. South
Las Vegas, NV 89109
(702) 734-0410
Hotel/casino operator

Claridge Hotel and Casino Corp.
Indiana & Boardwalk
Atlantic City, NJ 08401
(609) 340-3400
Hotel/casino operator

Comdata Network Inc.
5301 Maryland Wy.
Brentwood, TN 37027
(615) 370-7000
Gaming industry commercial
lender

Concorde Gaming Corp.
3290 Lien St.
Rapid City, SD 57702
(605) 341-7738
Video lottery route operator

Creator Capital Inc.
595 Howe St., Suite 1115

Vancouver, British Columbia
V6C 2T5
Canada
(604) 689-1515
Gaming devices for international
air flights

Crown Casino Corp.
2415 W. Northwest Hwy., #103
Dallas, TX 75220
(214) 352-7561
Riverboat casino operator

Elsinore Corp.
P.O. Box 370
Las Vegas, NV 89101
(702) 385-4011
Hotel/casino operator

Gaming World International Ltd.
438 Line Ave.
Ellwood City, PA 16117
(412) 758-2461
Indian gaming developer and
manager

Gemini Inc.
P.O. Box 1060
Las Vegas, NV 89125
(702) 477-3000
Hotel/casino operator

Global Gaming & Technology Inc.
2575 S. Highland Dr.
Las Vegas, NV 89109-1113
(702) 732-1414
Computer gaming machine
manufacturer

Gold River Hotel and Casino Corp.

2330 Paseo Del Prado, Suite 104
Las Vegas, NV 89012
Hotel/casino operator

Grand Casinos Inc.
13705 1st Ave. North
Plymouth, MN 55441
(612) 449-9092
Hotel/casino developer and
operator

GTECH Holdings Corp.
55 Technology Wy.
West Greenwich, RI 02817
(401) 392-1000
Gaming Consultant

Harveys Casino Resorts
P.O. Box 128
Lake Tahoe, NV 89449
(702) 588-2411
Hotel/casino operator

Hilton Hotels Corp.
9336 Civic Center Dr.
Beverly Hills, CA 90209
(310) 278-4321
Hotel/casino operator

Holly Products Inc.
360 Crider Ave.
Moorestown, NJ 08057
(609) 234-1450
Gaming table and slot cabinet
manufacturer

Hollywood Casino Corp.
13455 Noel Rd., #2200
Dallas, TX 75240
(214) 386-9777
Casino operator

Hotel Investors Corp.
11845 W. Olympic Blvd., #560
Los Angeles, CA 90064
(310) 575-3900
Hotel/casino operator and real
estate investor

**Innovative Gaming
Corp. of America**
12700 Industrial Park Blvd.,
Suite 60
Plymouth, MN 55441
(612) 557-674
Video gaming machine designer
and manufacturer

**International Game
Technology Inc.**
5270 Neil Rd.
Reno, NV 89502
(702) 686-1200
Slot machine and computer
gaming manufacturer

**International Gaming
Management Inc.**
1550 Utica Ave. South,
Suite 500
Minneapolis, MN 55416
(612) 546-8140
Video gaming machine
wholesaler and gaming route
operator

ITT Corp.
1330 Ave. of the Americas
New York, NY 10019
(212) 258-1000
Hotel/casino operator

Jackpot Enterprises Inc.
1110 Palms Airport Dr.
Las Vegas, NV 89119

(702) 263-5555
Gaming route and casino operator

Lone Star Casino Corp.
1 River Wy., Suite 2550
Houston, TX 77056
(713) 960-9881
Hotel/casino operator

M & R Investment
4045 S. Spencer St., #206
Las Vegas, NV 89119
(702) 732-7474
Real estate developer and casino
investor

Mast Keystone Inc.
4673 Aircenter Cir.
Reno, NV 89502
(702) 827-8110
Slot machine and video gaming
machine manufacturer

Merv Griffin Resorts
1133 Boardwalk
Atlantic City, NJ 08401
(609) 344-6000
Hotel/casino operator

MGM Grand Inc.
3799 Las Vegas Blvd. South
Las Vegas, NV 89109
(702) 891-3333
Hotel/casino operator

Mikohn Gaming Corp.
6700 S. Paradise Rd., #E
Las Vegas, NV 89119
(702) 896-3890
Progressive jackpot systems
operator

Mirage Resorts Inc.
3400 Las Vegas Blvd. South
Las Vegas, NV 89109
(702) 791-7111
Hotel/casino operator

Monarch Casino and Resort Inc.
3840 Baker Ln.
Reno, NV 89509
(702) 825-3355
Hotel/casino operator

National Gaming Corp.
339 Jefferson Rd.
Parsippany, NJ 07054
(201) 428-9700
Hotel/casino operator

Palace Casinos Inc.
124 Lameuse St.
Biloxi, MS 39530
(601) 432-8888
Dockside casino developer

Paul-Son Dice and Card Company Inc.
2121 Industrial Rd.
Las Vegas, NV 89102
(702) 384-2425
Dice and playing cards
manufacturer

Pratt Hotel Corp.
13455 Noel Rd., Suite 2200
Dallas, TX 75240
(214) 386-9777
Hotel/casino operator

President Riverboat Casinos Inc.
130 W. River Dr.
Davenport, IA 52801

(319) 328-8000
Riverboat and dockside casino
operator

Primadonna Resorts Inc.
P.O. Box 19129
Jean, NV 89019
(702) 382-1212
Hotel/casino operator

Promus Companies Inc.
1023 Cherry Rd.
Memphis, TN 38117
(901) 762-8600
Hotel/casino operator

Rio Hotel and Casino Inc.
P.O. Box 14160
Las Vegas, NV 89114
(702) 252-7733
Hotel/casino operator

Riviera Holdings Corp.
2901 Las Vegas Blvd. South
Las Vegas, NV 89109
(702) 734-5110
Hotel/casino operator

Sahara Gaming Corp.
2535 Las Vegas Blvd. South
Las Vegas, NV 89109
(702) 737-2111
Hotel/casino operator

Sands Regent Hotel Casino
345 N. Arlington Ave.
Reno, NV 89501
(702) 348-2200
Hotel/casino operator

Scientific Games Inc.
1500 Bluegrass Lakes Pkwy.
Alpharetta, GA 30201

(404) 664-3700
Lottery ticket manufacturer

Showboat Inc.
2800 Fremont St.
Las Vegas, NV 89104
(702) 385-9141
Hotel/casino operator

Shuffle Master Inc.
10921 Valley View Rd.
Eden Prairie, MN 55344
(612) 943-1951
Casino card shuffling machine
manufacturer

Sodak Gaming Inc.
405 E. Omaha St.
Rapid City, SD 57701
(605) 341-5400
Slot and gaming machine
distributor

**Southwest Casino &
Hotel Corp.**
2001 Killebrew Dr., Suite 345
Minneapolis, MN 55425
(612) 853-9990
Casino operator

Sports Tech Inc.
2900 S. Highland Dr., #18C
Las Vegas, NV 89109
(702) 735-7774
Custom gaming software and
video production designer

Starwood Lodging
11845 W. Olympic Blvd., #550
Los Angeles, CA 90064
(310) 575-3900
Hotel/casino operator and real
estate investment trust

Station Casinos Inc.
2411 W. Sahara Ave.
Las Vegas, NV 89102
(702) 367-2411
Hotel/casino operator

Stratosphere Corp.
2000 Las Vegas Blvd. South
Las Vegas, NV 89104
(702) 382-2000
Casino and vacation club operator

Union Plaza Hotel and Casino Inc.
P.O. Box 760
Las Vegas, NV 89125
(702) 386-2110
Hotel/casino operator

United Gaming Inc.
4380 Boulder Hwy.
Las Vegas, NV 89121
(702) 435-4200
Gaming route and casino operator, and gaming machine manufacturer

Video Lottery Technologies Inc.
2311 S. 7th Ave.
Bozeman, MT 59715-6502
(406) 585-6600
Gaming video terminal manufacturer

Wico Holding Corp.
6400 West Gross Point Rd.
Niles, IL 60714
(708) 647-7500
Gaming machine parts manufacturer

Winners Entertainment Inc.
30448 Rancho Vieso Rd., Suite 110
San Juan Capistrano, CA 92675
(714) 222-2220
Hotel/casino operator and commercial property management

WMS Industries Inc.
3401 N. California Ave.
Chicago, IL 60618
(312) 728-2300
Video lottery terminal and video game manufacturer, hotel/casino operator

Subject Index

Author Index

NUMBERS FOLLOWING HEADINGS REFER TO ENTRIES

Mason, Paul M. 665, 728, 785
Massachusetts. Senate Audit and
     Oversight Bureau 448
Massachusetts. Senate
     Committee on Post Audit and
     Oversight 449, 867
Mayo, Ann M. 244
McAvoy, Kim 143
McCabe, Michael H. 450, 564
McCarthy, John J. 451
McCormack, Patrick J. 365
McCulloch, Anne Merline 295
McDowell, Douglas J. 649
McGowan, Richard 620
McGurrin, Martin C. 651, 652,
     880
McKay, Nancy 225
McKee, Jamie 144
McLaughlin, John 366
McMillen, Jan 498
McQueen, Patricia A. 13, 59
Medley, Keith Weldon 729
Meier, Barry 60, 819
Meier, Kenneth J. 553
Merin, Kenneth D. 518
Meyer, Gerhard 881
Michaelis, Laura 367
Michigan Indian Gaming
     Enterprises 226
Michigan State Legislature.
     Special Ad Hoc Committee to
     Study Legal Gambling on
     Indian Reservations 261
Midwest Hospitality Advisors
227
Midwestern Legislative
     Conference. Council of State
     Governments
          See Council of State
          Governments. Midwestern
          Legislative Conference
Milan, Monica L. 452
Milanowski, Joseph D. 550

Mills, John R. 61, 453, 454
Mills, R.G.J. 145
Milt, Harry 677
Minnesota. Department of
     Gaming 499
Minnesota. Department of
     Human Services, Mental
     Health Division 647, 779
Minnesota Gambling Control
     Board 62, 417, 500
Minnesota House of
     Representatives, DFL Caucus
     Research 489
Minnesota House of
     Representatives, Research
     Department 214, 258, 514,
     515, 516
Minnesota Indian Gaming
     Association 228, 229
Minnesota Institute of Public
     Health 759, 820
Minnesota. Senate Counsel and
     Research 365
Mirage Resorts, Inc. 146
Misrach, Richard 730
Mississippi Institutions of
     Higher Learning, Center for
     Policy Research and Planning
     368
Mississippi. Legislature 501
Mitler, Ernest A. 455
MN Planning 230, 231
Mobile, Alabama. Gaming Task
     Force 565
Mobilia, Pamela 821
Mok, Waiman P. 731
Montana. Legislative Council
277
Montana. Office of the
     Legislative Auditor 456
Monteau, Harold 204
Moody, Eric N. 457
Moody, Gordon E. 732

W

Wagenaar, Willem Albert 775, 835
Walke, Roger 335
Walker, Michael B. 836, 837
Walker, Reid 336
Walkoff, Neil E. 594
Walkup, Carolyn 642
Walters, Glenn D. 838, 839
Walters, Laurel Shaper 392, 413
Walton, Roger Alan 91
Wapato, Timothy 271, 322
Ward-Smith and Company 256
Warker, Kimberly J. 595
Warrior, Robert Allen 337
Waters, Gary A. 92
Watson, Jerome R. 93
Weatherford, Mike 178
Weinblatt, J. 845, 856
Weinstein, Adam K. 884
Welles, Chris 840
Wendler, Kathryn A. 475
Wexler, Arnold 803
Whalen, Jeanne 179
Wheeler, Sharon K. 65
Whyte, William F. 706
Wiegand, Steve 338
Wilhite, Ed 414
Wilkins, Beth M. 257
Will, George F. 841
Williams, John 258, 514, 515, 516
Williamson, Lonnie 393
Wilson, Jerome L. 339
Wisconsin Legislative Fiscal
 Bureau 477
Wisconsin. Legislative Reference
 Bureau 505, 517
Witcher, Gregory 643
Wolf, John D. 776
Wolfe, Frank 180
Wolff, Phyllis 842

Woolner, Ann 873
Worsnop, Richard L. 259, 596, 777

Y

Yesalis, Charles E. 740
Yoshihashi, Pauline 94, 182, 183

Z

Zazzali, James R. 518
Zeiger, Jeffrey 670
Zelio, Judy 209, 340
Zeller, Laurie Hirschfield 644
Zendzian, Craig A. 874, 875
Zimmerman, Art 477
Zimmerman, Kevin 184, 645

ABOUT THE AUTHORS

Thomas R. Mirkovich is assistant collection development and management librarian at the University of Nevada, Las Vegas, and the selector of library materials for the William F. Harrah College of Hotel Administration and the College of Business and Economics. He earned his B.A. with Distinction in history and political science and his M.L.S. from the University of Washington.

Allison A. Cowgill was Head of Reference Services at the Nevada State Library and Archives, Carson City, Nevada from 1987 to 1995. She is now the Social Sciences Librarian/Coordinator of Government Documents at the University of Denver. She has undergraduate degrees in sociology and English from the University of Colorado and an M.L.S. from the University of Denver.